POLITICAL INTELLIGENCE

AND THE

CREATION OF MODERN MEXICO,

1938–1954

AARON W. NAVARRO

POLITICAL INTELLIGENCE
AND THE
CREATION OF MODERN MEXICO,
1938–1954

THE PENNSYLVANIA STATE UNIVERSITY PRESS
UNIVERSITY PARK, PENNSYLVANIA

LIBRARY OF CONGRESS
CATALOGING-IN-PUBLICATION DATA

Navarro, Aaron W., 1973–
Political intelligence and the creation of modern Mexico,
1938–1954 / Aaron W. Navarro.
p.   cm.
Includes bibliographical references and index.
ISBN 978-0-271-03705-9 (cloth : alk. paper)
1. Mexico—Politics and government—1946–1970.
2. Mexico—Politics and government—1910–1946.
3. Presidents—Mexico—Election—History—20th century.
4. Intelligence service—Political aspects—Mexico—History—20th century.
5. Mexico—Armed Forces—Political activity—History—20th century.
6. Political parties—Mexico—History—20th century.
7. Opposition (Political science)—Mexico—History—20th century.
8. Partido de la Revolucion Mexicana—History.
9. Partido Revolucionario Institucional—History.
10. Civil-military relations—Mexico—History—20th century.
I. Title.
F1235.N38 2010
324.272′05—dc22
2010004667

The Pennsylvania State University Press is a member of the
Association of American University Presses.

It is the policy of The Pennsylvania State University Press
to use acid-free paper. Publications on uncoated stock satisfy
the minimum requirements of American National Standard for
Information Sciences—Permanence of Paper for
Printed Library Material, ANSI z39.48-1992.

This book is printed on Natures Natural, which contains 50% post-consumer waste.

To my FATHER & MOTHER

Contents

Illustrations

Acknowledgments

The pursuit and completion of this project, evolving as it has over the past fourteen years, would not have been possible without the support of a wide host of institutions and people. The lists that follow are necessarily incomplete, for no doubt my debts range wider and my thanks strike deeper than the words here may convey. From the beginning of this project, I counted on the support of the History Department at Harvard University. This aid was supplemented by the strong community and financial resources (including summer travel grants) of the David Rockefeller Center for Latin American Studies, where I spent several years as a graduate student associate. I am also thankful for the support of the Jacob Javits Fellowship, the Mellon Fellowship in Latin American History, and the Ford Foundation Dissertation Fellowship. In Mexico, I was very fortunate to join the Colegio de México as a visiting scholar.

For research support, I thank the staffs of the Benson Latin American Collection, University of Texas at Austin; the Harvard University Libraries; the National Archives and Records Administration Archives II, College Park, Maryland; the Archivo Manuel Gómez Morín, Mexico City; the Secretaría de la Defensa Nacional, Mexico City; the Hemeroteca "Manuel Sobreira Galindo" of *El Universal*, Mexico City; the Hemeroteca Nacional, Universidad Nacional Autónoma de México (UNAM), Mexico City; the Special Collections Division, University of Tennessee at Martin; and the Harry S. Truman Library and Museum, Independence, Missouri.

In Mexico, the bulk of my research time was spent in the Archivo General de la Nación in Mexico City, where Roberto Beristaín first guided me to the collection of intelligence documents that were, at the time, newly opened to researchers and that form the core of this book. The staff of Gallery Two at the AGN, led by the mighty Joel, made the trip to the archives each day worthwhile by offering me unfettered access to the documents along with their friendship. The long stays in Mexico City were more enjoyable for the camaraderie of my *compañeras de archivo*: Dina Berger, Ann Blum, Susan Deeds, Susan Gauss, and Nichole Sanders. It was my good fortune to meet them, along with so many other interesting scholars, during breaks from our respective projects. I have also been fortunate to gain the friendship of Elisa Servín, whose work on *henriquismo* informed much of this project and whose generosity as a scholar is unmatched. Finally, the family of Enrique and Cathie Pani provided both comfort and friendship by opening their home to me at crucial points in this project.

Javier Garciadiego coordinated my affiliation with the Colegio de México. He also introduced me to General de Brigada (D.E.M.) Luis Garfias Magaña, who had served for many years as the official historian of the Mexican Army and director of its archives. Garfias gave generously of his time to answer my questions, discuss military issues, and plumb his deep memory for personal recollections of some of the subjects of this book. I appreciated that Eugenia Meyer not only accepted me (informally) into her graduate seminar on the military in Mexican history at the UNAM but also took it upon herself to shepherd my long-standing requests to consult the archives of the Secretaría de la Defensa Nacional. In the end, I gained entrance through her intercession. Alejandro de Antuñano Maurer and his staff at the Fundación Miguel Alemán provided crucial information for the period of the 1940s and powerful images for this book. Throughout, I have enjoyed the insight and encouragement of Juan Enríquez Cabot, whose logistical support in Mexico City and intellectual fire in Cambridge were critical to the success of this project.

The staff of the Fideicomiso Archivos Plutarco Elías Calles y Fernando Torreblanca deserves a special measure of thanks. A first-class archive, housing core collections of materials on Mexico in the 1920s and 1930s as well as the private archive of Joaquín Amaro, it is led by the able and generous hands of Norma Mereles de Ogarrio and Amalia Torreblanca. They aided my search for housing and, after the tragedy that nearly took the lives of my dear friend Carmen and her parents (as well as my own), offered a refuge from the uncertainty that followed. They became the center of my sphere in Mexico City, and I cherish the friendships formed with the good people there.

The process of producing this book was a very enriching experience, and I count myself lucky to have had the guidance of Sandy Thatcher at Penn State University Press. The incisive comments I received from the anonymous outside readers forced me to rethink the structure and rationale of the book. Julie Schoelles was a superb editor in every respect. The book is certainly better for the effort that these individuals put into its revision, though they bear no blame for the flaws that remain.

Henry Dietz and Mauricio Tenorio have been intellectual mentors to me since they oversaw the first stirrings of this project as my undergraduate honors thesis at the University of Texas at Austin. It has been my incredible luck to learn from them over the years and to count them as friends. Many other individuals affected this project through running discussions of shared interests, probing questions, or collaborative work. I thank them for their very useful input over the years and apologize to anyone I may have forgotten: Alison Adams, Michiel Baud, Mike Bernath, Brian DeLay, Oliver Dinius, Jorge Domínguez, Ben Fallaw, Aurora Gómez, Sarah Jackson, Hal Jones, Gil Joseph, Claudio Lomnitz, Martha Loyo, Graciela Márquez, Kevin Ostoyich, Erika Pani, Andrew Paxman, Enrique Plasencia de la Parra, Monica Rankin, Bertha Rosas Baruch, Elspeth Rostow, Walt Rostow, Terry Rugeley, Laura I. Serna, Peter H. Smith, William Suarez-Potts, David J. Weber, and Julia Young. *A todos, les agradezco.*

I have had the great fortune to learn from three of the most accomplished historians of Mexico. Friedrich Katz has been a generous and graceful interrogator of my project and has never stopped short in offering his time and insight to make it better. His encyclopedic knowledge of Mexico and its historiography opened many of the fruitful paths this book explores. John Coatsworth continually amazes me with both his relentless determination to sharpen arguments and his wry sense of humor. His penetrating analysis of my arguments, based on a deep expertise in Latin American affairs, unquestionably made this book stronger. Jack Womack has been an unfailing supporter of my research since the beginning. His decency, precision, and charm are the backbone of a body of scholarly work that is a model of clarity. I cannot claim that this project is a reflection of his mastery of Mexican history, but none of the good would be here if not for his hand.

Finally, I thank my family for the support they have provided throughout the course of this project. Although my parents were not always certain what I did all day with my stacks of papers and old books, their dogged support of my goals offered solace in the hard times. For all of their sacrifices, too many to name, I dedicate this volume to them.

The newest collaborator on this project is also the smallest. I thank my young daughter Alice for being such a joy, offering perspective and providing timely motivation to finish this book. Most of all, I am compelled to offer the last and greatest gratitude to my wife, Laura. In our many years together, we have traversed a long and difficult path: our lean and overworked college days, starting life over (still lean) in a strange place, the inevitable strains imposed by the pursuit of our aspirations, and all the time spent apart. Her persistence in her own career and dedication in supporting mine made all of this possible. Words, now, fail.

November 22, 2008
Dallas, Texas

Acronyms

CFE	Comisión Federal Electoral
CISEN	Centro de Investigación y Seguridad Nacional
CNC	Confederación Nacional Campesina
CROM	Confederación Regional Obrera Mexicana
CTM	Confederación de Trabajadores de México
DC	Departamento Confidencial
DFS	Dirección Federal de Seguridad
DGIPS	Dirección General de Investigaciones Políticas y Sociales
FPPM	Federación de Partidos del Pueblo Mexicano
MID	Military Intelligence Division
OIP	Oficina de Información Política
OSS	Office of Strategic Services
PAN	Partido Acción Nacional
PARM	Partido Auténtico de la Revolución Mexicana
PCM	Partido Comunista Mexicano
PConstM	Partido Constitucionalista Mexicano
PDM	Partido Democrático Mexicano
PNR	Partido Nacional Revolucionario
POCM	Partido del Obrero y Campesino Mexicano
PP	Partido Popular
PR	Partido de la Revolución
PRAC	Partido Revolucionario Anti-Comunista
PRM	Partido de la Revolución Mexicana
PRI	Partido Revolucionario Institucional
PRUN	Partido Revolucionario de Unificación Nacional
SIS	Special Intelligence Service
STFRM	Sindicato de Trabajadores Ferrocarrileros de la República Mexicana
UNAM	Universidad Nacional Autónoma de México
UNS	Unión Nacional Sinarquista

INTRODUCTION

MEXICAN POLITICS IN THE TWENTIETH CENTURY HAVE been dominated by two complementary paradigms: the rhetoric of the Mexican Revolution (1910–20) and the existence of an "official" party. The Mexican Revolution has enjoyed a long and voluminous historiography throughout the nine decades since the violence ended. The "official" party, founded as the Partido Nacional Revolucionario (PNR) in 1929, reformed as the Partido de la Revolución Mexicana (PRM) in 1938, and called the Partido Revolucionario Institucional (PRI) since 1946, has not received the same level of historical scrutiny. While the importance of the revolution as a historical period is self-evident, the development of a party based on the political aspirations of the surviving revolutionary elites has not generally sparked as much historical interest.

The PRI was not a Mesoamerican Marduk, born whole and spitting (electoral) fire in 1929. Structural changes in the party as it transformed from PNR to PRM to PRI reflected shifting domestic political realities as well as a changed international environment. The PNR began as an agglomeration of competing interests, political ambitions, and personal feuds that operated under a basic principle: political conflicts would be negotiated within the party. But the strength of the PRI as an institution through the second half of the century derived from the appearance of unity and the unwavering certainty of its leaders, a veneer that was meant to inspire confidence and reinforce the supposedly disinterested values of party politicians. The appearance of political unity and bureaucratic competence dissolved with the government's tardy and weak response to the disastrous 1985 Mexico City earthquake. Soon after, Cuauhtémoc Cárdenas's defection from the PRI to the leftist opposition and his strong presidential challenge in 1988 signaled the waning of the era of single-party dominance. The victory of Vicente Fox, candidate of the conservative Partido Acción Nacional (PAN), in the presidential election of 2000 marked a watershed in the political history of the country, as executive power moved peacefully into the hands of an opposition party for the first time.

This book is an analysis of opposition politics in Mexico. The aim throughout is to strike a new path into the discussion of the long dominance of a single party in Mexican politics. After the PNR came into existence in 1929 as a reaction to the political chaos issuing from both the Mexican Revolution and president-elect Álvaro Obregón's assassination, the country was seemingly in the thrall of a monolithic party bureaucracy. Much academic writing has followed this line of argument as well, unnecessarily simplifying a complex reality. Crucial to the present analysis is the argument that the PNR was not completely dominant in electoral politics from 1929 onward. Much as the weaknesses of a levee are revealed by the rampage of floodwaters and are then rebuilt and strengthened at the most vulnerable points, so too did the PNR and its successors learn from its challengers. As it faced and defeated opposition movements, the party leadership learned which elements of internal party rules and federal elections law needed tinkering with to avoid similar challenges in the future. The PNR and its successors also openly appropriated the portions of an opposition candidate's platforms that were most popular. Throughout the period from 1929 to 1952, the PNR experienced a very steep learning curve. The fact that from 1952 to 1988 there was very little electoral opposition suggests that the party leadership learned its lessons well.

This project seeks to amend the view of a monolithic party dominating elections since 1929 by examining the ongoing struggles within the dominant party and analyzing the consequences of those conflicts, namely opposition presidential campaigns. These campaigns are crucial for at least two major reasons. First, the emphasis on presidential contests derives from the fact that the president of Mexico has generally been the chief negotiator of political conflict in the country. That is, he has been, for the length of his term, the arbiter of all manner of high-level disputes. The president is emphatically not an all-powerful force, someone who rules by decree, or the issuer of commands that are always heeded. Indeed, this book explicitly rejects the idea of presidentialism as it is usually understood in the Mexican case. The president may have been the *jefe de los jefes,* but his position was only marginally stronger than other elites because of his official standing, which did not guarantee compliance. The old colonial maxim *obedezco pero no cumplo* ("I obey but do not comply") continues to be a guiding force in modern Mexican politics. Further, one need only consider the substantial power of some of the men who never felt the need to run for president (sugar magnate Aarón Sáenz, for example) to understand that the office itself only provides a seat at the head of the table; it does not ensure fealty. Often more power rests with those behind the office than the person in it.

Still, the struggle for the presidency provides a unique opportunity every six years to peer inside political machines and electoral alliances in an attempt to understand the lay of the land. Unlike the usual ambiguity of political life, an election is Manichaean in nature, a zero-sum game. During the presidential elections presented in this book (1940, 1946, and 1952), stalwarts of the dominant party decided to challenge the very system that they had once supported through opposition campaigns. These fractures within the party demonstrated its weakness at an early stage and its failure to accommodate strongly dissenting political views. The opposition campaigns also show the frailty of the PRM/PRI at a time when most academic studies consider it to already be an "official party" or monolithic in structure and effect. The challenges provided the impetus for structural changes of the party, carried out by visionary leaders such as Miguel Alemán, Ernesto Uruchurtu, and Rodolfo Sánchez Taboada. Thus, the threat of electoral opposition from renegade high-level operatives forced the PRM/PRI leadership to clarify the party's internal discipline, deal with the military once and for all, and create a force of political control that would all but guarantee the party leadership's continuation in power.

This study engages two distinct literatures beyond traditional Mexican historiography, one on intelligence and intelligence services and the other on the military in politics. In the first case, the arguments here do not so much differ from the existing intelligence literature as add to it, in large part due to the relative dearth of analyses of the Latin American intelligence services. The current literature concentrates heavily on what may be termed the "master" services: the United States, British, Russian, German, and Japanese agencies that dominated up to and, in some cases, after World War II. The "apprentice" services, in peripheral areas, enter the literature mainly as corollaries or outgrowths of the master agencies. The logic of this structure is clear: for example, no discussion of Estonia's *Kaitsepolitseiamet* can ignore the role that German and then Soviet intelligence played in its development. For Latin American cases, the dynamic is similar, although the United States is usually the master service on which the apprentices are modeled. But the literature on Latin American intelligence services has not kept pace with that of other apprentice agencies.

"We know little—almost nothing—about the Mexican intelligence services. This ignorance is not only absurd but dangerous."[1] So wrote Sergio Aguayo Quezada, a leading scholar of the Mexican intelligence services, in 1996. This was no doubt true then, and the situation has improved only marginally in the intervening years, though there appears to be a light on the horizon.[2] Mexico has since made the transition from the electoral dominance of the PRI to the semblance of a multiparty democracy. This political shift

---

1. Sergio Aguayo Quezada, "Intelligence Services and the Transition to Democracy in Mexico," in *Strategy and Security in U.S.-Mexican Relations Beyond the Cold War,* ed. John Bailey and Sergio Aguayo Quezada (San Diego: Center for U.S.-Mexican Studies, University of California at San Diego, 1996), 139.

2. The existing historical literature on Mexican intelligence agencies is slim, with only a few works dedicated to the topic. These include: Sergio Aguayo Quezada, *La charola: Una historia de los servicios de inteligencia en México* (Mexico City: Grijalbo, 2001); Harry Thayer Mahoney and Marjorie Locke Mahoney, *Espionage in Mexico: The Twentieth Century* (San Francisco: Austin and Winfield, 1997); María Emilia Paz Salinas, *Strategy, Security, and Spies: Mexico and the U.S. as Allies in World War II* (University Park: Pennsylvania State University Press, 1997); W. Dirk Raat, "U.S. Intelligence Operations and Covert Action in Modern Mexico, 1900–1947," *Journal of Contemporary History* 22, no. 4 (October 1987): 615–38; Leslie B. Rout Jr. and John F. Bratzel, *The Shadow War: German Espionage and United States Counterespionage in Latin America During World War II* (Frederick, Md.: University Publications of America, 1986). Other very interesting studies with information on the development or operations of Mexican intelligence include: Barry Carr, *Marxism and Communism in Twentieth-Century Mexico* (Lincoln: University of Nebraska Press, 1992); John F. Chalkley, *Zach Lamar Cobb: El Paso Collector of Customs and Intelligence During the Mexican Revolution, 1913–1918* (El Paso: Texas Western Press, University of Texas at El Paso, 1998); Friedrich Katz, *The Secret War in Mexico: Europe, the United States, and the Mexican Revolution* (Chicago: University of Chicago Press, 1981); Stephen R. Niblo, *War, Diplomacy, and Development: The United States and Mexico, 1938–1954* (Wilmington, Del.: Scholarly Resources, 1995); Friedrich E. Schuler, *Mexico Between Hitler and Roosevelt: Mexican Foreign Relations in the Age of Lázaro Cárdenas, 1934–1940* (Albuquerque: University of New Mexico Press, 1998). There is also the fascinating collection of interviews with the late master of Mexican intelligence: Gregorio Ortega, ed., *Fernando Gutiérrez Barrios: Diálogos con el hombre, el poder y la política* (Mexico City: Planeta, 1995). An exemplary work on Brazil is Martha Huggins, *Political Policing: The United States and Latin America* (Durham: Duke University Press, 1998). Huggins ably handles the development of the secret police in Brazil and its financial and training relationship with the United States.

provided the necessary impetus to finally open to researchers the long-guarded collections of intelligence files at the Archivo General de la Nación in Mexico City. The archive of the Dirección General de Investigaciones Políticas y Sociales (DGIPS), one of the main intelligence bureaucracies, was opened in 1999. The collection consists of nearly three thousand boxes of intelligence files for the period from 1920 to 1985. When I was conducting research for this book, the DGIPS archive was completely disorganized and without a proper catalogue of materials. Lacking reference materials, I consulted the collection box by box in a time-consuming but ultimately very enlightening process. Much of the argument about the structure and culture of the intelligence services in Mexico springs from such a thorough acquaintance with the documents.

A second collection of intelligence documents was opened too late to add greatly to this project. The massive archive of the Centro de Investigación y Seguridad Nacional (CISEN), complete with card catalogue and fully digitized, opened to researchers in 2002. The remnants of the DGIPS and the Dirección Federal de Seguridad (DFS), the other key domestic intelligence agency, were consolidated in 1985 after the abuses perpetrated by the agencies during Mexico's "dirty war" of the 1970s came to light. The CISEN was the direct descendant of these services, created in 1989 to provide greater transparency and accountability. The collections of the DGIPS and the CISEN offer historians of modern Mexico an entirely new viewpoint on political and social developments during the period.

My approach in this book has been to approximate the historical trajectory of Mexican politics in this period by a process of triangulation. Mexican intelligence documents as described above form the first leg. The second leg of evidence is drawn from U.S. government documents. The bureaucracies of the Central Intelligence Agency, Federal Bureau of Investigation, Military Intelligence Division, Office of Strategic Services, and State Department produced voluminous and sometimes very cogent reports detailing economic, social, and political developments in Mexico. The third evidentiary leg consists of newspaper accounts and editorials, published memoirs, campaign flyers and other propaganda, and eyewitness accounts.

The documents of the DGIPS collection are cited here in a standard format, including box number, internal file number, *expediente,* and page numbers (if available), as well as dates and places. Such a format may seem too detailed, but the continuing reorganization of the DGIPS archive demanded it. Although the collection of boxes may by now be renumbered, the notes herein refer to the old system, which should be preserved for future reference. In all cases for the DGIPS archive, I have included a place name for a document only when it was filed from outside of Mexico City. Also, lacking the original file number scheme, I nonetheless provide numbers in the hope that the future discovery or re-creation of such a guide may make the notes here even more useful. Although from the formation of the Departamento Confidencial in 1918 onward there were several name changes, I refer to this main Mexican intelligence service throughout as the DGIPS for the sake of simplicity. The DFS, since it was formed only after World War II, is treated separately. Chapter 4 offers an explanation of the early history of these agencies.

The nature of intelligence documents is often conditional or tentative. Agents may present information without the benefit of context or even specific knowledge of the persons involved. Likewise, it may be difficult for supervisors to correctly identify the pertinent morsels of intelligence in the sea of reports produced daily. This reality affects the way that historians can utilize intelligence archives. Many of the DGIPS reports contained information regarding rumors that were prevalent among various communities. For example, a theft of arms and ammunition from the Colegio Militar in early 1952 was quickly linked in the rumor mill to a supposed rebellion, allegedly because the perpetrators were "unconditional supporters" of Luis Alamillo Flores.[3] The central fact of the report, the theft of arms and ammunition, faded into the background of the more compelling political possibility: the rumor of rebellion. This rumor was all the more fertile since Alamillo Flores functioned as a close advisor to the opposition presidential candidate Miguel Henríquez Guzmán. In all, the report focused not on attempting to resolve the crime against the Colegio Militar, but on the potential political disturbance deriving from the rumor of rebellion. Although there are uncertainties regarding the intelligence documents utilized here, the problem of bias appears in the use of any primary source. The tremendous advantages gained from these reports are the opportunity to read the considered analyses of interested Mexican officials writing about their own political reality and to see the variety of opinion feeding into the intelligence bureaucracy of the federal government.

3. *Novedades,* Jan. 7, 1952; Report, Jan. 6, 1952, Archivo General de la Nación, Dirección General de Investigaciones Políticas y Sociales (AGN-DGIPS), Box 24, File 10, 2.1/061.8/10, p. 163.

Rumors can attest to the popular beliefs of certain segments of a population where they may be current. In the case of the DGIPS files, however, the interest of the historian is not so much the creation of the rumor and its effect in society, but the decision to report the rumor and the influence it has on any official who reads about it. In the period from 1918 to the early 1940s, agents had to develop their own ideas about what was worth reporting, how to present it, and how it might affect their superiors. But after World War II, each Mexican intelligence agent was charged with being the "eyes and ears of the President," constantly reporting facts or suspicions that might have a bearing on national politics.[4] High intelligence officials, cabinet members, and the president himself in turn read and digested the reports streaming in from around the country. Since they could base decisions on that intelligence, they had to trust that it was either accurate or at least plausible. Returning to the theft of arms in 1952, the rumor of an Henríquez link was no less interesting because it was uncorroborated. The importance of the rumor lay in the fact that some part of the public heard it or even believed it. The same was true among high-level consumers of the intelligence reports: reported rumors were important insofar as they were read and believed. The problem of rumors in intelligence reports was not one of objective truth, but of subjective perception. The continuing threat assessments and rumors coming in from field agents had a cumulative effect on the behavior of the officials who received them.

The second large theme addressed in this book is the issue of the military in politics. For Latin America, as with most other regions, this topic has been the province of political science. Mexico maintains an air force and a navy alongside the much larger army. Throughout this study, the army is the focal point because, unlike other Latin American cases, the navy and air force never provided the leadership or prestige that the army did in Mexican history.[5] Thus, when reference is made to military officers or soldiers, the reader may assume that these are members of the army and not the other services.

4. *El Universal,* Jul. 17, 1948.

5. The case of Mexico's involvement in World War II through the deployment of Air Force Squadron 201 is an exception to this general rule. Also, Argentina, Brazil, and Chile had better geostrategic reasons for developing strong naval forces: Argentina because of her long connection to the British trading empire, and Brazil and Chile for their long coastlines. Mexico, for better or worse, has often relied on the naval power of the United States for coastal protection and has generally been a nation of land battles. See Robert L. Scheina, *Latin America: A Naval History, 1810–1987* (Annapolis, Md.: Naval Institute Press, 1987).

The Spanish word *militares* is often used interchangeably to indicate both members of the armed forces generally and a group of ranking officers in particular. In the first case, the translation would be "soldiers" or "military men." The second case could be translated as "military officers" or simply "officers." These are imprecise translations at best since they do not adequately capture the specific contextual meanings that can be associated with the term in the original language. Moreover, the basic meaning of the word *militar* is something or someone related to the military. Very few items in my research materials refer to *soldados,* which specifically means soldiers, or *oficial,* which literally means officer. For the purposes of this project, I have rendered the term *militar(es)* as either "soldier(s)," "the military," or, if the context warrants, "military officer(s)." Although this removes some of the nuance of the original language, it also more accurately conveys the meaning of the sources.

The existing literature on the army in Mexican politics has developed a rather too facile explanation of civilianization, a process that made Mexico the exception in Latin America, with no military governments or coups since 1945. (For comparison, Latin America as a whole has had over one hundred coup attempts and almost every country has dealt with a military government over that period.) Edwin Lieuwen, who studied the process explicitly in his 1968 book *Mexican Militarism,* concluded neatly that "the elections of 1940 finally ended the political sway of the generals of the Revolution."[6] This explanation fails to deal with the fact of continuing political activity among the officer corps throughout the 1940s and into the 1950s, finally abating after the 1952 presidential elections and the U.S.-sponsored coup in Guatemala in 1954. It is true in retrospect that the break in military dominance came in 1940, after the political opposition had been beaten at the polls and Manuel Ávila Camacho removed any remaining authority from the military sector within the PRM. However, the officers who supported the presidential aspirations of Henríquez in 1946 (and again in 1952), or the powerful revolutionary generals who met secretly in 1948 to plot political change, or Octavio Véjar Vázquez, who argued for the political rights of soldiers as Mexican citizens, all seem to belie Lieuwen's easy interpretation. The rules of Mexican politics were not entirely clear (then or now), and it took over a decade for the importance of the 1940 election to be fully appreciated, a period that also

6. Edwin Lieuwen, *Mexican Militarism: The Political Rise and Fall of the Revolutionary Army, 1910–1940* (Albuquerque: University of New Mexico Press, 1968), xiii.

hastened the retirements of many of the older and more recalcitrant officers. This book is in part an analysis of the historical process that Lieuwen so quickly glossed over: how the Mexican military lost its authority in political matters and subjugated itself to a single-party dominant electoral system ruled by civilians.

In the discussion of political leaders and presidential candidates, another problem of language presents itself. The word "elite" derives from the Latin *eligere*. Therefore, members of the elite are literally a "chosen" group, different from and above other groups. The problem in Mexico from the revolution forward was that there were competing groups of elites, each vying for greater political and economic authority. This project deals with several elite groups at once, accepting the existence of dominant and nondominant elites. How is this possible? There were elite groups that chose poorly in these presidential elections, most of all the opposition candidates themselves, and they often fell into a sort of political purgatory after the voting. This does not imply that they lost their elite status, only that they lost their share of dominance. Moreover, the cases of political rehabilitation presented in chapters 1, 3, and 5 suggest the difficulty of definitively losing elite status in Mexican politics.

Chapter 1 explores the presidential election of 1940 and the collision of the PRM candidate, General Ávila Camacho, with two opposition candidates, Generals Juan Andreu Almazán and Joaquín Amaro. While Almazán represented a coalition of business leaders, conservative social groups, and some factions of the army, Amaro counted on the support of former president Plutarco Elías Calles and his political machine. This dual threat from the Right threatened the political strategy of the newly formed PRM and offered an alternative to the left-leaning policies that had defined the administration of Lázaro Cárdenas. The "conservative wave" that carried Almazán and Amaro in the election of 1940 brought with it the danger that right-leaning revolutionary veterans could effectively subvert the long-term stability of the PRM by competing for power in elections. *Almazanismo* represented the reaction to the increasingly hegemonic behavior of the PRM and the best chance for the opposition to scotch the nascent dominance of that party. Almazán's defeat in 1940 provided an important set of lessons for PRM leaders, who continued refining the political system to their benefit through changes in both internal party rules and national electoral laws, and it offered the opportunity to further perfect the political machinery that would provide lasting access to power.

Chapter 2 analyzes the theme of the military in Mexican politics. From the 1930s to the 1950s, the Mexican military declined in political status and eventually became one of the most exceptional cases in Latin America: a national army removed from politics. While military officers maintained control of national politics in the immediate aftermath of the Mexican Revolution, the efforts of Calles and Álvaro Obregón to systematize national politics transformed the traditional methods of exercising influence into a more modern structure. The creation of the PNR, and its reformations into the PRM and then the PRI, afforded the dominant elites the opportunity to shift acceptable political speech from the realm of violence to that of parties and elections. As the revolutionary generation of officers aged and the education gap between young military and civilian leaders grew, the federal bureaucracy became increasingly controlled by civilians. These leaders, especially under the administration of Miguel Alemán, effectively co-opted the new generation of military elites by offering leadership positions within the newly expanding national security apparatus and secret police. In this way, the praetorian impulses of the military officers could be sated in the service of civilian political goals, including the elimination of electoral opposition.

Chapter 3 examines the presidential election of 1946 and the beginning of a new era of civilian control of government. The particular rhetoric of democracy surrounding the end of World War II provided a unique window of opportunity for civilian ascendance in Mexican politics, embodied in the presidential contest between two nonmilitary candidates: Miguel Alemán of the PRM and Ezequiel Padilla. The perception of increasing civilian control was cemented after Alemán's victory, as the military sector of the PRM was drowned in the massive popular sector of the PRI during the party's reformation in 1946. Alemán staffed his administration with a large number of university-educated civilians and walked a fine line between curbing the military and appeasing it. His decision to bring a new generation of military officers into the leadership of the DFS in 1947 signaled a willingness to cede strategically important posts without relinquishing executive control. Indeed, the success of the dominant civilian elites in creating a single-party dominant system depended on the committed work of the military officers who ran the intelligence community. This set of roles made Mexico an outlier in the region, as civilian government was institutionalized alongside the increasing professionalization of the intelligence services.

Chapter 4 outlines the history of the Mexican intelligence services from 1918 to the present and describes changes in the professional methods that agents used. The creation of the DFS is taken as a case study of the interplay between domestic and international interests and the increasing professionalization of the Mexican intelligence services. As methods improved, agents began to see themselves as extensions of the party in power, gradually aligning their work with the greater strategic goals of the PRI. In this way, although the Mexican intelligence services could deal with international threats reasonably well, they were more often utilized in the battle against domestic political opposition to the PRI. Thus, the creation of the DFS was a signal policy success for Miguel Alemán, as the new president was able to parlay his warm relations with President Truman into direct funding and training aid. In this specific case, we see Alemán having it both ways: appeasing the Cold War aims of the United States and the domestic political needs of the PRI. The intelligence bureaucracy operated as a political police force for the PRI and became one of the crucial tools that party leaders could use to deal with challenges from within and from without.

Chapter 5 argues that the presidential election of 1952 represented the first time that the adjustments made by the PRI to electoral law, internal candidate selection, and domestic intelligence gathering operated at their full potential. Party discipline was enforced as never before as the PRI, under Sánchez Taboada, cracked down on *futurismo* by candidates such as Henríquez.[7] Even Alemán failed in his attempts to gain reelection and to impose his successor on the PRI. The costs of working outside of the PRI surpassed the limits of most Mexican elites, most of whom chose to take their chances within the bounds of the dominant party after 1952. Finally, the military settled into the role of pillar of the state, solidifying the alliance of civilian leadership and military staffing that defined the Alemán-era intelligence bureaucracy. In all, the Henríquez campaign of 1952 signified the end of three related characteristics of postrevolutionary Mexican politics: the *cardenista* revolutionary ideology, the influence of the military in national electoral politics, and the existence of opposition parties. With the loss of Henríquez, Mexican politicians and generals fully realized the primacy of the PRI in electoral contests and acceded to its dominance.

This book, in short, posits an alternative lifespan for the "official" party's dominance in Mexican politics. Rather than looking to the foundation of the

---

7. *Futurismo* is the informal process in which potential candidates for office across the political spectrum, in this case the presidency, test the political waters. Such potential candidates usually attempt to line up support among unions, factions of the PRI, and in various sectors of the public. It is literally "futurism"—looking to the future to calculate one's chances for succeeding in a political race.

PNR in 1929 as the starting point for such control, my analysis argues that the PRI's dominance was only cemented in the aftermath of the 1952 presidential election. This study thereby offers a new viewpoint on the political transition that occurred in Mexico during the 1940s. The transformation of the PRM into the PRI, the removal of the military from electoral politics, the resettlement of younger officers in the intelligence services, and the inculcation of a new discipline among political elites all produced the conditions that allowed for the dominance of a single party structure for decades. As leaders of the PRI became more adept at negotiating political disputes and running the electoral machine, the costs for any elite attempting to oppose it at the polls became too high to reasonably fathom.

ONE

MISSED OPPORTUNITY
The Election of 1940

THE PRESIDENTIAL ELECTION OF 1940 was a defining moment in the development of the modern Mexican political system. The 1930s had seen a shift away from the conservative policies of Plutarco Elías Calles, especially in the oil and agrarian expropriations of the Lázaro Cárdenas administration. Cárdenas's move to the Left was opposed in the 1940 election by various elements of the Right. Although Juan Andreu Almazán fielded the main electoral opposition, several other military officers exhibited presidential aspirations, a complement to heavy influence that private citizens brought to bear.[1] The Mexican government and U.S. observers viewed armed rebellion as a constant threat. Almazán led a campaign that emphasized the disastrous economic, diplomatic, and political consequences resulting from the Cárdenas policies. He argued against the perpetuation of the dominant Partido de la Revolución Mexicana (PRM). On July 7, 1940, the presidential election proceeded with a high voter turnout across the country. Official returns gave Almazán far fewer votes than PRM candidate Manuel Ávila Camacho. Popular calls for rebellion against this allegedly fraudulent vote count were legion, but Almazán chose instead to leave the country. He went first to Cuba, to

---

1. Other precandidates with military credentials in the 1940 cycle included Generals Joaquín Amaro, Bonifacio Salinas, and Manuel Perez Treviño. Private citizens exerting influence over the presidential succession included Antonio Díaz Soto y Gama, Manuel Gómez Morín, and the industrialist Emilio Madero.

rendezvous with U.S. diplomats at the Pan-American Conference, on his way to the Baltimore–Washington, D.C., area, where he seemingly intended to press his connections with the Franklin D. Roosevelt administration. When negotiations failed and U.S. vice president-elect Henry Wallace attended the inauguration of Ávila Camacho on December 1, 1940, the electoral challenge of *almazanismo* passed into history.

Origins of the Conservative Wave

The Cárdenas administration had deeper worries than the United States in 1940. Within Mexico, elements of the Right had formed several groups of important size and influence to challenge the reformist agenda of the president. As a U.S. Army attaché concluded in 1939:

> The present political set-up in Mexico appears to the casual observer to be seated firmly in the saddle and to have the situation well in hand. Actually this is far from the truth, and all of the "ins," including the high officials of the P[artido] N[acional] R[evolucionario], are experiencing a severe attack of the jitters. The President and his advisers have, as a result of their radical ideas, alienated the sympathy and support of many powerful Mexicans, such as: Calles, Cedillo, Amaro, Rodríguez, Almazán, Morones, Portes Gil, Ayala, etc. In addition there are many others who, for financial or other reasons, appear to support Cárdenas when actually their sympathies lie elsewhere.[2]

From land reform to the rolling back of religious power, Cárdenas succeeded in alienating and angering sizeable domestic constituencies during his administration.

Seven groups in opposition to *cardenista* programs came together in the presidential campaign of General Juan Andreu Almazán in 1940. These included the Monterrey industrialists, railroad workers, segments of the army, the Camisas Doradas, the Sinarquistas, the Partido Acción Nacional (PAN), and Joaquín Amaro's Partido Revolucionario Anti-Comunista (PRAC). Almazanismo was the single most important political force in Mexico in 1939–

---

2. Summary, [Military Intelligence Division, Jan. 1939], National Archives and Records Administration, Washington, D.C. (NARA), Record Group 165, Box 2454, File 3000.

40, after the group led by Cárdenas himself. The development of the Almazán campaign, his alliances with the main groups of the Right, and his defeat by the electoral machinery of the dominant party were all key developments in the political history of Mexico between Álvaro Obregón's death in 1928 and the outbreak of World War II. This period set the stage for the eventual electoral dominance of the PRI, as the party leaders learned how best to deflect or defeat disaffected elements of the elite and close off avenues of political dissent.

Almazán began his campaign for the presidency under fairly propitious circumstances. The president in office was a divisive figure, inspiring either adoration or disgust among different sectors of the Mexican populace. Lázaro Cárdenas, for his many virtues, provided a very inviting target for criticism from the Right. Cárdenas had distributed far more land under the Constitution of 1917 than any of his predecessors—nearly fifty million acres in all, representing 80 percent of Mexico's arable land. He had focused his administration on the fulfillment of the "promises of the Revolution" in the form of myriad social policies and government entitlements that were either small or absent before 1934. Finally, his expropriation of the oil industry in 1938 had alienated two of the great world powers, the United States and Britain, at a time when the international situation was in deep flux. Each of these policy decisions opened Cárdenas, and his party's next candidate, to withering attacks from the conservative opposition.

The Mexican political rules, too, seemed to invite democratic challenges. Especially after the unpleasant experience of the Saturnino Cedillo rebellion in 1938–39, revolutionary veterans began to look for nonviolent means of contesting political authority.[3] In July 1939, Heriberto Jara, president of the Executive Committee of the PRM, gave an interview to the press that opened the door to challenges from the likes of Almazán and Amaro. The newspaper headline stated that "internal acts of the Party should not be confused with the electoral act itself. . . . The National Council of the Party declares that there is equality of conditions among its members."[4] This announcement appeared to give equal footing to all comers in the internal party caucus and negate the idea that the PRM candidate was elected de facto after the nomination. The veneer of democracy was maintained as discontented politicians were drawn into the fray.

3. The details and implications of the Cedillo rebellion are treated in greater detail later in this chapter and in chapter 2.

4. *Excélsior,* Jul. 13, 1939.

There was, however, a simple rationale for allowing the contenders to fight it out for the party nomination: if the leaders of the PRM could contain any political challenges to the internal caucus, they would be able to shield such bitter divisions and acrimonious disputes from the eyes of the public. They would also be in a position to "rightfully" deny the aspirations of the challengers once they were defeated in the rounds of candidate selections in the party committees. This strategy rested on an assumption of discipline: that the challengers would accept the deals struck in the end and withdraw for the sake of party unity. In this, the leaders of the PRM were either mistaken or very cunning. Neither Almazán nor Amaro accepted the choice of Ávila Camacho as the presidential candidate, and each launched a presidential campaign wholly outside the PRM. If the PRM was caught unawares, then it was a serious political miscalculation. If the PRM had anticipated this action and allowed it to happen to isolate them, then it was a devious move indeed. Either way, the PRM could attack the opposition ruthlessly under the banner of revolutionary unity.

The project of political consolidation guided by Cárdenas could not risk derailment by the opposition, especially from the Right. Almazán's position at the head of conservative forces in Mexico fueled his campaign. The continuing strength of conservative groups in Mexican politics, echoes of the Cristero revolt of the 1920s and the Cedillo rebellion, allowed Almazán to amass enormous political influence and force the PRM into a more conservative political stance than the Cárdenas record to 1937 would have suggested.[5] Prior to the election of 1940, U.S. officials clearly discerned "a trend towards a somewhat more conservative government in Mexico and probably a government more favorably inclined to American interests."[6] Thus, while Almazán was denied the electoral victory he likely attained in 1940 and earned the lasting enmity of conservative groups throughout Mexico for eschewing "revolution" to protect that victory, he should be recognized as an important force shaping the strategies pursued by the PRM leadership groups. His efforts in the campaign of 1940 accelerated the pendulum swing in Mexican politics back to the Right, a process visible in the administrations of Ávila Camacho and Miguel Alemán.

5. Friedrich E. Schuler, *Mexico Between Hitler and Roosevelt: Mexican Foreign Relations in the Age of Lázaro Cárdenas, 1934–1940* (Albuquerque: University of New Mexico Press, 1998). Schuler puts the turn to conservatism in the Cárdenas administration in 1937.

6. Summary of Report from Ft. McIntosh to G-2, Ft. Sam Houston, San Antonio, Apr. 28, 1939, NARA, Record Group 165, Box 2460, File 3020.

Almazán pursued intensive negotiations with elements of the Cárdenas group before announcing his independent candidacy. On April 22, 1939, Almazán met Cárdenas in Reynosa before they traveled together the next day to Chipinque, Almazán's mountaintop estate high above Monterrey, for a private dinner. Almazán duplicated this schedule on May 7 by traveling to Reynosa to meet with Secretary of Defense Jesús Agustín Castro and again returning to Chipinque for a formal dinner. Finally, days later, Almazán visited Cárdenas in El Palmito, Durango.[7] The timing of these visits belies simple social occasions; they were clearly opportunities for Almazán to press his case for the PRM candidacy at the highest levels of the administration. In this he demonstrated his cognizance of the obvious advantages of carrying the PRM nomination and, importantly, his eagerness to become the new standard-bearer of the party. Only when he was rejected by the PRM did Almazán press his case from the opposition.

Almazán realized that conducting an opposition campaign against the PRM machinery was dangerous. In a published statement in 1939, he argued, "Thirty years of skepticism about electoral matters has left me in the position that my intervention in them offers me nothing to gain and the danger of losing everything." His critics argued in a similar vein, "[Almazán] is an individual who since 1920 has been taking advantage of not only guarantees from the government but also a privileged position whereby he has enriched himself . . . The ultimate goal of his campaign is to secure the continuation of his personal prosperity for the future . . . The Number One Contractor of the administrations since 1920, who became a millionaire thanks to the prebends he has monopolized and still controls, is the last person who would have the moral authority to censure the government."[8]

Almazán derived an opulent lifestyle from government concessions and construction contracts.[9] One of his most visible projects was the new military

7. Report, [unidentified agent] to DGIPS, May 13, 1939, Monterrey, Archivo General de la Nación, Mexico City, Dirección General de Investigaciones Políticas y Sociales (AGN-DGIPS), Box 187, 2.1/311.1/5, Vol. 1.

8. "Thirty years of skepticism": "El Gral. Almazán habla a la Nación," Jul. 25, 1939, Monterrey, AGN-DGIPS, Box 188, 2.1/311.1/5, Vol. 5; "continuation of his personal prosperity": Speech, Diputado Manuel Jasso in León, Guanajuato, La Prensa, Feb. 21, 1940, AGN-DGIPS, Box 189, 2.1/311.1/5, Vol. 9.

9. See, for example, Elizabeth Borton de Treviño to McCombs, Jul. 3, 1939, Monterrey, Holland McCombs Papers, University of Tennessee at Martin, Special Collections, Box 46, File 22; also, James W. Wilkie, The Mexican Revolution: Federal Expenditure and Social Change Since 1910 (Berkeley and Los Angeles: University of California Press, 1967).

city at Monterrey built to house the Seventh Military Zone command structure, which he had headed since 1926.[10] This installation was one of the finest in all of Mexico, and Almazán reaped substantial profit from its construction.[11] More profitable still was the contract awarded to Almazán's "Anahuác" company to build the Pan-American Highway section from Laredo to Mexico City, a distance of some 750 miles.[12] As one reporter put it in 1939, "The busy general is always building something; sometimes for himself, sometimes for the government, sometimes for his men, sometimes for the tourist, sometimes for all four at once."[13] U.S. consular officials laconically judged that "his record in business administration and construction carries considerable weight."[14] After the revolution, Almazán became virtually indispensable in large construction projects and military defense in his adopted home state of Nuevo León.[15] Almazán had singular power within Mexico because of his large capital reserves, revolutionary stature, and military rank. He was the quintessential product of the revolution, a man risen from relative obscurity to the revolutionary pantheon, a man who parlayed his revolutionary credentials into political influence, which brought government contracts and wealth, thus reinforcing his political power. By 1920, Almazán was one of the giants of the revolutionary generation and had two decades to exploit the cycle of influence before the election of 1940 arrived. No one could doubt his wealth, power, or influence when the question of Cárdenas's succession came to the fore.

But even his own supporters saw cause for concern about Almazán's reliability if rebellion were to occur, since he "had too much wealth invested in the Republic, which would be lost in case of defeat."[16] And his wealth provided a good excuse for the apathy or suspicion of some Mexicans who

10. Service record of Juan Andreu Almazán, Mar. 6, 1928, Archivo Histórico de la Secretaría de la Defensa Nacional (AHSDN), Cancelados, General de División Juan Andrew Almazán, XI-111/1–114, pp. 539–44.

11. General de Brigada (D.E.M.) Luis Garfías Magaña (Ret.), interview with author, Nov. 10, 2000, Mexico City.

12. Edwin Lieuwen, *Mexican Militarism: The Political Rise and Fall of the Revolutionary Army, 1910–1940* (Albuquerque: University of New Mexico Press, 1968), 134.

13. McCombs to Thomas Krug (*Time*), Sep. 5, 1939, McCombs Papers, Box 46, File 22.

14. Summary of Report from Ft. McIntosh to G-2, Ft. Sam Houston, San Antonio, Apr. 28, 1939, NARA, Record Group 165, Box 2460. File 3020.

15. The ancestral home of the Almazán clan was the state of Guerrero.

16. Memo, Daniels to Secretary of State, 812.00/30927, Feb. 2, 1940, in *Confidential U.S. State Department Central Files. Mexico: Internal Affairs, 1940–1944. Part I: Political, Governmental, and National Defense Affairs* (Frederick, Md.: University Publications of America, 1987), Reel 1.

"would not forget that in the shadow of all the administrations Almazán had amassed millions of pesos."[17] Indeed, throughout the campaign of 1940, accusations persisted against the director of the Banco de México for helping Almazán extract the nation's wealth from the Treasury "by way of leonine contracts."[18] Just as Cárdenas became a champion of the poor, Almazán was seen as hopelessly tied to his government contracts and substantial wealth.

The U.S. diplomatic community could not accurately discern the political landscape in the 1940 presidential cycle and actively debated which outcome would best serve U.S. interests: "It is too early to forecast the future political outcome, but at present it appears General Almazán has a stronger following than General Camacho. If this situation continues, and there is a free election, he will probably be elected president. . . . In the event he is not elected, yet is possessed of the conviction that the greater portion of the masses supported him, force may be used to secure that which an election failed to do. There is always the possibility that General Almazán and President Cárdenas have already come to a secret agreement concerning the future control of Mexico."[19]

Initially, the staff of the U.S. Military Intelligence Division (MID) could not perceive a popular trend one way or the other toward Ávila Camacho or Almazán's opposition campaign. Complicating the situation further was the assumption at MID that military force, in the form of an armed rebellion, was recognized as an available and viable means of enforcing political claims in Mexico. Finally, beneath the political and military analysis lay the possibility that all of the rhetoric and movement was simply a ruse, a masterwork of deception, intended to reinforce the power of both Cárdenas and Almazán while addressing the domestic and international need for the appearance of democracy and fair play. As the United States attempted to maintain official neutrality in the Mexican presidential contest, debate raged over which candidate, Almazán or Amaro or Ávila Camacho, would best serve U.S. interests in the long run.

17. Report, Insp. 12 to DGIPS, Aug. 21, 1939, AGN-DGIPS, Box 188, 2.1/311.1/5, Vol. 4.

18. *El Popular,* Jun. 27, 1940, AGN-DGIPS, Box 190, 2.1/311.1/5, Vol. 16. The original wording in Spanish, "contratos leoninos," is a play on words, suggesting a role for Almazán's brother Leonides in the steady provision of government construction business.

19. Military Attaché Report 9162, Gordon H. McCoy to War Department, Mexico City, Aug. 29, 1939, in Robert Lester, *U.S. Military Intelligence Reports. Mexico, 1919–1941* (Frederick, Md.: University Publications of America, 1984), Reel 4, Frames 216–19.

The natural power center for Almazán's campaign was in the state of Nuevo León, especially in its industrial and financial center Monterrey, where Almazán enjoyed an exceptionally long tenure as commander of the Seventh Military Zone. His connections to the "entrepreneurial interests of the Mexican north that considered the General as one of their own" enforced his claim to political predominance in the state.[20] Even along the U.S.-Mexico border, there was "a real burning desire to see him elected as President of Mexico."[21] Yet Almazán received strong criticism for his links to the Monterrey industrialists and their contributions to his campaign. In April 1939, reports circulated that the industrial elite of the city had offered to support his candidacy with the astronomical sum of eight million pesos. He was further reported to have strong ties to the leaders of the Cervecería Cuauhtémoc and the Vidriera Monterrey, two of the largest industrial concerns in the nation. In a speech in Guadalajara toward the end of the campaign, Almazán disputed the veracity of these long-standing rumors, saying, "The rich do not help me. . . . Eighty percent [of expenses] are from my own funds and the other twenty percent are from friends."[22] Nevertheless, throughout the campaign, the image of Almazán as a revolutionary tycoon playing in politics endured.

Allied to Monterrey businessmen were U.S. business interests, most often through Texas connections, a fact that proved powerful in the battle for the appearance of U.S. support. A U.S. reporter in Mexico wrote that "[U.S. vice president John Nance] Garner himself has made no move towards the Almazán elements, but some of the big Garner supporters in Texas are also big Almazán sympathizers."[23] Meanwhile, Mexican intelligence reported that it was Garner who had encouraged Almazán to seek the presidency in the first place. Finally, U.S. banks had allegedly promised Almazán "all the money that is necessary" to conduct his presidential campaign.[24] Even if such

20. Albert Michaels, "Las elecciones de 1940," *Historia Mexicana* 21, no. 1 (Jul.–Sep. 1971): 109.

21. Report, Maj. Malcolm Lindsey, Ft. Sam Houston, to War Department (G-2), May 15, 1940, NARA, Record Group 165, Box 2460, File 3020.

22. Links to the Monterrey industrialists: Draft report, Insp. Rincón C. to DGIPS, [Mar. 24], 1939; industrial elite of the city: Report, Insp. 19 to DGIPS, Apr. 14, 1939 (both located in AGN-DGIPS, Box 187, 2.1/311.1/5, Vol. 1); largest industrial concerns in the nation: Report, Insp. 15 to DGIPS, Jun. 21, 1939, AGN-DGIPS, Box 188, 2.1/311.1/5, Vol. 2; "rich do not help me": Report, Insp. 9 to DGIPS, Jun. 2, 1940, Chihuahua, AGN-DGIPS, Box 190, 2.1/311.1/5, Vol. 15.

23. McCombs, Jul. 31, 1939, McCombs Papers, Box 46, File 22.

24. Seek the presidency: Report, [unidentified agent] to DGIPS, May 13, 1939, Monterrey, AGN-DGIPS, Box 187, 2.1/311.1/5, Vol. 1; "all the money that is necessary": Report, Insp. 19 to DGIPS, Jun. 24, 1939, AGN-DGIPS, Box 188, 2.1/311.1/5, Vol. 2.

information only circulated as rumor, the very fact that it circulated at all with any credibility, demonstrated by the need of Mexican agents to urgently report it to their bosses, meant that Almazán enjoyed at least the *appearance* of powerful connections, which in turn could provide political leverage. Almazán's ability to attract moral support and hard cash from the rich and connected appeared to stretch across the northern border to the highest levels of the U.S. government as well.

Almazanismo took different forms and attracted different followers throughout Mexico, according to the reports of Mexican agents. In Chiapas, it was depicted as a front for "Sinarquistas and Reactionaries," bureaucratic shorthand for radical conservatism.[25] In Guadalajara, some groups and villages that had been granted *ejidos* reportedly kept their support for almazanismo close to the vest for fear of punishment or losing their lands. In the same area, Mexican intelligence estimated that 80 percent of workers in the Confederación de Trabajadores de México (CTM), especially railroad workers, supported Almazán, as did 90 percent of Catholics and most women.[26] The Partido Veracruzano del Trabajo also reportedly supported Almazán's campaign, and Orizaba was noted as "one of the regions where almazanismo is the most rooted." In Matamoros, Almazán could count on the support of "independent elements" and a large part of the popular sector.[27] In short, in the vision of Mexican agents attempting to compile a composite of national sympathies, Almazán's supporters were not limited to his base in Monterrey or to some sort of regional stronghold. Rather, those elements of Mexican society disaffected with the Cárdenas administration, regardless of geographic location or professional affiliation, found ideological solace in the Almazán campaign and gave his movement national scope.

The voluminous ranks of the Mexican bureaucracy were not immune to almazanista organizing, contrary to the usual belief that government workers loyally vote for those who pay them. More troubling for one agent than the adhesion of workers from the Treasury Office in Mexico City was the sinking realization that "the movement of people is all the time more numerous."

25. Report, Insp. Thivol to DGIPS, Apr. 5, 1940, Tuxtla Gutiérrez, AGN-DGIPS, Box 30, File 4, 2.1/062.2(72)/2, p. 3.
26. Report, Insp. Alemán Pérez to DGIPS, Apr. 28, 1940, Guadalajara, AGN-DGIPS, Box 30, File 4, 2.1/062.2(72)/2, pp. 41–42.
27. "Most rooted": Report, Insp. 7 to DGIPS, May 14, 1940, Orizaba, AGN-DGIPS, Box 30, File 4, 2.1/062.2(72)/2, pp. 49–52; "independent elements": Report, Inspector Reina to DGIPS, May 31, 1939, Matamoros, AGN-DGIPS, Box 185, 2.1/311.1.1/2, Vol. 3.

One legislator threatened to evict almazanista officeholders from all branches of the government, arguing that their political allegiance "tacitly locates them in an antagonistic position with the Government, for whom they work, thus committing a disloyalty *and a crime*."[28] As evident in the language of the agent filing the report, there was increasing currency and acceptance of the idea that there was decreasing political latitude within the electoral system. Fear of a fifth column of almazanistas within the government, especially in crucial sectors that dealt with business, transportation, or labor issues, made the presidential campaign of 1940 especially polarizing.

In his attack on the cardenista power base within organized labor, especially the CTM, Almazán derived great strength and legitimacy from the support of railroad workers.[29] A government agent argued this tacitly when he described how almazanistas were spreading propaganda "among their own supporters" by agitating in train stations. This activism was echoed by passengers around the conservative stronghold of León, Guanajuato, who put up pro-Almazán propaganda in the train cars themselves.[30] The support of citizens in León was of special interest since it was also the traditional center of the ascendant conservative movement of the Sinarquistas.[31] In Monterrey, Almazán found very strong backing among the railroad workers, including Local 19 of the national railroad union, the Sindicato de Trabajadores Ferrocarrileros de la República Mexicana (STFRM). The Comisión Ferrocarrilera in Monterrey confirmed their support in a campaign strategy meeting with Almazán in July 1939.[32] Critics of Almazán's business practices derided his use of active military units in the construction of the Ferrocarril del Sureste line, a project from which he personally derived profit. Yet, in August 1939, the workers who had labored on the project published a full-page ad in

28. "Movement of people": Report, Insp. 19 to DGIPS, Jun. 27, 1939, AGN-DGIPS, Box 188, 2.1/311.1/5, Vol. 2; "antagonistic position": *Excélsior,* Jul. 17, 1940, AGN-DGIPS, Box 191, 2.1/311.1/5, Vol. 17, emphasis added.

29. McCombs to David Hulburd (*Time*), Aug. 2, 1939, McCombs Papers, Box 46, File 22; Report, Insp. 20 to DGIPS, Jun. 3, 1939, AGN-DGIPS, Box 187, 2.1/311.1/5, Vol. 1.

30. "Among their own supporters": Report, Insp. 7 to DGIPS, Feb. 23, 1939, AGN-DGIPS, Box 184, 2.1/311.1/2, Vol. 2; propaganda in the train cars: Report, Insp. Meneses to DGIPS, Feb. 24, 1939, León, AGN-DGIPS, Box 187, 2.1/311.1/5, Vol. 1.

31. See, for example, Daniel Newcomer, *Reconciling Modernity: Urban State Formation in 1940s León, Mexico* (Lincoln: University of Nebraska Press, 2004).

32. Backing among the railroad workers: Report, [unidentified agent] to DGIPS, May 13, 1939, Monterrey, AGN-DGIPS, Box 187, 2.1/311.1/5, Vol. 1; campaign strategy meeting: Telegram, Insp. Castro Reina to DGIPS, Jul. 19, 1939, Monterrey, AGN-DGIPS, Box 188, 2.1/311.1/5, Vol. 2.

Excélsior defending Almazán from his detractors and claiming that they were treated fairly by their former employer. In July 1940, Almazán replied that it was Ávila Camacho himself, as secretary of national defense, who gave him permission to use military units as construction crews on the Sureste line.[33] Further, the organic law of the armed forces from 1926 "provided for the use of military resources in the construction of communications networks and public works that had some correlation with the overall needs of the military."[34] Due to their strategic position in both economic and military terms, railroad workers were a crucial constituency during any political contest, electoral or otherwise. Therefore, Almazán's apparent alliance with large numbers of these workers made his presidential challenge even more dangerous to the PRM.

The Organized Right: Dorados, Sinarquistas, and Panistas

Almazán reputedly controlled a large proportion of the activists on the Right in Mexico as well.[35] In an interview with the U.S. consul in Ciudad Juárez, Nicolás Rodríguez confided that "should the situation so resolve itself as to make such action advisable, his Camisas Doradas would support the candidacy of General Juan Andreu Almazán." The Camisas Doradas was a paramilitary group on the Right that was quite capable of resorting to violence. U.S. military officials likewise debated whether a "shift of this body under Calles' influence to the candidacy of Almazán might result in his election." The reports from U.S. consular officials that fascist activities were "considered stronger in North Mexico," a region more closely associated with almazanismo, fueled the belief that Almazán was somehow in league with these forces. More troubling for the U.S. analysts was the uncorroborated but persistent information that German agents had "infiltrated

33. Full-page ad: *Excélsior,* Aug. 5, 1939, AGN-DGIPS, Box 188, 2.1/311.1/5, Vol. 2; permission to use military units: *La Prensa,* Jul. 5, 1940, AGN-DGIPS, Box 191, 2.1/311.1/5, Vol. 17.

34. Specifically, Article 81 of the *Ley Orgánica del Ejército y la Armada* supplied the legal outline of the activity in which Almazán was engaged. See Stephen J. Wager, "The Mexican Army, 1940–1982: The Country Comes First" (PhD diss., Stanford University, 1992), 269.

35. Letter, "Costas" to "Pérez Sánchez," Mar. 25, 1939, Monterrey, AGN-DGIPS, Box 187, 2.1/311.1/5, Vol. 1.

into the various organizations of the Almazán Headquarters."[36] A confidential assessment of the Mexican press classified both of the major Mexico City dailies, *Excélsior* and *El Universal,* as "pro-Almazán."[37] The U.S. Embassy was well aware of links between newspapers sympathetic to the almazanista cause and German sponsorship. Among the media outlets receiving subsidies from both Almazán and the German state were *Hombre Libre, Omega, El Sinarquista, Mexico Nuevo,* and *La Semana.* Links between some of the media outlets and Franco's Spain were also noted.[38] Still, other U.S. officials questioned the veracity of attributing fascist tendencies to Almazán. The reports from U.S. observers in Mexico presented no definitive evidence for formal ties between Mexican groups and European fascism. However, there were enough indicators, tentative as they might be, to provoke concern in Washington. In all, Almazán's seemingly close ties to the quasi-fascist Right in Mexico was cause for alarm among U.S. officials who worried that the building conflict in Europe could seep across the U.S.-Mexico border.

Almazán drew additional support from more traditionally conservative and Catholic elements in Mexico. As early as 1935, the archbishop of Durango pledged that "in case of any serious trouble arising in Mexico, all Catholics in the Republic would gladly place their resources and their lives in his hands."[39] In Iguala, Guerrero, an Almazán campaign rally was attended by both "disaffected" citizens and a "great quantity of old nuns."[40] The majority of Chiapan smallholders and clerics reportedly favored the Almazán campaign, an indication of the continuing dominance of the clergy in the state or perhaps the echo of ties to the counter-revolutionary government of Alberto

36. "His Camisas Doradas": Report, Blocker to Secretary of State, Jul. 8, 1939, Ciudad Juárez; "shift of this body" and "considered stronger in North Mexico": Summary of Report from Ft. McIntosh to G-2, Ft. Sam Houston, Apr. 28, 1939; "infiltrated into the various organizations": Military Attaché Report 9328, Gordon H. McCoy, Apr. 16, 1940, Mexico City (all located in NARA, Record Group 165, Box 2460, File 3020).

37. Boal to Secretary of State, Jun. 13, 1940, Mexico City, NARA, Record Group 165, Box 2450, File 2810, Despatch 10801. The assessment was researched by Bernard S. Redmont, then of the Graduate School of Journalism at Columbia University. For more information in this vein, see Bernard S. Redmont, *Risks Worth Taking: The Odyssey of a Foreign Correspondent* (Lanham, Md.: University Press of America, 1992).

38. Report, McGurk to Secretary of State, Sep. 30, 1941, Mexico City, NARA, Record Group 165, Box 2450, File 2810, Despatch 13884.

39. Military Attaché Report 5838, Lt. Col. H. E. Marshburn to Military Intelligence Division (MID), Jan. 19, 1935, NARA, Record Group 165, Box 2455, File 3020.

40. Report, Insp. 20 to DGIPS, Jul. 12, 1939, Iguala, AGN-DGIPS, Box 185, 2.1/311.1/2, Vol. 4.

Pineda.[41] The pattern was much the same in Pachuca, Hidalgo, where the Partido Laborista Mexicano (PLM), the middle class, small merchants, and non-agrarista peasants supported Almazán. In the state of Colima, the reverse held true; almazanismo was weak "above all because there is not the high number of religious folk that exist in other places."[42] Throughout the country, Almazán could measure his support as easily by the size of Sunday morning Masses as by any kind of polling data. In areas marked by strong Catholic traditions, almazanismo flourished, while in less devout regions citizens tended to distance themselves from the Almazán campaign.

Outside of the traditional stronghold of León, Guanajuato, the Unión Nacional Sinarquista (UNS) was reported to be powerful along the U.S.-Mexico border, especially in ports of entry. This influence, closely mirroring Almazán's own popularity among border agents, gave an important appearance of danger should civil war erupt and the importation of arms from the United States become necessary, as in the rebellions of 1923 and 1929.[43] In one example, former army general Fausto Ruiz and his brother Sóstenes were accused of having stockpiled arms in Chiapas to lead the Sinarquistas in a rebellion. In Manzanillo, Mexican agents reported that all of the navy and customs personnel were almazanistas. And a large group of uniformed customs agents attended an Almazán rally in Piedras Negras in May 1940.[44] Again, Almazán's presumed ties to such a well-armed and organized group

41. Report, Insp. Pérez to DGIPS, Nov. 18, 1939, Mapastepec; Report, Insp. Pérez to DGIPS, Nov. 21, 1939, Tonalá; Report, Insp. Pérez to DGIPS, Nov. 28, 1939, Las Casas (all located in AGN-DGIPS, Box 185, 2.1/311.1/2, Vol. 5); Prudencio Moscoso Pastrana, *El pinedismo en Chiapas, 1916–1920* (Mexico City: n.p., 1960). Pineda welcomed Félix Díaz to the state of Chiapas and aided his operations against the Carranza government, thus staking his political fortunes to a nostalgic conservatism.

42. Pattern was much the same: Report, Insp. 5 to DGIPS, Jan. 11, 1940, Pachuca; "high number of religious folk": Report, Insp. Pérez to DGIPS, Jun. 15, 1940, Manzanillo (both located in AGN-DGIPS, Box 185, 2.1/311.1/2, Vol. 6).

43. U.S. State Department, 812.00/30906, "Resumé of Conditions in Mexico During December, 1939," Jan. 15, 1940, in *Confidential U.S. State Department Central Files, Mexico, 1940–1944, Part I,* Reel 1; Report, Lt. Col. A. W. Roffe to Commanding General, Ft. Sam Houston, San Antonio, Oct. 9, 1940, NARA, Record Group 165, Box 2458, File 3020; Report, R&A No. 843, "The Sinarquista Movement in Mexico," Jun. 1943, p. 19, NARA, Record Group 226. Arms imports from the U.S. were crucial during the periods of the French Intervention and the Mexican Revolution, as well.

44. Stockpiled arms: Report, Insp. 20 to DGIPS, Apr. 1, 1940, Tuxtla Gutiérrez, AGN-DGIPS, Box 189, 2.1/311.1/5, Vol. 11; navy and customs personnel: DGIPS Chief Arriola to Secretary of the Navy, Jul. 23, 1940, AGN-DGIPS, Box 191, 2.1/311.1/5, Vol. 17; uniformed customs agents: Report, Insp. 46 to DGIPS, May 29, 1940, Torreón, AGN-DGIPS, Box 190, 2.1/311.1/5, Vol. 14.

gave pause to policy makers, on both sides of the border, as they attempted to discern the appropriate path forward.

Allied to the Catholic thrust of Almazán's campaign was a decided effort to involve Mexican women in the political equation. Such appeals were a mixture of traditional gender roles and optimism about future political rights. Many campaigns since the 1920s had proceeded with similar strategies, relying on women's influence even though they could not vote in national elections until after the 1952 presidential cycle. Pro-Almazán activists in Saltillo argued that the women of Coahuila represented the "guarantee of the progress of the nation," as well as the hopes of all Mexican women to enjoy and exercise the political and civil rights they deserved.[45] General Francisco Coss, at one time a "die-hard Carrancista," reached out to women in Sabinas, declaring at a rally that they should go to the polls to protect the voting boxes and to "compel their husbands" to vote for Almazán.[46] In Colima, women undertook the task of going house to house during the campaign, arguing the almazanista case and making a list of supporters, all the while competing for prizes for the most rapid progress.[47]

The almazanistas' post-election political strategy also depended on women's efforts. Female supporters of the Partido Revolucionario de Unificación Nacional (PRUN) approved a resolution at almazanista headquarters in Mexico City to "visit barracks to invite the troops to take part in the rebellion," but were admonished not to write down any of their plans. Similarly, in Michoacán, up to two hundred women attended an almazanista meeting where they learned that they were responsible for convincing their male relatives of "the obligation that they have as patriots to save the country from ruin."[48] Although their role in the almazanista effort was clearly ancillary, women represented an important component of the effort to play upon traditional conservative elements of Mexican culture in the electoral campaign, and they did what they could, short of voting, to ensure an Almazán victory.

Despite the close affinity of social goals, the emphasis on local action in lieu of coordinated electoral activity marked a central breaking point between

45. "Llamado de Saltillo," *El Siglo de Torreón,* Apr. 7, 1939.

46. Report, Insp. 46 to DGIPS, May 29, 1940, Torreón, AGN-DGIPS, Box 190, 2.1/311.1/5, Vol. 14. Coss's *carrancista* streak is discussed in Friedrich Katz, *The Life and Times of Pancho Villa* (Stanford: Stanford University Press, 1998), 378.

47. Report, Insp. Alemán Pérez to DGIPS, Apr. 20, 1940, Colima, AGN-DGIPS, Box 190, 2.1/311.1/5, Vol. 12.

48. "Visit barracks": Memo, DGIPS, Aug. 2, 1940; "save the country from ruin": Report, Insp. 7 to DGIPS, Sep. 2, 1940 (both located in AGN-DGIPS, Box 191, 2.1/311.1/5, Vol. 18).

the UNS and the Almazán campaign. While members of the UNS were encouraged to fulfill their civic duties, there was not a concerted effort to turn out the vote for particular candidates. This precluded any formal offer of electoral support by the UNS as an organization, but individual members could, and very likely did, vote for conservative candidates. For example, in Guerrero, the large concentration of Sinarquistas generally aligned themselves with the Almazán candidacy, although they refrained from early propaganda campaigns in his favor.[49] The Sinarquistas were predominantly anti-Cárdenas, if not explicitly pro-Almazán. Nevertheless, the latent conservatism of Almazán's campaign found a useful echo in the activist language of Sinarquismo's faithful.[50]

Manuel Gómez Morín, one of the founders of the PAN, was widely viewed as both the spokesman and leading intellectual of the conservative movement in Mexico. Though he was not affiliated with the UNS, his articles and opinions appeared in the Sinarquista magazine *Orden,* as well as mainstream media outlets.[51] Orators at the 1940 PAN convention in Tampico synthesized the complaints of many on the Right, describing a nation subjected to "a revolution bloody and cruel in its youth, degenerated in its maturity into a political racket [and] a democracy prostituted to the breeding of political 'hold-up men.' "[52] In general, Gómez Morín and the PAN wanted less centralized government, a greater degree of municipal autonomy, and a respect for traditional conservative values. The PAN platform opposed "the existence of an official party . . . the coercion effected on labor groups . . . the attempted partisan use of the Army . . . [and] the entire mechanism of official and semi-official propaganda aimed towards imposition." This laundry list of the political system's ills, each of them aimed at increasing the hegemony of the PRM, found a simple solution in the official PAN ideology.

49. Report, Insp. Castro Reina to DGIPS, Oct. 16, 1939, AGN-DGIPS, Box 188, 2.1/ 311.1/5, Vol. 5.

50. For further elaboration of this point, see Servando Ortoll, "Catholic Organizations in Mexico's National Politics and International Diplomacy (1926–1942)" (PhD diss., Columbia University, 1987); also, Aaron W. Navarro, "Opposition and Dominance in the Mexican Presidential Election of 1940: The Challenge of Almazanismo" (paper presented at the 24th International Congress of the Latin American Studies Association, Dallas, Texas, March 28, 2003).

51. Report, R&A No. 843, "The Sinarquista Movement in Mexico," Jun. 1943, p. 114, NARA, Record Group 226.

52. U.S. State Department, 812.00/30894, Memo, Consul Collins to Secretary of State, Jan. 11, 1940, Tampico, in *Confidential U.S. State Department Central Files, Mexico, 1940–1944, Part I,* Reel 1.

"Citizen's action," Gómez Morín concluded, "is the only road to salvation that the country has."[53]

In spite of Gómez Morín's call to action, the aversion of the PAN to electoral processes made its participation in the election of 1940 a rather conditional affair. Indeed, the PAN's stance on the value of electoral processes was a conflicted one. On one hand, a PAN bulletin declared, "We do not think that the vote itself can ever be the true road to the solution of the nation's problems . . . [and] affirm the superior value of the human being and of principles that will never be subject to a vote." After the elections, the PAN was also quick to point out that the party had "objectives that went beyond the merely electoral." Yet, on the other hand, the PAN understood the necessity of elections and that they would continue to be essential to the Mexican process. To reach their political and social goals in the long term "the proper road in our legal system is that of elections."[54]

If there had to be elections, the PAN argued that they should be effective and fair. The electoral system, as the *panistas* saw it, "only authorizes the existence of transitory gangs [*pandillas*] formed for elections . . . [and] is a well-conceived instrument of falsification, its persistence, even within the childish and primitive field of our public institutions, is a national disgrace." This criticism extended naturally to the PRM and the concept of an "official party" in Mexico. The PAN could not allow "the symbiosis between the party and the State," arguing that "they are two different institutions, their goals are distinct." When the union between a political party and the state solidified, the PAN argued, the party would cease to be a "communion of political ideals and become an antechamber of power."[55] Reading the views and predictions of PAN founders such as Gómez Morín, it is astonishing how astute and accurate their criticisms of the ascendant system were.

53. "Existence of an official party": Report, "Acción Nacional. Programa Mínima de Acción Política (Tercera Comisión)," Sep. 1939, Archivo Manuel Gómez Morín (AMGM), Fondo Acción Nacional, Vol. 1, File 14; "citizen's action": Report, "Informe del Comité Organizador a la Asamblea Constituyente y la Convención," Oct. 4, 1939, AMGM, Fondo Acción Nacional, Vol. 2, File 26.

54. "True road to the solution": Memo, PAN, [Oct. 1940], AMGM, Fondo Acción Nacional, Vol. 4, File 47; "beyond the merely electoral": Report, PAN convention, Sep. 1940; "proper road in our legal system": PAN Committee report, "Elecciones presidenciales," 1939 (both located in AMGM, Fondo Acción Nacional, Vol. 39, File 220).

55. "Existence of transitory gangs": Memo, PAN, [Oct. 1940]; "communion of political ideals": "Papel pendiente," [1940] (both located in AMGM, Fondo Acción Nacional, Vol. 4, File 47).

What the PAN sought was responsible political life, battles fought on the field of principles and ideas rather than personalities and rhetoric. The most effective way to take part in politics was "in the Constitution and the life of the political parties." For the PAN, a political party was "a community of conviction in a system of ideas that correctly interpret man and society . . . [and] not a voracious construct that prepares assaults on positions of authority in order to abuse them." Rather, it should be "an organized and active force of opinion . . . the Nation organized against the powerful to limit it in its excesses, contain it in its abuses, direct it in political goals." A political party, in sum, was "the natural link between man, any man dedicated to his work, and the political life of the country."[56] The PAN leaders' conception of parties, and political participation in general, contrasted starkly with the model exemplified by the rival PRM, which sought to swallow up whole sectors of the population for the sake of electoral hegemony. The struggle between the PAN and the PRM in this early stage seemed the story not so much of David and Goliath as Pangloss and *The Prince*.

The PAN did not present a forceful picture when it was founded. As U.S. ambassador Josephus Daniels noted, "It is a party to be watched, but cannot be considered more than a nuisance to the [Cárdenas] Administration."[57] But Gómez Morín and his advisors understood the necessity and strategy of political opposition and how it would be used to foment the "complete national renovation" they sought. In November 1939, as the Cárdenas administration was pushing a plan through Congress to federalize education, Gómez Morín argued that it was a ploy "to see how far they ought or not worry about the opposition." Moreover, if the opposition did not fight vociferously on this issue, the administration "[would] have won a key battle and also know[n] that it could go much further, in electoral matters as well as its other proposals." Gómez Morín was willing to step into the breach to oppose what he viewed as an increasingly overreaching government from arrogating still more power to itself. Such actions earned the PAN support among those groups who had tired of the package of reforms engendered by the Cárdenas administration and did not wish to see them continued under a successor regime. By February 1940, the PAN was the most organized and extensive independent political group in the northern state of Chihuahua.[58]

56. "Papel pendiente," [1940], AMGM, Fondo Acción Nacional, Vol. 4, File 47.

57. U.S. State Department, 812.00/30927, Memo, Daniels to Secretary of State, Feb. 2, 1940, in *Confidential U.S. State Department Central Files, Mexico, 1940–1944, Part I*, Reel 1.

58. "Complete national renovation": PAN Convention, Sep. 1940, AMGM, Fondo Ac-

It was obvious to all that Almazán was the presidential candidate most closely aligned with the PAN's long-term political goals, but the posture of the PAN in the election was anything but assured. The cycle of debate within the PAN over an endorsement of Almazán offers a crucial viewpoint on the potential gains and losses in 1940. Miguel Palacios Macedo, an influential official from the Banco de México, wrote to Gómez Morín that "Acción Nacional has nothing to gain and much, very much, to lose if it puts itself in with the mountain of almazanista parties." The PAN was threatened with an almazanista inundation if it declared its support too soon. Even a general statement of common principles that approximated the Almazán platform, Palacios Macedo argued, "would be seen as the beginning of the unification of the independent groups . . . and one of the first acts of the almazanista campaign." Any attempt to rectify these impressions would only "attract the hostility of the other groups and demonstrate the disunity that is rampant in the opposition camp."[59] Palacios Macedo, like many panistas, did not strictly oppose supporting Almazán in the presidential contest but, rather, feared the submersion of the newly constituted PAN organization and principles in what was essentially a personalist campaign. The decision about whether to endorse Almazán as a candidate or not proved to be a thorny ideological proposal for the PAN leadership.

The PAN convention in October 1939 solidified support for the Almazán campaign. This support was "to make clear the necessity of beginning the complete renovation of public life in Mexico, counting the electoral process as an episode in this larger battle, which is not a conflict of personalities, but rather of . . . two different concepts of life, society and the Fatherland." The PAN had a larger vision for Mexican politics than just electoral contests—one that encompassed every facet of daily life. Efraín González Luna argued that "the politician of Acción Nacional is a politician of constant political activity, doing politics in his house, his office, the street, his conversations with friends. . . . Our political action is an organic activity, not episodic."[60] Given

ción Nacional, Vol. 39, File 220; "worry about the opposition" and "won a key battle": Letter, Gómez Morín to González Luna, Nov. 7, 1939; extensive independent political group: Letter, Gómez Morín to González Luna, Feb. 17, 1940 (both located in AMGM, Fondo Corresponde-ncia, Personal, Correspondencia Particular: Efraín González Luna, 1935–1965).

59. Letter, Palacios Macedo to Gómez Morín, Jun. 23, 1939, AMGM, Fondo Correspon-dencia, Personal, Correspondencia Particular: Miguel Palacios Macedo, 1921–1941.

60. "Complete renovation of public life": Report, "Informe del Comité Organizador a la Asamblea Constituyente y la Convención," Oct. 4, 1939, AMGM, Fondo Acción Nacional, Vol. 2, File 26; "politician of constant political activity": Speech of Efraín González Luna to first regional PAN conference, Jan. 8, 1940, Tampico, AMGM, Fondo Acción Nacional, Vol. 2, File 39.

the pervasive nature of PAN's organizing and activity, it survived the election of 1940 while Almazán's PRUN, based on a vague conservative agenda and a charismatic figure, did not.

The PAN was unique among the movements on the Right in that it formally supported Almazán's candidacy in the presidential election of 1940. None of the other groups were organized or overtly political enough to present such unified endorsement. The PAN membership voted to back Almazán, over the objections of Gómez Morín, during their national conference in Mexico City.[61] When the PAN finally did declare its support, at least one close advisor to Gómez Morín broke professional and personal ties: "I cannot now accept the position of shameful almazanista, which is the only thing the members of the PAN are, after the absurd agreements they have just made."[62] Palacios Macedo and Gómez Morín had been close friends for many years, but after this letter they never spoke or wrote to each other again.[63] Soon after, Gómez Morín advised that the PAN leadership should be thinking about not only what was necessary to win the election but also what kind of responsibilities the party would have if they won. Still, there was an undercurrent of indecisiveness among the directors of the PAN since, as late as May 1940, González Luna discussed what the limits of the PAN collaboration with independent parties should be.[64] The alliance between the almazanistas and the PAN was as uneasy as it was unequal.

Candidates and Nominations

The Almazán campaign, in combination with the formation of the PAN, demonstrated a truism of postrevolutionary Mexican politics that U.S. military intelligence perceptively discerned: "Rivalries of opposing factions within the Government party have been of greater significance in internal and international affairs than any agitation emanating from opposing political

61. U.S. State Department, 812.00/30899, Memo, Daniels to Secretary of State, Jan. 10, 1940, in *Confidential U.S. State Department Central Files, Mexico, 1940–1944, Part I*, Reel 1.

62. Letter, Palacios Macedo to Gómez Morín, Sep. 20, 1939, AMGM, Fondo Correspondencia, Personal, Correspondencia Particular: Miguel Palacios Macedo, 1921–1941.

63. I thank Angelica Oliver of the Archivo Manuel Gómez Morín for her insights on this point.

64. Responsibilities the party would have: Letter, Gómez Morín to González Luna, Nov. 7, 1939; undercurrent of indecisiveness: Letter, González Luna to Gómez Morín, May 13, 1940 (both located in AMGM, Fondo Correspondencia, Personal, Correspondencia Particular: Efraín González Luna, 1935–1965).

parties."[65] That is, the most dangerous challengers were the stalwarts of the PRM who turned on their masters and sought to take charge of the developing system for their own benefit. When these internal rivalries became open conflicts, the most common tactic of the PRM was to expel the opposition members from the party ranks, thereby denying them the lucrative political and financial benefits that membership conferred. Many almazanistas were purged from the PRM in this way in late June 1940, just weeks before the presidential elections.[66] The formal revocation of membership in the PRM was meant to publicly besmirch the reputations and long-term prospects of nonconformist elements of the party.

The most crucial political contests within the PRM involved the issue of candidate selection. In these battles, the choice of a presidential candidate weighed heaviest of all. The cardenistas realized the necessity of confronting the threat of Almazán's campaign directly. Two generals close to Cárdenas wanted to "begin propaganda towards the unification of the elements now wandering dispersed" and argued that he needed "to see the danger of the reaction grouped around General Almazán and find a serious [de peso] candidate to confront almazanismo." Manuel Ávila Camacho did not seem to fit that bill.[67]

News from Veracruz in 1939 was decisive. Miguel Alemán resigned as governor of the state in order to direct the presidential campaign of Ávila Camacho. This association aligned the interests of the avilacamachista Puebla group with that of the Veracruz group in a way that would persist through the 1940s. One report suggested that heavy political and personal influence was brought to bear as Generals Cándido Aguilar, Maximino Ávila Camacho, and Arturo Campillo Seyde prevailed upon Alemán to accept the position and lead Manuel Ávila Camacho's campaign.[68] Yet Alemán's selection was

65. Summary, "Source: G-2," Feb. 14, 1939, NARA, Record Group 165, Box 2454, File 3000.

66. *La Prensa,* Jun. 25, 1940; *Excélsior,* Jun. 18, 1940 (both located in AGN-DGIPS, Box 190, 2.1/311.1/5, Vol. 16).

67. Report, Insp. G[utiérrez] to DGIPS, Aug. 29, 1939, AGN-DGIPS, Box 188, 2.1/311.1/5, Vol. 4.

68. Aguilar had been a stalwart of the revolutionary group around Carranza, only to side erroneously with de la Huerta in the 1923 rebellion, before being reintegrated into the dominant elite and holding legislative positions from his native state of Veracruz. He was a federal senator from Veracruz when Alemán was convinced to lead Manuel Ávila Camacho's campaign. Maximino Ávila Camacho was the candidate's brother, the muscle of the family operations, and governor of Puebla at this juncture. Campillo Seyde was a close friend of Alemán's father and young Miguel's legal mentor. See Roderic Ai Camp, *Mexican Political Biographies, 1935–1993,* 3rd ed. (Austin: University of Texas Press, 1995).

not free of controversy. The Veracruz connection drew pressure from other groups within the state. Former state governor Adalberto Tejeda, who ran for president on the Mexican Communist Party ticket in 1934, was reportedly active in planning another opposition candidacy to challenge the avilaca-machista majority in formation.[69] In the end, Mexican agents went so far as to report, probably erroneously, that even one-time presidential hopeful and cardenista Francisco Múgica was joining the Almazán campaign as a protest against the imposition of Ávila Camacho.[70] A strong view grew within the intelligence bureaucracy that there was widespread disaffection with the prospect of an Ávila Camacho administration.

Nevertheless, Ávila Camacho constructed his candidacy on the back of both official support and intense political negotiation. In a coded telegram, a Mexican intelligence agent described how Ávila Camacho had secretly promised to maintain old *cedillista* bureaucrats in their positions without prejudice, if they would work to get him elected.[71] This deal was struck in October 1938, before Cedillo's death at the hands of federal troops, and it is unclear how many chose to keep their government sinecures via a change in political allegiance. In May 1939, the positions of several of the key cabinet secretaries, including those of agriculture, labor, and foreign relations, vis-à-vis the presidential election, were mainly undecided. The notable exceptions were communications and public works, where the presidential aspirations of former secretary Múgica lived on through the efforts of his successor, Melquíades Ángulo, and the president's office, which had already been organized to support Cárdenas's first choice.[72] By 1939 in Aguascalientes state, old cedillistas had begun to form Ávila Camacho committees to advance his candidacy, reportedly outshining the nascent campaigns of Almazán, Gildardo Magaña, and Rafael Sánchez Tapia in both enthusiasm and sheer numbers.[73]

Ávila Camacho utilized his position as the PRM candidate to form a wide base of political support through state patronage networks. He steadily built

69. Draft report, Insp. Thivol to DGIPS, Jun. 19, 1939, Veracruz, AGN-DGIPS, Box 185, 2.1/311.1/2, Vol. 3. See also Camp, *Mexican Political Biographies, 1935–1993*, p. 691.

70. Report, Insp. Gutiérrez to DGIPS, Aug. 2, 1939, AGN-DGIPS, Box 188, 2.1/311.1/5, Vol. 2.

71. Telegram, Insp. 4 to DGIPS, Oct. 19, 1938, San Luis Potosí, AGN-DGIPS, Box 184, 2.1/311.1/2, Vol. 1.

72. Report, Insp. 19 to DGIPS, May 6, 1939, AGN-DGIPS, Box 184, 2.1/311.1/2, Vol. 2.

73. Letter, Gustavo I. Guerra to Insp. Thivol, May 6, 1939, Aguascalientes, AGN-DGIPS, Box 184, 2.1/311.1/2, Vol. 2. Magaña and Sánchez Tapia were both active early in the presidential campaign but retired from the contest before election day.

alliances with traditional groups such as the CTM and the Confederación Nacional Campesina (CNC), but his influence extended through individual states as well, including the "official machinery of the State [of Nuevo León]." Indeed, reports indicated that the state government of Nuevo León was discounting one day of salary from each two-week pay period for the Ávila Camacho campaign. Such activity on Almazán's home turf became easier after he took official leave from his position as commander of the Seventh Military Zone at Monterrey, as required by the electoral law. Almazanistas claimed to have intercepted a message from Ávila Camacho to the Treasury of Oaxaca, requesting thirty thousand pesos to supplement the ten thousand pesos already paid monthly. This was in addition to the "large amounts" (*fuertes sumas*) flowing from the state-owned Petróleos Mexicanos into the Ávila Camacho campaign.[74] Ávila Camacho's support from government sources may have been double-edged, as Ambassador Daniels observed: "[it] caused the conservative elements in Mexico to turn against the General and offered an opportunity for General Almazán to secure a large following."[75] For those elements of the population wary of the marriage of official and personal fortunes, Almazán's self-funded effort seemed preferable to Ávila Camacho's apparent shaking down of various government entities and federal workers.

However, the struggle for political ascendancy was not just a matter of Ávila Camacho versus Almazán (and Amaro). The political conflict within the PRM became visible in April 1940 as the Ávila Camacho group maneuvered to defang the threat of a potential Cárdenas power play. Throughout the election season, rumors had been rampant that Cárdenas might seek to provoke a state of emergency, perhaps by inciting Amaro or Almazán to rebellion, in order to continue in power. The U.S. Federal Bureau of Investigation (FBI) reported that, after a six-hour conference, Maximino Ávila Camacho and the San Luis Potosí power broker Gonzalo N. Santos decided that Manuel should "definitely demand a 'show-down' relative to President Cárdenas' intentions." The message was that "if President Cárdenas attempted to 'double cross' General [Ávila] Camacho by causing an emergency

74. "Official machinery": Report, [unidentified agent] to DGIPS, Jul. 3, 1939, Monterrey, AGN-DGIPS, Box 185, 2.1/311.1/2, Vol. 3; one day of salary: Report, Insp. 15 to DGIPS, Jun. 21, 1939, AGN-DGIPS, Box 188, 2.1/311.1/5, Vol. 2; "large amounts": Report, Insp. 7 to DGIPS, Nov. 4, 1939, AGN-DGIPS, Box 188, 2.1/311.1/5, Vol. 6.

75. U.S. State Department, 812.00/30927, Memo, Daniels to Secretary of State, Feb. 2, 1940, in *Confidential U.S. State Department Central Files, Mexico, 1940–1944, Part I*, Reel 1.

in the country and remaining in power himself or by the imposition of another candidate at the last moment, *the [Ávila] Camacho people intended to fight*."[76] That Ávila Camacho's political backers "intended to fight" the very political machine that they were utilizing was an extraordinary situation. It demonstrated the inherently hostile and severely complicated political terrain on which these historical actors moved. It also presented a picture of an evolving political group, then called a party, that was unable to prevent even its own elite (for the sake of democratic form) from cutting one another's throats.

In the midst of these events, the Cárdenas administration was well aware of the danger of an alliance between Almazán and forces on the Right. Mexican intelligence concluded that "unspeakably secret in the extreme are the almazanista activities with the counter-revolutionary elements in Mexico, but also undoubtedly true is that they are always seeking the means to strengthen those ties."[77] Amaro also nurtured informal allegiances with the various groups of the Right, and his party, the PRAC, offered aid to those who "have publicly manifested anti-communist tendencies and . . . know how to advance the aspirations of the opposition."[78] Yet more dangerous than his links to elements of the Right was his long-standing connection to former president Plutarco Elías Calles, in exile since 1935. U.S. reports in 1937 indicated that Calles was "actively interested in opposition plans."[79] A Mexican agent in Ciudad Juárez similarly concluded that it was Calles who was determining Amaro's political strategy.[80] The connection between Amaro and Calles provided a nostalgic alternative for Mexican voters, offering the undoubted patriotism of Amaro and the political sagacity of Calles.

Amaro saw the problem of Mexican politics in the persistence of personalism. He argued that only by selecting a single candidate at a national convention of all "independent and opposition elements [representing] . . . great

76. Memo, J. E. Hoover to Col. J. M. Churchill, G-2, War Department, Apr. 13, 1940, NARA, Record Group 165, Box 2460, File 3020. Emphasis added. Ávila Camacho was sometimes shortened to "Camacho" by U.S. observers unfamiliar with Mexican naming conventions.

77. Memo, DGIPS, Aug. 28, 1940, AGN-DGIPS, Box 191, 2.1/311.1/5, Vol. 19.

78. Memo, titled "Opinión" and signed by Amaro, Feb. 28, 1940, Fideicomiso Archivos Plutarco Elías Calles y Fernando Torreblanca, Archivo Joaquín Amaro (FAPEC-AJA), Campaña Política, 1939–1940, File 020200, PRAC.

79. Summary, [MID, Jan. 1939], NARA, Record Group 165, Box 2454, File 3000.

80. Telegram, Insp. Martínez Flores to DGIPS, Sep. 11, 1940, Ciudad Juárez, AGN-DGIPS, Box 191, 2.1/311.1/5, Vol. 19.

currents of public opinion" could the tradition of factional conflict and division be precluded. He believed that such a procedure would "make possible the creation of a true national independent party capable of assuming the responsibility of the national destiny." This contrasted with the machinations of the politicians within the PRM who "had arrogated to themselves the role of great electors in the selection of the candidate, unnecessarily creating a mood of acute personalism."[81] Amaro was setting himself up as a candidate poised to unify the nation under the old banner of the revolution and all that it implied.

With clarity, Amaro argued that "everything that causes political confusion and disorganization tends to favor the *continuista* goals of the group of demagogues trying to keep illegally clinging to power."[82] The danger that imposition presented was clear to Amaro, not only because it was being attempted so openly, but because it was "at odds with the will of the nation."[83] His discontent with the policies of the Cárdenas administration was such a cause of concern that "he [was] being watched very carefully and everyone with whom he talk[ed was] being questioned by officials of the Presidential Staff." At least in 1939, U.S. officials judged that "more concern [was] felt over Amaro's probable actions than was experienced during Cedillo's activity in San Luis Potosí."[84] Amaro's idealistic vision of multiparty politics in Mexico, coupled with his allegiance to the old Calles machine, made his challenge to the political system in many ways as robust as Almazán's.

Amaro's campaign was centered on a keen opposition to the Cárdenas policies that were leading Mexico toward an "inevitable disaster." In Querétaro, Amaro challenged the emerging electoral machinery of the PRM, arguing that "the greatest danger for the immediate future of our country is that the regime is trying to perpetuate itself by way of imposition." He was philosophical about the level of civic participation in Mexico, echoing PAN and UNS platforms, and claimed that the death of the "civic spirit" was the fault not of the people but of "the men that dedicate themselves to those political tasks without the necessary tact and understanding of them." More

---

81. Memo, titled "Esquema" [basic ideas of Amaro, 1940], FAPEC-AJA, Campaña Política, 1939–1940, File 020200, PRAC.

82. Ibid.

83. Statement of Amaro, Jan. 1940, FAPEC-AJA, Campaña Política, 1939–1940, File 020200, Querétaro.

84. Military Attaché Report 8922, William. F. Freehoff, Mexico City, Feb. 17, 1939, NARA, Record Group 165, Box 2460, File 3020.

specifically, he blamed "the existence of an Official Party, that degenerates politics [and] suborns the conscience," for the poor state of the civic spirit in Mexico.[85]

Amaro had grand ideas about the nature and necessity of democracy in Mexico. He argued that "to institute a democratic regime, liberty for citizens to elect their government is indispensable [and that] a Single Official Party that is arbitrary slays aspirations and liberty and nullifies the participation of citizens in the political functioning of the country." Only with liberty could "the diverse tendencies in society organize themselves into political parties [which], always acting within the law, can win and lose battles in the great field of civics, without compromising the stability of the Nation, or breaking the public order." But he was not blinded by ideology, in a conventional sense, stating that "the politician is a man of action and not of ideas." Amaro was "fighting for the existence of a national government, strong in substance, respected morally, aloof from dishonorable compromises, and safe from the danger of coups and uprisings." More than a simple contest of personalities, the election to Amaro was a "collision of ideals, aspirations and systems of government."[86] Amaro's quest was not unlike that of PNR and PRM planners; he desired a stable government, a depoliticized army, strong national sovereignty, and a triumphant postrevolutionary nationalism. He was simply not willing to achieve such a goal at the expense of real, deep, functional democracy.

Likewise, Amaro sought to combat what he perceived as a pervasive communist threat within the highest circles of the Mexican government. Such

85. "Inevitable disaster": Undated speech [Mar. 1939]; "greatest danger for the immediate future": Statement, Jan. 1940 (both located in FAPEC-AJA, Campaña Política, 1939–1940, File 020200, Discursos, Folder 1); "civic spirit": Letter, Amaro to General de Brigada Juan Antonio Domínguez A., Feb. 29, 1940, FAPEC-AJA, Campaña Política, 1939–1940, File 0514, Durango, Asuntos relacionados con entidades políticas; "existence of an Official Party": Interrogatorio al Sr. Gral. Joaquín Amaro, [1940], FAPEC-AJA, Campaña Política, 1939–1940, File 0514.

86. "Institute a democratic regime": Unsigned draft, "Democracia, debe instituirse la democracia en México," [1939], FAPEC-AJA, Campaña Política, 1939–1940, File 0514; "diverse tendencies in society": "Amaro ofrece una convivialidad al Gral. Pérez Treviño con motivo de su onomástico: La oposición define los propósitos que persigue," Jun. 23, 1939, FAPEC-AJA, Campaña Política, 1939–1940, File 0514, Clipping book; "man of action": Draft with MS notes, "El Libro Blanco del Partido Revolucionario Anti-Comunista," [1939], FAPEC-AJA, Campaña Política, 1939–1940, File 0514; "existence of a national government": Questionnaire for *Estampa* magazine, May 1940, FAPEC-AJA, Campaña Política, 1939–1940, File 0514, Entrevistas; "collision of ideals": "Amaro ofrece una convivialidad al Gral. Pérez Treviño con motivo de su onomástico: La oposición define los propósitos que persigue," Jun. 23, 1939, FAPEC-AJA, Campaña Política, 1939–1940, File 0514, Clipping book.

claims were an outgrowth of the policies of the Cárdenas government, especially in terms of the large-scale redistribution of lands in *ejidos* and the na-
tionalization of the oil industry. "The communist penetration and influence
in the official sphere is no mystery . . . [and] the inspiration of the present
administration is communistic [*comunizante*]." The PRAC was organized to
work against the communistic tendencies allowed by the Cárdenas government through administrative sins of both commission and omission. Beyond
the obvious actions of Cárdenas in this field, another figure singled out for
criticism was Vicente Lombardo Toledano, head of the CTM, whom Amaro
classified as a "social danger and traitor to the country." Lombardo's efforts
in labor organizing and his presumed sympathy for Soviet policy made him
a convenient and increasingly frequent target. Amaro went further, remarking that "the Mexican people are not communist and do not want a democracy of workers, they want a democracy of Mexicans." Amaro's ideological
isolationism played well alongside his revolutionary credentials, even if it did
not accurately represent Mexican reality.[87]

Like Amaro, Almazán recognized the importance of the international conflicts surrounding World War II for Mexico and sought to position himself as
an experienced leader ready to enter the field of foreign relations. In March
1940, well before the United States entered World War II, Almazán argued,
"If in my country I have fought and continue to fight for a democratic
government, and if the antecedents of democracy in Mexico are the Consti-
tutions of the United States, France, and England, my conviction and my
sympathies are with the countries that are now defending the cause of democracy in the world, because I firmly believe that it is the cause of Human-
ity." He contrasted his position with the functionaries of the PRM, whom
he accused of being "instruments of Hitler and Stalin . . . [and] turning the
country over to the totalitarian countries." According to Almazán, Mexico
"must be prepared because if the totalitarians win the war in Europe, the
invasion of Mexico is a certainty." This appeal was clearly meant for U.S.
ears, as Almazán described his fight as one that would punish "the misguided

87. "Communist penetration and influence": Questionnaire for *Estampa* magazine, May
1940, FAPEC-AJA, Campaña Política, 1939–1940, File 0514, Entrevistas; administrative sins:
Lic. Mario Somohano Flores, "El PRAC ante los problemas nacionales," FAPEC-AJA, Campaña Política, 1939–1940, File 0514; "traitor to the country": Questionnaire for *Estampa* magazine, May 1940, FAPEC-AJA, Campaña Política, 1939–1940, File 0514, Entrevistas;
"democracy of Mexicans": Draft with MS notes, "El Libro Blanco del Partido Revolucionario
Anti-Comunista," [1939], FAPEC-AJA, Campaña Política, 1939–1940, File 0514 (this file outlines major policy positions of the PRAC).

leaders . . . who want to make Mexico into a center of agitation against the United States of America." Such declarations were at odds with the more frequent popular representations of Almazán as a "fascist" leader aligning himself with more nefarious European mentors. Almazán's stated vision was a Mexico with "the same kind of government as the United States so that it can take its rightful place among the democratic nations of Latin America."[88]

The lack of enthusiasm among U.S. diplomats for the Almazán campaign was puzzling. Almazán was very careful to mark out relatively strident positions on issues of importance to the United States, such as the fight against fascism and the need for democratic institutions. Moreover, he adhered to the principle of U.S. hegemony in the hemisphere in a way that raised suspicions among some Mexican nationalists. Nevertheless, Almazán went to great lengths to present himself as a staunch friend of the United States and a man who could be counted on to lend support in the growing world conflict. However, his attempts to position himself close to the U.S. agenda were not sufficient to gain the support of Washington officials. Perhaps the power of the United States to influence events in Mexico was much weaker than normally assumed, or perhaps the United States prized stability more than ideology.

Almazán and Amaro shared important goals in the election of 1940. Amaro and the PRAC viewed Almazán's manifesto "with sympathy given that it demonstrates his desire to fight for effective suffrage and his resolution to combat imposition." Amaro argued that "the development of this campaign is bringing us to the definition of the situation, and fortunately only two camps remain: official imposition and democratic opposition."[89] Such a Manichean struggle would have been disastrous for the PRM since it would have divided the country roughly in half. This analysis was not lost on U.S. observers. When Almazán's political party (PRUN) was formed in 1940, Ambassador Daniels immediately pondered whether it would join forces with

88. "Antecedents of democracy": *Excélsior,* Mar. 13, 1940, AGN-DGIPS, Box 189, 2.1/311.1/5, Vol. 11; "instruments of Hitler": Report, Insp. 1 to DGIPS, May 12, 1940, Monterrey, AGN-DGIPS, Box 190, 2.1/311.1/5, Vol. 13; "invasion of Mexico": Report, Insp. 46 to DGIPS, May 29, 1940 Torreón, AGN-DGIPS, Box 190, 2.1/311.1/5, Vol. 14; "misguided leaders": Report, Insp. 1 to DGIPS, May 12, 1940, Monterrey, AGN-DGIPS, Box 190, 2.1/311.1/5, Vol. 13; "rightful place among the democratic nations": *Excélsior,* Sep. 7, 1940, AGN-DGIPS, Box 191, 2.1/311.1/5, Vol. 19.

89. "Desire to fight": "El PRAC opina sobre el manifiesto del General Almazán," Aug. 3, 1939, signed by Pérez Treviño and Amaro; "two camps remain": "Amaro habla de la Guerra Europea y de la política mundial," Sep. 30, 1939 (both located in FAPEC-AJA, Campaña Política, 1939–1940, File 0514).

Amaro and the PRAC. A few days later, the U.S. Embassy presumed that fellow presidential contenders Amaro and Sánchez Tapia would submerge their campaigns in the wave of almazanismo.[90] This echoed a Mexican intelligence report that foresaw former *callista* Manuel Perez Treviño, yet another early candidate for the presidency, and Amaro joining forces with Almazán's campaign.[91] The ongoing State Department obsession with potential Mexican upheaval prompted Daniels to blithely opine that once Almazán returned from a campaign trip "his position will be known with regard to the possibilities of carrying on a revolution."[92] The overheated, but persistent, fascination of U.S. observers with revolutions aside, it was clear that a political realignment was under way.

The ideological and political links between Almazán and the old callista ranks were numerous, manifesting themselves in the attempted fusion of the Almazán and Amaro candidacies. In Campeche, holdover callista (and thereby *amarista*) bureaucrats expressed optimism that Almazán would "continue protecting them" if he should win, a belief that spurred some of them to actively support his candidacy.[93] But it was a confluence of conservative political and social viewpoints that fueled the attempted unification of the campaigns, as seen in a draft statement on the matter by Amaro. Both campaigns were "inspired by the urgent need to take energetic measures to save the country and correct the confusion evident in several aspects of the national life."[94] When generals in Latin America refer to "energetic measures" to save the country, civilian governments usually tremble. Importantly, neither Amaro nor Almazán was referring to coup attempts. In a crucial shift in mentality—the transition from violence to elections as the accepted form of political speech—both Amaro and Almazán were interested in policy prescriptions, not barracks revolts.

90. Daniels immediately pondered: U.S. State Department, 812.00/30898, Memo, Daniels to Secretary of State, Jan. 10, 1940; wave of almazanismo: U.S. State Department, 812.00/30906, "Resumé of Conditions in Mexico During December, 1939," Jan. 15, 1940 (both located in *Confidential U.S. State Department Central Files, Mexico, 1940–1944, Part I,* Reel 1).

91. Report, Insp. 19 to DGIPS, Dec. 5, 1939, AGN-DGIPS, Box 188, 2.1/311.1/5, Vol. 6.

92. U.S. State Department, 812.00/30927, Memo, Daniels to Secretary of State, Feb. 2, 1940, in *Confidential U.S. State Department Central Files, Mexico, 1940–1944, Part I,* Reel 1.

93. Report, Insp. Rincón C. to DGIPS, Mar. 14, 1939, Campeche, AGN-DGIPS, Box 187, 2.1/311.1/5, Vol. 1.

94. Draft, "Proyecto de Amaro para una unificación con Almazán," Jun. 1939, FAPEC-AJA, Campaña Política, 1939–1940, File 0514. This draft was typewritten on Amaro's personal letterhead.

The draft was an outline of the most fundamental principles embodied in the political life of the nation, and the sketch here is only an overview. Amaro's draft argued for the defense of private property and the judicious application of expropriation powers; against the system of collective land-holding, unless it could increase productivity; for the reformation of the government bureaucracy into a rational and effective entity in the service of the citizenry (i.e., no nepotism or corruption); against the insular world of public works construction; for a cost-benefit analysis of all public works projects; for the sanctity of freedom of expression in a democracy; for the continuing improvement of the armed services; for the equality of the branches of government; for a diplomatic policy "based in reality"; and for the ultimate responsibility of the president for all actions undertaken by his government.

When the union of the two main opposition groups became imminent in January 1940, even elements within the Secretaría de Gobernación recognized that "a united front of all the opposition parties will result in a strong electoral force . . . [and] General Almazán had a great deal more sympathy among the public than did General Ávila Camacho."[95] Among military men, "those below the rank of colonel, however, including the enlisted men, felt that Almazán would do more for the army than Ávila Camacho, and they favored the PRUN candidate."[96] The strong support of the public at large and elements of the rank and file in the army gave the Ávila Camacho campaign pause. Moreover, the Cárdenas administration worried that the perceived strength of a unified opposition would "result in the addition of many new followers," a kind of political snowball effect. The PAN was viewed as a potentially serious swing factor in the election of 1940, if only the main opposition candidates, Almazán and Amaro, could resolve their differences and mount a united campaign.[97] But the possibility of such a united opposition collapsed almost as soon as it arose.[98]

Almazán's perceived timidity in criticizing the Cárdenas administration impeded the potential unification of the Almazán and Amaro campaigns. In

95. U.S. State Department, Memorandum of Conversation with Ricardo Rubio (secretary of Gobernación), Raleigh Gibson, Jan. 12, 1940, in *Confidential U.S. State Department Central Files, Mexico, 1940–1944, Part I*, Reel 1.

96. Lieuwen, *Mexican Militarism*, 135.

97. "Many new followers": U.S. State Department, 812.00/30906, "Resumé of Conditions in Mexico During December, 1939," Jan. 15, 1940; potentially serious swing factor: U.S. State Department, 812.00/30899, Daniels to Secretary of State, Jan. 10, 1940 (both located in *Confidential U.S. State Department Central Files, Mexico, 1940–1944, Part I*, Reel 1).

98. See Aaron W. Navarro, "La fusión fracasada: Almazán y Amaro en la campaña presidencial de 1940," *Boletín del Fideicomiso Archivos Plutarco Elías Calles y Fernando Torreblanca* 49, 2005.

October 1939, Amaro contended, "There is the argument that if this man [Almazán] realizes the historic moment, all of the opposition parties could be unified. . . . Unfortunately events have followed a different path. General Almazán's manifesto was lukewarm, diffuse and without the attacks on the administration that the people were expecting. . . . Naturally, it has been impossible for the opposition to consolidate and unify in strength and the only one responsible for this phenomenon is General Almazán."[99]

Another issue was Almazán's presumed weakness among the Amaro crowd, who viewed his candidacy as a "pantomime . . . a masquerade [and] a farce" that wasted the energy of opposition-minded voters in 1940. As early as October 1939, advisers within the PRAC argued internally that Almazán was fundamentally mistaken when he "thought that his personality was above the environment of opposition and ran with the pretension that the whole world would join his ranks unconditionally." Such an attitude fit well with *personalismo,* which Amaro dismissed as a critical flaw in Mexican politics. After the proposed coalition collapsed and well into 1940, Amaro weighed his own electoral campaign in a clear political calculus: would his campaign strengthen or weaken the chances of defeating the cardenista group?[100] If Amaro ran as a presidential candidate, he would more likely siphon votes from Almazán than from Ávila Camacho, perhaps enough to assure the latter's victory. Yet Amaro also believed that something deeper than bald political calculation was at stake in the election of 1940: at issue was the future course of Mexican democracy.

The nature of Mexican government aside, members of Amaro's inner circle began to desert the PRAC in early February 1940. The fracturing of the putative alliance between Almazán and Amaro, along with lagging popularity on the campaign trail, placed the Amaro campaign on very shaky ground. Senior advisors began to resign their positions in the party in order to lend support to the Almazán campaign. By February 8, rumors abounded suggesting that Amaro himself would join the Almazán campaign, not least to head

99. Memo, Oct. 13, 1939, FAPEC- AJA, Campaña Política, 1939–1940, File 020200, Discursos, Folder 1.

100. "Masquerade [and] a farce": Statement by Ing. Zeferino R. Reyes, Feb. 19, 1940, FAPEC-AJA, Campaña Política, 1939–1940, File 020200, Campaña pro-Amaro, San Luis Potosí; "environment of opposition": Unsigned memo, "Opinión de amigos de Amaro y del PRAC," Oct. 6, 1939, FAPEC-AJA, Campaña Política, 1939–1940, File 020200; "clear political calculus": Interview with José C. Valadéz for *Hoy* magazine, Mar. 1940, FAPEC-AJA, Campaña Política, 1939–1940, File 020200, Entrevistas.

the forces already prepared for an armed movement after the election.[101] This last bit of rumor played on the idea current throughout the 1940 campaign that Amaro was by nature a gifted military commander and tactician while Almazán was mainly a businessman in uniform. The Amaro organization in Jalisco officially switched its allegiance to Almazán in February, adding to Amaro's bad news. In March, a group of Amaro supporters in Torreón reluctantly moved to support Almazán, arguing that he was the only viable opposition candidate and that "the leaders of the PRAC have done nothing effective to combat imposition."[102] By April 1940, Sánchez Tapia was set to end his presidential campaign in order to offer his allegiance and supporters to the Almazán campaign.[103] In all, the early months of 1940 showed a developing inevitability surrounding Almazán's status as the main opposition contender set against the "imposition" of Ávila Camacho by the PRM. During these dark days, there were practical considerations for Amaro and his supporters. If Amaro was not going to oppose the PRM on election day, he had to find a way to keep faith with his movement's supporters and also guard his personal interests. In meetings at the end of July 1940, according to a Mexican intelligence report, Amaro and his advisors discussed how to simultaneously guarantee the safety of their investments, wealth, and property in Mexico while fleeing to the United States to avoid the appearance of participation in any armed movement. The same report argued that Calles was working behind the scenes because there was "an understanding" between Almazán and Amaro.[104] Whether this "understanding" referred to post-election power sharing or some sort of nonaggression pact between the two men, as it turned out Almazán had precious little to offer after the votes were tallied.

101. Senior advisors began to resign: Report, Insp. 7 to DGIPS, Feb. 3, 1940; rumors abounded: Report, Insp. 7 to DGIPS, Feb. 8, 1940 (both located in AGN-DGIPS, Box 189, 2.1/311.1/5, Vol. 8).

102. Allegiance to Almazán: Letter, Lic. Daniel Benitez (president of Jalisco State Committee for Amaro) to Organizaciones Almazanistas de Jalisco, Feb. 12, 1940, Guadalajara, FAPEC-AJA, Campaña Política, 1939–1940, File 020200, Organizaciones Almazanistas del Estado de Jalisco; "combat imposition": Letter, Rodríguez to Celso Valdespino, Mar. 16, 1940, Torreón, FAPEC-AJA, Campaña Política, 1939–1940, File 020200, Tomás Rodríguez de la Fuente.

103. Report, Insp. 12 to DGIPS, Apr. 25, 1940, AGN-DGIPS, Box 190, 2.1/311.1/5, Vol. 12.

104. Report, Insp. G[utiérrez] to DGIPS, Aug. 1, 1940, AGN-DGIPS, Box 191, 2.1/311.1/5, Vol. 17. Present at the meeting of Amaro and his advisors were Ing. Luis L. León, General Manuel Pérez Treviño, Lorenzo Tapia (brother of General Jose Maria Tapia), Ing. Jose Torres Navarrete (a PRAC official), former diputado Delfín Cepeda, and Enrique Rodríguez.

The Campaign Trail

The Almazán rally in Monterrey in May 1940 was a key stop in the campaign homestretch. The crowd present at the rally provided an interesting look at the type of support on which Almazán relied during his campaign: "Forty percent of the people were women, among them were some of the well-dressed class that are not usually at rallies; ladies, old women, young 'society' girls, some in cars and others on foot; these groups were the most aggressively almazanista. The other sixty percent was made up of men of all social classes: well-dressed and young men, who, judging by their clothing were from the richer families, were the majority, so that the groups of peasants and workers were the minority."[105] The composition of the rally attendees meshed with popular views that Almazán was allied with the economically privileged in society, carried the banner for traditional conservative elements like the Catholic Church, held views that were often stridently anti-cardenista, and offered little of interest to peasants and most workers. Such supporters were useful in a general election, but not as numerous as those citizens who were members of industrial and peasant unions.

On the day of Almazán's campaign rally in Monterrey, all of the union locals linked to the PRM were held in meetings, in order to keep them away from the gathering and preclude any spontaneous defection to the PRUN. Seeking to drum up support from all other corners, the PRUN printed coupons in the regional newspapers valid for free transportation to and from Monterrey for those who wished to attend the rally. Militant avilacamachistas did their best to disrupt Almazán's plans, and at least one special train of supporters could not reach the city because a bridge had been burned in advance of it.[106] Such interference by government agents was common in the 1940 campaign and subsequent election cycles as well.[107] Even Almazán's supporters among the elite faced physical intimidation and violence. Generals Gustavo León and Alfredo Lezama, both revolutionary veterans and men of a certain status in society, were assaulted on a train to Hermosillo on the way to an Almazán rally, though their attackers did not enter any of the coaches

---

105. Report, Insp. 1 to DGIPS, May 12, 1940, Monterrey, AGN-DGIPS, Box 190, 2.1/ 311.1/5, Vol. 13.

106. Ibid.

107. See chapter 4 for further discussion of the methods used by agents of the DGIPS and DFS to combat opposition movements.

full of U.S. citizens.[108] The almazanistas were well aware of the physical threat to Almazán himself during campaign trips and appearances. A Mexican agent in Guadalajara described the fears of physical attack among the almazanistas as a "mania."[109] Such apprehensions about Almazán's safety proved to be accurate assessments.

One security strategy that the almazanistas and other opposition campaigns utilized was to simply avoid announcing their candidate's arrival in a locale.[110] Another was to actively seek police protection in advance of any threat. For instance, in May 1940, Leonides Almazán requested protection of the family compound in Coyoacán from the chief of police directly. His fears about an attempt on his brother seem reasonable when weighed against intelligence reports from the campaign trail in the north, where a federal agent noted dryly that "as is known, attempts will be made on his life."[111] The treatment of such threats as common knowledge suggested that everyone involved in the campaign, on both sides, was well aware of the danger.

In June 1939, while campaigning in his adopted home turf of Monterrey, Almazán faced a very well-organized attempt on his life. Intelligence reports stated that six to eight men had stopped Almazán's car and began firing their guns, somehow failing to kill or even injure the candidate. Further, a note not relating to the attempt itself but signed by Maximino Ávila Camacho, the PRM candidate's brother, was found on the person of one of the perpetrators caught after the incident.[112] In August 1939, almazanistas argued that Ávila Camacho supporters "already had a group of gunmen ready so that one of them might get the opportunity to assassinate General Almazán upon his arrival [in Mexico City]." Further ties between the Ávila Camacho campaign and the threat to Almazán's life were revealed in September 1939. A report from a federal agent in Puebla detailed a long-standing plot, masterminded by then-governor Maximino Ávila Camacho, to assassinate Almazán during his campaign stop in the city of Puebla through some variety of accident,

108. *Excélsior,* Apr. 24, 1940, AGN-DGIPS, Box 190, 2.1/311.1/5, Vol. 12. Lezama was a luminary in the Mexican Air Force, referred to as "Mexico's air ace." See *Time,* Aug. 26, 1940.

109. Report, Insp. Alemán Pérez to DGIPS, Mar. 26, 1940, Guadalajara, AGN-DGIPS, Box 189, 2.1/311.1/5, Vol. 10.

110. See, for example, Report, Insp. 18 to DGIPS, Jul. 28, 1939, AGN-DGIPS, Box 188, 2.1/311.1/5, Vol. 2.

111. Family compound in Coyoacán: *Excélsior,* May 27, 1940; "attempts will be made on his life": Report, Insp. 46 to DGIPS, May 29, 1940, Torreón (both located in AGN-DGIPS, Box 190, 2.1/311.1/5, Vol. 14).

112. Report, Insp. 12 to DGIPS, Jun. 24, 1939, AGN-DGIPS, Box 30, File 3, 2.1/062.2(72)/1, p. 7.

either a car crash or a severe train derailment.[113] This particular plot was apparently never put into operation.

The actual attempt on Almazán in Monterrey in June 1939 was not an isolated incident. During his campaign travels in Michoacán in February 1940, Almazán was again the subject of an assassination attempt. In a media interview, General Alfredo Serratos, a former member of the old federal army and one-time defense secretary during the revolution who had become an important Almazán supporter, described the scene. He said that five men wearing sarapes with machine guns hidden beneath them assaulted the home of Francisco Barbosa, where Almazán was staying after a night of dinner and dancing. The number of assailants differed significantly in the official statement of the PRUN regarding the matter, although the general outlines of the plot remained the same. The PRUN leadership claimed that up to one hundred men opened fire on the house where Almazán was staying and accused the perpetrators of "the lack of political sense or culture." They argued that "if the assassins from below, paid by the assassins up above, manage to complete their sinister tasks . . . this would be the surest path toward the definitive breakdown of imposition and an indelible stain on the government of the Republic." Almazán, soldier that he was, was reportedly "forcibly subdued by friends as he struggled to rush outside and return fire." Leonides Almazán, in a statement to the attorney general, revealed what he perceived as the complicity of the Ávila Camacho group in the attempt. He outlined how Antonio Figueroa and Ignacio Morales worked with other confederates to activate the plot. Figueroa was gainfully employed as the driver for Graciano Sánchez, one of the founders of the CNC and a staunch ally of Cárdenas. Morales, known colloquially as "El Compa Nacho," had ties to Alemán and often aided him with special assignments. The link between this assassination plot and known associates of both the Cárdenas and Alemán groups did nothing to assuage the fears of the almazanistas for their candidate's safety. Nevertheless, Cárdenas ordered Secretary of Gobernación Ignacio García Téllez to conduct an investigation of the matter, and he sent several "confidential agents" to do the work.[114]

113. "Group of gunmen": Report, Insp. Rincón C. to DGIPS, Aug. 24, 1939, AGN-DGIPS, Box 188, 2.1/311.1/5, Vol. 4; longstanding plot: Report, Insp. Rincón C. to DGIPS, Sep. 2, 1939, Puebla, AGN-DGIPS, Box 185, 2.1/311.1/2, Vol. 4.

114. Five men wearing sarapes: *La Prensa*, Feb. 13, 1940; "lack of political sense" and "assassins from below": *La Prensa*, Feb. 9, 1940; "forcibly subdued by friends": *San Antonio Light*, Feb. 9, 1940; special assignments: *La Prensa*, Feb. 13, 1940; "confidential agents": *San Antonio Light*, Feb. 9, 1940. (The results of this investigation were not evident in the archives at the time of this study.)

Another significant incident occurred as Almazán arrived in Hermosillo for a campaign stop as election day neared.[115] At the PRM offices, where the Sonoran chief of police was spotted by eyewitnesses, a loudspeaker announced the imminent arrival of Almazán as well as the need for the workers of Sonora to "punish the reactionary candidate *in an expressive way.*" A group called "El Huarache" had been prepared for the attack, carrying clubs disguised as banner staffs into the train station. These were confiscated by federal troops at four in the afternoon, as they tried to avert a violent confrontation. But another loudspeaker exhorted members of the Huarache group to "make their presence felt to Almazán," and the clash with almazanistas in the station began in force. Skirmishes between the groups continued through the sweltering hours of the late afternoon. When Almazán's train arrived at 7:30 P.M., the Huarache group approached the platform, only to be turned back by several explosions determined to be the work of Almazán's military escort. This escort had accompanied Almazán since Nogales and was credited with saving him from the Huarache aggression in Hermosillo. Almazán continued on to his rally in the town center, still harried by the Huarache group, and asked his followers to restrain themselves in order to allow the army to perform its duty of keeping order. His speech attacked longtime Sonoran political heavyweights such as Governor Anselmo Macías Valenzuela, a career military officer, and Alejo Bay, a cardenista standing as the PRM candidate for the Senate. While Almazán spoke, an aide who had accompanied him to the microphone was struck in the head by a stone and injured.[116]

Once the raucous meeting ended, Almazán and his retinue, worse for the wear, retired to the home of General Jesús Bórquez for the night. Numerous federal troops guarded the home, allowing no one to enter or leave, while Almazán was secluded with his key advisers through the night. The intelligence agent traveling with Almazán captured the mood inside the house and offered a surprisingly strong critique of the government's actions: "The partiality and connivance of the Interim Governor and the head of the garrison have raised fears of an assassination attempt against Almazán. . . . The lack of strong guarantees of safety have made me fear for my life and I suggest as a temporary measure that you bring federal troops from Sinaloa in order

115. Letter, McCombs to David Hulburd (*Time*), Jun. 20, 1940, McCombs Papers, Box 46, File 19.

116. Report, Town Official Ildefonso Martinez Mora to DGIPS, Jun. 17, 1940, Hermosillo, AGN-DGIPS, Box 190, 2.1/311.1/5, Vol. 16. Emphasis added.

to calm this situation. . . . If the Defense Department does not effect an immediate change in the Chief of the Military Zone, bloody events will develop and the blame will fall directly on the Federal Government."[117] The agent was writing from self-interest, since his personal safety had been threatened along with that of Almazán's group, but he also made a policy prescription. The PRM could either dial back the inflammatory rhetoric that led to outbreaks of violence like he had just seen or risk creating a greater sense of animosity among sectors of the population that were still uncommitted to a political program. Such analyses were rare at this stage of the development of Mexico's intelligence community—when most agents were still relatively green—although not apolitical. This report offered a glimpse of the politicization that would develop during the 1940s and emerge in full force in the election of 1952 and, of course, afterward in the complicated struggles of the 1960s.

Almazán and his supporters throughout the country, and outside of it, were harried and threatened in ways both serious and mundane. While the most spectacular obstructions were assassination attempts, riots, and exchanges of gunfire, most of the tactics used against the almazanistas were more boring, though not to say less effective. There occurred daily assaults in the media, refusals of permits to march in political rallies, roadblocks (both literal and bureaucratic), and the ever-present reality of infiltration.[118] "It is noticeable that intimidation is being openly practiced by them [the government] as a means of furthering their ends and gunmen are being hired for this purpose throughout the Republic."[119] The use of obstruction and violence in the campaign of 1940 prefigured the increasing sophistication of such behavior in the following decades.

Anticipating further security threats as the election neared, Almazán sent his family to New York City in May 1940. His fears were soon confirmed, as the supporters of Ávila Camacho detonated a terror campaign throughout the country against almazanista sympathizers. An attack of avilacamachistas on "defenseless people" in Zitácuaro forced Secretary of Gobernación Garcia Téllez to send a telegram to Conrado Magaña, the interim governor of

117. Worse for the wear: ibid.; "partiality and connivance": Report, Insp. 22 to DGIPS, Jun. 16, 1940, Hermosillo, AGN-DGIPS, Box 190, 2.1/311.1/5, Vol. 15.

118. See AGN-DGIPS, Box 187, 2.1/311.1/5, Vol. 1, for further examples.

119. Military Attaché Report 9328, Gordon H. McCoy, Apr. 16, 1940, Mexico City, NARA, Record Group 165, Box 2460, File 3020.

Michoacán, urging an investigation and legal action.[120] Soon after, an army colonel in Acámbaro, Guanajuato, was accused of shooting several citizens, alleging that they were almazanistas and "rebel agents." The federal agent investigating this incident concluded that the victims "had not participated in politics or belonged to any group."[121] In Mérida, bombs were set off at the entryways of the homes of several leaders of the Almazán campaign. While no one sustained injury, it was widely believed in the city that these bombings were the work of "the CHEKA of Governor [Humberto] Canto Echeverría."[122] The easy implication of the PRM and its associates in such cases of political violence, whether the belief was accurate or not, demonstrated the public perception that the increasingly dominant party thrived on a steady diet of dirty tricks.

The campaign of violence seemed to be succeeding in Colima by the middle of June 1940. One Mexican agent reported that "the almazanista element in general is completely cowed [acobardado] and I think that they will abstain from voting on election day . . . There is great demoralization here especially among the peasants." This success, he continued, was due in no small part to the support of the key police officials and public employees. In Guadalajara in early March 1940, another report described Almazán's supporters as "very numerous, very sure of their triumph and even prideful." Yet by the end of the month, as the activists continued working for the campaign, local authorities increasingly targeted them for arbitrary imprisonment and other harassment.[123] When the almazanistas did organize to post propaganda and hold a meeting in Mérida in May 1940, the posters were torn down by the city police and the rally, held in front of the army garrison, was broken up by city authorities who fired shots in the air for emphasis. At

120. Further security threats: Telegram, Insp. Martínez to DGIPS, May 20, 1940; "defenseless people": Telegram, DGIPS Chief Garcia Téllez to Int. Gov. Conrado Magaña, May 20, 1940 (both located in AGN-DGIPS, Box 190, 2.1/311.1/5, Vol. 13).

121. Telegram, Insp. Urrutia L. to DGIPS, Jun. 13, 1940, Morelia, AGN-DGIPS, Box 190, 2.1/311.1/5, Vol. 15. The accused was Col. Roberto Calvo Ramtrea, head of the Eighteenth Batallion in Acámbaro.

122. Report, Insp. 36 to DGIPS, Jun. 13, 1940, Mérida, AGN-DGIPS, Box 190, 2.1/311.1/5, Vol. 15. The leaders whose homes were targeted were Lic. Martínez Palma, Lic. Esquivel Fernandez, and the head of the Almazán campaign in the city, a Sr. Sarlat.

123. "Great demoralization": Report, Insp. Alemán Pérez to DGIPS, Jun. 20, 1940, Colima, AGN-DGIPS, Box 190, 2.1/311.1/5, Vol. 16; "sure of their triumph": Report, Insp. 11 to DGIPS, Mar. 3, 1940, Guadalajara, AGN-DGIPS, Box 189, 2.1/311.1/5, Vol. 10; arbitrary imprisonment: Report, Insp. Alemán Pérez to DGIPS, Mar. 21, 1940, Guadalajara, AGN-DGIPS, Box 189, 2.1/311.1/5, Vol. 11.

the same time, outside the PRUN headquarters in Torreón, an altercation broke out between almazanistas and avilacamachistas that left two dead and six wounded. What began as verbal insults and a fistfight escalated to an exchange of gunfire.[124] The situation in San Luis Potosí was much the same. Governor Reynaldo Pérez Gallardo was accused of turning a blind eye to the "avilacamachista fury" unleashed upon Almazán's supporters in the state.[125] With election day approaching, the security situation was spiraling out of control.

As the level of physical violence neared a crescendo, the PRM saturated the Mexico City dailies with verbal attacks on the Almazán campaign and arguments outlining its treasonous nature. One such manifesto appeared in *Excélsior* just weeks before the polls opened:

> But its enemies [i.e., of the PRM], the organized reaction lined up behind the millionaire candidate, take part in this electoral contest . . . [but] all hope of success is tied to a state of alarm, a break in the order that they claim to defend; that interrupts the tranquillity and peace of the people and propitiates . . . the establishment of a dictatorial and oppressive regime, enemy of the liberty that they claim to defend. . . . If by other very evident and clear reasons there did not already exist enough foundation to qualify the actions undertaken by the almazanistas as a treason to the Nation, the argument above is sufficient cause to accuse them, as we do today, of committing a crime against the entire Nation and betraying the Nation.[126]

The PRM essentially argued that if the almazanistas did not exist then there would be no need to violently repress them. A single party dominant system, such as the PRM was cobbling together, would provide the "order" and "tranquility" that the populace desired. The case against Almazán was presented forcefully by another group, whose lawyer, Lic. Roberto Atwood, was the former head of Mexican intelligence in the Dirección General de Investigaciones Políticas y Sociales (DGIPS). This group declared that Almazán had ties to "totalitarian powers like Italy, Japan and probably Germany,"

---

124. Posters were torn down: Draft report, Insp. Cirerol to DGIPS, May 28, 1940, Mérida; altercation broke out: Report, Insp. 46 to DGIPS, May 28, 1940, Torreón (both located in AGN-DGIPS, Box 190, 2.1/311.1/5, Vol. 14).

125. *La Prensa*, Jun. 29, 1940, AGN-DGIPS, Box 190, 2.1/311.1/5, Vol. 16. Advertisement placed by "un grupo de almazanistas."

126. *Excélsior*, Jun. 19, 1940.

reprising the old attack line that he was a fascist, and it accused him of attempting to replace the popular government of Mexico with a regime offering privileges to the elite, trotting out his business record as proof of his priorities.[127] The longevity of such arguments suggests how persuasive they could be to voters and strategists alike.

The position of the United States, though formally neutral, became a factor in how the candidates positioned themselves. At the outset of the campaign, Almazán's pronouncements hinted that "he will probably be the biggest Americanophile that has ever held the presidency of Mexico."[128] In 1935, Almazán suggested to a U.S. official that "he realized fully that just as no Mexican Administration can endure without the permission of the United States, neither can Mexico look forward to a hopeful future without the friendship of America."[129] How was it that a candidate popularly perceived as more amenable to U.S. interests and long-term goals could fail to gain the support of Washington? How could the United States support a candidate like Ávila Camacho, who, as one observer acerbically noted, "does not possess a great deal of force and is mentally sluggish"?[130]

The support of U.S. politicians could confuse the political spectrum. A U.S. Secret Service agent in Laredo claimed that Almazán not only was the most popular candidate in the United States but also had the support of Wendell Willkie, who would help him if he won his presidential campaign against Franklin D. Roosevelt. A Mexican agent analyzed the situation differently, arguing that President Roosevelt supported Almazán since they were "compadres."[131] Still another source in the U.S. military argued that Almazán was waiting for the U.S. election results and "hopes to secure the support of Willkie if Willkie is successful, and that if President Roosevelt is re-elected he would attempt to persuade him to resume his 'moral' support."[132]

127. *El Popular,* Aug. 22, 1940, DGIPS, Box 191, 2.1/311.1/5, Vol. 17. The group was the Coalición de Partidos de las Izquierdas Revolucionarias de la República Mexicana.

128. McCombs report, Jul. 31, 1939, McCombs Papers, Box 46, File 22.

129. Military Attaché Report 6273. H. E. Marshburn to MID, Jul. 12, 1935, NARA, Record Group 165, Box 2455, File 3020. Since the report paraphrases conversation, there is some question about whether Almazán used the rather problematic word "permission" when referring to U.S. support.

130. Summary, [MID, Jan. 1939], NARA, Record Group 165, Box 2454, File 3000.

131. Support of Wendell Wilkie: Report, Insp. 15 to DGIPS, Jun. 21, 1939, AGN-DGIPS, Box 188, 2.1/311.1/5, Vol. 2; "compadres": Report, Insp. 19 to DGIPS, Jun. 7, 1939, AGN-DGIPS, Box 187, 2.1/311.1/5, Vol. 1.

132. Report, Lt. Col. A. W. Roffe to Commanding General, Ft. Sam Houston, San Antonio, Oct. 15, 1940; Report, Lt. Col. Frederick Laherty [Ft. Ringgold] to Commanding General, Ft. Sam Houston, Oct.12, 1940 (both located in NARA, Record Group 165, Box 2458, File 3020).

The United States was not oblivious to the role that it could play in Mexico in 1940. Reports indicated that the United States was taking advantage of the conflict in Mexico to exact conditions from each side, knowing that the Mexican contenders considered U.S. support crucial to a defensible electoral victory and a legitimate government. Ávila Camacho convened a meeting of high PRM members to hear a translation of a *Washington Post* article that declared the position of the United States on prohibiting Almazán from importing weapons across the border in order to "foment a revolution."[133] Both Ávila Camacho and Almazán went to great lengths to convince the United States that the new Mexican administration would be opposed to further expropriations and in favor of greater foreign investment.

Post-Electoral Reckoning

Election day came and went, and in the end Almazán was soundly defeated at the polls. Official figures gave Ávila Camacho 2,176,641 votes to Almazán's paltry 151,101.[134] A contemporary observer noted that "Mexican election laws and machinery are such that actual popular support and approval have little to do with the final outcome."[135] Of course, Mexican elections have generally been the site of vote fraud in one form or another, and 1940 was no exception. While the official tally certainly underestimated the Almazán total, archival evidence does not support claims by almazanistas then (and now) that the election was stolen outright. Given the kind of documentation that survives, the nature of the bureaucracy that created it, and the weight of accumulated political hyperbole surrounding any such conflict, a definitive claim either way would be practically impossible.

Regardless of the reported vote tally, it was immediately evident that the almazanistas were not prepared to meekly accept what they viewed as the ultimate imposition, a fraud of epic proportions, and a betrayal of revolutionary ideals. A report circulating in September 1940 outlined preparations for a general strike to protest the actions of the Cárdenas administration in the

133. Report, Insp. G[utiérrez] to DGIPS, Sep. 10, 1940, AGN-DGIPS, Box 191, 2.1/311.1/5, Vol. 19. Among those present at the meeting were Ávila Camacho, Col. Leandro Sánchez Salazar, General Pablo Quiroga, General Heriberto Jara, and Lic. Ezequiel Padilla.

134. *Excélsior,* Jul. 6, 1952. Information summary of past election results drawn from *Diario de los debates,* the official publication of the Cámara de Diputados.

135. Letter, McCombs to Thomas Krug (*Time*), Jul. 23, 1939, McCombs Papers, Box 46, File 22.

elections and to support Almazán's presidential claim. Almazanistas further pressed their advantage when they specifically spoke of a widespread strike on the railroad system in protest of the imminent official announcement of Ávila Camacho's electoral victory that same month.[136] The Almazán campaign stretched from the street to the union hall to the international media. Meanwhile, the avilacamachistas continued to attack Almazán in an attempt to delegitimize his claims to victory. When asked by a U.S. journalist why the avilacamachistas continued their campaign in the press after the election, Almazán replied laconically, "Because they lost."[137] The PAN, defending the candidate it endorsed, stated bluntly that "the entire Nation, in overwhelming voting, condemned the administration, rejected imposition, chose General Almazán as President of the Republic and . . . elected independent candidates."[138] Yet these early efforts at contesting the results were countered by Ávila Camacho's courting of U.S. influence. In early August 1940, Alemán "unofficially" visited Undersecretary of State Sumner Welles, presumably carrying a business-friendly message on behalf of Ávila Camacho.[139] The decision of the United States in November 1940 to send vice president elect Henry A. Wallace to the inauguration of Ávila Camacho essentially destroyed any remaining hopes within the Almazán camp of victory. Rodolfo Neri, one of the PRUN's senior strategists, left San Antonio to visit Almazán "to get orders as to whether [to] close up and give up."[140] And Cárdenas, ever the tactician, left General Miguel Henríquez Guzmán as zone commander in Monterrey on inauguration day, just in case any problem should arise.[141]

Mexican intelligence agents compiled a report at the end of August 1940 that tried to outline the "probable tactics" of an almazanista rebellion. Arrests of secondary and tertiary level leaders of the PRUN had declined, since most officials at that level did not have the money to flee abroad and had either been rounded up or had given up. After sending his senior leaders to different parts of Mexico and going to the United States, Almazán was expected to

136. Outlined preparations: Report, Insp. G[utiérrez] to DGIPS, Sep. 4, 1940, AGN-DGIPS, Box 191, 2.1/311.1/5, Vol. 18; pressed their advantage: Telegram, Insp. 7 to DGIPS, Sep. 12, 1940, AGN-DGIPS, Box 191, 2.1/311.1/5, Vol. 19.

137. La Prensa, Jul. 13, 1940, AGN-DGIPS, Box 191, 2.1/311.1/5, Vol. 17.

138. PAN Convention, Sep. 1940, AMGM, Fondo Acción Nacional, Vol. 39, File 220.

139. Mobile Press, Aug. 29, 1940, AGN-DGIPS, Box 191, 2.1/311.1/5, Vol. 18.

140. Telegram, McCombs to Thomas Krug (Time), Nov. 15, 1940, McCombs Papers, Box 46, File 23.

141. Lt. Col. W. D. Styer [Cmdr. Ft. McIntosh, Laredo] to G-2, Ft. Sam Houston, [San Antonio], Nov. 23, 1940, NARA, Record Group 165, Box 2458, File 3020.

raise the hopes of the faithful. However, the agents figured that after a few days "the subversive temperature of the almazanistas would drop again . . . [since] Almazán speaks without danger, outside the country, where he has security, comfort and resources, while the rest here within the country are to suffer the consequences of what their leader says and does." General José Mijares Palencia, Almazán's campaign manager, was expected to continue to coordinate military commanders, "except in reality not doing anything effective but creating alarm."[142]

In the same report, Mexican agents projected a cross-country trip for Almazán, from New York to Philadelphia to Washington, D.C., then to Niagara Falls, Chicago, San Francisco, and finally Alaska. This trip would have the dual purpose of camouflaging Almazán's potentially subversive plans and shielding him from calls to return to Mexico to defend and aid his supporters. He was thought to be headed ultimately for San Antonio, where it seemed he might settle once the electoral conflict was finished. The agents concluded that "this itinerary can be changed for any other, since the purpose is to not be in a set location and let the time pass without any concrete agreements, while his friends in Mexico do what they can."[143]

In fact, after the election Almazán boarded the U.S. steamship *Mexico* at Veracruz on July 18, headed for Havana. Once in Cuba, he downplayed any assertions that his voyage had political implications or aspirations: "I am a simple tourist, plenty of beaches, plenty of rest, and a bit of cinema." His rhetorical misdirection in Havana could not be mistaken for a lack of confidence, as he stated, "I will be President of the United States of Mexico next December 1st, I have obtained 90 percent of the votes." Almazán seemed to be betting that such statements would eventually win over Mexican citizens and foreign governments by creating an air of inevitability. Yet some took his vagaries immediately after the election as "the best proof that Almazán recognizes that he lost the elections by a huge majority."[144]

The reasons for Almazán's trip to Havana were several. An especially persistent and credible rumor argued that Almazán had attempted to arrange a meeting with U.S. Secretary of State Cordell Hull, who was attending the Pan-American Conference in Havana at the time. Almazán dismissed this as

142. Memo, DGIPS, Aug. 28, 1940, AGN-DGIPS, Box 191, 2.1/311.1/5, Vol. 19.

143. Ibid.

144. Headed for Havana: *La Prensa*, Jul. 19, 1940; "simple tourist": *Excélsior*, Jul. 25, 1940; "United States of Mexico": *Excélsior,* Jul. 27, 1940; "best proof": *La Prensa*, Jul. 19, 1940 (all located in AGN-DGIPS, Box 191, 2.1/311.1/5, Vol. 17).

"mere coincidence."[145] A phone tap, coordinated by Mexican intelligence, recorded Almazán telling Neri that Cuban president Fulgencio Batista had welcomed him to the island and that "at this moment Leonides is having dinner with Roosevelt in Washington."[146] The implication of this message was clear: Almazán was relying on the United States to provide the leverage he needed to displace Ávila Camacho's claim to the presidency. In this tactic, his brother's long familiarity with the Washington social scene, nurtured during years of medical training at Johns Hopkins University, was combined with the Almazán family's larger circle of business and military contacts. This strategy was intended to outflank Cárdenas and Ávila Camacho in a way that would remind U.S. policy makers *who* had expropriated *what* only two years before and reinforce Almazán's own determination to pursue a more collegial foreign policy with the United States.

Aside from the threat of armed intervention after the election, the Almazán campaign had another strategy to confront the PRM, one that Mexican intelligence agents fully expected: the PRUN would install a rump congress to recognize Almazán's victory. Neri suggested in late July 1940 that the rump congress would be held "at any cost" either in Mexico City or in Chihuahua, where almazanista sentiment was strong, and that "any movement that takes place will not be against General Cárdenas but against the usurpation of Ávila Camacho."[147] This crucial distinction gave firm ground to those who had benefited from the Cárdenas reforms or participated in Cárdenas's cult of popularity but were interested in breaking with the PRM over the issue of Ávila Camacho's "imposition." Given the efforts of the rump congress, one almazanista broadside also explicitly called on the army to take sides in the electoral aftermath: "the moment has come when the Army must decide its future, putting itself squarely on the side of legality or accepting usurpation."[148] Such a call to arms was partially a threat to the PRM by loyal almazanista commanders and partially a reminder to politically minded officers that their role in politics would be degraded further under continued PRM rule, a signal that was remarkably prescient.

145. Persistent and credible rumor: *El Popular,* Jul. 22, 1940; "mere coincidence": *Excélsior,* Jul. 27, 1940 (both located in AGN-DGIPS, Box 191, 2.1/311.1/5, Vol. 17).

146. Memo, DGIPS, Aug. 2, 1940, AGN-DGIPS, Box 191, 2.1/311.1/5, Vol. 18.

147. Memo, DGIPS, Mexico City, Aug. 2, 1940 (citing DGIPS report of Jul. 27, 1940), AGN-DGIPS, Box 191, 2.1/311.1/5, Vol. 18.

148. Boletín Almazanista, [Sep.] 1940, FAPEC-AJA, Campaña Política, 1939–1940, File 020200, Juan Andreu Almazán.

High-ranking almazanista advisors continued to meet in August 1940 to decide when and where a rump congress should be convened. The decision from one such meeting was reportedly that the almazanista congress would be convened in the chambers of the National Congress the day before the recognized Congress was scheduled to meet. In this way, it would make the installation of the recognized Congress very difficult.[149] Another report indicated that plans were being made to convene the assembly in Montemorelos, Nuevo León, where the legislators could meet with security and declare Almazán president. The El Paso press reported rumors circulating within the Mexican exile community that a "military junta" was forming in the city. Other reports indicated that almazanistas were being warned to remain in hiding and avoid capture until September 1, the date that they should be in Mexico City for the installation of the almazanista congress.[150] One report went so far as to speculate on persistent rumors that the almazanista congress was being held in a conference room of the U.S. Embassy in Mexico City. The location of Almazán through these crucial weeks was of great importance. Many supposed schemes involved Almazán's home state of Guerrero, rather than his adopted stronghold in Nuevo León. One report advised that Almazán could possibly land at Zihuatanejo and then go to Chilpancingo to declare himself president and install his government. This report resulted in increased military security patrols in Chilpancingo and surrounding towns to guard against any agitation, even though all of the key almazanistas were absent from the state.[151] All of these rumors, and it is important to classify them as such, had a similar punch line: a rump congress on Mexican soil would declare Almazán president and precipitate a constitutional crisis. With two rival presidents, each claiming legitimacy as the next leader of the country, the almazanistas would create time for further maneuver, demonstrate to foreign powers (especially the United States) that the PRUN was serious about procedural democracy, and reinforce the claim that Ávila Camacho was being imposed against the will of the Mexican people.

149. Report, Insp. 24 to DGIPS, Aug. 10, 1940, AGN-DGIPS, Box 191, 2.1/311.1/5, Vol. 17.

150. Convene the assembly: Telegram, Insp. 7 to DGIPS, Sep. 12, 1940; "military junta": El Paso Times, Sep. 12, 1940 (both located in AGN-DGIPS, Box 191, 2.1/311.1/5, Vol. 19); remain in hiding: Report, Insp. G[utiérrez] to DGIPS, Aug. 20, 1940, AGN-DGIPS, Box 191, 2.1/311.1/5, Vol. 17.

151. Persistent rumors: Report, Insp. 10 to DGIPS, Sep. 3, 1940, Chilpancingo; declare himself president: Report, Insp. 25 to Garcia Téllez, Aug. 22, 1940, Hermosillo; increased military security patrols: Report, Insp. 10 to DGIPS, Sep. 3, 1940, Chilpancingo (all located in AGN-DGIPS, Box 191, 2.1/311.1/5, Vol. 18).

On September 1, 1940, the "almazanista Congress of the Union" was constituted "outside the official chamber, for lack of guarantees [of safety]." The lawyer José Castro Estrada served as president of the lower chamber, and the Senate was led by Rafael Zubarán Capmany, a revolutionary veteran who had been rehabilitated after helping lead the de la Huerta revolt of 1923.[152] As Castro Estrada addressed the assembly, his speech was broadcast on live radio at the same time that Cárdenas was speaking to the "official" Cámara de Diputados in Mexico City. Castro Estrada rejected any argument that the almazanista congress was illegal and criticized Cárdenas for not addressing the "legitimate Congress constituted here" as the Constitution prescribed.[153] General Héctor F. López, the second in command of the PRUN, was named "Presidente Substituto Constitucional" by the rump congress. On September 22, he issued a statement outlining his program of government. López also, for reasons unknown, confided to a U.S. informant that the almazanistas planned to sabotage the National Railroad and the oil pipeline from Tampico to Mexico City at the end of September as a show of force, although this never came to pass. The strength of the almazanista congress's claim to legitimacy was difficult to judge. The analysis from Ft. McIntosh in Laredo pointed out "certain contradictory indications," including the fact that "many wealthy Mexicans who have in the past invariable [sic] supported the winning faction are still openly almazanista."[154] This report, and the simple fact that many people who, up to 1940, were regarded as savvy politicians continued to fight in favor of Almazán's claim, demonstrated exactly how serious the conflict was and made it difficult to dismiss their actions as frivolous or misguided.

152. "Almazanista Congress of the Union": Statement of Octavio Ortiz Medina, secretary of bureaucratic action of PRUN, Excélsior, Sep. 2, 1940; president of the lower chamber: La Prensa, Sep. 2, 1940 (both located in AGN-DGIPS, Box 191, 2.1/311.1/5, Vol. 18). Other leaders of the Cámara de Diputados were Ignacio Andraca Malda, Hermenegildo Gutiérrez, Jose Maria Rodríguez de la Fuente, Pedro Julio Pedrero, Alberto Perera Castillo, and Juan Abarca Pérez. Among the other leaders in the Senate were Lic. Daniel Benitez, Jesus E. Ortiz, Adolfo Cienfuegos y Camus, Jesus Ramírez Mendoza, and Alfonso Gómez Morentin. Interestingly, Castro Estrada was a classmate of Miguel Alemán at the National Law School; this may have aided his rehabilitation after 1940, which culminated in a seat on the Supreme Court from 1952 to 1967. See Camp, Mexican Political Biographies, 1935–1993, 141.

153. La Prensa, Sep. 2, 1940, AGN-DGIPS, Box 191, 2.1/311.1/5, Vol. 18.

154. Sabotage the National Railroad: Summary, G-2/2657-G-842, MID, May 20, 1941, NARA, Record Group 165, Box 2460, File 3020; "many wealthy Mexicans": Report, Lt. Col. W. D. Styer to G-2, Ft. Sam Houston, San Antonio, Sep. 7, 1940, NARA, Record Group 165, Box 2458, File 3020.

Almazán's success as a businessman and military commander in Nuevo León opened him to long-standing accusations of plotting a post-election rebellion. Already, in June 1939, one critic argued that Chipinque, Almazán's hilltop compound, was "a cabaret for the rich built with the sweat of soldiers . . . [as well as] a fortress where all Monterrey knew that Almazán has arsenals of weapons and ammunition, laid away to confront the Cárdenas regime." The criticism extended to Acapulco, which Almazán also reputedly controlled and where he allegedly maintained vast stockpiles of weapons and supplies for the coming conflagration in which he would "destroy everything the Revolution has achieved."[155] U.S. analysts dealt with similar information, and FBI chief J. Edgar Hoover himself reported in April 1940, "The Camacho leaders firmly believe that a revolution is inevitable and are preparing for same."[156] During the campaign, Almazán remarked in Ciudad Juárez that the city "was the cradle of the revolution of 1910 and has to be the cradle of the revolution of 1940." This remark led one Mexican agent to surmise that the El Paso/Ciudad Juárez area would be a starting point for Almazán's post-election strategy, whatever it might be. The threat was more real since only one army garrison was stationed in Chihuahua and the large Compañía de Palomas de Terrenos y Ganados was on good terms with Almazán and controlled unguarded borderlands.[157]

During their short-lived negotiations to join forces in the campaign, Almazán and Amaro had reportedly formed a military compact for the overthrow of the PRM government should Ávila Camacho be declared the winner of the election. Under their written agreement, Almazán would operate in the north and Amaro in the center, directing from Michoacán.[158] This document has a special credibility since it comes not from public perception or federal agents, but from the Amaro group directly: it was an internal document of the PRAC. The U.S. and Mexican agents monitoring events came to similar conclusions about the plan, without the benefit of the PRAC memorandum. Other generals allegedly involved in the potential revolt were Francisco Gonzales, Marcelo Caraveo, Francisco Bórquez, Roberto Cruz,

155. Report, [unidentified agent] to DGIPS, Jun. 25, 1939, Monterrey, AGN-DGIPS, Box 185, 2.1/311.1/2, Vol. 3.

156. Memo, J. E. Hoover to Col. J. M. Churchill, G-2, War Department, Apr. 13, 1940, NARA, Record Group 165, Box 2460, File 3020.

157. Report, Insp. Martinez Flores to DGIPS, Aug. 21, 1940, Ciudad Juárez, AGN-DGIPS, Box 191, 2.1/311.1/5, Vol. 17.

158. Report, Huétamo, Michoacán, Apr. 8, 1940, FAPEC-AJA, Campaña Política, 1939–1940, File 020200, Documentos Confidenciales.

Alfredo Lezama, and Gustavo León.[159] Mexican intelligence reported that Almazán had sent Caraveo to Chihuahua and Cruz to Sonora in August 1940 to begin military operations.[160] Almazán considered the dispersal of his troops to various regions under loyal commanders to be to his benefit "since in this way they could serve him better than if they were concentrated in any one military zone."[161] A strategic consideration was posed by another agent, who reported that the armed movement would begin in earnest in the rural southeast, where bad communications would both prevent quick government reprisals and prolong the life of the struggle in order "to give time to the timid to decide to join the movement."[162] The U.S. consul in Nuevo Laredo reported persistent rumors that 80 percent of the army supported Amaro and that "Amaro was considered to be a stronger man than Almazán."[163] FBI sources concluded that "more than sixty percent of the officers of the regular army are supporters of General Juan Andreu Almazán." An FBI agent, returning from Mexico City, stated, "Almazán will be practically forced into an open revolt by his followers . . . [but] if Almazán does not head a revolt, Amaro will."[164] Still other investigations by the U.S. Army pointed to a solo campaign by Amaro since "Almazán can't and won't turn the trick" and reinforced the point that "in case Almazán will not head a revolt that Amaro will."[165] Amaro confused the situation further when he announced, "The PRAC like myself is working within the law. . . . If someone is spreading

159. Memo, J. E. Hoover to Col. J. M. Churchill, G-2, War Department, Apr. 13, 1940, NARA, Record Group 165, Box 2460, File 3020.

160. Memo, DGIPS, Aug. 28, 1940 (citing DGIPS report of Aug. 23, 1940), AGN-DGIPS, Box 191, 2.1/311.1/5, Vol. 19.

161. U.S. State Department, Aguirre, "Memorandum of Conversation with Captain (Ret.) Thomas Ward, U.S. Army," Jan. 19, 1940, in *Confidential U.S. State Department Central Files, Mexico, 1940–1944, Part I*, Reel 1.

162. Report, Insp. Galván to DGIPS, Aug. 10, 1940, AGN-DGIPS, Box 191, 2.1/311.1/5, Vol. 17.

163. U.S. State Department, 812.00/30904, Wormuth to Secretary of State, Jan. 19, 1940, Nuevo Laredo, in *Confidential U.S. State Department Central Files, Mexico, 1940–1944, Part I*, Reel 1.

164. "Sixty percent of the officers": Memo, J. E. Hoover to Col. J. M. Churchill, G-2, War Department, Apr. 13, 1940; "forced into an open revolt": Report, Maj. Malcolm Lindsey, Ft. Sam Houston, San Antonio, to G-2, War Department, Apr. 29, 1940 (both located in NARA, Record Group 165, Box 2460, File 3020). The FBI agent returning from Mexico City was Gus T. Jones.

165. U.S. State Department, unnumbered memo, Bursley to Duggan, Jan. 22, 1940, in *Confidential U.S. State Department Central Files, Mexico, 1940–1944, Part I*, Reel 1; Report, Maj. Malcolm Lindsey, Ft. Sam Houston, San Antonio, to G-2, War Department, May 15, 1940, NARA, Record Group 165, Box 2460, File 3020.

subversive propaganda, they should be punished, whoever they are."[166] Such widespread discussion, rumor, and planning for a post-election revolt provided a source of leverage for the opposition, who could potentially destabilize the country. Conversely, it proved what the PRM had said all along—that the opposition simply would not play by the rules or respect the vote.

Amaro saw the conflict between Almazán and the PRM as inevitable by the end of August 1940. Sensing an opportunity, he argued that the two sides would weaken each other to the extent that "the PRAC could be the decisive factor in the dispute and take the winning side." This strategy led Amaro to call upon his followers to renew their work for the party and strengthen their political bonds in anticipation of the opportunity. He also decided that supporting Almazán was no longer an option. Rather, in a style worthy of Machiavelli, he had to use the state of crisis so that "the PRAC will be in a position to triumph, taking advantage of the conflict to facilitate the return to power of General Calles."[167]

This strategy of moving into the political breach seemed to be papered over only a few days after it was first reported. Mexican agents concluded that "despite the differences between Amaro and Almazán, thanks to the intervention of mutual friends, they have agreed to provoke disturbances with subversive tendencies . . . and Amaro notified his followers in Sonora, Sinaloa and Chihuahua to be in contact with General Cruz, in order to unify their action in the North." But at a meeting of callista loyalists, leaders declared that Amaro was only "flirting" (*coqueteando*) with both Almazán and Ávila Camacho to gain position and that Amaro would certainly control the situation when the real conflict began due to his support within the army. Mexican intelligence viewed Amaro's vacillation as a key weakness that would "make it easy to disperse."[168] Amaro was certainly attempting to play his hand wisely by never fully pledging his movement to either side. Yet his public posture and connections to the old Calles machine made his support worth the trouble for either Almazán or Ávila Camacho to secure.

166. Draft of comments by Amaro, "Amaro hace declaraciones sobre supuestas actividades subversives," Feb. 22, 1940, FAPEC-AJA, Campaña Política, 1939–1940, File 0514.

167. Memo, DGIPS, Aug. 28, 1940 (citing DGIPS report of Aug. 23, 1940), AGN-DGIPS, Box 191, 2.1/311.1/5, Vol. 19. The same report remarked that Manuel Peláez had similar aspirations and was headed for the Huasteca Veracruzana to press his case.

168. Memo, DGIPS, Aug. 28, 1940 (citing DGIPS report of Aug. 26, 1940), AGN-DGIPS, Box 191, 2.1/311.1/5, Vol. 19.

In August 1940, Amaro reportedly met privately with L. L. Anderson and A. R. Carruthers, representatives of the oil giant Royal Dutch Shell. This report, coupled with other investigations showing Almazán in contact with Huasteca oil representatives and Amaro with El Aguila oil managers, led Mexican agents to conclude that the Almazán-Amaro group had made a deal with the foreign oil companies "to provoke a domestic conflict that will be favorable to their interests." The presence of senior foreign oil representatives H. W. Sampson, J. N. S. Longe, C. H. L. Chase, and F. L. Armstrong in Mexico City and their "anti-government" forces on the ground in the oil regions did nothing to assuage fears within the administration that these companies might attempt to take by force what they lost by law in the 1938 expropriation.[169] With the compensation issue still being negotiated in 1940 and the bad feelings on all sides, the possibility of intrigue on the part of international petroleum concerns could not be taken lightly.

The U.S. War Department was so concerned "that the country is drifting towards a revolution" that the assistant chief of staff at G-2 (Intelligence) researched the points arguing for and against the possibilities of such violence. Reasons against the possibility of revolution included the armed militancy of unions and agrarians in support of the government, doubts about whether the rank and file of the army would follow the generals in a coup attempt, and the financial support of Spanish refugees (rumored to have $50 million in gold stashed away in Mexico). Two other arguments bore closer inspection: first, that Cárdenas had transferred military leaders from positions of power and replaced them with loyalists; second, and most hopefully, "the fact that the Government has put down the last two revolutions with comparative ease: Escobar [in] 1929, Cedillo [in] 1938." Arguing for the possibility of revolution were the worsening economic condition of the country, the collective effort of conservatives to defend their interests, and the presumption that "the Army officers, especially the older ones, hate Cárdenas." Most simplistically, and stereotypically, was the idea that "the Mexican is a poor loser and would not hesitate to attempt to win an election by force if he felt he had a good chance of success." All of these "facts" were presented to the War Department leadership to aid in forming judgments about the eventual outcomes of the 1940 election. Underlying them all was the sentiment that revolution in Mexico was never far away, in the past or in the future.[170]

169. Ibid.
170. Memo, Col. E. R. W. McCabe to Chief of Staff, War Department, Aug. 16, 1939, G-2/2657-G-732, in Lester, *U.S. Military Intelligence Reports. Mexico, 1919–1941,* Reel 4, Frames 213–15.

Though largely the preoccupation of U.S. news editors, businessmen, and diplomats, the threat of physical violence or "revolution" in Mexico following the election of 1940 was not completely unfounded. Indeed, the traffic in arms had been a source of great interest for Mexican and U.S. agents for many years. Nicolás Rodríguez, leader of the quasi-fascist Camisas Doradas, reportedly had a large cache of weapons and ammunition in Mission, Texas, that he could put in play in Mexico if needed. Almazán supposedly kept great quantities of matériel stashed on both sides of the U.S.-Mexico border to support his candidacy with force.[171] This report held credence owing in large part to Almazán's long tenure as zone commander in Monterrey, a time when he was able to thoroughly ensconce himself in the highest circles of the political and business elite in the Mexican North and Texas. In Acapulco, Mexican intelligence reports indicated that a Mr. Stephens and a Mr. Todd as well as their wives, U.S. citizens all, were active in transporting munitions through the port and were a danger for organizing among the port workers.[172] The rumors of weapons caches and rebellious intentions, duly inflated by political strategists, fanned the apprehension present along the U.S. side of the border, "where they talk of nothing else but the next revolution in Mexico."[173]

Not all of the talk of revolution came from outside the Almazán campaign. One Almazán advisor predicted in April 1939 that the imposition of Ávila Camacho in the election of 1940 would likely provoke a revolt, given that so many of the principal army generals supported Almazán.[174] Another observer noted the predominance of support for Almazán among the lower ranks as well, "who saw him as an illustrious soldier, a man of order, who would watch out for the interests of the Army."[175] Almazán himself promised in a campaign speech in Nuevo Laredo that if he was elected president he would "do [his] duty and defend to the death the will of the Mexican people."[176] Almazán later

171. Large cache of weapons: Report, Insp. 7 to DGIPS, Jan. 7, 1939, AGN-DGIPS, Box 142, 2.1/310.1(725)/1; great quantities of matériel: Report, Insp. Rincón C. to DGIPS, Apr. 12, 1939, AGN-DGIPS, Box 187, 2.1/311.1/5, Vol. 1.

172. Memo, DGIPS, Aug. 28, 1940 (citing DGIPS report of Aug. 28, 1940), AGN-DGIPS, Box 191, 2.1/311.1/5, Vol. 19. The women were also active in the almazanista feminist league.

173. Letter, Noriega to Amaro, Apr. 29, 1940, FAPEC-AJA, Campaña Política, 1939–1940, File 020200, Lic. Jose Luis Noriega.

174. Report, Insp. 19 to DGIPS, Apr. 24, 1939, AGN-DGIPS, Box 187, 2.1/311.1/5, Vol. 1.

175. Letter, Lic. Ulloa to Gómez Morin, Jul. 3, 1939, AMGM, Fondo Acción Nacional, Vol. 39, File 220.

176. Report, Insp. 1 to DGIPS, May 21, 1940, Monterrey, AGN-DGIPS, Box 190, 2.1/311.1/5, Vol. 14.

stated to a San Antonio paper, "If the Cárdenas administration ignores the law and denies me the right to take office, then they are the instigators of an uprising, if one occurs."[177] After the election, Carlos Lavín, an almazanista and friend of the governor of Morelos, allegedly incited the people of the Tetecala region to "be ready with your weapons for the call at any moment."[178] And days before the inauguration, almazanistas continued to "stoutly maintain that there will be a revolution on his behalf."[179] Claims from the almazanistas and Almazán himself of the probability of a post-election revolt tended to lend credence to the belief, current among PRM and U.S. officials alike, that some sort of armed conflagration was due to break out.

Almazán's access to the tools of violence, mainly significant numbers of armed men, made the threat of revolution more plausible. A 1939 report by the U.S. military argued that "If all, or even a fair part, of the opposition should crystallize around and in support of one man . . . it would be able easily to overthrow the government."[180] An internal Mexican intelligence memorandum named six regiment- and battalion-level officers who were prepared to support Almazán in an uprising.[181] For example, longtime Almazán loyalists Lt. Col. Tiburcio Garza Zamora and Col. Herón Ramírez continued to be active in the Reynosa area in August 1940, where their attempt to have Almazán's post-election Havana speech printed on leaflets was quashed by the local military chief.[182] Soon after, an agent in Toluca reported that almazanistas were attempting to join state police forces to form a "hard-core almazanista fifth column." Almazán allegedly controlled six groups of federal troops stationed in Mexico City, as well as a fair number of Mexico

177. *San Antonio Light,* Jun. 15, 1940.
178. DGIPS Memo, DGIPS, Aug. 28, 1940 (citing DGIPS report of Aug. 28, 1940), AGN-DGIPS, Box 191, 2.1/311.1/5, Vol. 19.
179. Report to G-2, Ft. Sam Houston, San Antonio, Nov. 23, 1940, NARA, Record Group 165, Box 2458, File 3020.
180. Summary, [MID, Jan. 1939], NARA, Record Group 165, Box 2454, File 3000.
181. Memo, DGIPS, Aug. 2, 1940, AGN-DGIPS, Box 191, 2.1/311.1/5, Vol. 18. The officers included Col. Rosendo Cuevas Rojas, Seventieth Regiment, Autlán de la G., Jalisco; Col. Enrique Sáenz Mejía, Seventy-first Regiment, Tocolotlán, Jalisco; Col. Rafael Cancino P., Seventy-second Regiment, Cocula, Guerrero; Col. Rafael Moran González, Seventy-third Regiment, Chiapas; Col. Ignacio Angulo V., Seventieth Battalion, Taxco, Guerrero; Col. Catarino Melendez M., Seventy-first Battalion, Huamúchil, Sinaloa.
182. Report, Insp. 5 to DGIPS, Sep. 1, 1940, Reynosa, AGN-DGIPS, Box 191, 2.1/311.1/5, Vol. 18. When Almazán was zone commander in Monterrey, Garza Zamora was the army chief in Reynosa and was given the concession to run the electric utility there. In 1940, he stood as a PRUN candidate for diputado.

City police officers.[183] All of these reports, alarmist though they may have been, pointed to the possibility of Almazán backing his claim to the presidency with considerable popular support and armed might.

Another element of the threat of revolution was the willingness to use force as a political tool. By February 1940 in Veracruz, PRUN advisors gave the impression that "if the federal government does not recognize General Almazán's triumph, the question of the presidency will be decided by violence."[184] By the autumn of 1940, the PRUN office in Mexico City hinted that the "general uprising" would occur on September 15. This date would coincide symbolically with Mexican Independence Day on September 16. After the election, rumors spread that Higinia Cedillo (sister of the late Saturnino) was organizing groups around Ciudad del Maíz, San Luis Potosí, to protest in Mexico City on September 1. This plan was reportedly "developed with the connivance of the political leaders of the PRUN."[185]

The accusation of preparing for an armed confrontation, however, was as easily directed at the PRM as at Almazán. In Zacatecas, Almazán flatly rejected the notion of planning a rebellion, saying that his supporters were not "a bunch of imbeciles to do such a thing, since in reality it is the impositionists themselves who are giving out weapons." In Jalisco, General Marcelino Garcia Barragán, who became secretary of national defense in 1964, and several congressmen took charge of distributing arms to avilacamachistas. PRUN supporters in Mexico City had argued darkly during the campaign that the government was preparing to stage a revolt in order to blame and discredit the almazanista movement. A corollary of this theory for some was the notion that a pre-election staged revolt would be a pretext for suspending the vote and allowing Cárdenas to remain in power.[186] In his widely reported

183. "Hardcore almazanista fifth column": Report, Insp. 12 to DGIPS, Aug. 19, 1940, Toluca, AGN-DGIPS, Box 191, 2.1/311.1/5, Vol. 17; six groups of federal troops: Memo, DGIPS, Aug. 2, 1940, AGN-DGIPS, Box 191, 2.1/311.1/5, Vol. 18.

184. Report, Insp. 2 to DGIPS, Feb. 11, 1940, Veracruz, AGN-DGIPS, Box 190, 2.1/311.1/5, Vol. 15.

185. "General uprising": Report, Insp. G[utiérrez] to DGIPS, Sep. 6, 1940; "connivance of the political leaders": Report, Insp. Pérez Aldama to DGIPS, Aug. 30, 1940, San Luis Potosí (both located in AGN-DGIPS, Box 191, 2.1/311.1/5, Vol. 18).

186. "Bunch of imbeciles": Excélsior, Mar. 4, 1940, AGN-DGIPS, Box 189, 2.1/311.1/5, Vol. 10; distributing arms to almazanistas: Report, Insp. Alemán Pérez to DGIPS, Jun. 1, 1940, Guadalajara, AGN-DGIPS, Box 190, 2.1/311.1/5, Vol. 15; stage a revolt: Draft report, Insp. Tena to DGIPS, [May 1940], AGN-DGIPS, Box 190, 2.1/311.1/5, Vol. 13; pretext for suspending the vote: Report, Insp. Alemán Pérez to DGIPS, Jun. 1, 1940, Guadalajara, AGN-DGIPS, Box 190, 2.1/311.1/5, Vol. 15.

speech in New York City in September 1940, Almazán charged that thou-
sands of Spanish refugees were being brought to Mexico for less than human-
itarian reasons: "these Communists will not only strengthen Lombardo and
his Stalinist movement, but, being trained soldiers, all can be used against any
popular uprising."[187]

The federal government was clearly concerned about the possibility of an
armed conflict with the almazanistas after the election. The army garrison in
Ciudad Juárez, officials worried, had only one company of troops, rendering
it "impotent to confront any movement at a given time." Moreover, the
customs office at Juárez was reported to be 30 percent almazanista. The
DGIPS recommended that the government replace all of the customs personnel in the north, owing to a strong core of almazanista sympathizers. Rumors
of an almazanista rebellion in Palomas or Ojinaga surfaced days later but were
never corroborated or disproved. Almazán reportedly ordered one almazanista, Lt. Col. Cruz Villalba, a follower of Caraveo, to set up a local committee
in Palomas to facilitate communications across the border.[188] All signs pointed
to the real possibility of an armed revolt and perhaps a successful one.

After the election, the government policy of terror against the almazanistas
continued. A U.S. reporter opined that "the government is apparently bearing
down on opposition, taking sort of a stand of 'either [join] us or else.'" He
further stated that the government had a clear plan "to snuff out almazanismo
and all its works." "All sorts [of] punitive measures" were taken against almazanistas through the autumn of 1940, including the disappearance of, among
others and most intriguingly, Higinia Cedillo. Information from Mexican intelligence indicated the suspicion "that her subversive activities had something to
do with it." Through it all, rumors circulated that local bosses were "reporting
non-existant [sic] revolts here and there" to raise their profile with the federal

187. San Antonio Evening News, Sep. 3, 1940, AGN-DGIPS, Box 191, 2.1/311.1/5, Vol.
18. The article also noted, "As an indication of the situation here, most newspapers voluntarily
censored Almazán's New York statement, and the United Press draft of it mysteriously failed to
arrive after it had been received over the government radio." The responsibility for this turn of
events is unclear.

188. "Impotent to confront any movement": Memo, DGIPS, Aug. 2, 1940; customs office
at Juárez: Telegram, Insp. Conrado Meili to DGIPS, Sep. 3, 1940, Ciudad Juárez (both located in
AGN-DGIPS, Box 191, 2.1/311.1/5, Vol. 18); strong core of almazanista sympathizers: Memo,
DGIPS, Aug. 28, 1940; rumors of an almazanista rebellion: Report, Insp. 1 to DGIPS, Sep. 6,
1940, Ciudad Juárez (both located in AGN-DGIPS, Box 191, 2.1/311.1/5, Vol. 19); local committee in Palomas: Memo, DGIPS, Aug. 2, 1940 (citing DGIPS report of Jul. 27, 1940), AGN-
DGIPS, Box 191, 2.1/311.1/5, Vol. 18.

government.[189] Even the belief in a phantom revolt conditioned the behavior and influenced the PRM response to perceived almazanista aggression.

Almazán's support was not limited to Mexican territory. Early in the campaign, a Mexican agent in Monterrey indicated that many followers of Almazán were concentrated in the Monterrey region, but also "on both sides of the border." These connections allegedly contained dangerous elements funded by "fascist American capitalists." In Weslaco, Texas, Almazán's popularity was reportedly comparable only to that of Franklin D. Roosevelt and Clark Gable.[190] A clandestine shortwave radio station broadcast pro-Almazán messages in San Antonio, managing to elude detection by government scanners. Along the U.S.-Mexico border, especially the Texas section, arms, intelligence, and funds flowed more or less freely across the line. However, the debate was far from one-sided; in San Antonio La Prensa questioned the propriety and ability of Almazán to judge the fairness of the elections, given his ongoing implicit threat of "agitation," and announced its opposition to "all attempts to subvert order [in Mexico] and to ruin the country."[191]

San Antonio was a source of arms as well as political cover. Mexican Army major Blas Tijerina Cárdenas, an almazanista sympathizer, took delivery of eight .30–30 rifles out of an order of one hundred fifty in September 1940. The same report indicated that "a suspicious plane has been flying from San Antonio towards Mexico, almost certainly carrying contraband weapons." Customs officials who suspected the flights were ferrying guns into Mexico noted a similar plane and turned the issue over to U.S. authorities for investigation. At Specia Plumbing and Hardware, a man named Mayer placed an order for one hundred .30–30 rifles, arousing the suspicion of a Mexican agent working in the area, who notified the local authorities with the "hope that they confiscate the weapons and charge him with subversive activities." The customs office in Nuevo Laredo reported to the Mexican consul in San

189. "Bearing down on opposition": Letter, McCombs to Thomas Krug (Time), Nov. 13, 1940; "snuff out almazanismo" and "punitive measures": Telegram, McCombs to Thomas Krug (Time), Nov. 15, 1940; "subversive activities": Draft letter, McCombs to Thomas Krug (Time), Nov. 15, 1940; "non-existant revolts": Telegram, McCombs to Thomas Krug (Time), Nov. 15, 1940 (all located in McCombs Papers, Box 46, File 23).

190. "Both sides of the border" and "fascist American capitalists": Letter, Jesús M. Costas S. [Inspector Jose M. Clavé] to Isidro Pérez Sánchez [IPS], Mar. 18, 1939, Monterrey, AGN-DGIPS, Box 187, 2.1/311.1/5, Vol. 1; Almazán's popularity: Memo, Jefe de Migración Andrés Guerra G. to Garcia Téllez, May 20, 1940, Matamoros, AGN-DGIPS, Box 190, 2.1/311.1/5, Vol. 16.

191. Clandestine shortwave radio station: La Prensa, Jul. 25, 1940; "attempts to subvert order": La Prensa, Jul. 4, 1940 (both located in AGN-DGIPS, Box 191, 2.1/311.1/5, Vol. 17).

Antonio the activities of an American named H. S. Lebman, who had ordered one hundred carbines for the almazanistas, allegedly had ties to the
Chicago and New York underworlds, and maintained a substantial supplemental arsenal.[192] The provision of arms in the United States and their trans-
port to almazanista loyalists in Mexico was one of the most crucial subjects
of Mexican surveillance efforts abroad.

The reunion of almazanista supporters in San Antonio did much to create
the impression that the city would be the center of any organized rebellious
activities. The local press described "a quiet but steady flow of almazanistas
to the United States." Neri reportedly met confidentially with the Mexican
consul Omar Josefe to discuss the potential for violence in Mexico.[193] Luis N.
Morones, former head of the Confederación Regional Obrera Mexicana
(CROM) and an old ally of Calles, was among the Mexican politicians operating in San Antonio by the end of August 1940. The arrival of senior Almazán
advisor José Mijares Palencia in the city days later caused a flurry of speculation from a Mexican agent stationed there. Even the Mexican consuls became
involved as the Laredo office telephoned the San Antonio office to begin
surveillance of revolutionary veteran Leopoldo Dorantes upon his arrival in
the city. By mid-September, a host of key almazanista leaders were assembled
in San Antonio, including Neri, Dorantes, Francisco Cárdenas, Gabino Vizc-
arra, and Joaquín Muñoz. To fully organize the effort, Almazán had rented
an entire floor of a downtown hotel and only "recognized almazanistas"
were allowed entrance.[194]

The selection of San Antonio as a focus of almazanista exiles was not
unusual. For many years, the city had been a refuge for Mexican political
exiles. During the fall of 1940, Francisco Cárdenas stayed at the home of

192. "Suspicious plane": Summary, DGIPS, Sep. 14, 1940 (based on Report, Insp. Ruiz
Russek to DGIPS, Sep. 14, 1940, San Antonio); "hope that they confiscate the weapons":
Report, Insp. 31 to DGIPS, Sep. 16, 1940, San Antonio; substantial supplemental arsenal: Report, Insp. 31 to DGIPS, Sep. 18, 1940, San Antonio (all located in AGN-DGIPS, Box 191,
2.1/311.1/5, Vol. 19).

193. "Quiet but steady flow": San Antonio Evening News, Sep. 3, 1940, AGN-DGIPS, Box
191, 2.1/311.1/5, Vol. 18; potential for violence: Telegram, Insp. González Ramírez to DGIPS,
Sep. 9, 1940, Nuevo Laredo, AGN-DGIPS, Box 191, 2.1/311.1/5, Vol. 19.

194. Mexican politicians operating in San Antonio: Report, Insp. 31 to DGIPS, Sep. 1,
1940, San Antonio; flurry of speculation: Report, Insp. 31 to DGIPS, Sep. 4, 1940, San Antonio;
surveillance of revolutionary veteran: Report, Insp. 31 to DGIPS, Sep. 5, 1940, San Antonio
(all located in AGN-DGIPS, Box 191, 2.1/311.1/5, Vol. 18); host of key almazanista leaders:
Report, Insp. 31 to DGIPS, Sep. 16, 1940, San Antonio; "recognized almazanistas": Excélsior,
Sep. 11, 1940 (both located in AGN-DGIPS, Box 191, 2.1/311.1/5, Vol. 19).

declared almazanista Matilde Elizondo, where meetings with *La Prensa* publisher Ignacio Lozano and other Almazán supporters were held.[195] The community of exiled Mexicans in San Antonio formed a focal point for political activism. Indeed, many within the group had relocated to San Antonio in part to escape political aggression.[196] Some of the pro-Almazán members of the San Antonio group filed a formal complaint with the Cárdenas administration demanding a thorough accounting for the events surrounding an attempt on Almazán's life at Zacapú, Michoacán.[197] Exiled Mexican activists were every bit as energetic as those that remained in their homeland. As the political battle in Mexico heated up in the autumn of 1940, the United States was not the only option for political exiles: Honduras and Venezuela extended offers of political asylum to the almazanistas.[198]

By operating in the United States, Almazán could avoid much, but not all, of the surveillance set up by Mexican agents. It also allowed him easier access to perhaps the most strategic exile there was: former president Calles. In September 1940, Calles was spotted on the way to San Antonio after allegedly having discussions with Almazán in El Paso. Almazanistas offered no comment on the rumors when they appeared in the press. Further reports indicated that Calles was traveling incognito, such that his contacts in El Paso did not know that he was coming and his friends in Los Angeles did not know that he had left. This seemed to lend credence to the belief that Calles and Almazán, perhaps through the intervention of Amaro, had overcome their former mistrust of one another and "coordinated a secret alliance with ulterior motives for action in Mexico."[199] Such an alliance would have allowed Almazán to claim his electoral victory and Calles to visit his revenge upon Cárdenas.

From New York, Almazán continued his withering verbal assault on the PRM. He criticized the Cárdenas administration's searches of homes in the name of security as proceeding from "a justifiable fear that the people of

195. Report, Insp. 31 to DGIPS, Sep. 23, 1940, San Antonio, AGN-DGIPS, Box 191, 2.1/311.1/5, Vol. 19.

196. For more information on the Mexican exile community in San Antonio, see Richard A. Garcia, *Rise of the Mexican-American Middle Class: San Antonio, 1929–1941* (College Station: Texas A&M University Press, 1991).

197. *San Antonio Light,* Feb. 15, 1940.

198. Report, Insp. G[utiérrez] to DGIPS, Aug. 28, 1940, AGN-DGIPS, Box 191, 2.1/311.1/5, Vol. 18.

199. Calles was spotted: Report, Insp. Martínez Flores to DGIPS, Sep. 12, 1940, Ciudad Juárez; no comment on the rumors: *Excélsior,* Sep. 11, 1940; "secret alliance with ulterior motives": *La Prensa,* Sep. 13, 1940 (all located in AGN-DGIPS, Box 191, 2.1/311.1/5, Vol. 19).

Mexico are sick of racketeer government, sick to the point of revolt with or without my leadership." He claimed that upon his return to Mexico he would challenge "not constituted authority, but bold defiance of the people's will by as ruthless a crew of racketeers as ever cursed a country."[200] By casting his struggle as a defense of "the people's will," Almazán hoped to attract citizens to his cause who may not have voted for him but still believed in fair play.

Yet the political strength of almazanismo quickly dissipated following the election of 1940. Almazán's vagabond path from Mexico to Cuba to Baltimore to New York, and back again, did little to inspire confidence in his followers, including the ill-fated General Andrés Zarzosa, who was killed in an apparent rebellion in Monterrey. A U.S. official observed concisely that "every day the Almazán leaders remain out of the country the General's strength is diminishing."[201] By mid-September, Emilio Madero had been relieved of his position at the head of the PRUN for suggesting that the party was "paralyzed" by the lack of communication with Almazán abroad, and some in the press declared almazanismo "rudderless."[202] In October, "the feeling of almazanistas [was] one of fear and worry, engendered by Almazán's long stay in the United States and the lack of action on the part of his followers."[203]

The belief that Almazán had much to lose in any confrontation with the PRM was given new life in August 1940. Almazán either signed over or sold at token prices at least fifteen pieces of his financial and business interests. This was taken as a sign that he indeed planned to rebel against the government. Further reports alleged that Almazán had been paid eight million pesos, an amount owed him for sundry government contracts pending, and had deposited all of it in foreign banks, along with the proceeds of the sale of all of his real estate holdings in Mexico. Almazán reportedly deposited U.S.$300,000 in a New York bank in mid-September.[204] It seemed that Almazán was cashing out.

200. *El Paso Herald-Post,* Sep. 3, 1940; *La Prensa,* Sep. 4, 1940 (both located in AGN-DGIPS, Box 191, 2.1/311.1/5, Vol. 18).

201. U.S. State Department, Memo, Blocker to Secretary of State, Sep. 12, 1940, Ciudad Juárez, in *Confidential U.S. State Department Central Files, Mexico, 1940–1944, Part I,* Reel 2.

202. *La Prensa,* Sep. 21, 1940, AGN-DGIPS, Box 191, 2.1/311.1/5, Vol. 19. Columnists Pedrero and Jorge Prieto Laurens demanded Madero's resignation.

203. Report, Lt. Col. A. W. Roffe to Commanding General, Ft. Sam Houston, San Antonio, Oct. 9, 1940 (based on report from Ft. Huachuca, near Nogales), NARA, Record Group 165, Box 2458, File 3020.

204. Planned to rebel against the government: Memo, DGIPS, Aug. 2, 1940; eight million pesos: Report, Insp. 7 to DGIPS, Aug. 26, 1940, Morelia (both located in AGN-DGIPS, Box

The efforts at compromise between almazanistas and the government hinted at the corrupting influence of money in politics. As one U.S. intelligence officer noted, "Any ideal or patriotic purpose or movement can be stopped in Mexico if there are sufficient silver bullets."[205] Notable supporters began to jump ship as Ávila Camacho's inauguration neared, often asking to be reinstated in their military or bureaucratic capacities. Almazanistas and "voluntary exiles" in the Nogales area were promised immunity and allowed to return to Mexico in late November 1940, ahead of inauguration ceremonies on December 1.[206] This process of reintegration was echoed in the elections of 1946 and 1952 as personal survival took precedence over ideology, friendship, or political allegiance.

After the 1940 campaign, the United States could not help but preserve a keen interest in the Sinarquista movement. The Spanish legation in Guatemala was reported to be a clearinghouse for Axis intelligence activity, a theory reinforced by British intelligence studies on the connection between Falangists and Sinarquistas in Mexico.[207] With active units residing on U.S. soil, the U.S. Office of Strategic Services (OSS) reported in 1943 that "the UNS encourages Mexicans in the United States to resist assimilation and is laying the groundwork for an irredentist movement." This threat was in addition to the "inevitabl[e] attempt to overthrow the . . . friendly and allied Mexican government," which would result in "a long and disastrous civil war to which the United States could not remain indifferent."[208] The concerns of the United States were linked to World War II as well. "The once obscure movement has grown to such proportions that it might conceivably affect the stability of the Mexican government and its ability to discharge its international commitments."[209] The persistence of groups like the UNS became a major factor in the U.S. decision to train and fund Mexican intelligence during and after World War II.

191, 2.1/311.1/5, Vol. 18); U.S.$300,000 in a New York bank: Report, Insp. Ruiz Russek to DGIPS, Sep. 12, 1940, San Antonio, AGN-DGIPS, Box 191, 2.1/311.1/5, Vol. 19.

205. Naval Attaché Report 304–40-R, W. M. Dillon, Mexico City, Sep. 30, 1940, NARA, Record Group 165, Box 2460, File 3020.

206. Supporters began to jump ship: Report to G-2, Ft. Sam Houston, San Antonio, Nov. 23, 1940; "voluntary exiles": Report, Col. L. D. Davis to G-2, Ft. Huachuca, Nov. 30, 1940 (both located in NARA, Record Group 165, Box 2458, File 3020).

207. Summary, MID, May 29, 1942, NARA, Record Group 165, Box 2453, File 2950.

208. Report, R&A No. 843, "The Sinarquista Movement in Mexico," Jun. 1943, p. vi, NARA, Record Group 226.

209. Ibid., 1.

The disaffected groups within the almazanista movement were also judged to pose a potential threat to U.S. security. Such a group was "a fertile field for the agents of foreign nations to use. . . . The groundwork of their organization is laid, and they are partially armed." The almazanistas returning from their U.S. exile were still seen as a powerful political group that could either work for honorable goals or "be very harmful to the interest of their own country, as well as the United States, if allowed to be influenced by subversive elements." Indeed, though the threat of "revolution" had passed, U.S. officials viewed the situation as "more serious than before, in view of the subversive activities of foreign agents."[210]

Yet the conservative forces that coalesced in the 1940 electoral season did not disappear after inauguration day. In 1941, the FBI reported that a group of almazanistas was planning a secret assembly to be headed by military officials.[211] As late as 1942, candidates for Congress from Durango were writing letters to Amaro asking for his support in their campaigns.[212] The fact that the Ávila Camacho administration took up many of the professed goals of the Sinarquistas attests to the dominant elite's awareness of the power of forces on the Right and the need to address their grievances.[213]

Among the devoted PAN members and dedicated conservatives linked to the Almazán challenge, there was a continuation of the goals that had fueled almazanismo in the first place. In 1941, an agent in Acapulco reported, "It seems that the opposition parties are trying to unify their groups so that at a given time the parties can form a single front." News from Guerrero positing a unification of the main opposition parties, PAN and the Sinarquistas, tended to support this contention.[214] Yet without a clear and finite goal, such as an election, whether such a unified conservative front could have been formed, prospered, or even survived was unclear.

The PAN continued its rhetorical assault on the prevailing political norms and the detrimental economic condition that the country faced. One deep

210. Report, Col. L. D. Davis to G-2, Ft. Sam Houston, Ft. Huachuca, Nov. 30, 1940, NARA, Record Group 165, Box 2458, File 3020.

211. Summary, G2/2657-G-842/117, MID, Jun. 7, 1941, NARA, Record Group 165, Box 2460, File 3020. The source for this summary was noted as an FBI report of Jun. 2, 1941.

212. FAPEC-AJA, Campaña Política, 1939–1940, File 020200, Durango, PRAC.

213. Report, R&A No. 843, "The Sinarquista Movement in Mexico," Jun. 1943, p. 27, NARA, Record Group 226.

214. "Opposition parties are trying to unify": Report, Insp. 53 to DGIPS, Nov. 3, 1941, Acapulco, AGN-DGIPS, Box 23, File 1, 2.1/061.7(725.1)/2, p. 40; news from Guerrero: Report, Insp. 53 to DGIPS, Nov. 1, 1941, Iguala, AGN-DGIPS, Box 23, File 1, 2.1/061.7(725.1)/2.

problem panistas identified was "the existence of an abyss between the real Mexico and the official Mexico, that false concept of Nation and State that is the basis and the pretext for the internal shredding of Mexico's public life caused by an obscure succession of lies, violent acts and repressions." Nor did the PAN refrain from excoriating the electoral system itself: "Only the excruciating lethargy of the Mexican citizenry, the monopoly of power in the hands of the most ridiculous ignorance, [and] the ruffianism that has become a fixture in Mexican politics, can explain how there still exists in Mexico a body of law so foolish, so incongruous, so ineffective, as that relating to electoral procedures."[215] Of course, this set of laws, constructed and perfected by the PRM leadership over years, was the very tool that would be used to weaken and undermine political challenges for years to come. The PAN resisted attempts by the Ávila Camacho administration to restrict its activities: "It cannot and should not fall to the judgment of any *caciquillo* our right to profess the doctrine that we have proclaimed and to peacefully pursue an organization of citizens around this doctrine."[216] Win or lose—and the losing was just beginning—the PAN was determined to voice its opinions and attempt to shape the direction of national policy.

Following the defeats of 1940, the almazanistas pursued different strategies. Some sought the protection of the ascendant political group surrounding Ávila Camacho. Others attended the court of Alemán, already constructing his power within Gobernación. Some, like Almazán himself, retired more or less quietly to private life, content in their still considerable wealth and social standing if not in popular image. A U.S. reporter had wondered in 1939, "Almazán must have had good reasons to get off his gravy train and sit himself on top of this dump of dynamite that could explode into a civil war."[217] Yet the available evidence indicates that Almazán was never fully weaned from government contracts.

Reports surfaced even before the election that a quiescent Almazán in defeat "would be given the contract of building the highway from Cd. Juárez to Mexico City and from thence to the Guatemalan border."[218] Already in

215. Memo, PAN [Oct. 1940], AMGM, Fondo Acción Nacional, Vol. 4, File 47.

216. Letter, PAN to González Gallo (personal secretary of the president), Aug. 22, 1941, AMGM, Fondo Acción Nacional, Vol. 6, File 56.

217. McCombs, Jul. 31, 1939, McCombs Papers, Box 46, File 22.

218. Wormuth to Secretary of State, May 22, 1940, Nuevo Laredo, NARA, Record Group 84, Mexico City Consulate, Confidential Records, Box 6.

August 1940, reports were circulating among the almazanistas that their candidate had sealed a very lucrative contract with the outgoing Cárdenas administration to build the Pan-American Highway.[219] Another observer commented that "the Almazán party will remain strong enough to demand important concessions." In 1942, one U.S. official went so far as to claim that "there were no reprisals after the inauguration of the successful candidate and General Almazán was permitted to retire to private life without being molested in any way by any official or even political group." This appraisal was in marked contrast to a Military Intelligence Division (MID) report from October 1940 that "reprisals, dismissals and even assassinations are reported in the ranks of known Almazán followers who hold Government jobs."[220] The line between the elite and the rest was distinctly drawn in the aftermath of the 1940 election. Elite almazanistas had sufficient wealth, social and family connections, and political skills to weather the storm and reintegrate themselves into their accustomed societal roles. For lower-ranking sympathizers, however, the line between loyalty and betrayal was much more strictly enforced.

Amaro made peace with the administration by the end of 1941, informing Ávila Camacho that he was "absolutely disposed to collaborate with your Government in whatever role you indicate to me." In reaching out to the president, Amaro advanced the argument that "the Executive should avoid at all cost that the other branches of government are unconditionally submissive to his will." He also reminded Ávila Camacho of the need to "keep the Army on its high level and have it always apart from the field of politics."[221] Ávila Camacho took this advice in stride, especially given the geopolitical realities of World War II. The need for revolutionary solidarity during the war became clear, and some revolutionary generals, including those who had broken away at some point, were called back into service to help defend the

219. Report, Insp. 7 to DGIPS, Aug. 5, 1940, AGN-DGIPS, Box 191, 2.1/311.1/5, Vol. 17.

220. "Important concessions": Report, Lt. Col. W. D. Styer to G-2, Ft. Sam Houston, Ft. McIntosh, Sep. 7, 1940, NARA, Record Group 165, Box 2458, File 3020; "no reprisals after the inauguration": Cross reference of Report 241 from Consul Waterman, Mar. 31, 1942, Monterrey, NARA, Record Group 165, Box 2456, File 3020; "dismissals and even assassinations": Report, Lt. Col. A. W. Roffe to Commanding General, Ft. Sam Houston, San Antonio, Oct. 9, 1940, NARA, Record Group 165, Box 2458, File 3020.

221. Letter, Amaro to Ávila Camacho, Dec. 1, 1941, FAPEC-AJA, Correspondencia Personal, 1935–1945, File 030100, Gral. Manuel Avila Camacho.

nation. Abelardo Rodríguez became head of the military zone of the Gulf of Mexico, Múgica became head of the Third Military Zone (Baja California Sur), and Amaro became head of the military zone for the Isthmus of Tehuantepec. "By 1942, the division between revolutionary generals evident during the presidential succession seemed to have disappeared."[222] In reincorporating the dissident generals, Ávila Camacho followed a durable tradition in elite Mexican politics. He correctly judged that the value of the senior officers in command positions or advisory roles was greater than the satisfaction he might achieve through mothballing their careers. Almazán chose the path of lucrative retirement, however, and never returned to active duty.

It is clear that the presidential contest in 1940 presented an existential threat to the cardenista program and marked a "dividing line" in the development of the Mexican political system.[223] Before the election of 1940, the dominant political group surrounding Cárdenas managed to enforce a nearly radical menu of policies aimed at fulfilling the promises of the revolution. In the main, these efforts succeeded in the sense that vast amounts of land were redistributed, foreign holdings in the oil industry were nationalized, and the demands of the revolutionary generation were held paramount. The evident electoral fraud that took place in 1940, it has been argued, could be seen as necessary to maintain the legacy of the cardenista administration into that of Ávila Camacho. This would not be a case of policy continuity but, rather, a transferral of revolutionary legitimacy. In this view, a resounding victory in the reported vote totals would offer outgoing support for Cárdenas at the same time that it provided Ávila Camacho with solid footing for his own term in office.[224] Such a theory does not account for ideological shifts or fundamental policy differences; it only tracks the weighty issue of authority.

In fact, when the dust settled after the presidential cycle of 1940, something new was afoot in the nation. Even though there existed a defiantly diverse and powerful opposition movement led by Almazán, "the axis of conflict within Mexican society shifted from polarization based on class antagonisms to a struggle between two vertical coalitions, each dominated by

222. Arturo Sánchez Gutiérrez, "Los militares en la década de los cincuenta," *Revista Mexicana de Sociología* 50, no. 3 (1988): 276.

223. Michaels, "Las elecciones de 1940," 80. The concept of 1940 as a "dividing line" in modern Mexican political history is evoked in many of Michaels's writings on the topic.

224. Lorenzo Meyer, "La revolución mexicana y sus elecciones presidenciales, 1911–1940," in *Las elecciones en México: evolución y perspectivas,* ed. Pablo González Casanova (Mexico City: Siglo XXI, 1985), 96.

conservative factions."[225] A more moderate faction had taken power under the aegis of the Ávila Camacho administration and embarked on a program of more conservative policies aimed at expanding the economy, chastening labor militancy, and reassessing the old cardenista prescriptions. And almazanismo demonstrated the power and size of the constituency on the Right that the PRM could no longer ignore. As the U.S. State Department averred, "Ávila Camacho, however, has declared himself as favoring conservatism and has declared that his policies will be anti-communistic, anti-Nazi, and anti-Fascist, to meet the demands of the people and to counter his opponent, Almazán. He has declared himself as a good Catholic and pro-American, with a definite program of cooperation with the United States. This has drawn to him a large following of conservatives who otherwise would have helped Almazán. It has lost him the more radical votes."[226] Ávila Camacho's turn to the Right following the election essentially appeased the Catholic, conservative, and business elements that had found hope in almazanismo.[227] In this light, the election of 1940 can be seen as "a requiem for Cardenismo."[228] During, but especially after, the campaign, Ávila Camacho made significant portions of the conservative wave his own.

While the perception of the electoral contest generally underlined the spectacle of revolutionary veterans fighting for power, the more subtle calculus of political positioning was at work as well. This development can be read at least two ways. On one hand, it demonstrated the savvy and early dominance of the PRM in elections, since Ávila Camacho was able to co-opt sections of Almazán's platform and use them to get elected. On the other hand, this process showed that the visible opposition during the campaign of 1940, in the form of almazanista rallies and long lines of voters, was a force to be reckoned with and one that was not going to dissolve on its own. In this vein, the opposition movements of Almazán and all the other elements of the conservative wave in 1940 effectively manipulated the platform of the PRM to the right in a way that might not otherwise have been possible.

225. Nora Hamilton, *The Limits of State Autonomy: Post-Revolutionary Mexico* (Princeton: Princeton University Press, 1982), 265.

226. Roscoe Gaither to ACS, G-2, War Department, Oct. 10, 1940, NARA, Record Group 165.

227. U.S. State Department, 812.00/31492, Memo, Daniels to Secretary of State, Oct. 9, 1940, in *Confidential U.S. State Department Central Files, Mexico, 1940–1944, Part I,* Reel 2.

228. Alan Knight, "The Rise and Fall of Cardenismo, c. 1930–c. 1946," in *Mexico Since Independence,* ed. Leslie Bethell (Cambridge: Cambridge University Press, 1991), 301.

Without the pressure from these conservative forces, beginning in 1938, Cárdenas might well have been able to impose Francisco Múgica as his successor and oversee a continuation of his social and economic policies. Yet the fight in the election of 1940 was over control, not ideology, since cardenista policy had already been brought low.

The opposition campaigns of Almazán and Amaro struck a heavy, but not mortal, blow against the developing electoral machinery of the PRM. These candidacies posed a serious threat to the evolving organization and discipline of the party and "represented a true challenge to the regime, not least since the main figures of Almazán and Amaro counted on strong support within the Army."[229] The fear of an opposition movement that was both organized and potentially violent caused tremendous consternation for PRM strategists and foreign observers alike. Equally troubling was the fact that the PRM in 1940 had not achieved the mastery of electoral forms and public reprisal that would mark its tenure during the years of high dominance in the 1960s and 1970s. Instead, the strategists within the party in 1940 "either did not know how or [were] unable to respond to its opponents within the rules of the liberal democratic game and instead turned to a mixture of repression and fraud." This portrait of electoral incompetence, of an organization that "neither knew nor was prepared to confront substantive electoral opposition," is an unfamiliar one for students of modern Mexican politics. It is also accurate.[230]

As much as the PRM had created control mechanisms through the counting of votes in Gobernación and the obstructionist tactics of domestic intelligence agents, the election of 1940 put at stake precisely everything that had been built to that point. The nature of the threat was dire as "the Almazán candidacy constituted a direct attack on the corporate party structure; an Almazán victory would probably destroy it, since the hierarchy of domination and clientelism on which it was based depended on access to state power."[231] Had Almazán achieved the presidency, he could have starved the patrons of the PRM of their contracts and funding, essentially breaking their hold on so many clients throughout the system. Indeed, an Almazán victory could have signaled a new clientelist system focused on the prerogatives of the almazanistas and their supporters. In this analysis, the PRM was in a

229. Hans Werner Tobler, *La Revolución Mexicana: Transformación social y cambio político, 1876–1940* (Mexico City: Alianza, 1994), 654.

230. Meyer, "La revolución mexicana y sus elecciones presidenciales," 98–99.

231. Hamilton, *Limits of State Autonomy,* 266.

vulnerable and tenuous position, susceptible to opposition movements springing from a shared revolutionary pedigree. The opposition in 1940 had both the opportunity to strike a decisive blow against the emerging electoral machine of the PRM and the means to do it. Yet the tenacious appetite for continuity within the PRM trumped even the powerfully arrayed forces of the opposition, and the most tantalizing chance to destroy the PRM machinery in its infancy was lost.

The election of 1940 was a wake-up call for strategists within the PRM to get their house in order, to reformulate internal rules for nomination and candidate selection, and to determine a process for co-opting the palatable portions of opposition platforms. As the party structure was transformed, "internal democracy became almost non-existent and the official platforms of the PRM were one by one turning more moderate."[232] The efforts of the PRM to redefine the contours of the nomination process left little room for elements radically opposed to the dominant policy thrust. From the 1940 cycle onward, "the pre-electoral period, more than the election itself, was always the decisive moment in the transmission of power."[233]

The opposition challenges in 1940 opened a learning process for the dominant elites within the PRM, as party strategists worked ceaselessly to perfect the mechanisms that could cement electoral control. In this process, the challenges from Almazán and Amaro forced a fundamental reevaluation of party strategy that would be useful in 1946, which provided lessons for 1952, and so on. As the machinery of the party was streamlined, the key objective of the PRM (and later the PRI) became not so much legitimating itself through electoral victory as "disciplining its members so that the internal struggle for power did not ruin the system."[234] The internal metamorphosis of the PRM, including the enforcement of rules governing intraparty conflicts, reflected the realization among the dominant elites that enduring influence was within reach if only the price of opposition could be raised high enough. The process begun in 1940 and completed in 1952 effectively closed the door to even those opposition figures most able to pay. Crucially, the dominant elite of the PRM "made clear its intentions to maintain a monopoly on political power and, at the same time, publicly embrace all the ideals of a political democracy."[235] The dual strategy of thoroughly dominating electoral contests while

232. Luis Javier Garrido, *El partido de la revolución institucionalizada: La formación del Nuevo Estado en México, 1928–1945* (Mexico City: Siglo XXI, 1986), 356.

233. Meyer, "La revolución mexicana y sus elecciones presidenciales," 98.

234. Ibid.

235. Michaels, "Las elecciones de 1940," 80.

adhering to the façade of procedural democracy proved to be the durable patrimony of the party elite.

In the end, Almazán was widely viewed as having given up too easily, allowing himself to be shunted aside. An editorial argued that "General Almazán is responsible for having intoxicated [*embriagado*] the Mexican nation with a promise that neither he nor anyone could have fulfilled."[236] Though declines of political and economic power were evident among the almazanistas after the election, many Mexicans paid for their political opposition with their lives. General Zarzosa was killed in a firefight outside his home in Monterrey in October 1940, which the PRUN claimed was little more than a political assassination.[237] Many other almazanistas, not nearly so famous, died for the cause as well. Almazán's failure in 1940 was the last true opposition campaign that stood a chance of winning in the rough world of Mexican presidential politics. The challenges of Ezequiel Padilla and Miguel Henríquez Guzmán in the years to come would only serve to discredit the role of pro-U.S. diplomacy and the Mexican Left as viable power centers and thereby reinforce the newly hardened discipline imposed by the PRM leadership.

Almazán's ability to ride the conservative wave in the election of 1940 intensified the pressure of his campaign on the PRM. As Cárdenas sought to build a more consolidated and encompassing party, there was less room for electoral opposition, especially from within the highest ranks of the army. The challenge of almazanismo, then, was the threat that a conservative coalition, under the leadership of military stalwarts with revolutionary credentials, could construct a viable political alternative. This would have spelled doom to Cárdenas and all of the politicians attached to his political project. That Almazán was defeated, almazanismo contained, and the demands of the Right appropriated by the Ávila Camacho and Alemán administrations demonstrated the political savvy of the PRM leadership and the indirect power of opposition politics in Mexico.

236. *El Universal,* Jan. 30, 1941.
237. McCombs report, Oct. 3, 1940, McCombs Papers, Box 46, File 22; *Excélsior,* Oct. 2, 1940; *El Universal,* Oct. 2, 1940; *La Prensa,* Oct. 2, 1940.

TWO

THE CANDIDATE ON HORSEBACK
The Military in Mexican Politics

IN A REGION THAT HAS WITNESSED dozens of military governments, hundreds of attempted coups, and no small amount of military intervention in politics since World War II, Mexico stands out as an exceptional country. Contrary to the Latin American saying that "the highest *military* rank is the presidency," Mexico in the postwar period has experienced no military governments, not a single coup attempt from within the armed forces, and a decided lack of political activity by the military.[1] The only other Latin American country to lay claim to a similar streak is Costa Rica, which solved the problem of praetorianism by abolishing its armed forces in 1948. By the early 1950s, Mexico was able to bring the military under firm civilian control, transform it into a more professional fighting force, and effectively scotch the political aspirations of the officer class, all the while reducing the percentage of GDP spent on national defense.

This chapter examines the process from the 1930s to the 1950s by which the Mexican military lost the political preeminence that it had enjoyed since at least the late eighteenth century. The prestige of the military officer as a political entity survived even after the revolution destroyed the old federal army. In 1929, revolutionary veterans solidified their control of political

---

1. Saying quoted from Eric A. Nordlinger, *Soldiers in Politics: Military Coups and Governments* (Englewood Cliffs, N.J.: Prentice-Hall, 1977), 6. Emphasis in original.

mechanisms through the creation of the Partido Nacional Revolucionario (PNR). This party's subsequent reformations into the Partido de la Revolución Mexicana (PRM) in 1938 and the Partido Revolucionario Institucional (PRI) in 1946 ironically served to subsume and marginalize the once formidable political powers of the revolutionary generation within an organization that became overwhelmingly civilian.

The military elite reacted to these shifts in political process in several ways. First, as the election of 1940 demonstrated, they formed political parties and ran as opposition candidates in elections, beginning the transition from armed to electoral rebellion. Almazán and Amaro launched rhetorical (but not armed) attacks against the undemocratic and "impositionist" tendencies of the federal government as it became more tightly aligned with the bureaucratic needs of the PRM/PRI. Second, military officers held secret meetings to discuss their views and to create a forum for military points of view on political issues. Notably, these discussions did not focus on planning for armed rebellion, since this had been effectively discarded as a viable form of political speech after the 1938 rebellion of Saturnino Cedillo. Third, as the case of Octavio Véjar Vázquez in this chapter will show, they mounted a defense of the political rights of soldiers as Mexican citizens. Véjar Vázquez, a leading scholar of military law, faced a court martial in 1951 when he argued that every Mexican citizen, specifically including soldiers, had the right to run for office, openly profess his political beliefs, and generally operate as a free citizen of a free country without the constraints imposed by a centralizing and increasingly authoritarian "official" party. These three reactions tended to strengthen the position of the civilian leaders of the PRM/PRI over time, as the officers were defeated in the electoral sphere, driven from the public square, and criminalized for demanding political equality.

The reactions of these military officers to the loss of long-held political authority signaled the shift in Mexico that set it apart from the rest of Latin America: the institution of lasting civilian control of government without military intervention. Two factors made it possible. First, the increasing gap in education and professional training between top bureaucrats and military officers reinforced the "graying" of the revolutionary generation. For instance, beginning with the election of Miguel Alemán in 1946, the influx of civilian lawyers into government posts outpaced that of revolutionary officers. Second, as the federal government and the PRM/PRI became more closely entwined, elements of the military provided security to the new political system by leading and staffing the domestic intelligence services. This role, while not as prominent as elective office, allowed the military to wield considerable power within the party bureaucracy in a *nonelectoral* way. By 1954, the deal between the two groups had been cemented: the civilians had firm control of the electoral machinery of the country, and the military had an essential role to play in supporting and defending them.

The study of the military in Latin American politics has produced a large literature, with analyses of this topic written primarily by political scientists. Historical treatments are generally more recent, and the exception to the rule. The work of Edwin Lieuwen was the first to focus on the unique quality of civil-military relations in Mexico. His 1968 book, *Mexican Militarism: The Political Rise and Fall of the Revolutionary Army, 1910–1940,* argued that the political power of the revolutionary army was harnessed within the confines of the PNR and later diluted as the party was transformed into the PRM. Lieuwen marked the election of 1940 as the moment when the traditional political power of the Mexican Army was crippled.[2]

For Lieuwen, five factors tended to depoliticize the Mexican Army: "(1) internecine warfare amongst the rival generals, (2) professionalization of the young and middle-rank officers, (3) development of civilian power counterpoises, particularly labor and peasants, (4) institutionalization of the political system from 1928–1940, and (5) the key role of General Cárdenas himself in bringing about the depoliticization result."[3] In this schematic explanation, Lieuwen took account of the military rebellions of the 1920s and 1930s, the reforms Amaro propagated in the military academies, the rise of mass organizations within the PNR and the formation of the party itself, and the seemingly mystical role of *cardenismo* in the whole affair. In short, Lieuwen aimed to explain how the Mexican Army was transformed by 1940 from one of the least professional and most political Latin American militaries into a very professional group with little direct influence in politics.

While Lieuwen's analysis is a cogent interrogation of the period, his overall explanation suffers from three main problems. First, it does not explain the continuing importance of opposition elements within the military after 1940. As chapter 5 will demonstrate, the military still considered itself a primary political force throughout the late 1940s and during the election of

2. Edwin Lieuwen, *Mexican Militarism: The Political Rise and Fall of the Revolutionary Army, 1910–1940* (Albuquerque: University of New Mexico Press, 1968), xiii.

3. Edwin Lieuwen, "Depoliticization of the Mexican Revolutionary Army, 1915–1940," in *The Modern Mexican Military: A Reassessment,* ed. David Ronfeldt (San Diego: Center for U.S.-Mexican Studies, University of California at San Diego, 1984), 52. Lieuwen's chapter provides a clear summary of his earlier 1968 work.

1952, with the defeat of Miguel Henríquez Guzmán being simply one of several possible outcomes. Second, Lieuwen argues too forcefully for the formal and informal authority of Cárdenas: "He [Cárdenas] eliminated Plutarco Elías Calles and Joaquín Amaro in 1935, Saturnino Cedillo in 1938, arranged for the electoral defeat of Juan Andreu Almazán in 1940, and then he himself retired, leaving politics to the official party and the civilian bureaucracy."[4] This interpretation makes Cárdenas into something of a political superman, unchallenged by societal forces or rivals, able to effect deep political changes at will. Such a heavy presidentialist interpretation leads to a third weakness in Lieuwen's analysis: it is deterministic in its conclusions. The Mexican Army *did* suffer a substantial loss of political (i.e., electoral) influence after 1940, but Lieuwen only argues that this was the case; he does not explain the historical process of how it came to be. While agreeing in principle with many of Lieuwen's conclusions, the purpose of this chapter, and the narrative chapters by example, is to offer the kind of historical explanation that earlier scholars have not provided.

More recent attempts to analyze the Mexican military have offered new insights. The most useful—indeed the standard reference work on the topic—remains Roderic Camp's *Generals in the Palacio*. Camp provides a fascinating overview of promotion patterns, generational groups, and the extant literature on the topic, as well as a summary of his exhaustive biographical research on Mexican elites. He argues suggestively that "the military did not withdraw from politics in the 1930s and 1940s; rather, the postrevolutionary military had never, in the true sense of the word, intervened in political affairs in the first place."[5] Revolutionary leaders were simply pursuing their political interests through the form of political speech *du jour,* which during the revolution meant armed and public violence. When that form of political speech became discredited after the Cedillo rebellion, revolutionary leaders in the opposition moved on, however belatedly, to the new arena: political parties and elections.[6] Camp argues further, and quite to the point of much of the present book, that up to 1934 "many prominent military leaders were thinking of their own political and personal interests rather than the military's interests as a corporate body."[7] This idea that an individual's own interests

---

    4. Lieuwen, *Mexican Militarism,* xiii.

    5. Roderic Ai Camp, *Generals in the Palacio: The Military in Modern Mexico* (New York: Oxford University Press, 1992), 7.

    6. This argument is more fully developed in chapter 1.

    7. Camp, *Generals in the Palacio,* 19.

take precedence over their corporate identity, public image, or ideological leanings pervades the argument of the present work.

The predominance of the military in civil and political affairs did not begin or end with the Mexican Revolution. Derived from the knightly traditions of Reconquista Spain and codified in 1768 during the Bourbon reforms of Charles III, the *fuero militar* essentially created a separate judicial system for members of the army and their dependents—no small matter in a legalistic and hierarchical society. Crimes alleged against a soldier or his dependent could be resolved through a court system staffed with military officials, rather than the usual civilian courts. The fuero militar also more firmly attached soldiers to a privileged position in society, on par with the Catholic Church, whose members had their own fuero. However, "since it extended some protection to non-elite sectors rather than exclusively to wealthy residents, it was considered more dangerous than other privileged jurisdictions."[8]

The fuero militar was not absolute or immutable. Members of the army could lose their fuero or its protections in a number of ways, including "malfeasance while holding public office . . . disrespect or resistance to civil magistrates . . . and frauds against the royal treasury." Particularly to the point here were two other offenses that could put a soldier beyond the pale: "participation in public riots [and] sedition."[9] These actions against established public order, originally conceived as treachery against the king, took on new meaning as the types of offense that twentieth-century opposition officers in Mexico were accused of committing in the course of their electoral campaigns. During and after the elections of 1940 and 1952, the dominant political elites portrayed the opposition military candidates as seditious, disloyal, and unpatriotic, despite their long and often storied service to the state. Almazán, Amaro, and Henríquez each had performed more notable service to the state than the PRM or PRI candidate who opposed them. The elites' rhetoric relied heavily on the perceptions of the traditional role of the military in society as protector and guardian of national institutions, a perception reinforced in the curricula of the reformed Mexican military academies. In a bit of irony, it was Amaro himself who had worked so diligently to instill the

<hr/>

8. Christon I. Archer, *The Army in Bourbon Mexico, 1760–1810* (Albuquerque: University of New Mexico Press, 1977), 125. Corona del Rosal defines the term *fuero* as "jurisdicción" (jurisdiction). See Alfonso Corona del Rosal, *La guerra, el imperialismo, el ejército mexicano* (Mexico City: Grijalbo, 1988), 254.

9. Lyle N. McAlister, *The "Fuero Militar" in New Spain, 1764–1800* (Gainesville: University of Florida, 1957), 7.

new professionalism in military cadets in the 1920s, only to see that system used against him in the 1940 election.

Returning to the late colonial period, military officers also gained the social and economic protection of *preeminencias,* privileges that effectively shielded them from bankruptcy, taxation, and levies. In combination, the institution of the fuero militar and the preeminencias created a specific group of subjects not only professionally and socially, but legally and economically. As McAlister argued, "The possession of special privileges enhanced its [i.e., the military's] sense of uniqueness and superiority, and at the same time rendered it virtually immune from civil authority. . . . A large proportion of officers and men regarded military service as an opportunity for the advancement of personal interests rather than as a civic obligation." A career in the army thus became an attractive opportunity for the ambitious and, often, the poor. Just as important as the actual provisions of the fuero militar were the protections that soldiers *presumed* to have and sought to use to their advantage.[10] While clogging the courts with claims, their presumption of immunity offered a strong foundation for Mexico's later tradition of impunity, especially in the officer corps.[11]

The transition to independence in Mexico effectively removed any restraint on the military in politics. "Until the abdication of Ferdinand VII in 1808, the troublemaking potential of the military was held in check by a long tradition of loyalty to the crown. . . . [After independence] this limitation was removed and the army emerged as an autonomous and irresponsible institution."[12] Through the nineteenth century, the military destabilized and restabilized national politics repeatedly.

McAlister argued that "the privileges granted to the Army of New Spain were probably the most important factor in the creation of a praetorian tradition in Mexico." However, in the twentieth century, the Mexican military has not continued in this tradition. Even Nordlinger's argument that "military officers become praetorian soldiers when they threaten or use force in order to enter or dominate the political arena" is valid only if we accept the postrevolutionary army as a true military corps. Moreover, Loveman's analysis that "military officers, as guardians of the mythically eternal, are virtually

10. Protection of *preeminencias:* McAlister, *Fuero Militar,* 8; "possession of special privileges": ibid., 15; protections that soldiers *presumed* to have: see, for example, ibid., 55–58.

11. For examples of abuses of the fuero militar by soldiers, see Archer, *Army in Bourbon Mexico,* 126–27.

12. McAlister, *Fuero Militar,* 15.

secular priests of *la patria*" does not fit the Mexican case after 1940.[13] Thus, the postrevolutionary Mexican Army up to 1946 was more a group of armed civilian politicians than a consolidated association of like-minded military officers.

Politicians in Mexico City had always been aware of the danger of a military uprising in the provinces. Porfirio Díaz initiated the practice of rotating military zone commanders in order to prevent the development of local loyalties or regional power bases. In 1923, Álvaro Obregón raised the number of military zones from twenty to thirty-five in order "to fragment further the regional military commands and thus reduce the danger of a challenge to the central government."[14] And Cárdenas used the strategy of frequently transferring military commanders to great effect.[15]

After the revolution, several serious armed rebellions occurred within the army. The de la Huerta revolt in 1923 involved 50 percent of the generals, 20 percent of the officer corps (roughly three thousand), and 40 percent of the standing troops (roughly twenty-three thousand). The Gomez-Serrano rebellion in 1927 counted twenty generals and about 20 percent of the standing troops. The Escobar rebellion in 1929 attracted over 30 percent of the officer corps and almost 50 percent of the standing troops.[16] The Cedillo rebellion of 1938, smaller in its numbers of officers and troops, nonetheless posed a clear threat to the Cárdenas project of political consolidation.[17] The new discipline learned from these events was, as Lieuwen correctly noted, "the precedent that an officer's career profited by his remaining loyal to the constituted government in times of rebellion."[18] This discipline allowed the transition from a mainly amateur officer corps born of the revolution to a professional military force. Crucially, this professional force did not take effective control of the Mexican Army until the 1940s, when cadets trained

13. "Creation of a praetorian tradition": McAlister, *Fuero Militar*, 15; "dominate the political arena": Nordlinger, *Soldiers in Politics*, 3; "guardians of the mythically eternal": Brian Loveman, *For la Patria: Politics and the Armed Forces in Latin America* (Wilmington, Del.: Scholarly Resources, 1999), xviii.

14. Rotating military zone commanders: Lieuwen, *Mexican Militarism*, 2; "reduce the danger of a challenge": ibid., 69.

15. The "mecánica cardenista" was crucial to political stability in the Cárdenas period. See Alicia Hernández Chávez, *Historia de la Revolución Mexicana, 1934–1940: La mecánica cardenista,* Historia de la Revolución Mexicana 16 (Mexico City: Colegio de México, 1979).

16. Lieuwen, "Depoliticization of the Mexican Revolutionary Army," 52–53.

17. For the best treatment of the Cedillo rebellion, see Dudley Ankerson, *Agrarian Warlord: Saturnino Cedillo and the Mexican Revolution in San Luis Potosí* (DeKalb: Northern Illinois University Press, 1984).

18. Virginia Prewett, "The Mexican Army," *Foreign Affairs* 19, no. 3 (April 1941): 612.

under Amaro's military education reforms began to achieve leadership positions and revolutionary veterans began to retire from service.

Military experience gradually lost its status as a defining trait of political elites as the twentieth century progressed. Camp concluded that "beginning with General Porfirio Díaz in 1884 until 1988, of 2,613 nationally prominent politicians and state governors, one in five had risen to the rank of lieutenant colonel or higher in the National Guard or armed forces." However, he also proved that the rate of change was not constant in this period and accelerated in the presidential transition of 1946, when the percentage of officeholders with military backgrounds dipped from 19 to 8 percent and the cabinet was devoid of officers for the first time. This analysis underscores the declining importance of officers in cabinet and other high posts from the revolution onward, for both demographic and political reasons. By one calculation, "between 1934 and 1970 only 12 percent of the posts within 'the inner circle of Mexican politics' have been held by soldiers."[19]

The Mexican case after the revolution was one of a sort of creeping civilianization, driven in no small part by the simple passage of time: eventually the revolutionary generation would die out. Schloming noted that already, in the period from 1928 to 1934, "former generals, who had acquired power by force of arms or wielded influence by the effective threat to resort to arms, came to shift their bases of support from troops and personally loyal comrades-in-arms to public opinion, organized groups of peasants and workers, and party organizations."[20] During the decade after the revolution, the growth of organized sectors of civilian society, such as the Confederación Nacional Campesina (CNC) and the Confederación de Trabajadores de México (CTM), forced the military to reach out to them for political support. In the exchange, the military officers became less likely to use violence and crept further along the path of civilianization.

A key to the civilianization of politics was the shift from armed to electoral rebellion as the primary mode of political speech among military officers. Although the spoils of the revolution had gone to the leaders who arrogated

19. "Nationally prominent politicians": Camp, *Generals in the Palacio*, 66; rate of change: ibid., 67–69; "inner circle of Mexican politics": Gustavo Hernández Enríquez, "La movilidad política en México" (licenciatura thesis, Facultad de Ciencias Políticas y Sociales, Universidad Nacional Autónoma de México, 1970), 2:670–73, cited in Guillermo Boils, *Los militares y la política en México, 1915–1974* (Mexico City: El Caballito, 1975), 47.

20. Gordon Clark Schloming, "Civil-Military Relations in Mexico, 1910–1940: A Case Study" (PhD diss., Columbia University, 1974), 192.

power through violent action, the trend after 1920 was to discourage such activity in favor of organized political stumping to win votes. The demands of electoral democracy, such as it existed in the 1920s forward, forced military officers out of the business of coups and (back) into the business of patronage. While officers had previously derived their political authority from heroics in the revolution, that was only a necessary credential for entry into the group of the political elite after 1920. The political calculus changed as civilians then began to appropriate "the revolution" as a central motif in their electoral platforms. Indeed, as Schloming argued, "one of the crucial transformations in Mexican politics was the adoption by civilians after 1920 of a revolutionary ideology that had been largely monopolized by military men in the revolutionary period of 1910 to 1920."[21] The rhetoric and shared experience of the revolution became the foundation of the political organization that most clearly defined Mexican history after 1929: the PNR.

The organizing committee of the PNR began its work on December 4, 1928, and the party met for its first convention in Querétaro on March 1, 1929. It represented "an alliance of the triumphant groups and *caudillos,* who decided to reconcile [*dirimir*] their arguments in the heart of a political organization that was capable of surmounting the differences between its members and thereby achieve that armed struggle would cease to be the path for determining the succession in leading the nation."[22] The PNR represented political negotiation in a country that had so recently settled such disputes on the battlefield. More than that, the centralization of political decision making in the PNR offered the opportunity to consolidate electoral strength. The U.S. ambassador was forthright when discussing the new political party: "They are not interested in promoting cultural relations or economic relations between the two countries. They are interested in putting a man into office and then getting the most individual profit out of it that they can."[23] The essentially realistic goals of the new PNR served over the long run to tame the power of the revolutionary leadership by subjecting it to nomination and electoral processes increasingly controlled by civilians.

21. Ibid., 19.

22. Organizing committee of the PNR: Lieuwen, *Mexican Militarism,* 102; "triumphant groups and caudillos": Gloria Fuentes, *El ejército mexicano* (Mexico City: Grijalbo, 1983), 284.

23. U.S. State Department, 812.00/7–3145, Memo, Messersmith to Carrigan, Jul. 31, 1945, in *Confidential U.S. State Department Central Files. Mexico: Internal Affairs, 1945–1949. Part I: Political, Governmental, and National Affairs* (Frederick, Md.: University Publications of America, 1987), Reel 1.

The needs and composition of the political elite changed through the 1930s, affected by the world economic depression, the political match between Calles and Cárdenas, and the expropriation of foreign oil holdings. The PNR's reorganization into the PRM in 1938 signaled an important shift in the role of the military in politics. The new structure divided the body politic into four corporate sectors: labor, agrarian, popular, and military. This arrangement gave the military authority out of proportion to its numbers, assuaging doubts among senior officers that political power was being shared too generously. However, it also strengthened military ties to the government since the military was, unlike the other sectors, already a direct dependency of the state. With the formation of the PRM, the military was doubly lashed to the ship of state, both as its formal protector and its political partner.

Before the reorganization, there was still the danger that the military leadership could define its interests along different lines than the party—the path to rebellions and *coups d'état*. By incorporating the military directly into the party (and in a strong position), "the party helped to unify civilian and military elements, channeling their respective interests." The formation of the military sector of the PRM drew inspiration from the long tradition of military participation in politics as well as the newly reinforced prerogatives of the revolutionary generation. These military officers were accustomed to having a voice in the political decisions of the country, not least "because after all, they had made the Revolution." Cárdenas defended the decision this way: "We are not involving the army in politics, it is already involved. . . . We are reducing its influence to one out of four votes."[24] The civilians thus obtained an important point of leverage against military aspirations, which could be offset by the more numerous peasant or labor sectors if the need arose. The very structure of the PRM facilitated the subordination of military leaders to the decisions of the party.

The PRM actively encouraged the forms of democratic debate and opposition, while always hewing to an enforced consensus. It voiced confidence that the military could responsibly exercise its political rights "within the Party . . . not with the purpose of substantial force or enforced superiority, but with the ample spirit of *civismo*."[25] In all, it was better for politically

24. "Respective interests": Camp, *Generals in the Palacio,* 22; "made the Revolution": Arturo Sánchez Gutiérrez, "Los militares en la década de los cincuenta," *Revista Mexicana de Sociología* 50, no. 3 (1988): 271; "one out of four votes": quoted in José Luis Piñeyro, *Ejército y sociedad en México: Pasado y presente* (Puebla: Universidad Autónoma de Puebla, 1985), 56.

25. Partido de la Revolución Mexicana, *Convocatoria para la Asamblea Constituyente del nuevo partido* (Mexico City: PRM, 1937), 36.

minded soldiers to operate within the confines of the party than to have such a movement outside of the organization. Granted political space within the increasingly civilian-dominated PRM, officers could attempt to change the direction of the country through political and electoral means, rather than resorting to armed violence. Yet not all officers welcomed the inclusion of the military within the PRM. Most important, for Amaro, was that the "infiltration of politics in the Army signifies its moral ruin [and] . . . would demolish the only bulwark of order."[26] The official incorporation of the military as a sector of the PRM represented, at least to Amaro, a cheapening of what he regarded as the one truly selfless organization in the country.

The inclusion of the military as a sector of the PRM in 1938, the dilution of its authority in 1940, and the dissolution of the military sector of the PRI in 1946 were all steps in an improvised but coherent strategy to normalize Mexican politics. As McAlister noted, "while the Mexican military were indeed 'tamed' and professionalized, this could only have been accomplished because at a more basic level they were first admitted into the system, then absorbed, and finally outnumbered." The old methods of acquiring power through force of arms turned into a new path, which led necessarily through the political committees of the PRI. True especially after 1940, Camp argued that "the political elite created such a strong sense of discipline and such complete and comprehensive control over the state apparatus that dissident civilians never sought allies among military officers."[27] Control of the "state apparatus" included patronage networks, government jobs, the intelligence bureaucracy, and, the *sine qua non* of political control, the electoral machinery. In short, after 1940, civilians held so much procedural power through the growing electoral controls of the PRM that the old reliance on revolutionary service became an afterthought. What mattered most from 1940 on was the ability to win elections.

As chapter 1 demonstrated, the presidential election of 1940 was unique in the history of twentieth-century Mexico. It pitted military candidates against one other in a political climate that demanded party organization, the

---

26. Manifiesto a la nación, Jun. 1940, Fideicomiso Archivos Plutarco Elías Calles y Fernando Torreblanca, Archivo Joaquín Amaro (FAPEC-AJA), Campaña Política, 1939–1940, File 020200, Manifiesto.

27. " 'Tamed' and professionalized": Lyle N. McAlister, Anthony P. Maingot, and Robert A. Potash, *The Military in Latin American Sociopolitical Evolution: Four Case Studies* (Washington, D.C.: Center for Research in Social Systems, 1970), 245; "strong sense of discipline": Roderic Ai Camp, "Mexico," in *The Political Role of the Military: An International Handbook,* ed. Constantine P. Danopoulos and Cynthia Watson (Westport, Conn.: Greenwood Press, 1996), 276.

enunciation of ideas on domestic, international, and even philosophical issues, and a formal disavowal of violence as a means of acquiring influence. This atmosphere of political combat contrasted sharply with the professional expertise of the various candidates in the art of war. In the end, Almazán and Amaro lost and, although Ávila Camacho won the much-disputed vote in 1940, the real action happened behind the electoral scenes.

After 1940, Mexico did not exhibit military influence in high-level electoral contests, or persist in its own long tradition of coups d'état as a form of political speech. Rather, its political elite engaged in a national project to diminish the power of the military, subsume the military's political demands in the larger mire of party platforms, and systematically decrease the opportunities for dissenting viewpoints outside of the party structure. It was this transformation, begun with the shot that killed Cedillo in 1939 and ending with the *rendimiento* of Almazán in late 1940, that chastened the political aspirations of a generation of military officers and set Mexico on a unique path among Latin American nations. The U.S. Military Intelligence Division (MID) closely observed the unsettled political situation in Mexico leading up to the presidential election of 1940 and seemed to understand its complexity.[28] U.S. officials correctly identified the internal threat from dissident military officers within the PRM, well before the open break between Amaro, Almazán, and the party. The analytical acumen of the MID allowed the United States to generally avoid embarrassing entanglements or untenable allegiances during the campaign.

Well aware of the danger of such an internal struggle for the presidential candidacy, the PRM purged many almazanistas in late June 1940, scarcely weeks before the presidential elections.[29] In particular, the Secretariat of Public Education expelled almazanista employees in a move characterized as a "foolish attack" by those who foresaw for the PRM "a gloomy future in which it cannot continue using [*usufructando*] the Revolution."[30] The denial of PRM membership was not simply a cancellation of political allegiance. In a system increasingly defined by single-party cronyism in jobs and contracts, being ejected from the PRM was akin to burning a meal ticket.

28. Summary, "Source: G-2," Feb. 14, 1939, National Archives and Records Administration, Washington, D.C. (NARA), Record Group 165, Box 2454, File 3000.

29. *La Prensa*, Jun. 25, 1940.

30. *Excélsior*, Jun. 18, 1940, Archivo General de la Nación, Mexico City, Dirección General de Investigaciones Políticas y Sociales (AGN-DGIPS), Box 190, 2.1/311.1/5, Vol. 16.

As difficult as the 1940 election was for the opposition, the fact that military officers generally accepted the validity of elections and national parties as the proper vehicles of politics signaled an important advance. As Schloming argued for the postrevolutionary period, "the price of survival [for the military] seems to be willingness to become political entrepreneurs and political institution-builders within a civilian framework of legitimacy and by characteristically civilian political means."[31] Personalistic parties had been commonplace in Mexico and would continue to form a part of the political spectrum. Yet the political parties formed by Almazán and Amaro during the campaign of 1940 were different from those of the past. The PRUN and the PRAC were intended to be national parties aimed at advancing the candidacies of politicians who adhered to a program more strictly ideological than the PRM. Further, the leaders of the PRUN and the PRAC explicitly supported democratic forms and institutions as a means of developing Mexican politics beyond the old revolutionary, and often violent, power struggles.

Emblematically, in the election of 1940 Almazán presented himself as a loyal military man who had not succumbed to the corrupting power of political machinations around him. In a speech at Monterrey in August 1939, he said, "I have been proud since I was a student and since I went off to the Revolution, that I have never had the friendship of politicians. For me this has been a satisfaction, because I have not mixed with those who in the name of the Revolution and the proletariat, enslave and exploit the proletariat." The emphasis on the power of elections to effect change in Mexico was a marked difference from the past. Almazán declared in Nuevo Laredo that "the way for the Mexican people to solve their problems is . . . to vote for who they want to win, not for who the impositionists want." Continuing eloquently, he argued, "The only moment that the government is in the hands of the people, in which the people truly govern, is the day that it chooses its leaders, voting and ensuring that vote is respected."[32] Such statements on the campaign trail portrayed at once his determination to attack the antidemocratic tendencies of the PRM machinery under construction and the internalization of the rhetoric employed by the PRM, placing trust in

31. Schloming, "Civil-Military Relations in Mexico," 34.
32. "Friendship of politicians": Report, Insp. Castro Reina to DGIPS, Aug. 1, 1939, Monterrey, AGN-DGIPS, Box 188, 2.1/311.1/5, Vol. 2; "vote for who they want" and "hands of the people": Report, Insp. 1 to DGIPS, May 21, 1940, Monterrey, AGN-DGIPS, Box 190, 2.1/311.1/5, Vol. 14.

elections rather than armed force to resolve political disputes. Almazán excoriated the leadership of the PRM in order to score political points during the
campaign, but did so under the ground rules that the PRM had established.

Amaro used his presidential campaign to rail against the PRM's emerging
dominance, declaring that "the ease with which the enormous bureaucratic
machinery has been converted into an tool of imposition to quiet the expres-
sions of genuine public opinion has convinced me that the country needs a
profound renovation of its political procedures." An example of this censorship was the refusal of the major Mexico City dailies to print Amaro's paid
advertisement of New Year's greetings in 1940.[33] This seemingly pedestrian
level of political control exerted by the PRM provoked Amaro into deeper
criticisms of the system arrayed against him. In a later statement, he advanced
criticisms of the Cárdenas administration on several levels: "the total of the
regime has been: in political terms, take to the extreme the corruption of
procedures, preparing the imposition of a new President who represents *conti-
nuismo,* contrary to the will of the people; in material terms, to sow ruin,
ending the prosperity that was ascendant when this administration began. In
spiritual terms, to undermine the social order, fomenting class hatred and
attacking paternal authority, by which it attacks the family, foundation of the
Fatherland [*Patria*]."[34] This kind of blistering rhetoric was typical of Amaro
throughout the campaign, as he sought to portray the PRM as both undemocratic and, in a philosophical sense, un-Mexican. In so doing, Amaro tried to
adjust the terms of the debate among the candidates to ones that favored his
strengths as a military leader.

Importantly, Amaro also spoke during the campaign of "the necessity of
organizing the opposition in a political party, seeking in this a form of expression within the law of opinions contrary to the government." The shift from
military to electoral opposition was essential to Amaro's view of the future
of Mexican politics. He, like Almazán, was shaped by the trend toward civil-
ian-style electoral groupings rather than highly personalistic or charismatic
movements centered on revolutionary credentials alone. Amaro distilled his

33. "Enormous bureacratic machinery": Manifiesto a la Nación, Jun. 1940, FAPEC-AJA,
Campaña Política, 1939–1940, File 020200, Manifiestos; Amaro's paid advertisement: "Mensaje
del PRAC a la Nación," typewritten draft of statement by Amaro, Jan. 1, 1940, FAPEC-AJA,
Campaña Política, 1939–1940, File 0514. The statement of New Year's greetings was subsequently published on flyers for distribution.

34. Manifiesto a la Nación, Jun. 1940, FAPEC-AJA, Campaña Política, 1939–1940, File
020200, Manifiestos.

political strategy in a statement issued at the outset of his campaign. He declared, "In other times, we were obliged to go to the fields of battle to fight in defense of our ideals; at present, the same obligation carries us to the civic battle, using the citizen's rights granted to us by the Constitution."[35] This rhetorical device, using the metaphor of "battle" to describe the old and the new arenas of conflict, exemplified the shift from armed to electoral rebellion as the preferred mode of political speech. Again, like Almazán, Amaro accepted that the political conflict under way would be determined under the new rules established by the PRM.

Yet the shift from armed to electoral rebellion was a difficult transition for men accustomed to the prerogatives of power. Schloming argued that a key component of the process of civilianization was the climate that "encourages military politicians to see themselves as spokesmen, with a responsibility to a defined civilian constituency and/or a defined set of political principles."[36] Amaro recognized this need during the campaign of 1940, declaring that "soldiers should leave our arms at the thresholds of the political parties, because these arms were given to us solely for the defense of the country and not in order to convert the Army into a faction."[37] The generalized movement away from armed rebellion and toward the forms and organizations of electoral contests was a crucial (and slow) transition that laid the groundwork for the later subjugation of the military's political influence.

Almazán and Amaro were not alone in calling for effective parties, elections, and democratic forms in Mexico. The formation of the Partido Acción Nacional (PAN) in 1939 reflected the desire among a group of intellectuals on the Right to create a new political party from the ground up, a party rooted in the idea of strong families and good citizenship. The PAN based its long-term strategy in the civic rehabilitation of the entire person, the so-called eternal struggle, in order to create an ever-growing group of citizens thoroughly dedicated to the core conservative principles of the party.[38] In counting the betterment of the individual more important than a seat in

35. "Expression within the law": "Amaro ofrece una convivialidad al Gral. Perez Treviño con motivo de su onomástico: La oposición define los propósitos que persigue," Jun. 23, 1939; "fight in defense of our ideals": "El General Amaro decide actuar en la política," Mar. 7, 1939 (both located in FAPEC-AJA, Campaña Política, 1939–1940, File 0514, Clipping book).

36. Schloming, "Civil-Military Relations in Mexico," 60.

37. La Prensa, Mar. 9, 1940, AGN-DGIPS, Box 192, 2.1/311.1/6.

38. See Michael Ard, An Eternal Struggle: How the National Action Party Transformed Mexican Politics (New York: Praeger, 2003).

Congress, the PAN provided an interesting counterpoint to the PRUN and the PRAC, which formed expressly to advance political candidacies. Nevertheless, the PAN joined them in a shared disdain for impositionist tactics and the prospect of the PRM's continuing dominance of political life.

After 1940, the subjugation of opposition movements did not fit with public avowals of democratic freedom. Yet it was a project that elements within the PRM considered necessary. The election of 1940 demonstrated to the PRM elite that opposition movements could disrupt the new political machinery and that violence echoing from one side of the country to another, across state and party lines, could destroy all that the revolution had seemingly wrought. Beyond the question of electoral contests and political parties, the issue of armed conflict as a form of political speech still lingered. The Cedillo rebellion was a looming background to the conflict between the Cárdenas administration and the electoral challengers, Almazán and Amaro. Higinia Cedillo had obviously not forgotten the treatment that her brother received in 1939, and during the campaign she had supported Almazán. After the election, she sent Melchor Ortega two Hotchkiss machine guns for use in a rebellion, along with a note asserting that she herself had attempted to assassinate Cárdenas to avenge her brother but was disarmed before being shown into his office.[39]

The Cedillo rebellion had drawn a clear line between electoral politics and armed insurrection. The message seemed clear: armed rebellion would mean the financial and physical destruction of the rebel leader. However, this new rule was only clear in retrospect. How many politicians could reasonably have assumed that the de la Huerta revolt in 1923 would be the final one, or the Serrano and Gomez revolt of 1927, or the Escobar rising in 1929? Each of these appeared to mark a transition away from violence as a form of political speech, yet each was followed by another armed rebellion. After Cedillo's death, it was far from clear that his would be the last full-scale military revolt.

Talk of armed revolt suffused the campaign season of 1940, focusing naturally on the opposition candidates. In March 1940, intelligence reports suggested a shift away from electoral politics and back toward armed confrontation. In Guadalajara, the almazanistas were allegedly "ready for an armed movement and swearing that they will do it." Another Mexican agent reported that Almazán's supporters in San Luis Potosí "are no longer in a civic

---

39. Memo, DGIPS, Aug. 28, 1940 (citing DGIPS report of Aug. 26, 1940), AGN-DGIPS, Box 191, 2.1/311.1/5, Vol. 19.

electoral campaign, but rather are preparing an armed movement." The Mexican intelligence agents began to present a coherent picture of a real danger to policy makers in the president's office and, by extension, in the PRM leadership. As this impending peril developed in their reports, public statements from the candidates served to confirm the suspicions of the dominant elite. From New York, Almazán himself accused the Cárdenas administration of reprising its strategy against Cedillo, saying, "During the whole campaign, they have not scrimped on their efforts to force me and my followers into rebellion, so that they can hunt us and kill us as [they did] unlucky Cedillo." The great quandary was whether Almazán was committed to leading an armed rebellion when the time came. Among the skeptics of such an outcome was the editorial board in El Paso that expressed "doubt that there can be a successful Mexican revolution soon." This skepticism sprang from the scarcity of surplus weapons in the United States due to the war in Europe, as well as possible U.S. restrictions on export licenses in the Almazán case.[40]

Among some Mexican analysts, the threat assessment was relatively low since the level of presumed support for any sort of armed rebellion among the officer corps was weak. As one colonel put it, "Among the *activos,* retired and former military men, they are not in favor of a Revolution in the least, because it would be a situation without any advantage, in fact the opposite."[41] The high-ranking military leadership who could lead a large-scale revolt had everything to lose in any kind of political challenge outside the bounds of the new electoral game. By 1940, the men who had clambered up the social ladder in the revolution through perseverance, achievement, or luck were unwilling to risk their gains for simple political advancement. It was far better to maintain one's status in a corrupt system than lose everything in the quest for a just one. Moreover, the dynamic of the revolutionary era had been transformed. A U.S. intelligence official averred, "It is doubtful whether the rank and file of the Army would follow their military leaders in any revolt against President Cárdenas, or a candidate backed by him. . . . The military

---

40. "Ready for an armed movement": Report, Insp. 11 to DGIPS, Mar. 3, 1940, Guadalajara; "no longer in a civic electoral campaign": Report, Insp. 37 to DGIPS, Mar. 11, 1940, San Luis Potosí (both located in AGN-DGIPS, Box 189, 2.1/311.1/5, Vol. 10); "hunt us and kill us": *La Prensa,* Sep. 4, 1940; "successful Mexican revolution": *El Paso Herald-Post,* Sep. 5, 1940 (both located in AGN-DGIPS, Box 191, 2.1/311.1/5, Vol. 18).

41. Report, Insp. 24 to DGIPS, Oct. 4, 1940, AGN-DGIPS, Box 191, 2.1/311.1/5, Vol. 20.

leaders know this."[42] By as early as 1940, the military leadership was immunized against rebellion by their relative wealth and status, while the regular soldiers had lost their rebellious impulse in Amaro's professionalized academies.

The threat of rebellion after the election of 1940 (and again after the 1952 election) presents an interesting question. Nordlinger argued that "praetorianism (or military intervention) occurs when officers more or less overtly threaten to carry out a coup d'état unless certain demands are met, when they stage an unsuccessful coup, when a coup brings about or prevents the replacement of the government by another group of civilians, and, most important, when the officers themselves take control of the government."[43] In the case of 1940, as demonstrated in chapter 1, Almazán's followers intended to spark an armed rebellion, with or without their leader, to defend his presumed victory in the presidential election. The events leading to the death of General Andrés Zarzosa were the most obvious example of such preparations. For the case of 1952, as will be shown in chapter 5, the supporters of Henríquez alternated between a strategy of threatening armed rebellion and planning for a more clandestine interference in the country during Ruiz Cortines's tenure. By Nordlinger's definition, both Almazán and Henríquez would have been guilty of praetorianism, since they (or their followers) threatened rebellion. However, is it possible to be praetorian if one is simply attempting to defend political rights in an increasingly dysfunctional democracy?

The rebellion of those opposed to the PRM did not occur in 1940. This simple fact—that something *did not* happen—underscored everything that *did* occur during the campaign. The political speech of army officers had been constrained in 1940 to the language of parties and elections. Overt threats of armed violence, once a common element of political conflicts, became practically forbidden during the 1940 campaign. The rhetoric of revolutionary vigor became more attuned to the ideals of democratic rivalries than military credentials. As Lieuwen correctly concluded, "The significance of the 1940 elections was that these generals, after a severe struggle, were forced to surrender control of Mexico's political processes to civilian politicians."[44]

42. Memo, G-2/2657-G-732, Col. E. R. W. McCabe (assistant chief of staff, G-2) to G-2 Chief of Staff, Aug. 16, 1939, in Robert Lester, *U.S. Military Intelligence Reports. Mexico, 1919–1941* (Frederick, Md.: University Publications of America, 1984), Reel 4, Frame 213.

43. Nordlinger, *Soldiers in Politics*, 3.

44. Lieuwen, *Mexican Militarism*, 129.

These shifts in the substance and tone of political debate signaled a sea change in the political history of modern Mexico. It was the first step in the wider transformation that largely extricated the military from political life.

Thus, the political rules of the game for Mexican military officers underwent a deep transformation in the presidential election of 1940. Political conflict became an arena for the formation of political parties, elections were accepted as a venue for political conflict, and violence was renounced as a means of obtaining influence. Top-ranking army officers formed political parties and defended the necessity of free and fair elections. The new parties had platforms that argued for the central importance of strong democratic and electoral forms, railed against PRM abuses and "impositions," and tried to form electoral coalitions.

The pervasive violence and obstructionism, perpetrated on all sides, marked the transformation as incomplete. Nevertheless, the fact that the losers in the election of 1940 did not take up arms in the pursuit of power demonstrated how far the political rules had shifted. While military officers continued to play a role in political life in Mexico, they no longer had the viable option of threatening or fomenting armed movements as a way of gaining political advantage. Thus, the effects of the election of 1940 were the legitimization of parties and elections as the proper arena for political conflict and the distancing of Mexican politics from the armed action evident only two years before in the Cedillo rebellion. This transformation was the key to Mexican exceptionalism in Latin America, with Mexico's continuous civilian government standing in marked contrast to so many difficult cases of coups d'état and military governments in the hemisphere during the latter half of the twentieth century.

The Mexican case was no less interesting given that it was two army officers who moved the political system toward demilitarization: Cárdenas and Ávila Camacho. "Cárdenas had created and passed on a system that at last successfully blended the old and the new, reconciling leadership mobility with party monopoly, benefits for the masses with an essentially capitalist, middle-class controlled program of development, military representation with civilian control." Camp argued that "military political leadership, relying on the strength of their revolutionary credentials, opted to remove their peers from the political scene. They were not forced to abandon politics because of popular, civilian pressures." On campaign in 1939, Ávila Camacho stated that "members of the National Army should not intervene, directly or indirectly, in electoral politics."[45] After his election, he became even more strident in the attempt to tame the political ambition of the military elite.

The process of demilitarizing politics was a treacherous one. In his first month in office, Ávila Camacho eviscerated the military sector of the PRM in the name of professionalization. He then began referring to the army as depoliticized, which "became an excellent pretext for eliminating those 'not depoliticized' generals that could have created problems for his administration."[46] Next, he shifted his position on the military in politics, remarking that "electoral partisanship and political fervor are evidently incompatible with the high duties of the Army and Navy."[47] Throughout, Ávila Camacho maintained the call for national unity to address Mexico's real need during World War II, but also as a convenient political fig leaf for his assault on the military.[48]

Ávila Camacho had the support of U.S. officials in his efforts, particularly as the election of 1946 approached. U.S. ambassador George Messersmith professed deep confidence in Ávila Camacho's ability to handle the matter: "I believe that the President has sufficient control over the Army to keep them out of politics." To this, Secretary of State Dean Acheson replied, "I think you have made it clear that we may feel reasonably assured that the military will wish to stay out of politics; and that we may feel assured that President Ávila Camacho . . . will prevent any misuse of the military." There were other misgivings in the State Department, however: "While the Mexican Army is becoming a career army, made up of technical officers, it still has a great influence in political matters. *The Army is always interested in the Presidential elections.*"[49] These messages demonstrated the perception of Ávila Camacho as having a fairly tight leash on the military at the same time that U.S.

45. "Blended the old and the new": Schloming, "Civil-Military Relations in Mexico," 309; "revolutionary credentials": Camp, "Mexico," 273; "should not intervene": Luis Javier Garrido, *El partido de la revolución institucionalizada: La formación del Nuevo Estado, 1928–1945* (Mexico City: Siglo XXI, 1986), 355.

46. Eviscerated the military sector: José Luis Piñeyro, "Las fuerzas armadas en la transición política de México," *Revista Mexicana de Sociología* 59, no. 1 (1997): 169; "excellent pretext": Sánchez Gutiérrez, "Los militares en la década de los cincuenta," 273.

47. "Primer Informe de gobierno del presidente Ávila Camacho," *El Universal,* Sep. 2, 1941, p. 4, quoted in Jorge Alberto Lozoya, *El ejército mexicano, 1911–1965* (Mexico City: Colegio de México, 1970), 65.

48. For a fascinating analysis of this topic, see Halbert Jones III, " 'The War Has Brought Peace to Mexico': The Political Impact of Mexican Participation in World War II" (PhD diss., Harvard University, 2006); also, Luis Medina, *Civilismo y modernización del autoritarismo.* Historia de la Revolución Mexicana 20 (Mexico City: Colegio de México, 1979).

49. "Sufficient control": U.S. State Department, 812.00/9–1145, Memo, U.S. Ambassador to Secretary of State, Sep. 11, 1945, in *Confidential U.S. State Department Central Files,*

observers discerned an undercurrent of the old tradition of military influence in politics.

Geopolitical concerns reinforced Ávila Camacho's rhetorical assault on the military's role in politics. Once the oil controversy was settled and Mexico sided with the United States against the Axis, "foreign pressures on Mexico were reduced [making] the captivity [*cautiverio*] of the soldiers within the party unnecessary."[50] Given the pressures for solidarity imposed by World War II, Ávila Camacho saw his opportunity to more completely subdue the political aspirations of the officer corps and he took it. On January 18, 1946, the convention of the PRM declared the reconstitution of the party as the Partido Revolucionario Institucional (PRI) with a structure that officially denied sectoral status to the military and effectively diluted its electoral power.[51] One observer in the U.S. State Department described the reorganization as being "done with the hope of getting away from some of the bad odor in which the PRM has recently found itself."[52] Camp analyzed this situation starkly: "[the military] could either overthrow the civilian leadership class, identifying with dissident civilian elites, or it could overthrow civilian leadership altogether, replacing it with military officers."[53] As the military began to appreciate the new discipline inherent in the PRI structure, the choice quickly became an obvious one, and the revolutionary officers began to cast their lot with the civilian-dominated PRI.

A central element of this transformation was the military's acceptance of civilian dominance in political decisions. If, as Schloming argued, "successful civilianization depends upon the capacity of the military-political elite to create effective political institutions," then the formation and evolution of the PRM/PRI were the keys to the removal of the military from politics. As the PRM gained experience in government and the political luster of the revolutionary generation waned, a new dynamic emerged that aligned the interests (political and economic) of the civilian and military elite. This

---

Mexico, 1945–1949, Part I, Reel 1; "reasonably assured": U.S. State Department, 812.00/1–1246, Memo, Acheson to Messersmith, Jan. 12, 1946, in *Confidential U.S. State Department Central Files, Mexico, 1945–1949, Part I*, Reel 3; "career army": U.S. State Department, 812.00/3–2445, Memo, Raleigh Gibson to Secretary of State, Mar. 24, 1945, in *Confidential U.S. State Department Central Files, Mexico, 1945–1949, Part I*, Reel 1, emphasis added.

50. Lozoya, *El ejército mexicano*, 65.

51. Ibid., 68–69.

52. U.S. State Department, 812.00/1–1846, ARA memo, Ruth Mason Hughes, Jan. 18, 1946, in *Confidential U.S. State Department Central Files, Mexico, 1945–1949, Part I*, Reel 3.

53. Camp, "Mexico," 276.

change has sometimes been overstated in the political science literature. One author argued that Mexico "provides a unique example of a military leadership's transforming itself into a civilian political elite, simultaneously transferring the basis of power from the army to the civil state."[54] Though it was true that civilian authority became ascendant after 1946, the military elite did not "transform" itself in this period into a civilian elite but was in fact *replaced* by one.

The most visible aspect of the replacement on the political stage was the fact that no military candidate for president stood in the election of 1946. Although Henríquez figured as a serious contender, the PRM declined to support his candidacy, forcing him to bide his time until 1952. Yet the public debate over the succession galvanized opinion regarding the appropriate profession of any contender. When Ávila Camacho was asked in 1945 whether he favored a civilian successor, he replied that since the Constitution mandated civilian government the next president would have to abide by that regardless of his former career.[55] This statement, rather than answering the question, only gave the impression that if a soldier were to run and be elected, he would have to be careful to *act* like a civilian. In the end it was a moot point, as the postwar period focused attention on the primacy of "democratic" governments and the preference for civilian administrators.

The debate resurfaced leading into the presidential election of 1952. In 1950, Rodolfo Sánchez Taboada, himself an army general, made clear the intentions of the Alemán administration regarding the presidential succession. His argument established "the premise that the future President . . . should be a civilian. And a young civilian. Moreover, he clearly indicated to the military that they should refrain from political activity." In the same year, the new rules of the game were being clarified in the public discourse: "In the past it was enough to be a Division General—even better if you had command of troops—to constitute a decisive political factor in the electoral 'selection.' Now things have changed and the officers will have to elaborate great projects and adopt a program that will convince and infiltrate itself in popular opinion. . . . Yet it is evident to all, that civilianism [*civilismo*] occupies the preferred position and that it will be problematic for its opponents

54. "Successful civilianization": Schloming, "Civil-Military Relations in Mexico," 58; "transferring the basis of power": Camp, *Generals in the Palacio,* 6.

55. U.S. State Department, 812.00/5–1745, Monthly Political Report, Raleigh Gibson to Secretary of State, May 17, 1945, in *Confidential U.S. State Department Central Files, Mexico, 1945–1949, Part I,* Reel 1.

to defeat it within the political models that govern and enliven the Partido Revolucionario Institucional."[56] A column by General Mariano Montero Villar posited that there was little to be gained in the old argument of whether the president should be civilian or military: "Hitler and Mussolini were civilians, now Stalin too, and praetorianism held sway in their governments. Generals Cárdenas and Ávila Camacho are soldiers, and their governments have been eminently civilian."[57] In other words, the old dichotomy between civilian and military leaders ceased to have clear meaning in postwar Mexico; connections to the party were paramount.

The civilianization of the military was successful in large part because of the completion of reforms within the military academies. Lozoya argued that the new curricula of these schools increased professionalization and thereby fostered depoliticization. For Turner, it was the education of young officers in the military academies from 1920 to 1940 with a new ethic based on respect and support for civilian government that marked the transition from a tradition of political to apolitical soldiers. Ackroyd pointed to "a progression of loyalties, placing the nation, the state and its institutions, and finally the military in descending order of importance" when assessing the military's newfound loyalty. Building on the Amaro reforms of the 1920s, Camp concluded, officers were inculcated with a new respect for civilian authority that essentially precluded interventions in political matters.[58]

In contrast to other large Latin American militaries, like those of Argentina and Brazil, the modern Mexican military did not engage in a praetorian tradition. Crucially, the Mexican officer corps was never able to define for itself a view of the national interest apart from the view of the civilian PRI leadership. The danger, of course, was that "the moment the military draw this

56. Debate resurfaced: see, for example, "Presidente Civil o Militar Civilista," El Universal, Jul. 31, 1950, AGN-DGIPS, Box 999, File 2, Futurismo Presidencial, 1950–1952, Vol. 3; "refrain from political activity": Excélsior, Feb. 7, 1950, AGN-DGIPS, Box 803, Campaña Presidencial, Futurismo 1950–1952, Vol. 1; "constitute a decisive political factor": Excélsior, May 30, 1950, AGN-DGIPS, Box 803, Futurismo Político, Campaña Presidencial, 1952–1958, Vol. 2.

57. El Universal, Dec. 4, 1951, AGN-DGIPS, Box 24, File 3, 2.1/061.8/3. Montero Villar was unlucky in his political affiliations. He supported both the de la Huerta movement in 1923 and the Escobar movement in 1929. See Roderic A. Camp, Mexican Political Biographies, 1884–1935 (Austin: University of Texas Press, 1991), 148.

58. New curricula: Lozoya, El ejército mexicano, passim; ethic based on respect: Frederick C. Turner, "México: Las causas de la limitación military," Aportes 6 (Oct. 1967): 63; "progression of loyalties": William S. Ackroyd, "Military Professionalism, Education, and Political Behavior in Mexico," Armed Forces and Society 18, no. 1 (Fall 1991), ·86; inculcated with a new respect: Camp, Generals in the Palacio, 19–20.

distinction between nation and the government in power, they begin to in-
vent their own private notion of the national interest, and from this it is only
a skip to the constrained substitution of this view for that of the civilian
government."[59] But the PRI successfully enforced the discipline "that loyalty
to it, even to a given administration, is tantamount to loyalty to the state and
to the nation."[60] Indeed, as Ackroyd argues, "the mythology of the revolution encourages officers to think of nation and government as one. An attack
on the government would therefore be an attack on the revolution and the
nation."[61]

Along with the ethic of loyalty to the party went a powerful corollary:
opposition to the party was tantamount to betrayal. Camp wrote, "The military's sense of discipline concerning political participation or association with
the opposition, sometimes imposed through extreme measures, accompanied
that of civilian political leaders, who developed an almost untouchable loyalty
to and discipline toward a single party, the PNR and its successors."[62] Leaders
of the PRM and PRI drew upon the negative historical images of nine-
teenth-century praetorianism and postrevolutionary rebellions to, in essence,
shame any soldier who questioned the civilian politicians.

This process unfolded alongside the weeding out of rebellious officers
(i.e., 1923, 1927, 1929, 1938) and the graying of the revolutionary generation.
Part of each successive program to professionalize the military, beginning
with Amaro in the 1920s, was an effort to retire the "finger" generals. These
officers had been promoted to high ranks during revolutionary campaigns,
often on the whim of a victorious leader, for reasons of *méritos de campaña*.
By either simply forcing retirement upon these finger generals or requiring
that all officers apply to the secretary of national defense for confirmation of
their rank, the military and political elite could move the armed forces toward
greater efficiency and professionalization. Wager also notes that many senior
army officers had passed through state and federal elective offices before at-
taining high commands in the military, such as the secretary of defense position. This process of vetting officers in positions of less authority, along with
the practice of choosing candidates late in their careers, "helped to convince

59. S. E. Finer, *The Man on Horseback: The Role of the Military in Politics,* 2nd ed. (Baltimore:
Penguin, 1975), 23.

60. Camp, *Generals in the Palacio,* 10–11; also, Finer, *Man on Horseback,* 23.

61. Ackroyd, "Military Professionalism, Education, and Political Behavior," 91.

62. Camp, *Generals in the Palacio,* 34–35.

key political leaders that top military officials were loyal to the system and could be trusted to carry out presidential directives."[63]

The military was purposely kept at a disadvantage in terms of education. "Cárdenas could well perceive that a professional army need not necessarily be politically neutral, but an apolitical army must necessarily be professional," and as the political project of the PRM/PRI developed, the civilian leadership realized the necessity of training the military elite in a new way. For this reason, "the Mexican military educational system has basically two functions: to instill the values and norms necessary to function within the military institution and to teach necessary skills while restricting political knowledge, interest, and efficacy."[64]

Ackroyd found that differences in the military education of officers affect their behavior in civil-military relationships. In Mexico, officers were taught that civilians govern the nation while the military acts as the guarantor of national security. More recently, in Brazil and Peru, the officer corps was trained with the belief that it "is the institution that has the greatest capability of determining the interests of the people."[65] This disparity of priorities among the military curricula manifested itself in the diverse historical trends in the three countries, Brazil and Peru experiencing regular and long military interventions while Mexico had none.

The gap in education levels between military and civilian aspirants to political office—civilians often possessed more formal education beyond the high school level—also played a role in determining political ascendancy. In short, "the educational experience in Mexico . . . psychologically places the military below civilians in rank and inhibits military assumption of civilian roles."[66] There was a secondary dynamic as well, as graduates of the military academies began to edge out older officers for prime posts. During the Alemán administration, more of the younger officers who had not fought in the Revolution but had been educated at the Escuela Superior de Guerra were

63. Stephen J. Wager, "The Mexican Military: The Dilemma of Functioning in a One-Party System," in *Beyond Praetorianism: The Latin American Military in Transition,* ed. Richard L. Millett and Michael Gold-Bliss (Coral Gables: North-South Center Press, 1996), 114.

64. "Apolitical army": Talukder Maniruzzaman, *Military Withdrawal from Politics: A Comparative Study* (Cambridge, Mass.: Ballinger, 1987), 95; "Mexican military educational system": William S. Ackroyd, "Military Professionalism and Nonintervention in Mexico," in *Rank and Privilege: The Military and Society in Latin America,* ed. Linda Alexander Rodríguez, Jaguar Books on Latin America 8 (Wilmington, Del.: Scholarly Resources, 1994), 223.

65. Ackroyd, "Military Professionalism and Nonintervention," 224.

66. Ibid., 226–27.

promoted to leadership positions, including head of the Estado Mayor Presidencial and the Guardias Presidenciales. This dynamic was reinforced by
the reality that "many of these officers have no important political connections, nor independent income, nor have they articulated any particular desire
to get into politics."[67] As the old revolutionary generals aged, they lost their
luster as leaders and were supplanted in the political arena by ambitious young
civilians (often university educated) and in the military arena by the professionalized products of the Amaro-era system of academy training.

Further, the Mexican military was not trained in the administrative and
professional skills that would have allowed them to directly challenge the
increasingly technical governmental policies of civilian administrations. Military officers detected the "growing congruence of ideological orientation
between dominant civilian and military politicians such as to encourage military men to select managerial roles precisely because they perceive[d] their
political interests to be protected." Meanwhile, key officers were individually
co-opted into the civilian system by assigning them to civilian positions with
both their military pay and the civilian position's pay. This created loyal top
officers and simultaneously had a multiplier effect, showing other officers that
if they were loyal, they could expect to be rewarded in a similar manner."[68]
In the end, the subordination of the military to civilian authority, through
elaborate systems of reward and punishment, became one of the hallmarks of
the single-party dominant system in Mexico.

One way in which the civilian elite managed to turn the military away
from opposition movements or outright use of force was through a shifting
of the institution's primary mission. As Needler noted, "To prepare for the
defense of national borders seemed neither feasible nor sensible: against Mexico's northern neighbor, the United States, defense is hardly possible; against
her southern neighbor, Guatemala, defense is hardly necessary." Yet the mission of the Mexican Army since 1926 had been "to defend the integrity and
independence of the fatherland, to maintain the rule of the Constitution and

67. Promoted to leadership positions: Sánchez Gutiérrez, "Los militares en la década de
los cincuenta," 279; "no important political connections": Franklin D. Margiotta, "Civilian
Control and the Mexican Military: Changing Patterns of Political Influence," in *Civilian Control
of the Military: Theory and Cases from Developing Countries,* ed. Claude E. Welch (Albany: State
University of New York Press, 1976), 234.
68. "Congruence of ideological orientation": Schloming, "Civil-Military Relations in
Mexico," 19; "co-opted into the civilian system": William S. Ackroyd, "The Military in Mexican Politics: The Impact of Professionalism, Civilian Behavior, and the Revolution," *Proceedings
of the Pacific Coast Council on Latin American Studies* 12 (1985–86): 100.

its laws, and to conserve internal order." This was congruent with the trend throughout the Latin American region, where "defending *la patria* against internal and external threats is the historical mission claimed by Latin American armed forces." Wager wrote that "the civilianization of power took away the army's direct role in political decision making, and the country's new civilian leaders assigned the military the role of guarantor and protector of the overall system." A new organic law in 1971 formalized the dominance of civic action as the primary duty of the armed forces.[69]

Wager argued that the tradition of civic action as a primary role of the military was a major factor in the removal of officers from politics. By this logic, Cárdenas viewed military participation in infrastructure projects as a way to reach out to the more remote regions of the country, and "as an added advantage for political leaders, civic action kept officers busy, leaving them little time to mingle in politics." These projects advanced the agenda of the centralizing civilian administrators on two fronts: they promoted the beneficent image of the dominant PRM, and they headed off any latent political ambitions within the officer corps. A contemporary observer noted that "Mexico's army is not a parade-ground army. . . . [It] is a working army, and on its various internal fronts it wages a peacetime campaign all the year round."[70]

The relationship between military and civilian authorities did not have to be harmful to either party. One analysis discussed two simple corollaries of the civil-military pact formed in the 1940s: "absolute respect for the military institution . . . [and that] the military would respect with all their might civilian authority." Lieuwen argued along the same line that "there is a kind of gentleman's agreement between the civilian and military authorities whereby it is understood that army officers will be provided reasonable living standards. For these economic rewards the armed forces are expected to remain loyal to the PRI."[71] This interdependency worked to the advantage of

69. "Defense of national borders": Martin C. Needler, *Politics and Society in Mexico* (Albuquerque: University of New Mexico Press, 1971), 66; "independence of the fatherland": *Ley Orgánica del Ejército y la Armada Nacionales*, Mar. 15, 1926, quoted in Stephen J. Wager, *The Mexican Military Approaches the Twenty-first Century: Coping with a New World Order* (Carlisle Barracks, Pa.: Strategic Studies Institute, U.S. Army War College, 1994), 2; "defending *la patria*": Loveman, *For la Patria*, xi; "civilianization of power": Wager, *Mexican Military Approaches the Twenty-first Century*, 1–2.

70. "Added advantage for political leaders": Wager, *Mexican Military Approaches the Twenty-first Century*, 2; "parade-ground army": Prewett, "Mexican Army," 609.

71. "Absolute respect": *Siempre cerca, siempre lejos: Las fuerzas armadas en México* (Mexico City: Global Exchange, 2000), 16; "gentleman's agreement": Lieuwen, *Mexican Militarism*, 149.

both groups, as the military continued to enjoy some of the perquisites of power and the civilian masters of the PRI contented themselves with their formal political domination of the military.

Civilians extricated the military from the regular electoral machinery of the party, but not without some concessions. The party recognized that there were truly valuable, even gifted, politicians among the ranks of the military. Therefore, by 1941, a new line of discipline had been expressed: "those soldiers who have political skills would be able to participate as individuals but not as representatives of the Army." By requesting *licencia,* a type of formal leave from duties, soldiers could participate in politics without causing the problems associated with a campaign being run by an active duty officer. "No military, in short, can be shorn of political influence. . . . The issue is rather one of seeing limits within which members of the armed forces, and the military as an institution, accept the government's definition of appropriate areas of responsibility."[72] The process of requesting licencia gave officers the opportunity to indulge their political aspirations, but only allowed them such freedom under the supervision of the civilian leadership of the PRI. All involved also realized that what was granted could be easily taken away. Officers knew that they could only regain command of troops or a choice base assignment if they worked within the constraints imposed by the PRI. Any strident criticism of the party might mean permanent reassignment to a desk at headquarters without real responsibilities or, more painfully, the retraction of lucrative contracts. Inherent in the licencia system was the threat of reprisal.

The military enjoyed material benefits as part of the deal along with the civilian elite. As the economy grew after World War II, "the soldiers enjoyed an agreeable standard of living, such that they did not feel the need to intervene to correct imperfections in the national economy." The process leading to the "refunctionalization" of the political role of the military was crucial to the consolidation of the PRI after the election of Miguel Alemán in 1946. As a corollary of the military's subjugation to civilian authority, the civilian elite stayed clear of internal military matters while exercising a liberal policy of promotions. During the Alemán administration, military promotions counteracted the negative effect of decreasing military influence in elections:

72. "Participate as individuals": Sánchez Gutiérrez, "Los militares en la década de los cincuenta," 281; "shorn of political influence": Claude E. Welch Jr., *Civilian Control of the Military: Myth and Reality,* Special Studies 63 (Buffalo: Council on International Studies, State University of New York at Buffalo, 1975), 1.

"Alemán is the only president since 1946 to have ordered more promotions to general than to colonel; in fact, he promoted more officers to the rank of general in one year than [Adolfo] López Mateos did during his entire administration."[73]

Further, as Camp argued, "declining numbers of military officers in politics can increase the potential for greater isolation of the military from other groups, including politicians, and the development of a caste mentality." This dynamic was ameliorated in Mexico by the determination of civilian politicians to remain aloof from "internal" military matters, such as promotion, equipment, and salaries.[74] This tactic, which isolated the military but also allowed it great latitude in its own affairs, was a carefully managed balancing act that succeeded only as long as the civilian politicians kept a close budgetary rein on the military. In financial terms, the Mexican military has generally had a much lower budget as a percentage of GDP than most other Latin American militaries.

Despite advances toward the civilianization of politics and the professionalization of the military, the political aspirations of the officer corps were not so easily forgotten. One observer noted that "the impatience of the military officers . . . derives from a simple cause: their knowledge of the strength acquired by *civismo* and the consolidation of it as a political force."[75] In the late 1940s and into the 1950s, several episodes demonstrated the resolve of some military officers to protect the political rights that they believed had been wrongly taken from them.

In the first instance, a soldier was a Mexican citizen and as such was entitled to the basic political freedoms guaranteed in the Constitution of 1917. At the most basic level, he was entitled to vote. The opening statement of the founding assembly of the PRM made clear the political rights and obligations of soldiers in Mexico: "The members of the Army have, constitutionally, political rights and *the duty to exercise them.* . . . Therefore, incorporating them in an effective way is precisely to facilitate for them the use of the legal norms for the effective completion of their *obligations as citizens.*"[76] In fact, in

73. "Agreeable standard of living": Turner, "México," 59; "refunctionalization" of the political role: Boils, *Los militares y la política en México,* 47; "more promotions to general": Camp, *Generals in the Palacio,* 178.

74. "Potential for greater isolation": Camp, *Generals in the Palacio,* 73; aloof from "internal" military matters: see, for instance, Camp, *Generals in the Palacio,* 176–211.

75. *Excélsior,* May 30, 1950, AGN-DGIPS, Box 803, Futurismo Político, Campaña Presidencial, 1952–1958, Vol. 2.

76. Partido de la Revolución Mexicana, *Convocatoria para la Asamblea Constituyente,* 36. Emphasis added.

1952, the secretary of national defense ordered all military personnel to register to vote, without specifying which group to support or outlining the limits of political participation.[77]

Beyond the fundamental act of voting, there was a thornier question as to whether a soldier could participate in politics or political campaigns. Officially, the policy was quite clear, even emanating from President Ávila Camacho in a decree of December 3, 1945, that announced the prohibition of soldiers participating in political matters without *licencia*.[78] An editorial titled "Politics without Uniforms" argued the point this way: "the military men that want to intervene in politics should retire from the service; even then, they should refrain from wearing the uniform . . . and these prohibitions do not diminish or harm the right of members of the Army to vote individually and express their will at the polls, not as soldiers, but rather as civilians; that is, as components of a democratic community where caste, privilege and the supremacy of force are abolished."[79] In this statement, the newspaper effectively underlined the new dichotomy in political participation, a line which ran directly through a citizen's status as civilian or military.

The army regulations governing *licencia* were meant to keep the military separated from political life, if only in a formalistic way: the generals remained generals, but they relinquished command of soldiers while they acted "politically." Elements within the army opposed such regulations, which essentially added a roadblock between them and their right as a citizen to express themselves freely in the political arena. In addition to maintaining fidelity to their official duties, "they do not believe that in order to defend their ideological positions they should have to request *licencia* ahead of time and separate themselves from the armed forces."[80] Nevertheless, newspapers during any given campaign season were littered with reports of who had requested *licencia*, since it was basically an announcement of political intentions.

The *licencia* process gave considerable leverage to the government and the PRM in terms of disciplining officers who challenged the political system under construction. During the campaign of 1940, the PRUN claimed that "soldiers who are truly deserving and have undisputed merit have been retired from the service or relegated to faraway posts simply because they are

77. *El Universal*, Feb. 18, 1952, AGN-DGIPS, Box 815, 2.1/52/375.

78. Lozoya, *El ejército mexicano*, 68.

79. *Excélsior*, Oct. 1, 1951, AGN-DGIPS, Box 24, File 3, 2.1/061.8/3.

80. *La Prensa*, Jul. 19, 1950, AGN-DGIPS, Box 999, File 2, Futurismo Presidencial, 1950–1952, Vol. 3.

sympathizers of Almazán's candidacy."[81] After the election, the Ávila Camacho administration countered the almazanista strength among army officers
with bureaucratic maneuvering. On September 12, 1940, the secretary of
national defense recalled to active duty a number of officers who had been
granted *licencia ilimitada* and cancelled the *licencia ordinaria* of other officers.
All of those affected had been members of the Almazán campaign, and most
figured in the supposed military preparations for a rebellion.[82] On October
1, 1940, military authorities began to open legal proceedings against the almazanista officers who had not returned for duty as ordered, charging them with
desertion.[83]

By 1951, the role of the military in political life was changing dramatically.
Requests for licencia to participate in opposition campaigns were routinely
denied.[84] In one high-profile case, Luis Alamillo Flores failed in his request
for licencia to aid the Henríquez campaign.[85] The Secretariat of National
Defense argued that any soldier, regardless of rank, was required to request
not just licencia but actual *discharge* from the army in order to then work
actively in political matters. In fact, over 150 officers soon retired from the
army to pursue political goals across the political spectrum, some as supporters
of presidential campaigns and others as candidates themselves for legislative
positions.[86] In October 1951, a group of officers received punishment for
violating rules of conduct embodied in the presidential order of December
24, 1945, which forbade participation in politics without proper authorization. The group had signed a letter of support for the PRI candidate, Adolfo
Ruiz Cortines, that was published in the daily newspapers.[87]

81. *Excélsior,* May 23, 1940, AGN-DGIPS, Box 133, 2.1/310/24, Vol. 1.

82. *La Prensa,* Sep. 13, 1940, AGN-DGIPS, Box 191, 2.1/311.1/5, Vol. 19. Among those
recalled were Brigade Generals Héctor F. López and Jose Mijares Palencia; Brigadier Generals
Leopoldo Dorantes Vázquez, Andres Zaragoza Verástegui, and Rodolfo Higareda Gudiño; Colonels Adrián Martinez del Rio, Adolfo Cienfuegos y Camus, Luis G. Segura García, Demetrio
Zúñiga Adame, and Herón Ramirez Garcia; Lieutenant Colonel Tiburcio Garza Zamora; and
Major Blas Tijerina Cárdenas.

83. *La Prensa,* Oct. 2, 1940, AGN-DGIPS, Box 191, 2.1/311.1/5, Vol. 19.

84. *La Prensa,* Aug. 17, 1951, p. 56, AGN-DGIPS, Box 24, File 3, 2.1/061.8/3.

85. Alamillo Flores reconciled with the government soon after the election, being promoted to division general on September 20, 1952. See Roderic Ai Camp, *Mexican Political
Biographies, 1935–1993,* 3rd ed. (Austin: University of Texas Press, 1995), 17–18.

86. Actual *discharge* from the army: *Excélsior,* Aug. 17, 1951; across the political spectrum:
Excélsior, Sep. 27, 1951 (both located in AGN-DGIPS, Box 24, File 3, 2.1/061.8/3).

87. *El Nacional,* Oct. 2, 1951, p. 77; *Zócalo,* Oct. 3, 1951 (both located in AGN-DGIPS,
Box 24, File 3, 2.1/061.8/3). The group included Generals Leobardo Tellechea, Francisco Luis
Castillo, Telesforo Morales, and (Lic.) Alfonso Caso; Colonels Ricardo Topete and Manuel Díaz
Hurtado; Lieutenant Colonels Antonio Astorga Meza, Eugenio Colís Reyna, and (Lic.) Juan
Covarrubias; and Captain Vidal Martínez Martínez.

The sword of military discipline could cut against the interests of the dominant party and provide grist for opposition claims of favoritism. In May 1940, the PRUN complained that General Adrian Castrejón had attended a PRM meeting in support of Ávila Camacho as a representative of the army and without proper licencia.[88] In 1952, the Federación de Partidos del Pueblo Mexicano (FPPM) supplied a list of active military officers who had signed a letter supporting the PRI, including the army's inspector general, Alejo G. González. The FPPM used this evidence to argue that in the future it expected that soldiers openly supporting any party would not be harassed or punished by the government.[89] In practice, however, those soldiers who supported the PRM/PRI, including the string of generals who served as head of the dominant party, were not penalized by the licencia system, while opposition elements received their punishment early and often.

As official harassment of military officers in the opposition continued, the process of political consolidation of the PRI kept pace. However, the change was not necessarily recognized in its depth right away, and it was not until the defeat of Henríquez in 1952 that the officer corps fully appreciated the discipline posited in 1940. Their uncertainty was reflected in the efforts of high-ranking generals in 1948 to form a new political party in order to "assure the prevalence of order, which according to them, could only be achieved with military leadership [la mano militar]."[90]

In August 1948, a group of army generals held a series of meetings to discuss the economic and political situation in Mexico. One of the leaders, Division General Antonio Rios Zertuche, pitched his idea of forming a new party to an impressive group of powerful politicians, including former presidents Ávila Camacho, Emilio Portes Gil, Abelardo Rodríguez, and Pascual Ortiz Rubio, and army heavyweights Generals Rodrigo Quevedo, Anacleto López, and Bonifacio Salinas.[91] Other important figures within the group included Joaquín Amaro, who was presumed by Mexican agents to be the leader, and Juan Barragán, who became one of the founding fathers of the

---

88. *Excélsior*, May 23, 1940, AGN-DGIPS, Box 133, 2.1/310/24, Vol. 1.

89. *El Universal*, Dec. 9, 1951, p. 86, AGN-DGIPS, Box 26, File 1, 2.1/061.8/15, Vol. 5. See also *El Popular*, Dec. 9, 1951, AGN-DGIPS, Box 808, File 6, 2.1/51/372.

90. Memo, DGIPS, Aug. 17, 1948, AGN-DGIPS, Box 24, File 3, 2.1/061.8/3.

91. Ibid. This meeting should not be misconstrued as one of disgruntled outsiders looking in—quite the opposite. In 1948, Rios Zertuche was such a stalwart of the dominant elite that he had recently been promoted to division general (1943) and served as Mexican ambassador to France (1945–46). See Camp, *Mexican Political Biographies, 1935–1993*, 592.

Partido Auténtico de la Revolución Mexicana (PARM).[92] Amaro went so far as to petition for licencia from the army in order to pursue his political aspirations, which reportedly included "the reconquest of power by the military."[93] The intense efforts at surveillance by the intelligence services proved ineffective for one simple reason: the participants were so well known that it was impossible to infiltrate the meetings. This additional layer of secrecy, beyond the basic fact of a meeting of such powerful (and political) generals, provoked fear in the minds of the civilian elite.

The goals of the group were consistent with the argument made by Rios Zertuche upon assuming command of operations in Sonora in the aftermath of the 1940 election: "since the Government of this state and the Military Zone are united to guarantee order, we soldiers will not tolerate any attempts to overthrow the current Government."[94] In short, Rios Zertuche did not suggest reinstituting military influence through force or threat of rebellion (i.e., praetorianism), but rather through the formation of a political party to advance the political interests of a recognized group in society. Rios Zertuche followed the example of Almazán and Amaro in 1940, and presaged Henríquez in 1952, playing by the new rules that demanded electoral supremacy in place of the old paths to power.

Some popular press sympathized with the efforts of this group of military officers to form a political party. One editorial argued that it defended "the necessity that the military elements form a solid bloc that can participate, within the law, in political contests." Another opined that it represented a preliminary attempt to gauge the reaction of other officers, in order that such groups could better prepare for future elections. However, the efforts of this group of officers faltered in the face of the results of the U.S. presidential election. Candidate Thomas E. Dewey supposedly harbored a more hard-line agenda for U.S.-Mexican relations that would have offered the military group the leverage necessary to reestablish the tradition of the military in high elective office.[95] His stunning defeat reinforced Alemán's political power, as his special relationship with Truman could be continued.

92. Memo, DGIPS, Sep. 27, 1948, p. 14; see also *La Prensa,* Oct. 22, 1948 (both located in AGN-DGIPS, Box 24, File 3, 2.1/061.8/3).

93. *La Prensa,* Feb. 25, 1948, AGN-DGIPS, Box 24, File 3, 2.1/061.8/3.

94. Report, Insp. Gutiérrez to DGIPS, Nov. 8, 1940, Nogales, AGN-DGIPS, Box 192, 2.1/311.1/5, Vol. 21.

95. "Solid bloc": *La Prensa,* Sep. 6, 1948; gauge the reaction: *La Prensa,* Sep. 7, 1948; hard-line agenda: *La Prensa,* Nov. 10, 1948, p. 23 (all located in AGN-DGIPS, Box 24, File 3, 2.1/061.8/3).

At the same time as the group was meeting, the rumored resignation of Secretary of National Defense Gilberto Limón caused a storm of debate over his replacement and, more importantly, who would get to make that decision. The civilian bureaucrats favored Ignacio Otero Pablos, while the officer corps argued for Amaro. One Mexican agent observed that "among some old revolutionaries the mention of Otero Pablos has not been well-received . . . since they do not see his military credentials as warranting such a promotion."[96] Otero Pablos later served as Mexican ambassador to Venezuela and head of the Tenth Military Zone at Irapuato.[97] Soon after the dispute, which ended when Limón stayed on as secretary of national defense until 1952, Luis Alamillo Flores lost his post as head of the Colegio Militar, went to Washington D.C. on a military commission, and then moved on to "an obscure post as head of an engine factory."[98] This turf battle between the civilian and military elite tested the unwritten arrangement that kept the army's business within army channels.

In the midst of the debate over the rights of soldiers in politics was Octavio Véjar Vázquez. Véjar Vázquez was a licenciado, a brigade general, the vice president of the Partido Popular (PP), and a recognized expert in the field of military law. A rumor circulating in 1945 that Véjar Vázquez was considering a run for the presidency, with the backing of the philosopher and 1929 presidential candidate José Vasconcelos as well as Efraín Brito Rosado, aroused skepticism by U.S. observers to whom "it hardly appears that his candidacy could really be taken seriously."[99] He was a professor of law at the Universidad Nacional Autónoma de México (UNAM), where he collaborated with such renowned scholars in the field of military jurisprudence as Roberto Calderón Serrano and Tomás López Linares. Along with López Linares, Véjar Vázquez published an annotated edition of the *Código de Justicia Militar*. Another of his publications in 1948 featured an introduction and a prologue written by, respectively, General Agustín Mercado Alarcón and Emilio Pardo

96. Memo, DGIPS, Aug. 17, 1948, AGN-DGIPS, Box 24.

97. *El Universal*, Jan. 30, 1952, AGN-DGIPS, Box 24, File 3, 2.1/061.8/3. Also, *La Prensa*, Jan. 12, 1952, AGN-DGIPS, Box 815, Campaña Presidencial, Jan. 1952.

98. Memo, IPS, Aug. 19, 1948, AGN-DGIPS, Box 24; *La Prensa*, Jan. 25, 1950, AGN-DGIPS, Box 803, Campaña Presidencial, Futurismo, 1950–1952, Vol. 1.

99. U.S. State Department, 812.00/7–1845, Memo, Thomasson to Secretary of State, Jul. 18, 1945, in *Confidential U.S. State Department Central Files, Mexico, 1945–1949, Part I*, Reel 1. Brito Rosado was an old school friend of Miguel Alemán, had been the secretary general of Almazán's PRUN in 1940, and was able to reconcile with the government well enough to be elected senator (PRI) from Yucatán in 1952. See Camp, *Mexican Political Biographies, 1935–1993*, 92.

Aspe, both of whom were sitting Supreme Court justices.[100] In short, few, if any, Mexican legal scholars could more ably interpret military law than Véjar Vázquez, who possessed far better qualifications to make such legal judgments than the political leaders within the PRI.

The root of Véjar Vázquez's ordeal was his intellectual honesty. In the heat of the presidential campaign and in a period when the civilian elite within the PRI attempted to paint Henríquez as a dangerous throwback to the military past, Véjar Vázquez argued simply that "soldiers are citizens and the only limitations they have on exercising their citizenship are those established by the Constitution."[101] By this interpretation, a soldier would only have to request licencia if he ran for office, not simply to participate in politics or support a candidate. Throughout the Véjar Vázquez controversy, the central questions remained: what were the proper political rights of soldiers, how were they allowed to exercise them, and what constraints (if any) were placed upon them?

Specifically, according to Véjar Vázquez, no law forbade wearing a military uniform at a political meeting. The only situation in which such a prohibition would exist, he argued, was in conjunction with "acts contrary to military honor." This proscription echoed the rules governing the colonial fuero militar. As a counterpoint, Véjar Vázquez reminded his critics that "forty uniformed *and armed* generals gathered in 1938 to form the Partido de la Revolución Mexicana . . . [and] in 1939 the 'Morelos' group of soldiers was formed to support the official candidate just as now the '20 de Noviembre' group has been formed for soldiers affiliated with the PRI."[102] Yet, "when General Véjar Vázquez accepted the presidency of Vicente Lombardo Toledano's Popular Party to fight the PRI, he was arrested and condemned by a military court for engaging in politics."[103] Véjar Vázquez faced a court martial

100. See Octavio Véjar Vázquez and Tomás López Linares, *Código de Justicia Militar: Anotado y concordado por los abogados Tomás López Linares y Octavio Véjar Vázquez* (Mexico City: Ediciones "Ateneo," 1948). Also, Octavio Véjar Vázquez, *Autonomía del derecho militar* (Mexico City: Editorial Stylo, 1948). Other publications by Véjar Vázquez establishing his standing in legal circles include: *Derecho procesal militar* (Mexico City: Ediciones Lex, 1947); *El ejército y sus tribunals,* 2 vols. (Mexico City: Ediciones Lex, 1944–46); and *Derecho penal militar* (Mexico City: Ediciones Minerva, 1944).

101. *El Popular,* Oct. 4, 1951, AGN-DGIPS, Box 24, File 3, 2.1/061.8/3.

102. "Acts contrary to military honor": *Zócalo,* Oct. 5, 1951; "forty uniformed *and armed* generals": *Zócalo,* Oct. 7, 1951, emphasis added (both located in AGN-DGIPS, Box 24, File 3, 2.1/061.8/3). For a listing of the military attendees at the 1940 PRM convention to select the party's presidential candidate, see AGN-DGIPS, Box 192, 2.1/311.1(72)/2.

103. Lieuwen, "Depoliticization of the Mexican Revolutionary Army," 61.

for "grave violations of the Law of Military Discipline," a law on which he was an acknowledged expert.[104]

But Véjar Vázquez went further when he attacked the PRI leadership directly, accusing it of hypocrisy in pursuing politically active military officers in the opposition. He stressed that "the PRI still has as President General Rodolfo Sánchez Taboada . . . and who has thought of indicting him?"[105] The contradiction between the tacit proscription of overt military participation in politics and the implicit approval of the presence of military officers in high positions within the PRI lacked resolution. A contemporaneous law thesis stated the apparently well-established premise that "not only is intervention in political acts against the government prohibited, but also acts *in favor* of it." The fact that revolutionary generals (Sánchez Taboada, Gabriel Leyva Velázquez, Agustín Olachea Avilés) held key PRI leadership positions only demonstrated that "men with military experience were still necessary for the exercise of power" while the party was in process of consolidation.[106] By the end of October 1951, the matter of military involvement in politics was settled. The Secretariat of National Defense granted licencia to Alamillo Flores and others to participate in politics and "liquidated" the legal case against Véjar Vázquez. But in April 1952, Véjar Vázquez remained active in his criticism of federal policy, as he faced charges of disobeying a superior order before a military tribunal.[107]

While the Véjar Vázquez case developed, another episode concerning the proper role of the military in politics was taking place. In a letter dated March 5, 1952, several high-ranking officers challenged Secretary of National Defense Limón to defend what they characterized as his "illegal and dangerous conduct" in regard to the political rights of soldiers. "The truth is that . . . soldiers are being made victims of a 'discrimination' that betrays a hostile and fickle [*tornadizo*] judgment when affiliates of the independent parties are involved, and a benevolent tolerance when sympathizers of the official candidacy are involved." The letter reported the denial of licencia to officers

104. *La Prensa,* Oct. 5, 1951, AGN-DGIPS, Box 24, File 3, 2.1/061.8/3.

105. *Zócalo,* Oct. 7, 1951, AGN-DGIPS, Box 24, File 3, 2.1/061.8/3.

106. "Intervention in political acts": Javier Bazán Pérez, "El ejército en la Constitución y en la política" (unpublished thesis, Facultad de Derecho y Ciencias Sociales, Universidad Nacional Autónoma de México, 1952), 49, emphasis added; "exercise of power": Sánchez Gutiérrez, "Los militares en la década de los cincuenta," 282.

107. "Liquidated" the legal case: *La Prensa,* Oct. 24, 1951, AGN-DGIPS, Box 24, File 3, 2.1/061.8/3; criticism of federal policy: *El Universal,* Apr. 8, 1952, AGN-DGIPS, Box 814, File 1, 2.1/52/374.

aligned with the opposition, the provision of licencia ilimitada when a request was for *licencia temporal* or when no licencia was requested at all, and transfers to undesirable commands or to the reserves, which precluded residence in Mexico City. It asserted the constitutional rights of soldiers as citizens: "we can vote and stand for election and meet to treat political matters of the country with no other limitation than to separate ourselves from active service for 90 or 180 days when we might be candidates in a popular election."[108] At this late date, the proper role of the military in Mexican political life was still very much an open question.

Limón responded to criticisms of his policies regarding military participation in politics by asserting that "all members of the Army are in equal conditions, in relation to the electoral campaign, whichever political party they are affiliated with." He added that all of them would have the opportunity to participate as long as they requested licencia, which the Secretariat of National Defense would grant as licencia ilimitada for everyone, regardless of political sympathies.[109] But Limón's assurances did not assuage the complaints of many senior officers in the opposition who continued to lambaste the policies that, they argued, militated against the political rights of soldiers as citizens.

Aid from the civilian political institutions was not forthcoming. In 1952, the Comisión Federal Electoral (CFE) voted four to one that it had no authority to intervene in the decisions of the Secretariat of National Defense regarding the political rights of soldiers.[110] The majority consisted of representatives of Gobernación (Ernesto Uruchurtu), the Senate (Gustavo Díaz Ordaz), the PRI (Adolfo López Mateos), and the PAN (Roberto Cossío y Cossío). The CFE member from the FPPM, Ezequiel Burguete, was the lone dissenting vote against the future secretary of Gobernación, the two future presidents, and the PAN member. Editorial opinion downplayed any lasting significance or shift of interpretation as a result of the disputes. One paper opined that the standoff centered on a simple principle: "to avoid members of the Army acting as such in political contests and using their military preeminence for or against any party."[111] This was the atmosphere that surrounded the presidential campaign of Henríquez in 1952.

108. *El Universal*, Mar. 20, 1952, AGN-DGIPS, Box 27, File 2, 2.1/061.8/15, Vol. 8, p. 89. The letter was signed by Division General Roberto Cruz; Brigade Generals Celestino Gasca, Luis Alamillo Flores, and Octavio Véjar Vázquez; Colonel Wenceslao Labra; and Lieutenant Colonel Miguel Bravo Carpintero.

109. *El Universal*, Apr. 17, 1952, AGN-DGIPS, Box 814, File 1, 2.1/52/374.

110. Ibid.

111. *Excélsior*, Nov. 12, 1951, AGN-DGIPS, Box 24, File 3, 2.1/061.8/3.

When Henríquez was passed over in 1950, a repetition of 1945, the roots of his disaffection with the increasingly dominant (and civilian) PRI began to strike deeper. He based his appeal to the military officer corps on lasting institutional and cultural ties: "It is precisely among the military element where the propaganda has taken special pains, invoking the argument that *militares* should be with *militares* and that Henríquez Guzmán comprises a hope for the Army, besides the fact that international events surrounding the war call for a *militar* in the Presidency."[112] This continuing political activity of army officers through the 1940s, including the Henríquez campaign of 1952, was the exception that proved the rule.[113]

In the election of 1952, the army continued to play a vital political role. The Dirección Federal de Seguridad (DFS) investigated the extent of military support for Henríquez's candidacy. The agency returned a report listing twenty pages, roughly three hundred names, of soldiers who were actively supporting the *henriquista* campaign, from division generals like Rios Zertuche down to First Sergeant Carlos Colín Portilla.[114] The PRI leadership was unwilling to grant any ground to the army in terms of political latitude. Rather, Sánchez Taboada warned the military to "follow the line of conduct signaled by the fulfillment of your duties." After the election of 1952, the new order that depended on the quiescence of the military in the civilian world of elections appeared consolidated. General Antonio Romero Romero, head of the Fifth Military Zone in Chihuahua, spoke for "the totality of the members of the Armed Forces [who] consider that the dark epoch of *asonadas* and *cuartelazos* has passed into history and who declare with pride that militarism and *caudillaje* have died forever."[115] The old habits of the revolutionary generation had been replaced by the close control of elections and candidates that would come to symbolize the dominance of the PRI.

The high-level defeat of the officers' political aspirations created a need for formalized participation in the newly consolidated system dominated by

112. *El Universal Gráfico,* Jun. 8, 1950, AGN-DGIPS, Box 803, Futurismo Político, Campaña Presidencial, 1952–1958, Vol. 2.

113. For a thorough treatment of Henríquez's presidential aspirations, see chapter 5. Also, Elisa Servín, *Ruptura y oposición: El movimiento henriquista, 1945–1954* (Mexico City: Cal y Arena, 2001).

114. Dirección Federal de Seguridad, *Henriquismo: 10. de octubre de 1950 a 30 de septiembre de 1951,* vol. 1, 288–308, Biblioteca Mexicana de la Fundación Miguel Alemán, Fondo Miguel Alemán Valdés, Dirección Federal de Seguridad.

115. "Fulfillment of your duties": *La Prensa,* Jun. 9, 1950, AGN-DGIPS, Box 803, Futurismo Político, Campaña Presidencial, 1952–1958, Vol. 2; "dark epoch": *Excélsior,* Oct. 23, 1952, AGN-DGIPS, Box 29, File 17, 2.1/061.8/15, Vol. 12, p. 246.

the PRI. After the election of 1952, Jacinto B. Treviño was instrumental in the formation of the PARM. Initially named "La Sociedad de Hombres de la Revolución," the group did not oppose the PRI but rather was "a forum in which veterans of the Revolution, who are no longer heeded by the government, would be able to express themselves and make themselves heard." The PARM could negotiate with the PRI, taking advantage of "the mechanism through which both military and non-military elements of the Revolutionary coalition could channel their political ambitions, secure access to government patronage, and be assured of a continuous voice at the highest policy-making levels."[116] Though never of great significance in electoral terms, the PARM served as a crucial venue for officers to indulge their political interests without actually operating within the larger national arena.

The military's loss of electoral opportunities and legitimacy after 1940 found a new balance with the position of prestige within the PRM and the PRI. Camp noted, "From December 1946 to December 1964, four generals, among Mexico's most important political-military officers, directed the government's party: Sánchez Taboada, Leyva Velázquez, Olachea Aviles, and Alfonso Corona del Rosal."[117] During the 1940s, the military lost positions in the cabinet and elected office and moved into "posts such as Secretary of National Defense, of the Navy, or in the headquarters of the police departments." The number of military officers serving as governors in the thirty-one states decreased from fifteen in 1948 to eight in 1953, six in 1959, three in 1965, and just one in 1972.[118] As chapter 4 will demonstrate, one of the main rewards the military received in exchange for its political withdrawal was a crucial extension of its role as national guardian: control of the intelligence services.

This trend, in combination with the economic dismemberment of Henríquez after the election of 1952, was an effective statement of the political discipline required of the military in the new PRI era. An important facet of this changing discipline was how and where soldiers in the opposition sought settlements with the government after their defeat. After the election of 1940,

116. "Heeded by the government": Sánchez Gutiérrez, "Los militares en la década de los cincuenta," 290–91; "elements of the Revolutionary coalition": Schloming, "Civil-Military Relations in Mexico," 244.

117. Camp, Generals in the Palacio, 79; see also Franklin D. Margiotta, Civilian Control of the Military: Patterns in Mexico, Special Studies 66 (Buffalo: Council on International Studies, State University of New York at Buffalo, 1975), 24–25.

118. "Posts such as Secretary of National Defense": Boils, Los militares y la política en México, 47; officers serving as governors: Margiotta, Civilian Control of the Military, 27.

the military supporters of Almazán filtered back into Mexico and went to Secretary of National Defense Jesus Agustín Castro to negotiate the terms of their reinstatement.[119] But by 1952 the dynamic had shifted and the henriquistas who sought a political settlement with the government went first, not to the secretary of national defense, but to President Ruiz Cortines himself. This change signaled the consolidated ascendance of the civilian elite over the military and the political life of the nation.

Those officers who participated within the party were selected to receive government contracts, party sinecures, and social prestige. Those who forced the issue of opposition and dissidence outside of party ranks faced severe economic and political reprisals. As one analysis concludes, "The Mexican pay-off matrix is designed for those who sit at the table." Another factor was perhaps more counterintuitive, given the history of the military in politics in other parts of Latin America. As Margiotta correctly observed, "One of the keys of nonintervention . . . was to keep the army involved in politics. Individual officers ran for political office, participated in party decisions, helped select candidates. Individual ambitions were channeled into formal institutions. The military elite was given a stake in the future of the government, which made them less likely to take matters into their own hands." By this logic, the Mexican military was kept out of politics by keeping officers in politics, and literally inside the dominant institution of the PRI. The increasing consolidation of electoral mechanisms under the PRM and the PRI was a factor in decreasing the influence of military officers in politics.[120] This discipline was at the root of PRI dominance from 1952 onward.

The period from 1938 to 1952 saw a substantial transformation of the political rules for the military in Mexico. The preferred modes of political maneuver became the formation of political parties, the acceptance of elections as a venue for political conflict, and the renunciation of violence as a means of obtaining influence. This change in the political affairs of the military manifested itself in the following ways. Key army officers and opponents of the PRM candidate in 1940 formed political parties and took the idea

119. *La Prensa,* Oct. 17, 1940, AGN-DGIPS, Box 115, 2.1/263.6(72)/3.

120. "Pay-off matrix": Irving Louis Horowitz, "Militarism and Civil-Military Relationships in Latin America: Implications for the Third World," in *Research in Political Sociology,* vol.1, ed. Richard G. Braungart and Margaret M. Braungart (Greenwich, CT: JAI Press, 1985), 86; "keys of nonintervention": Margiotta, "Civilian Control and the Mexican Military," 246–47; increasing consolidation of electoral mechanisms: Peter H. Smith, *Labyrinths of Power: Political Recruitment in Twentieth-Century Mexico* (Princeton: Princeton University Press, 1979), 95.

of participating in elections very seriously. They developed positions that championed the necessity of strong democratic and electoral forms in Mexico, argued against the "impositionist" tendencies of the PRM, and attempted to form electoral coalitions. However, the transformation was yet incomplete, as all sides were implicated in fomenting violence and threatening "revolution" during the campaign and its aftermath. The fact that no such rebellion occurred, as it had so recently in 1938 with Cedillo, was the crucial step forward. As Maniruzzaman argued, the campaign of 1940 responded to Cárdenas's challenge to "the politically minded and ambitious officers to come out of the barracks and to fight him on the ground of his own choosing—with political assembly . . . [and] to engage in combat on the political and electoral level."[121]

The second stage of this process was the gradual recognition of the new political rules by military officers through the 1940s and into the 1950s. As Smith put it, "by the 1940s, Mexico was on the road to creating its *rara avis*: an authoritarian regime thoroughly dominated, at its upper levels, by people of civilian background." Camp argued that "physically removing the military from political office is a first step, however small, in conveying to the population, the political leadership, and the officer corps itself, that the political arena is the purview of civilians, not military men."[122] The election of 1946 pitted the civilian candidate of the dominant PRM, Miguel Alemán, against the civilian opposition candidate, Ezequiel Padilla. This election, along with the reformation of the PRM into the PRI via heavy organizational maneuvers, spurred a crucial shift toward the civilianization of politics in Mexico, as discussed in chapter 3. The secret political meetings of high-ranking revolutionary generals in 1948 provoked the fear in the PRI bureaucracy that the army had not fully appreciated its removal from electoral politics. Serious intelligence efforts ascertained the nature, goals, and leadership of this group, as agents worked to undermine it. Véjar Vázquez, vociferously opposed the denial of political rights to soldiers, arguing that the removal of the military from sectoral politics within the PRI was an abrogation of their citizenship.

121. Maniruzzaman, *Military Withdrawal from Politics*, 97. Maniruzzaman rather naively argues further that Ávila Camacho considered his electoral victory a "popular mandate for civilian control of the military," a reading of events that may fit neatly with his thesis but not with the historical record. If anything, Ávila Camacho's election demonstrated the increasing ability of the PRM to control elections, the failings of the conservative candidacies of Almazán and Amaro, and the continuing political ambition within the military.

122. "Creating its *rara avis*": Smith, *Labyrinths of Power*, 95; "purview of civilians": Camp, *Generals in the Palacio*, 16.

His efforts in the late 1940s met with swift reproach and legal action by the government as it moved to silence dissent, especially within the ranks of the army. All of these incidents pointed toward the enforcement of a new discipline within the political (and military) elite: elections were a civilian matter, and the military was subordinate to the power of civilian government. From this viewpoint, Henríquez's opposition campaign in 1952 seemed a quixotic effort to restore the luster of military credentials on a political resumé, as well as to return Mexico to the heyday of the left-leaning, even "revolutionary," policies of the Cárdenas administration. In all, the attempts by military officers throughout the 1940s and into the 1950s to return the army to its former political stature were for naught. The civilian PRI had consolidated too much power, the revolution and its glamour were too far gone, and the needs of Mexico in the modernizing postwar era were far too great.

THREE

CIVILIAN ASCENDANCY
The Election of 1946

THE ELECTION OF 1946 took place at a crucial point in Mexican history. World War II had just ended, the reconstruction of Europe was commencing, and the invention of a new international system was under way. Through the presidency of Manuel Ávila Camacho, Mexico had moved away from the left-leaning policies of the 1930s toward a more balanced, even conservative, approach to social policy, economic planning, and international relations. Mexico had also provided much crucial manpower and raw material to the United States to aid the war effort, and the continuing presence of Mexican workers in the United States projected the old informal cross-border social, economic, and cultural exchanges well into the future. Moreover, although the Axis no longer threatened the country, quasi-fascist domestic movements such as the Unión Nacional Sinarquista (UNS) raised the stakes for the succession in 1946.

The political dynamics of Mexico had changed by 1946 as well. On January 9, 1946, the new Partido Revolucionario Institucional (PRI) was unveiled: a refurbished structure for the old political deals and rivalries consolidated through the postrevolutionary period. Just as it was for the Partido Nacional Revolucionario (PNR) and the Partido de la Revolución Mexicana (PRM), the key function of the PRI was the containment of political conflict. This mechanism, operating crucially through a freshly instilled discipline, allowed the PRI to present a unified front to the nation while brokering the political battles of the elite behind closed doors. However, the rebirth of the dominant political party did not signal the end of opposition political movements. Just as the election of 1940 had produced a spectrum of opponents offering different visions of the future, the election of 1946 demonstrated the breadth of political currents in Mexico.

This chapter will discuss the election of 1946 as a case study of the deeply changed political environment since 1940. Although the political spectrum in Mexico had remained wide, the viable paths to national political power narrowed. The election of 1946 was the first to pit only civilian candidates against each other, signaling a key shift in the dynamics of electoral contests. The military lost standing in the public imagination during the election, as well as its role within the dominant party. Since 1940, no military officer has run for president as a candidate of the PRI. Finally, the career of Alemán demonstrated the potential of civilian politicians, as he rose from governor of Veracruz to Ávila Camacho's campaign manager and secretary of Gobernación and then to president of Mexico. Beginning in the election of 1946, Gobernación became the most prized portfolio for those with presidential aspirations, and it would produce four of the next five presidents.

Gobernación was responsible for the negotiation of political matters as well as domestic security. Therefore, since 1918, the main Mexican intelligence bureaucracy operated within Gobernación and under its control. Through the early years, federal agents kept surveillance of political allies and enemies, performed investigative tasks of a general nature, and maintained information regarding foreigners in Mexico. After the shock of the Zimmermann telegram in 1917, U.S. authorities developed suspicions about the competence and cooperation of the Mexican intelligence bureaucracy. Although intensive U.S.-Mexico exchanges of training, funds, and information did not begin until the 1940s, the early period offered time to both countries to develop terms of engagement that would mollify concerns on both sides.[1]

During the 1930s and into the 1940s, the presence of foreign agents in Mexico began to alarm both the Mexican government and U.S. officials. British and German economic influence declined after World War I and U.S. influence grew, but some elements of Mexican society recoiled from the prospect of greater domination by their northern neighbor. Additionally, as the Spanish Civil War ended and World War II loomed, the activities of

---

1. See chapter 4 for a more detailed discussion of the early development of the Mexican intelligence services and the role of the United States in training and funding them, especially during and after World War II.

European and Asian networks in Mexico became a crucial concern of Mexican and U.S. authorities.

Mexican intelligence maintained close surveillance of suspected spies and other infiltrators among the German, Italian, and Japanese populations in Mexico before World War II and increased it during the war. Federal authorities received dozens of cases from local police forces, border agents, and the Mexico City Police.[2] U.S. military intelligence clearly indicated that "the Ávila Camacho regime is definitely anti-communist as well as anti-Axis." Moreover, the U.S. Military Intelligence Division (MID) concluded that "chaos and revolution, intermingled with fifth column leadership, will result unless Camacho receives backing from the United States."[3]

Several factors converged to raise this anxiety about Mexican security and the possibilities of an Axis threat from the south. During the war, Mexican authorities were vigilant in the surveillance and control of foreigners in the country. They initially focused on refugees from Spain after the civil war and their alleged communist activities. After the United States entered World War II in 1941, however, tracking the activities of German, Italian, and Japanese citizens in Mexico became a high priority.[4] In early 1941, reports demonstrated that "Japan is purchasing practically the entire output of mercury in Mexico and is paying approximately $20.00 above the market price for it." U.S. observers also analyzed the possibilities of fifth-column activity in Mexico, especially when they detected shipments of arms and ammunition crossing the U.S. border into Mexico bound for the Soconusco and Chiapas coffee regions, sites with large German populations. Finally, FBI analysts concluded that "prior to Mexico's declaration of war on the Axis on May 28, 1942, the network of German espionage in that country worked almost without opposition."[5] From the viewpoint of the United States, the threat of Axis activity in Mexico was all too real.

2. For examples of the surveillance of German and Japanese citizens, see Archivo General de la Nación, Mexico City, Dirección General de Investigaciones Políticas y Sociales (AGN-DGIPS), Box 123, 2.1/265.5/12—2.1/265.5/17, and Box 124, 2.1/265.5/18—2.1/265.5/24.

3. "Definitely anti-communist": Military Attaché Report 948, New York Office, Military Intelligence Division (MID), War Department General Staff, Apr. 29, 1941; "chaos and revolution": Memo, Headquarters Eighth Corps Area to Asst. Chief of Staff, G-2, War Department, May 15, 1941, Ft. Sam Houston (both located in National Archives and Records Administration, Washington, D.C. [NARA], Record Group 165, Box 2465).

4. Refugees from Spain: AGN-DGIPS, Box 315; German, Italian, and Japanese citizens in Mexico: for example, see AGN-DGIPS, Boxes 315–39, 738–49.

5. "Entire output of mercury": Military Attaché Report 849, New York Office, MID, War Department General Staff, Apr. 9, 1941, NARA, Record Group 165, Box 2465; detected shipments of arms: Report, "Possible Smuggling of Arms and Ammunition into Mexico," MID, Oct. 30, 1941, NARA, Record Group 165, Box 2462 (see note 24 below); "network of German

Gobernación was the center of domestic security efforts in Mexico and housed the main secret police bureaucracy, the Dirección General de Investigaciones Políticas y Sociales (DGIPS). As such, the DGIPS presented both a promising opportunity for U.S. officials hungry for surveillance and a potential breeding ground for foreign spies. U.S. officials learned with alarm that Alfonso González García, a high-level officer in the DGIPS, offered to "sell any record or arrange for citizenship papers and permanent resident cards for any foreigner for financial consideration." Three Mexican immigration agents, also bureaucratic subjects of Gobernación, reportedly met with George Nicolaus, the head of German intelligence operations in Mexico, in Guadalajara in May 1941. In October 1941, the U.S. naval attaché warned about a more specific threat of Axis sympathies within Gobernación. As an example, an FBI agent reported to Gobernación that German agents were operating a clandestine radio station in the state of Veracruz, but the site disappeared before an arrest could be made, suggesting that elements within Gobernación tipped off the German agents.[6] Alemán, as secretary of Gobernación, received severe criticism in 1943 from FBI chief J. Edgar Hoover, who wondered why he was unwilling to deal with the German threat and whether Alemán could even achieve that goal without losing control of his department.[7] Another analyst offered that Alemán "is responsible for what Gobernación has done to control the activities of Axis agents, but is thought to participate in and condone graft practices in connection with the arrests and subsequent release of enemy suspects."[8] The apparent equivocation of Alemán in the fight against Axis influence in Mexico gave U.S. observers pause and provided grist for those who believed he secretly aided the Nazi cause.[9]

---

espionage": Report, "German Espionage in Latin America," [Jan. 1946], 22, NARA, Record Group 226, Federal Bureau of Investigation (FBI), Special Services Unit (SSU), Box 3.

6. "Arrange for citizenship papers": Extract, "Mexico," [Oct. 1941] (citing FBI, Oct. 22, 1941; MID 201 Waring, E. N., Oct. 22, 1941); three Mexican immigration agents: Summary, "Miguel Alemán, Secretary of Gobernación," MID, Mar. 21, 1942 (citing U.S. Embassy Report 1288, May 27, 1941; Military Attaché Report 9856, May 26, 1941, Mexico City); clandestine radio station: Report, Naval Attaché, 545–41-R, Oct. 31, 1941, Mexico City (all located in NARA, Record Group 165, Box 2465).

7. Leslie B. Rout Jr. and John F. Bratzel, *The Shadow War: German Espionage and United States Counterespionage in Latin America During World War II* (Frederick, Md.: University Publications of America, 1986), 89.

8. Military Attaché Report 2761, Nov. 27, 1943, Mexico City, NARA, Record Group 165, Box 2465.

9. Alemán's alleged connections with the German network are discussed in more detail in the following pages.

Gobernación was not the only cause for concern. U.S. military intelligence officials reported in August 1943 that Ávila Camacho was apparently nurturing a close relationship with Axel Wenner-Gren, a Swedish financier who maintained a well-known friendship with Hermann Göring. The report indicated that at a weekly breakfast meeting with Ávila Camacho, Wenner-Gren "makes reports of his observations in Mexico and suggests courses of action indicated thereby" and that he "acted as godfather at the wedding of Maximino Ávila-Camacho's daughter." Wenner-Gren's close relationship with the Ávila Camacho brothers allowed him to emerge from wartime suspicions and actually begin manufacturing matériel to be sold to the U.S. Army.[10]

Up to 1943, German agents in Mexico were regular visitors to DGIPS offices in Gobernación; they "would come to [the chief's] office to discuss their problems with arrogant airs." After the Axis defeat at Tunis in May 1943, however, DGIPS chief José Lelo de Larrea noticed a change of attitude and predicted that many would then join anti-Nazi groups "to be in a more favored position after the defeat of Germany." Indeed, after Mexican intelligence uncovered Nicolaus and his colleagues and scotched the Nazi intelligence efforts in Mexico, the onus of Axis secret operations shifted. In the end, although "the Mexican Government believes that the German organization has been broken up . . . it is still essential to watch the Germans in case they attempt action during the later stages of the war."[11] The Mexican intelligence services maintained surveillance of the activities of German, Italian, and Japanese citizens in the country through the end of the war, at the same time that a new and in some ways more dangerous trend developed.[12]

After the Spanish Civil War ended in 1939, the Spanish Falange ramped up operations in Mexico to maintain surveillance of Spanish citizens abroad and expand its intelligence network overseas. Although Mexico outlawed the Falange in April 1939, U.S. observers were troubled by the fact that it had "succeeded in gaining direction of nearly all the Spanish casinos, clubs, commercial houses, and even the Spanish benevolent organizations." Through a

10. Report, MID, Headquarters Eighth Service Command, Aug. 12, 1943, Dallas, NARA, Record Group 165, Box 2465. After the war, Wenner-Gren played a major role in the creation of the telephone monopoly centered on Teléfonos de México.

11. Report, Gibson to Secretary of State, Jun. 16, 1943, Mexico City, NARA, Record Group 165, Box 2465.

12. For surveillance of and dossiers on German, Italian, and Japanese nationals in Mexico, see AGN-DGIPS, Boxes 113–15, 121–28, 311–39, 738–49, 2014.

system that blended intimidation, financial incentive, and nationalist appeal, the Falange attempted at an early stage to blend itself into the communities of Spanish refugees. For example, "all refugees in Mexico are kept under surveillance by the Falange and those in need are approached by Falange members who offer them financial and other help." By 1943, Lelo de Larrea informed the U.S. Embassy that the Falange was active in Mexico, "but only to a limited extent," and that the DGIPS had one known agent who came in among the refugees under surveillance. However, he could not rule out the possibility that more Spanish agents were operating under cover of the refugee communities. The FBI produced a lengthy report in December 1943 outlining Falange activities throughout the hemisphere and detailing its development in each individual country. The MID kept close watch on the activities of the Falange as well.[13]

In May 1940, J. Edgar Hoover strenuously denied reports that he "believed that the Axis was working to create an army of Fascist Spaniards in Mexico."[14] Hoover's FBI disagreed with the conventional wisdom, arguing that "no proof exists thus far as to the presence of Falange agents in Mexico who might possibly be paid either by the Spanish or German government for carrying on activities detrimental to the Allied cause." But by 1942, U.S. and British military intelligence agents were certain that Spanish Falangists were conducting espionage operations on behalf of the Axis powers and transmitting their reports through the Spanish legation in Guatemala. Moreover, "Argentine, Vichy-French, Portuguese and Swedish diplomats and attachés in Mexico are believed, with a fair degree of certainty, to use their codes and pouches in transmitting Axis information." U.S. authorities outside of the FBI knew very well that the Spanish Servicio de Inteligencia Militar (SIM) was taking over Nazi intelligence operations as the Mexican government dismantled the German network; one report stated, "The conclusion that the

13. "Spanish benevolent organizations": Report, "The Falange in the Other American Republics," Coordinator for Inter-American Affairs, Feb. 21, 1942, 2–3, NARA, Record Group 59, Entry 451b, Box 15; "surveillance by the Falange": ibid., 5; "only to a limited extent": Report, Gibson to Secretary of State, Jun. 16, 1943, Mexico City, NARA, Record Group 165, Box 2465; FBI produced a lengthy report: Report, "The Spanish Falange in the Western Hemisphere," FBI, Dec. 1943, NARA, Record Group 59, Entry 451b, Box 15; MID kept close watch: for example, see Military Attaché Report 2573, "Current Estimate of Falange Activities," Oct. 14, 1943, Mexico City, NARA, Record Group 165, Entry 188, Box 1002.

14. Francis MacDonnell, "The Search for a Second Zimmermann Telegram: FDR, BSC, and the Latin American Front," *International Journal of Intelligence and Counterintelligence* 4, no. 4 (1990): 494.

Falange in Mexico is primarily a German instrument for warfare against the United States is *inescapable.*"[15]

The threat from abroad dangerously dovetailed with a domestic movement: the Sinarquistas. A group founded on the ideals of the Christian betterment of its members and fervent nationalism, the UNS faced criticism as a quasi-fascist organization.[16] In December 1941, the U.S. Office of Strategic Services (OSS) believed that the Partido Acción Nacional (PAN) and the UNS were "the two most active and virile pro-Axis instruments . . . and directly or indirectly reflect the attitudes and interests of the Spanish Falange."[17] In 1943, Hoover wondered to what extent the PAN was "controlled, infiltrated, or financed by the Axis" and directed the civil attaché at the U.S. Embassy in Mexico City to report all relevant information to the. FBI as it was received.[18] Another OSS assessment argued that "the Sinarquista movement . . . represents the most immediate danger to United States interests."[19] Fears in the United States over the threat of fascist subversion in Mexico quickened U.S. pressure on the Ávila Camacho administration to deal effectively with the situation. Although no formal ties between the UNS and international fascism movements were discovered, the threat of a domestic movement sympathetic to fascist goals was unacceptable, especially during wartime. The DGIPS maintained careful surveillance of the UNS, not least out of domestic security concerns, but the movement enjoyed freedom to pursue its political goals.[20] The United States considered Mexican refusals to deal openly with the perceived threat of the UNS to be "exceedingly dangerous."[21]

15. "No proof exists thus far": Report, "The Spanish Falange in the Western Hemisphere," FBI, Dec. 1943, 114, NARA, Record Group 59, Entry 451b, Box 15; "codes and pouches": Summary, "Axis Transmission of Information and Censorship—Mexico," MID, War Department, May 29, 1942, NARA, Record Group 165, Box 2453; "German instrument for warfare": Report, "The Falange in the Other American Republics," Coordinator for Inter-American Affairs, Feb. 21, 1942, 6–7, 21–22, NARA, Record Group 59, Entry 451b, Box 15, emphasis added.

16. The UNS is also treated in chapters 1 and 4.

17. Memo, Vincenzo Petrullo to William J. Donovan, Dec. 22, 1941, NARA, Record Group 226, Entry 175, WASH-RA-INT-6, Box 1.

18. Memo, Hoover to [Civil Attaché, U.S. Embassy], Dec. 4, 1943, FBI Investigative File 64–22553–8, Partido Acción Nacional.

19. Memo, internal briefing to William J. Donovan, Dec. 30, 1941, NARA, Record Group 226, Entry 175, WASH-RA-INT-6, Box 1.

20. For example, see AGN-DGIPS, Boxes 770–75, for state-by-state coverage of UNS activities during 1943.

21. Memo, internal briefing to William J. Donovan, Dec. 30, 1941, NARA, Record Group 226, Entry 175, WASH-RA-INT-6, Box 1.

After the election of 1940, the UNS gained authority to develop its plans for a colony on the Baja California peninsula. UNS founder Salvador Abascal resigned his leadership of the national organization to pursue the project, conceived as a sort of Garden of Eden and demonstration of UNS principles all in one.[22] However, after Mexican authorities spotted and interdicted Japanese fishing vessels off the Baja California coast, speculation was rife that the boats were mapping the coast for possible docking locations and invasion routes. Thus, the development of the UNS colony sparked concern among U.S. observers who assumed that it was intended "to assist either clandestine Japanese bases which may already be established, or which the Japanese expect to establish in Lower California." Regardless, the report continued, "[the fact] that the Axis has a direct interest in the plan is undeniable."[23] In the end, the Sinarquista Garden of Eden, or Sinarcopolis, in Baja California failed to do anything but raise the suspicions of Mexican and U.S. authorities.[24]

Official distrust of the UNS project and the organization generally was not unfounded. Mexican agents uncovered a Sinarquista ring that successfully smuggled three million rounds of 38mm and 45mm ammunition and six hundred submachine guns across the border in the Nogales region in the month of August 1941 alone. A "special license" from the Secretariat of National Defense allegedly expedited the weaponry, although federal agents could not determine whether the license was authentic or falsified. The Sinarquistas stored the materiél in locations known to be controlled by Japanese spies in Soconusco. Moreover, one report detailed a list of members of other groups associated with the Sinarquista movement, including Manuel Gómez Morín of the PAN; Anicleto López of the Camisas Doradas; Augusto Ibañez Serrano, Franco's representative in Mexico; and elements of the German intelligence network, principally its chief, Nicolaus.[25] Habitually dismissive U.S. officials believed that such operations signaled a clear link between the UNS and outside aid since "no Mexicans alone are capable of managing such an organization without close supervision of foreign experts."[26]

22. Leonor Ludlow Wiechers, "La secularización e integración del sinarquismo a la vida política," *Revista Mexicana de Sociología* 50, no. 3 (Jul.–Sep. 1988): 206–207.

23. Memo, internal briefing to Donovan, Dec. 30, 1941, [Mexico City], NARA, Record Group 226, Entry 175, Box 1.

24. Pablo Serrano Álvarez, "El proyecto sinarquista de la colonización de Baja California (1941–1943)," *Revista de Indias* 54, no. 201 (1994): 439–58.

25. Memo, DGIPS, Aug. 21, 1941, AGN-DGIPS, Box 29, File 8, 2.1/061.9(72)/2, p. 2–3.

26. Memo, internal briefing to William J. Donovan, Dec. 30, 1941, NARA, Record Group 226, Entry 175, WASH-RA-INT-6, Box 1.

Despite the destruction of the German network in Mexico, the UNS appeared no less dangerous. The U.S. Embassy reported that the Sinarquistas were "believed to be working indirectly with the Nazi organization in Mexico" even after the crackdown against German agents.[27] Some reports specified government agencies shot through with Sinarquistas and other *quintacolumnistas,* one example being the accounting division of the Ferrocarril Interoceánico.[28] A U.S. State Department report declared that UNS members were, among other things, "violently pro-Axis, pro-Franco and anti-American."[29] Ambassador George Messersmith summarized the U.S. case in 1945 by arguing that "the danger in the Sinarquist movement lies in the fact that its membership is overwhelmingly made up of ignorant peasants who could easily be inflamed and of a very small group of fanatical and ill-balanced leaders who this Embassy does not believe can be trusted."[30] The old fears of revolution and anti-U.S. sentiment were joined in Messersmith's mind.

The conduct of World War II and the tensions associated with Axis activities in Mexico during the Ávila Camacho administration colored the political dynamics surrounding the election of 1946. Mexican voters took a clear interest in international events, if not in great detail then at least in the nationalistic support and pride deriving from Squadron 201, the Mexican air force group that fought in the Philippines with the Allies. Pressure from Washington on Mexican authorities to combat the Axis threat at home raised old debates about U.S. intentions and provoked a reaction against anyone who seemed to hew the U.S. line too closely.[31]

Miguel Henríquez Guzmán attempted to gain the PRM nomination by both trumpeting his revolutionary credentials and distancing himself from the

27. Memo, "Dangers Arising from Certain Domestic Groups in the other American Republics," ARA, Jan. 26, 1943, in volume titled *Reports Prepared by the Special Section of the Division of American Republics, Department of State, Vol. I, February 1942–February 1943,* 74, NARA, Record Group 59, Entry 451B, Box 13.

28. Letter, M. Gómez G. to Miguel Alemán (Gobernación), Jun. 10, 1942, AGN-DGIPS, Box 29, File 8, 2.1/061.9(72)/2.

29. Memo, "Dangers Arising from Certain Domestic Groups in the other American Republics," ARA, Jan. 26, 1943, in volume titled *Reports Prepared by the Special Section of the Division of American Republics, Department of State, Vol. I, February 1942–February 1943,* 73, NARA, Record Group 59, Entry 451B, Box 13.

30. Memo, 812.00/12–2045, U.S. Ambassador to Secretary of State, Dec. 20, 1945, Mexico City, in *Confidential U.S. State Department Central Files. Mexico: Internal Affairs, 1945–1949. Part I: Political, Governmental, and National Affairs* (Frederick, Md.: University Publications of America, 1987), Reel 3.

31. See Halbert Jones III, " 'The War Has Brought Peace to Mexico': The Political Impact of Mexican Participation in World War II" (PhD diss., Harvard University, 2006).

radicalism of the UNS.[32] Early supporters of Henríquez started to organize on his behalf, and as early as August 1944 a pro-Henríquez group had been formed in Chiapas. By February of the next year, university students in Morelia had created a similar organization to support Henríquez. Guadalajara, where he spent time as a young man and in military service, was the site of "intense activity" in favor of his potential candidacy. Henríquez also counted on support from military groups in Veracruz, including some of the top leadership. Other contenders for military support included former president Abelardo Rodríguez, who, in 1944, reportedly had a following among non-*cardenista* soldiers and had encouraged some of his colleagues to test the waters for a potential presidential bid.[33] Jesus Agustín Castro, the former secretary of national defense (1939–40), also competed for the support of the military in his own presidential bid.[34] However, Rodriguez and Castro were even less successful than Henríquez in their electoral ambitions.

At least as important as the support of the military, which still maintained a high level of political influence in 1946, was the position taken by former president Lázaro Cárdenas. During the Ávila Camacho administration, Cárdenas continued to play a major role in national politics. By serving as secretary of national defense during World War II, he managed to keep himself in the thick of international negotiations and project his domestic political influence. The U.S. Embassy believed that Cárdenas aimed to make Henríquez his preferred candidate for president in 1946. And while the U.S. State Department understood that Cárdenas's position did not provide enough power to impose his selection on the party, it was also clear that it allowed him sufficient leverage to block unwanted candidates.[35] Nefarious rumors abounded surrounding Cárdenas's support of Henríquez. One DGIPS agent

32. See chapter 5 for biographical information on Henríquez.

33. Pro-Henríquez group: Report, Insp. Alemán Pérez to DGIPS, Aug. 25, 1944, Tuxtla Gutiérrez; university students in Morelia: Telegram, Insp. 34 to DGIPS, Feb. 12, 1945, Morelia; "intense activity": Report, Insp. 21 to DGIPS, May 23, 1945, Guadalajara (all located in AGN-DGIPS, Box 2039, 2.1/A.G.D./818, Candidatura del General Miguel Henríquez Guzmán, 1944–1946); support from military groups in Veracruz: Report, Insp. Migoni to DGIPS, Oct. 7, 1945, Veracruz, AGN-DGIPS, Box 787, 2.1/45/282; following among non-*cardenista* soldiers: Telegram, Insp. Cervantes to DGIPS, Dec. 20, 1944, Tijuana, AGN-DGIPS, Box 2034, 2.1/A.G.D./818, Vol. 1.

34. Roderic Ai Camp, *Mexican Political Biographies, 1935–1993,* 3rd ed. (Austin: University of Texas Press, 1995), 142.

35. Preferred candidate for president: Memo, 812.00/2–1945, Messersmith to Grew (acting secretary of state), Feb. 19, 1945, Mexico City; block unwanted candidates: Internal memo, 812.00/6–1445, Carrigan (ARA), Jun. 16, 1945, Mexico City (both located in *Confidential U.S. State Department Central Files, Mexico, 1945–1949, Part I,* Reel 1).

reckoned Henríquez as a sort of stalking horse for Cárdenas in 1945. By this logic, once Henríquez announced his candidacy, the public would recognize the weakness of his campaign and open the door for Cárdenas to return to the presidency.[36] The U.S. Embassy echoed this sentiment two months later, forwarding reports that Henríquez was simply providing cover for a Cárdenas power play.[37] Other rumors in July 1945 indicated that Cárdenas intended to leave his post as the secretary of national defense to engage in political efforts around the presidential elections, and his sympathies were widely believed to lay with Henríquez.[38] Throughout, as would again be the case in 1952, Cárdenas refused to make any definitive statements to resolve the matter and Henríquez settled for playing up the possibilities of the situation.

Supporters of Henríquez physically agitated against the candidacies of both Padilla and Alemán in Veracruz in June 1945. Only two months later, however, local *padillistas* began to discuss the proposed consolidation of the Henríquez and Padilla efforts. This project was a dead letter soon after, as the DGIPS agent on the case concluded oddly that the two candidates were only "platonic" friends and that, in fact, *henriquistas* were defecting to the cause of Alemán instead of Padilla. But by October 1945, padillistas and henriquistas in Veracruz had begun advertising their intent to "begin a powerful offensive," though the possibilities for real trouble were scarce since "in reality, they only have a few followers." By August 1945, the DGIPS counted Henríquez out and agents began to focus their energies on the Padilla and Alemán campaigns.[39]

When the presidential campaigns began in early 1945, Padilla enjoyed an advantageous position. His duties as secretary of foreign relations, including the preparations for the Chapultepec Conference, offered an international stage for his intellectual and political skills. As a civilian, he presented a capable alternative to the tradition of soldiers in the presidency. In fact, one Mexican intelligence agent conceded in January 1945 that "Padilla is presently one

36. Report, Insp. Pérez Aldama to DGIPS, Jan. 22, 1945, Sonora, AGN-DGIPS, Box 787, 2.1/45/285.

37. Memo, 812.00/3–1645, Guy W. Ray to Secretary of State, Mar. 16, 1945, Mexico City, in *Confidential U.S. State Department Central Files, Mexico, 1945–1949, Part I*, Reel 1.

38. Report, Insp. 87 to DGIPS, Jul. 25, 1945, AGN-DGIPS, Box 2039, 2.1/A.G.D./818, Candidatura del General Miguel Henríquez Guzmán, 1944–1946.

39. Physically agitated: Report, Insp. Migoni to DGIPS, Jun. 25, 1945, Veracruz; discuss the proposed consolidation: Report, Insp. Migoni to DGIPS, Aug. 29, 1945, Veracruz; "platonic" friends: Report, Insp. Migoni to DGIPS, Sep. 1, 1945, Veracruz; "powerful offensive" and "few followers": Report, Insp. Migoni to DGIPS, Oct. 7, 1945, Veracruz (all located in AGN-DGIPS, Box 787, 2.1/45/282); counted Henríquez out: Report, Insp. 13 to DGIPS, Aug. 11, 1945, AGN-DGIPS, Box 750, File 3, 2.1/A.G.D./818, Vol. 1.

of the most viable people for the presidency . . . His international relations are firm and his position within the current government favors him notably over any other candidate."[40] When he was not chosen as the PRM candidate, he struck out on an opposition campaign backed by the newly formed Partido Democrático Mexicano (PDM).

Padilla was born December 31, 1889, in Coyuca de Catalán, Guerrero. Since Padilla's family had little wealth, it was his mind that allowed him to advance in life. He attended the Instituto Científico y Literario in Chilpancingo on scholarship until its closure in 1908, and then moved on to the Escuela Nacional de Jurisprudencia in Mexico City. He sided with Pancho Villa against Venustiano Carranza and was eventually jailed and exiled to Cuba and the United States.[41] On scholarship, Padilla attended the Sorbonne and Columbia University and thus spoke French and English fluently. Owing to his university studies, Padilla was considered "an authority on international law."[42] By 1925, he had risen to become the president of the Congress, representing Guerrero as a federal deputy. In 1928, he served as secretary of education and senator from Guerrero. Through his early political career, he received honorary doctorates from Columbia University, the University of Southern California, and the University of California at Berkeley, as well as universities in Guatemala, Havana, and Rio de Janeiro. But it was his deep involvement in the conferences of the Allied nations in Mexico City and San Francisco that earned him the highest stature on the world stage.[43] U.S. military intelligence analysts during World War II called him "one of the most far-sighted statesmen in Latin America."[44]

Beginning February 21, 1945, in Mexico City, the Inter-American Conference on Problems of War and Peace was meant "to study together the manner in which the countries of this Hemisphere can intensify their collaboration in the war effort and continue it, once peace is attained, for the benefit, not only of continental unity, but also of the preservation of peace

40. Report, Insp. 12 to DGIPS, Jan. 13, 1945, AGN-DGIPS, Box 750, File 3, 2.1/A.G.D./818, Vol. 1.

41. Salvador Mendoza, *Ezequiel Padilla: Breve apunte biográfico* (Mexico City: 1945), AGN-DGIPS, Box 750, File 3, 2.1/A.G.D./818, Vol. 1.

42. On scholarship: Military Attaché Report 2147, Jul. 2, 1943, Mexico City; "authority on international law": Extract, "Ezequiel Padilla, Secretary of Foreign Relations," MID, Dec. 16, 1941 (both located in NARA, Record Group 165, Box 2465).

43. Mendoza, *Ezequiel Padilla,* AGN-DGIPS, Box 750, File 3, 2.1/A.G.D./818, Vol. 1.

44. Military Attaché Report 2147, Jul. 2, 1943, Mexico City, NARA, Record Group 165, Box 2465.

in the world."[45] The Rio Treaty of 1947, which organized hemispheric collective security, found its "specific genesis" in the negotiations at Chapultepec.[46] U.S. secretary of state Edward Stettinius declared that Chapultepec marked a "historic turning point in the development of Inter-American cooperation for peace and security from aggression, and for the advancement of standards of living for all the American peoples." U.S. observers reported that Padilla's "brilliance" at the Chapultepec Conference had enhanced his possibilities for a strong presidential bid.[47] In fact, Padilla soared politically after Chapultepec and utilized his proximity to world leaders to demonstrate his ability to act presidential. Padilla waited until after Ávila Camacho's presidential address in September 1945 to officially launch his campaign since the speech was likely to touch on his efforts in representing Mexico at the San Francisco conference.[48]

Padilla's support derived from his personal achievements as well as his professional accomplishments. His biographer in 1945 wrote that "Padilla was not one of the countless examples of our heroic and improvised warriors of the Revolution. . . . [He] has gone to the masses, whose affliction he has felt in direct contact with them."[49] In the rhetoric of the time, Padilla could be understood as being *of* the revolution, as seen in his common touch, without having fought *in* the revolution. His humble beginnings sparked interest among the poor and rural citizens of Mexico, just as his international stature and lofty education gained adherents from the political elite.

As was common practice, Padilla counted on the efforts of political allies to gauge public interest before officially entering the campaign. To this end, Jorge Prieto Laurens, who had managed to stay in politics despite supporting the failed rebellions of de la Huerta in 1923 and Escobar in 1929, founded the Partido Nacional Democrático (PND) in July 1945 with the express intent of

45. Memo, 812.00/1–2445, Monthly Political Report, U.S. Embassy to Secretary of State, Jan. 24, 1945, Mexico City, in *Confidential U.S. State Department Central Files, Mexico, 1945–1949, Part I*, Reel 1.

46. John Child, *Unequal Alliance: The Inter-American Military System, 1938–1978* (Boulder: Westview, 1980).

47. "Historic turning point": Memo, 812.00/3–2145, Monthly Political Report, U.S. Embassy to Secretary of State, Mar. 21, 1945, Mexico City; "brilliance" at the Chapultepec Conference: Memo, 812.00/3–1645, Ray to Secretary of State, Mar. 16, 1945, Mexico City (both located in *Confidential U.S. State Department Central Files, Mexico, 1945–1949, Part I*, Reel 1).

48. Report, Insp. 42 to DGIPS, Jul. 23, 1945, AGN-DGIPS, Box 750, File 3, 2.1/A.G.D./818, Vol. 1.

49. Mendoza, *Ezequiel Padilla*, AGN-DGIPS, Box 750, File 3, 2.1/A.G.D./818, Vol. 1.

supporting Padilla's presidential aspirations.[50] Yet, by September 1945, the machinery of the Padilla campaign fell into disarray as funding became scarce. The Centro Director Pro-Padilla could not afford advertisements or even stamps for outgoing mail, and the only propaganda available were small stickers with a portrait of Padilla in miniature. The breakdown was temporary, though, as the Comité Pro-Padilla was formed on September 20, 1945, and injected new life into the briefly moribund campaign. On September 24, padillista candidates for the Senate were announced, including former *almazanista* Héctor F. López (Distrito Federal), Prieto Laurens (San Luis Potosí), and Antonio Díaz Soto y Gama (San Luis Potosí). On November 4, the Congreso Padillista convened in Iguala, Guerrero.[51]

Similar to the Almazán campaign of 1940, railroad workers provided significant support for the Padilla campaign. When a pro-Padilla group was formed in Tampico, most members claimed to be railroad workers and to have also formed the Comité Político-Ferrocarrilero Pro-Padilla. In Puebla, a railroad mechanic named José López led the Padilla campaign among organized labor groups in the state. Miners' associations began to donate money to the Padilla campaign in July 1945.[52] In Querétaro, the chief of railroad telegraph services for the Mexico City-Querétaro line headed padillista efforts, confirming the DGIPS assessment that "the party [PDM] has its greatest support among railroad workers."[53] As late as February 1946, Padilla was the only candidate working actively throughout the state of Querétaro to solidify support and gain new adherents. Padilla also enjoyed the support of dedicated organizations in Campeche, Chiapas, Chihuahua, and Yucatán.[54] His was a movement growing dynamically throughout various sectors of the country.

50. For background on Prieto Laurens, see Camp, *Mexican Political Biographies, 1935–1993*, 566; Report, Insp. 42 to DGIPS, Jul. 16, 1945, AGN-DGIPS, Box 750, File 3, 2.1/A.G.D./818, Vol. 1.

51. Small stickers with a portrait: Report, Insp. 23 to DGIPS, Sep. 11, 1945; briefly moribund campaign: Report, Insp. 35 to DGIPS, Sep. 20, 1945; padillista candidates for the Senate: *La Prensa Gráfica*, Sep. 24, 1945; Congreso Padillista convened: Telegram, Insp. 31 to DGIPS, Nov. 2, 1945, Acapulco (all located in AGN-DGIPS, Box 750, File 3, 2.1/A.G.D./818, Vol. 1). López was the head of the almazanista rump congress following the election of 1940. See chapter 1.

52. Claimed to be railroad workers: Report, Insp. 58 to DGIPS, Nov. 9, 1945, Tampico, AGN-DGIPS, Box 750, File 3, 2.1/A.G.D./818, Vol. 1; railroad mechanic: Report, Insp. 42 to DGIPS, Sep. 3, 1945, Puebla, AGN-DGIPS, Box 787, 2.1/45/289.

53. Miners' associations: Report, Insp. 42 to DGIPS, Jul. 19, 1945; "greatest support among railroad workers": Report, Insp. 24 to DGIPS, Nov. 9, 1945, Querétaro (both located in AGN-DGIPS, Box 750, File 3, 2.1/A.G.D./818, Vol. 1).

54. Only candidate working actively: Report, Insp. 24 to DGIPS, Feb. 21, 1946, Queré-

Some supporters of Henríquez defected to the Padilla campaign in July 1945 after noting the failure of Henríquez to gain the explicit support of Cárdenas. This development must have worried Alemán since it allowed the possibility that henriquismo and padillismo, however different in ideology, were not just personalist movements but rather popular movements that arose from disaffection with the policies of the Ávila Camacho administration and the strategies of the PRM. A report that the padillistas believed that "their candidate will be aided by a *mano poderosa*" provoked alarm in *alemanista* circles of the government at the time.[55] The fear of "revolution" was not limited to the usual fixations of the diplomatic corps or the policy community in Washington.

Padilla garnered support from traditionally conservative sectors of society. General Antonio Martínez worked on behalf of the PDM to gather funds from financial centers and to attempt to win influence with elements within the Catholic Church, an effort that included an interview with the archbishop of Mexico City, Luis Maria Martínez y Rodríguez. A week later, another agent seconded this information, adding that the archbishop was a "close friend" of General Martínez. A flyer from the Partido Femenil Nacional "Mujer" exhorted Mexican women to work against the efforts of the Alemán campaign since he was a communist, a Protestant, a Mason, and a supporter of the secular education "that is carrying our children towards Communism." A DGIPS report indicated that a UNS meeting in Guanajuato included cheering in support of Padilla. The UNS also provided a twenty-four-hour security detail for Padilla in August 1945, although the reporting agent averred that it might be part of a "double game," since the UNS leader Gildardo González was known to have some sympathies for the Alemán campaign.[56]

Conservative groups remained wary of Padilla's candidacy, however. Despite a report that the Confederación Regional Obrera Mexicana (CROM)

taro, AGN-DGIPS, Box 791, 2.1/46/390; support of dedicated organizations: Report, Insp. 42 to DGIPS, Nov. 10, 1945, AGN-DGIPS, Box 750, File 3, 2.1/A.G.D./818, Vol. 1.

55. Defected to the Padilla campaign: Report, Insp. 42 to DGIPS, Jul. 23, 1945; "aided by a *mano poderosa*": Report, Insp. 60 to DGIPS, Aug. 13, 1945 (both located in AGN-DGIPS, Box 750, File 3, 2.1/A.G.D./818, Vol. 1).

56. Elements within the Catholic Church: Report, Insp. 87 to DGIPS, Oct. 2, 1945; "close friend": Report, Insp. 30 to DGIPS, Oct. 10, 1945; "carrying our children towards Communism": Flyer, [1945]; cheering in support: Report, Insp. 42 to DGIPS, Jul. 23, 1945; "double game": Report, Insp. 38 to DGIPS, Aug. 31, 1945 (all located in AGN-DGIPS, Box 750, File 3, 2.1/A.G.D./818, Vol. 1).

and the Partido Laborista Mexicano (PLM) supported the Padilla candidacy, Luis Morones, at the PLM convention in July 1945, argued that the party should refrain from endorsing a candidate since things had only gone badly the last time when they backed Almazán.[57] And conservatives were distrustful of Padilla, not least because as attorney general he had led the prosecution of José de León Toral after Álvaro Obregón's assassination in 1928.[58] In short, Padilla could not hope to cement an alliance among conservative voters in 1946 because they either distrusted his credentials or his ability to defend the integrity of the vote.

And from the Left he was under outright attacks, most notably from labor leader Vicente Lombardo Toledano. Lombardo dismissed Padilla's presidential aspirations, saying, "Padilla is a Latin American Stettinius . . . [who] has about as much chance of becoming President as I have of becoming Emperor of Ethiopia."[59] But there Padilla fought back. He founded a new periodical, *Adelante,* in July 1945 specifically to "attack Communism and Vicente Lombardo Toledano."[60] Padilla also went on a rhetorical offensive, arguing publicly that under his watch "we will eliminate the communist tactics and influence hidden away in every corner of the administration."[61] Padilla's willingness to confront Lombardo signaled the vitality of the opposition, just as Lombardo's attacks demonstrated the level of the threat that the PRM felt from the opposition movement.

Throughout his campaign, Padilla relied on his close relations with the United States and long experience with foreign affairs to buoy his candidacy. In 1941, U.S. observers considered Padilla "one of the staunchest friends of the Democracies in the Cabinet" and noted that he "has gone even farther than the President in collaboration with the United States." U.S. observers recognized that Padilla was "very friendly toward the United States and devoted to the ideals of Pan-Americanism and democracy . . . [but] his open friendship for the United States has caused him to be quite unpopular in

57. Report, Insp. 42 to DGIPS, Jul. 23, 1945; Report, Insps. 20 and Rios Thivol to DGIPS, Jul. 25, 1945 (both located in AGN-DGIPS, Box 750, File 3, 2.1/A.G.D./818, Vol. 1).

58. Memo, 812.00/3–1645, Ray to Secretary of State, Mar. 16, 1945, Mexico City, in *Confidential U.S. State Department Central Files, Mexico, 1945–1949, Part I,* Reel 1.

59. Ibid.

60. Report, Insp. 42 to DGIPS, Jul. 19, 1945, AGN-DGIPS, Box 750, File 3, 2.1/A.G.D./818, Vol. 1.

61. Memo, 812.00/11–2845, Thomasson to Secretary of State, Nov. 28, 1945, Mexico City, in *Confidential U.S. State Department Central Files, Mexico, 1945–1949, Part I,* Reel 2.

many Mexican circles."[62] During the campaign, Padilla emphasized his connections to the United States, going so far as to have Daniel Ford, an FBI agent working through the U.S. Embassy, present at many political rallies. The reporting DGIPS agent reckoned that his presence was meant to suggest that Padilla was "the candidate that will be supported by the American Government in the next federal elections."[63] Nevertheless, U.S. observers handicapped the presidential race to Alemán's advantage in the early stages, owing mostly to his strength in Veracruz and, through his position in Gobernación, among state governors. Padilla ended up at a disadvantage, despite strong support in his native Guerrero, because of his close connection with U.S. policy.[64]

However, the United States did not write off Padilla from the outset. One senior State Department official argued that "he might conceivably at least come very close [to winning]." He certainly had the barely veiled support of Messersmith, who opined, "There is not a particle of doubt in my opinion that if there were to be a free election in Mexico tomorrow Padilla would be overwhelmingly elected . . . because he represents the opposition to the imposition."[65] Messersmith's open support of Padilla's candidacy may have sprung from their long personal relationship as much as the foreign minister's pro-U.S. policy stances. Notably, after Roosevelt and Ávila Camacho exchanged visits in Monterrey and then Corpus Christi in April 1943, Messersmith and Padilla "drove south together in high spirits, meandering through the provinces . . . [with] exhilaration over what they had helped bring about at Monterrey." Indeed, Messersmith's biographer described Alemán's selection as the PRM candidate as "one of the bitterest disappointments of his life." It seemed that "their intimate friendship and the near-perfect correlation of their views became liabilities for Padilla."[66]

62. "Staunchest friends" and "farther than the President": Extract, "Ezequiel Padilla, Secretary of Foreign Relations," MID, Dec. 16, 1941; "Pan-Americanism and democracy": Military Attaché Report 2147, Jul. 2, 1943, Mexico City (both located in NARA, Record Group 165, Box 2465).

63. Report, "Candidatura del Lic. Ezequiel Padilla," 1946, AGN-DGIPS, Box 2039, 2.1/A.G.D./818, Vol. 2.

64. Memo, 812.00/3–2445, Gibson to Secretary of State, Mar. 24, 1945, Mexico City, in *Confidential U.S. State Department Central Files, Mexico, 1945–1949, Part I*, Reel 1.

65. "Come very close": Memo, 812.00/7–245, Carrigan (ARA), Jul. 2, 1945, in *Confidential U.S. State Department Central Files, Mexico, 1945–1949, Part I*, Reel 1; "particle of doubt": Memo, 812.00/1–2546, U.S. Ambassador to Spruille Braden, Jan. 25, 1946, Mexico City, in *Confidential U.S. State Department Central Files, Mexico, 1945–1949, Part I*, Reel 3.

66. "Meandering through the provinces": Jesse H. Stiller, *George S. Messersmith: Diplomat of Democracy* (Chapel Hill: University of North Carolina Press, 1987), 196; "bitterest disappointments": ibid., 221; "intimate friendship": ibid., 222.

In contrast, at the outset of his career in high political office, Alemán evinced mixed reactions. He did have connections in Washington, mainly stemming from his position as director of Ávila Camacho's presidential campaign and then as secretary of Gobernación. In fact, after the disputed election of 1940, Alemán made a secret visit to U.S. undersecretary of state Sumner Welles to press the case for U.S. support of the incoming Ávila Camacho administration.[67] He also cultivated a personal friendship with U.S. vice president Henry Wallace and projected himself as a "moderate Revolutionary and not a Communist." In December 1941, the MID lumped Alemán together with "the Padilla group of sincere supporters of the United States and hemisphere defense" and reportedly believed "that the theories of Nazism have no place in Mexico." Finally, MID concluded that he was "one of the few Mexican politicians who is sincere in his desire to cooperate with the United States."[68] But Alemán's distance from communism and selection of friends in the U.S. government could not dilute the threat that U.S. officials perceived in the form of Axis intelligence and subversion activities in Mexico.

Accusations of German influence and graft within Gobernación were current before Alemán assumed leadership of the department.[69] Still, his apparent involvement in its more unsavory goings-on, especially those dealing with Axis influence, caused concern among U.S. observers. In late 1941, suspicions surrounding Alemán were high enough to warrant the "careful observation" by U.S. officials on the lookout for pro-Axis activity in Mexico. MID considered Alemán "very pro-Nazi" and someone who "places pro-Americans in certain positions in his Ministry merely to please the President."[70]

Alemán cultivated a reputation as a charmer and was "notorious for his women friends in the city." Numerous reports linked Alemán to the dancer (and alleged German spy) Hilda Kruger. U.S. military intelligence argued that

67. *Mobile Press,* Aug. 29, 1940, AGN-DGIPS, Box 191, 2.1/311.1/5, Vol. 18.

68. "Moderate Revolutionary": Military Attaché Report 2761, Nov. 27, 1943, Mexico City; "sincere supporters" and "desire to cooperate": Extract, "Miguel Alemán, Secretary of Gobernación," MID, [Dec.] 1941 (both located in NARA, Record Group 165, Box 2465).

69. Report, "Nazi, Communist and Other Foreign Agents in Mexico," Consul Robert G. McGregor Jr., Jun. 28, 1940, p. 28, NARA, Record Group 165, Box 2463.

70. "Careful observation": Summary, "Miguel Alemán, Secretary of Gobernación," MID, Mar. 21, 1942 (citing Office of Naval Intelligence [ONI], 209–41, Dec. 15, 1941); "very pro-Nazi" and "certain positions in his Ministry": Summary, "Miguel Alemán, Secretary of Gobernación," MID, Mar. 21, 1942 (citing Naval Attaché Mexico, 545–41-R, Oct. 31, 1941) (both located in NARA, Record Group 165, Box 2465).

she "exercises great influence over him."[71] For this reason, Mexican and U.S. agents maintained close surveillance of Kruger. In August 1941, as she moved from Washington, D.C., to New York and back to Mexico City, agents in both countries collaborated to track her telephone calls, follow her movements, and inspect her belongings at customs checkpoints. Since she was a dancer by training, she traveled with dresses and shoes, but always seemed to have new clothes, sometimes of the incorrect size, causing (somewhat bizarre) speculation among Mexican agents that messages could be transmitted within the garments themselves.[72] A U.S. agent remarked on the same trend, noting that a U.S. couple in Mexico City who were friendly with her would often "smuggle" dresses to Kruger's acquaintances in the United States, adding breathlessly, "God only knows what was hidden in those dresses."[73]

U.S. military intelligence concluded in 1942 that "there is no question but that she [Kruger] is engaged in dangerous espionage activities." More alarming was the belief that the Nazi agent Nicolaus was "kept in Mexico through Hilda Kruger's influence over Alemán who it is reported protects several such agents."[74] British intelligence efforts concluded that she was "a high-level propagandist rather than an espionage agent, and she used her influence to obtain privileges for Germans in Mexico." After fomenting a spate of revelatory reports in the press, the British took credit for collapsing her once widespread web of connections among high-ranking government officials.[75]

Accusations against Alemán were so stiff in 1943 that U.S. military officials claimed he had only "a precarious hold on the Ministry of Gobernación." He allegedly took bribes in the amount of U.S.$1000 per person "for facilitating the entry of 20,000 Jewish refugees to Mexico—particularly those Jews in Cuba who had been denied admittance to the United States." This charge was never corroborated, although other tales of corruption percolated

71. "Notorious for his women friends": Military Attaché Report 2761, Nov. 27, 1943, Mexico City; "exercises great influence": Summary, "Miguel Alemán, Secretary of Gobernación," MID, Mar. 21, 1942 (citing ONI Serial 134–41, Oct. 9, 1941) (both located in NARA, Record Group 165, Box 2465).

72. Memo, DGIPS, Aug. 21, 1941, AGN-DGIPS, Box 29, File 8, 2.1/061.9(72)/2, pp. 2–3.

73. Report, "Hilda Kruger," Apr. 17, 1942, NARA, Record Group 165, Box 2465.

74. "Dangerous espionage activities": Summary, "Hilda Kruger," MID, Apr. 17, 1942; "protects several such agents": Summary, "Miguel Alemán, Secretary of Gobernación," MID, Mar. 21, 1942 (citing Naval Attaché Mexico, Serial 530–41-R, Oct. 25, 1941) (both located in NARA, Record Group 165, Box 2465).

75. William Samuel Stephenson, ed., *British Security Coordination: The Secret History of British Intelligence in the Americas, 1940–45* (New York: Fromm International, 1999), 331.

through Gobernación. In 1943, DGIPS chief "[Lelo de] Larrea stated that he considers the Japanese in Mexico as the greatest danger," a position with which the U.S. Embassy concurred. He also confessed that "there have been attempts by the Japanese to bribe him and that on one occasion he had returned the bribe to the Japanese in his own office before some of his agents." This led the U.S. Embassy to conclude that Gobernación was "endeavoring to do all in its power to watch the activities of Axis agents."[76] U.S. officials remained extremely wary of Alemán's loyalty to the bilateral relationship.

Throughout the early 1940s, Alemán built a core group of supporters and used his position as head of the domestic intelligence services to his full advantage, essentially making himself an indispensable part of the political strategy of the PRM. As early as 1943, Alemán was being mentioned as a potential civilian successor to Ávila Camacho.[77] In January 1945, U.S. observers concluded that Alemán had "definite presidential aspirations." When longtime cardenista diplomat Francisco Castillo Nájera discussed his presidential aspirations with Ávila Camacho, the president reportedly told him that "there would be only one candidate in the next election and that he would be selected from the old Revolutionary group."[78] As the succession struggle developed, the connotation of "revolutionary" changed from charismatic soldier to civilian bureaucrat.

Within the Ávila Camacho administration, the succession renewed longstanding difficulties between the two major factions of the PRM. On one side was Cárdenas, who utilized his position as secretary of national defense to maintain substantial political influence. He also continued in his role as political godfather to a large group of local and regional political leaders who were holdovers from his administration. On the other side were the Ávila Camacho brothers, Manuel in the presidency and Maximino as secretary of public works. Just as Cárdenas had his brother Dámaso to conduct questionable deals, so too did Ávila Camacho have his brother Maximino,

76. "Precarious hold" and "Jewish refugees to Mexico": Report, MID, Headquarters Eighth Service Command, Aug. 12, 1943, Dallas; "Japanese in Mexico," "returned the bribe," and "watch the activities": Report, Gibson to Secretary of State, Jun. 16, 1943 (both located in NARA, Record Group 165, Box 2465).

77. Military Attaché Report 2761, Nov. 27, 1943, Mexico City, NARA, Record Group 165, Box 2465.

78. "Definite presidential aspirations": Memo, 812.00/1–1845, Hale to Secretary of State, Jan. 18, 1945, Mexico City; "only one candidate": Confidential Memo, Gibson to Secretary of State, Feb. 15, 1945, Mexico City (both located in *Confidential U.S. State Department Central Files, Mexico, 1945–1949, Part I,* Reel 1).

who "not only will receive the graft and split with the President later on, but also is the 'man behind the throne.' "[79] Maximino was a man of notorious temper, led the conservative wing of the PRM, and never trusted Cárdenas. The U.S. Embassy predicted that the battle to name the PRM candidate in 1946 would provide definitive evidence of who was stronger: Ávila Camacho or Cárdenas. In the end, it seemed that Maximino would have supported Padilla in 1946 as a foil to Cárdenas's influence, but "his death [in February 1945] weakened the political position of Lic. Ezequiel Padilla, strengthened that of Lic. Miguel Alemán, and removed an obstacle for General Lázaro Cárdenas."[80]

Soon after the PRM selected Alemán as its candidate, he began collecting endorsements from the Confederación de Trabajadores de México (CTM), Confederación Nacional Campesina (CNC), and other organizations.[81] Alemán's selection provoked surprise and not a little anxiety among U.S. observers, some of whom had steadily criticized him for his studied opportunism and presumed lack of understanding of world affairs. Ambassador Messersmith averred that "the fact that Cárdenas and Lombardo Toledano would support Alemán was one of the most unexpected developments that could have taken place." His explanation for the alliance stemmed from the idea that Lombardo was threatened by Padilla's increasing strength after the San Francisco conference and felt impelled to move quickly to devalue his political capital. As the ambassador put it, "It was the fear of Padilla that brought about this unholy alliance." Messersmith continued that Alemán went along with the deal "only because he felt that in accepting the bargain he assured himself of the Presidency" and that Cárdenas and Lombardo thought that "they have completely tied up Alemán and that he will be their instrument." Another report from inside the U.S. Embassy indicated two possibilities for the selection process: either Cárdenas was outsmarted by Lombardo, or Cárdenas had begun to fear Henríquez's independence and so chose a seemingly more pliable candidate.[82]

79. Military Attaché Report 849, New York Office, MID, War Department General Staff, Apr. 9, 1941, NARA, Record Group 165, Box 2465.

80. Provide definitive evidence: Memo, 812.00/3–1645, Ray to Secretary of State, Mar. 16, 1945, Mexico City; "weakened the political position": Memo, 812.00/3–2445, Gibson to Secretary of State, Mar. 24, 1945, Mexico City (both located in *Confidential U.S. State Department Central Files, Mexico, 1945–1949, Part I,* Reel 1).

81. Memo, 812.00/6–745, Messersmith to Secretary of State, Jun. 7, 1945, Mexico City, in *Confidential U.S. State Department Central Files, Mexico, 1945–1949, Part I,* Reel 1.

82. "Unexpected developments," "unholy alliance," and "accepting the bargain": Memo, 812.00/6–1445, Messersmith to Stettinius, Jun. 14, 1945, Mexico City; two possibilities for the selection process: Memo, 812.00/6–2545, Hale to Secretary of State, Jun. 25, 1945, Mexico

The padillistas tended to align Alemán very closely with the communist allegiances usually associated with Lombardo and the CTM. One agent reported that elements of the CTM would control the Secretariats of Gobernación, of Foreign Relations, and of Labor if Alemán was elected, a path that the padillistas considered ruinous. In Labor, the CTM would attempt to "sovietize" workers, while in Foreign Relations such an influence would lead Mexico into a foreign policy of the "extreme left." Lombardo realized the negative associations of the Partido Comunista Mexicano (PCM) and seconded its instruction that subsidiary movements, especially in Labor, call themselves "democratic" parties or organizations in order to avoid undue attention by U.S. observers.[83]

Despite the pro forma declarations of neutrality in the Mexican electoral matters, Messersmith made no secret of his great regard for Padilla and his disdain for Alemán. He considered Alemán "one who could be swayed too much by opportunistic considerations . . . [and] not a person who can be depended upon to take energetic measures." He continued that Alemán "is not unfriendly to us, but he is not very understanding of us . . . [and] his attitude is very opportunistic." Messersmith added, "While he is intelligent, he does not really have an understanding of what is going on and does not, I believe, have a clear understanding of the problems of his own country."[84] Messersmith's statements belied the early distrust of Alemán, although it gave way in later years as a mutually beneficial relationship developed between the United States and Mexico.

Beyond the confusion occasioned by Messersmith's personal friendship with Padilla lay a generalized feeling of resignation among U.S. observers of Alemán's campaign. In part, this was due to Alemán's indirect courtship of the United States, prompted by the "fear in the mind of Lic. Alemán that the United States might in some way support Padilla as opposed to him." Alemán *wanted* the United States to support him, secretly perhaps, but in a way that satisfied his need for credibility and the needs of the United States

City (both located in *Confidential U.S. State Department Central Files, Mexico, 1945–1949, Part I,* Reel 1).

83. Policy of the "extreme left": Report, Insp. 42 to DGIPS, Dec. 26, 1945; "democratic" parties or organizations: Report, Insp. 42 to DGIPS, Nov. 10, 1945 (both located in AGN-DGIPS, Box 750, File 3, 2.1/A.G.D./818, Vol. 1).

84. "Swayed too much": Memo, 812.00/4–845, Messersmith to Nelson Rockefeller, Apr. 8, 1945, Mexico City; "not unfriendly to us" and "understanding of the problems": Memo, 812.00/4–1945, Messersmith to Stettinius, Apr. 19, 1945, Mexico City (both located in *Confidential U.S. State Department Central Files, Mexico, 1945–1949, Part I,* Reel 1).

as a hemispheric power. One U.S. Embassy observer neatly summarized the key material advantage of a potential Alemán administration: "[his] conception of Mexican collaboration with the United States consists principally in permitting Americans to make investments in Mexico and engage in business there." The State Department also recognized the opportunity, concluding that "[Alemán] is too astute a politician and too opportunistic a man not to 'play ball' with us. . . . It does not seem unreasonable to assume that he could control the country and that *his control would not necessarily be detrimental to our interests.*"[85] Therefore, despite early worries about Alemán's commitment to fighting communist influence and malleable political beliefs, the prevailing opinion in circles of U.S. observers became a generally positive one.

Padilla attempted to turn postwar rhetoric to his advantage in the campaign. He argued in 1945 that "*nazifascismo* was hatred of the democracies, the contempt for the will of the people . . . [and] the democracy victorious during the war cannot be defeated during the peace." He extended his argument to the development of the dominant PRM in Mexico, railing against "the official machinery that the citizens pay for that is dedicated to weakening the fundamental rights of men, to supplanting the positive forms of the electoral process, and to falsifying the results of the genuine popular will."[86] Padilla's equation of totalitarian domination and the evolving electoral hegemony of the PRM machinery did not resonate well during the campaign, leading to charges that he was not only against the PRM but also, by implication, the revolution itself.

Election day presented few surprises. Padilla accused the PRI and the government of harassing opposition voters, manipulating the vote count, and refusing to abide by electoral laws. The case of Chiapas served as a blatant example: although it had one of the worst communications systems in the country and was a stronghold of the Padilla organization, the overwhelming vote for Alemán was reported in record time. Padilla fared better in Mexico City, although he lost there by almost 40,000 votes. In Mexicali, Padilla lost

---

85. "Fear in the mind of Lic. Alemán": Memo, 812.00/3–1645, Ray to Secretary of State, Mar. 16, 1945, Mexico City; "conception of Mexican collaboration": Memo, 812.00/7–2045, Ray to Secretary of State, Jul. 20, 1945, Mexico City; "too astute a politician": Internal Memo, 812.00/6–645, Carrigan (ARA), Jun. 6, 1945, emphasis added (all located in *Confidential U.S. State Department Central Files, Mexico, 1945–1949, Part I,* Reel 1).

86. Padilla statement to the press, Sep. 2, 1945, cited in *El respeto a la Voluntad Popular* (Mexico City: Comité Pro-Ezequiel Padilla, 1945), AGN-DGIPS, Box 750, File 3, 2.1/A.G.D./818, Vol. 1.

Table 3.1   Mexico City Voting Totals, 1946

District	Alemán	Padilla
1	8,832	8,118[i]
2	11,937	6,950[ii]
3	11,252	5,681[iii]
4	12,662	5,505[iv]
5	8,609	8,586[v]
6	20,450	6,586[vi]
7	9,564	8,983[vii]
8	9,424	6,526[viii]
9	9,777	7,919[ix]
10	9,296	9,140[x]
11	7,954	6,910[xi]
12	8,589	7,922[xii]
Total	128,346	88,826

[i] Report, Insp. 16 to DGIPS, Jul. 11, 1946, AGN-DGIPS, Box 750, File 1, 2.1/A.G.D./818, Vol. 2. All subsequent documents are located in this file.
[ii] Memo, Baig Serra to SEGOB, Jul. 12, 1946.
[iii] Report, Insp. 30 to DGIPS, Jul. 12, 1946.
[iv] Report, Insp. 51 to DGIPS, Jul. 12, 1946.
[v] Report, Insp. 20 to DGIPS, Jul. 12, 1946.
[vi] Report, Comisionado Pérez Aldama to DGIPS, Jul. 11, 1946.
[vii] Report, Insp. 71 to DGIPS, Jul. 12, 1946.
[viii] Memo, Baig Serra to SEGOB, Jul. 12, 1946.
[ix] Ibid.
[x] Report, Insp. 28 to DGIPS, Jul. 12, 1946; Memo, Baig Serra to SEGOB, Jul. 12, 1946.
[xi] Report, Insp. 63 to DGIPS, Jul. 12, 1946.
[xii] Report, Insp. 11 to DGIPS, Jul. 12, 1946.

by almost two votes to one.[87] In the Toluca region, Padilla only won 20,933 votes and suffered crushing defeat by Alemán's total of 136,797 votes. In Morelia, Alemán won 52,401 votes to Padilla's 21,147. In the state of Chihuahua, Alemán won 56,897 votes and Padilla 15,561.[88] Around Villahermosa, Alemán romped to victory with 33,386 votes versus Padilla's paltry 509.[89] The race was closer in Tampico and Ciudad Madero, where Padilla's

87. Reported in record time: Report, Insp. 23 to DGIPS, Jul. 10, 1946; two votes to one: Report, Insp. 70 to DGIPS, Jul. 12, 1946 (both located in AGN-DGIPS, Box 750, File 1, 2.1/ A.G.D./818, Vol. 2). Alemán won 14,066 votes to Padilla's 7,440 votes.
88. Padilla only won 20,933 votes: Telegram, Insp. Jara to DGIPS, Jul. 12, 1946, Toluca; Alemán won 52,401 votes: Report, Insp. 34 to DGIPS, Jul. 15, 1946, Morelia; Alemán won 56,897 votes: Telegram, Insp. 61 to DGIPS, Jul. 13, 1946, Ciudad Juárez (all located in AGN-DGIPS, Box 750, File 1, 2.1/A.G.D./818, Vol. 2).
89. Telegram, Insp. Rios Thivol to DGIPS, Jul. 14, 1946, Villahermosa; Telegram, Insp. Rios Thivol to DGIPS, Jul. 15, 1946, Villahermosa (both located in AGN-DGIPS, Box 750, File 1, 2.1/A.G.D./818, Vol. 2).

8,885 votes nearly equaled Alemán's 9,195.[90] By any standard, Padilla lost the election badly, and despite partisan complaints to the contrary, the level of fraud did not appear to be as severe as it was in 1940 (or would be in 1952). In large part, this derived from the inherent weakness of Padilla's candidacy and support for Alemán among the major revolutionary factions.

In retrospect, John Carrigan of the Inter-American Affairs (ARA) office of the State Department had the clearest vision of the situation in 1946. A full year before the voting, he wrote that "no matter how friendly toward us he [Padilla] might be, if his administration were unpopular, it would not turn out as much to our advantage as a popular administration which might be somewhat less friendly toward us [i.e., Alemán]."[91] Carrigan's recognition that Alemán was the less unpleasant choice for the United States in the immediate aftermath of World War II signaled a new understanding between the two countries. Alemán, whom U.S. observers roundly and routinely vilified during his early years in Gobernación, experienced a political rehabilitation of sorts after the election of 1946. His vices, including seeming collaboration with Axis elements during the war, were outweighed by his central virtues: firm control of a professionalizing domestic intelligence service and a willingness to support U.S. investments in the Mexican economy. During his administration, Alemán was able to provide a level of social, political, and economic security that would have been impossible with a Padilla regime.

The victory of Alemán in the presidential election of 1946 opened the door on a new era in Mexican politics. Scholars view his ascendance as the beginning of a period marked by robust economic growth, a dramatic shift toward civilian government, and the consolidation of electoral control. The structural foundations of the economic growth that Alemán oversaw were laid in the 1920s and 1930s. The organization of the Banco de México in 1925 for the first time institutionalized federal control over the money supply and allowed officials to manage monetary policy in a comprehensive fashion. In 1934, the government created the Nacional Financiera, S. A. (NAFINSA) in order to centralize authority over the distribution of federal funds in the developing industrial economy. Finally, the agrarian reforms based in the Constitution of 1917 and carried to their fullest extent during the Cárdenas

90. Telegram, Insp. 58 to DGIPS, Jul. 12, 1946, Tampico, AGN-DGIPS, Box 750, File 1, 2.1/A.G.D./818, Vol. 2.

91. Memo, 812.00/7-245, Carrigan (ARA), Jul. 2, 1945, in *Confidential U.S. State Department Central Files, Mexico, 1945–1949, Part I,* Reel 1.

administration broke down rural landowners' power over local workers, effectively freeing the labor market in such areas. These structural changes,
under way since the 1920s, provided the underpinnings for the economic
expansion that took hold during Alemán's term of office.[92]

Under Alemán, fundamental aspects of the Mexican political economy
were transformed and offered a new footing for the creation of lasting electoral dominance by the PRI. The Alemán administration coincided with a
global economic expansion after World War II, as countries retooled from
war industry and stockpiles of foreign reserves were made available for investment and consumption. These new pools of capital were directed toward
prime investment zones like Mexico in the postwar period, a nation that was
consciously and decisively turning away from the cardenista-style reforms of
the past and orienting federal policy in a pro-business line. Indeed, as one of
its overriding goals, the incoming Alemán administration aimed for "a new
national project that would put Mexico on the map and on the threshold of
joining the highly industrialized countries." In the effort to attract investment, it did not hurt that federal policy implementation was often matched
by increasingly warm relationships between Mexican officials and foreign
executives. From 1947 to 1952, Mexico received a staggering U.S.$3.7 billion
of foreign investment for projects in all areas of the economy. The heaviest
funding went to enterprises dealing in mining, electricity, and industrial manufacturing.[93] These investments, overseen by Alemán's bureaucracy, gener-
ated a sustained rise in productivity as new equipment and technology were
utilized to further Mexican economic expansion.[94] The macroeconomic
measure of the "Mexican Miracle" was an average annual GDP growth rate
of 6 percent from 1940 to 1970.[95] Economic growth on this scale was impressive and signaled the determination of the economic policy makers in Mexico
to foment and support foreign investments for the long term.

92. Roger D. Hansen, *The Politics of Mexican Development* (Baltimore: Johns Hopkins University Press, 1971), 35–36.

93. "New national project": Medina, Luis. *Civilismo y modernización del autoritarismo,* Hist-
oria de la Revolución Mexicana 20 (Mexico City: Colegio de México, 1979), 91; increasingly
warm relationships: Stephen R. Niblo, *War, Diplomacy, and Development: The United States and
Mexico, 1938–1954* (Wilmington, Del.: Scholarly Resources, 1995), 180–87; heaviest funding:
Bernardo Sepulveda and Antonio Chumacero, *La inversión extranjera en México* (Mexico City:
Fondo de Cultura Económica, 1973), 120.

94. For a detailed overview of the various sectors impacted by the massive foreign investments, see Blanca Torres Ramírez, *Hacia la utopía industrial,* Historia de la Revolución Mexicana
21 (Mexico City: Colegio de México, 1984).

95. Hansen, *Politics of Mexican Development,* 41.

The pursuit of macroeconomic growth under Alemán necessarily required serious efforts at political stabilization. Throughout the postrevolutionary phase, Mexican politics had been dominated by military leaders, many of whom had risen through the ranks during the decade of armed conflict. These revolutionary veterans used their charisma, access to violent means, and personal connections to maintain influence in national politics. Yet the transition from the Ávila Camacho government to the Alemán administration in 1946 "marked the evolutionary process from military to civilian control in a symbolic and concrete fashion." It was quite simply "the starting point for civilian rule in contemporary Mexico."[96] Not only was the office of president handed from a military officer to a civilian lawyer, but the entire system was shaken as a new group of advisors began to fill out the ranks of the government.

A novel element of the Alemán administration was the particular nature of the advisors and bureaucrats who were swept into the federal bureaucracy. One especially useful variable in analyzing the constitution of Mexican administrations is age cohorts. Mexican presidents have tended to stock their administrations with those of a similar age, and Alemán's cohort was generally too young to have participated in the revolution directly. Therefore, in his effort to staff the federal bureaucracy with his own people, Alemán created "a decisive generational break"; he filled his government with classmates from the Universidad Nacional Autónoma de México (UNAM) and other associates from a similar background. Alemán argued for the particular managerial and policy expertise of his appointees, but also underlined the need for new thinking. Veterans may have had revolutionary credibility, but in general they could not boast a firm command of increasingly complex political and economic strategies. The education gap between old revolutionary hands and university-trained professionals almost always favored the more educated civilians, giving them the upper hand in debates about governmental competence. Finally, the roster of Alemán's government reinforced the authority that his status within the party already accorded him. Thus, the Mexican bureaucracy after 1946 "was not a coalition government. . . . [It] was Alemán's personal instrument."[97] In these ways, Alemán was able to create an

96. "Symbolic and concrete fashion": Roderic Ai Camp, *Mexico's Military on the Democratic Stage* (Westport, Conn.: Praeger Security International, 2005), 25; "starting point for civilian rule": José Luis Reyna, "Las elecciones en el México institucionalizado, 1946–1976," in *Las elecciones en México: Evolución y perspectivas,* ed. Pablo González Casanova (Mexico City: Siglo XXI, 1985), 105.

97. "Decisive generational break": Roderic Camp, *Political Recruitment Across Two Centuries: Mexico, 1884–1991* (Austin: University of Texas Press, 1995), 50–51; favored the more edu-

administration that simultaneously shortchanged the traditional political prerogatives of the revolutionary generation and initiated a tectonic shift in the
composition of the dominant political elite.

Under Alemán's leadership, economic growth was matched with civilian
ascendance, offering the opportunity for further consolidation of electoral
control. The period from 1946 to 1970 was one of "professionalization of the
elite and political stability" deriving from the increasing reliance on university-trained civilians in the federal bureaucracy. Alemán strengthened his position as president by opening space for new civilian political groups, or
camarillas, within his administration. As these groups cycled through the various branches of the national government, each remained conscious of the
debt owed to its patron in the National Palace. This process afforded Alemán
and his successors the opportunity to supply benefits to up-and-coming
groups while maintaining relatively firm control over appointments. The
strategy was not without conflict, and "since the 1940s the struggle between
camarillas has found resolution through accommodation and equilibrium. . . .
[Thus] the competition is continuous." Still, even this competition between
political factions had positive ramifications for the dominant civilian elite. As
the PRM metamorphosed into the PRI in 1946, the party became even
more established as the clearinghouse for political office in Mexico, and party
officials acted as the gatekeepers for nominations. The process for selecting
candidates became "more centralized and less participative" with the sectors
of the party losing power and the Comité Ejecutivo Nacional (CEN) "being
charged with channeling and regulating all electoral activity." In sum, Alemán's election "represented the opening of a period of institutional continuity," and the tangible political results that marked his term signaled that the
PRI "had finished transforming itself."[98]

cated civilians: William S. Ackroyd, "Military Professionalism, Education, and Political
Behavior in Mexico," *Armed Forces and Society* 18, no. 1 (Fall 1991): 81–96; "Alemán's personal
instrument": Peter H. Smith, "Mexico Since 1946: Dynamics of an Authoritarian Regime," in
Mexico Since Independence, ed. Leslie Bethell (Cambridge: Cambridge University Press, 1991),
341.

98. "Professionalization of the elite": Francisco Suárez Farías, "La élite política," *Revista
Mexicana de Sociología* 50, no. 3 (Jul.–Sep. 1988): 307; conscious of the debt owed: see, for
example, Joy Langston, "Political Factors in the Mexican Political System: A Theoretical and
Comparative Examination" (PhD diss., Duke University, 1995); "accommodation and equilibrium": Peter H. Smith, *Labyrinths of Power: Political Recruitment in Twentieth-Century Mexico*
(Princeton: Princeton University Press, 1979), 51; "more centralized" and "channeling and
regulating": Reyna, "Las elecciones en el México institucionalizado," 102–3; "finished transforming itself": Jacqueline Peschard, "El PRI: Partido hegemónico (1946–1972)," in *El partido
en el poder: Seis ensayos* (Mexico City: Partido Revolucionario Institucional, IEPES, 1990), 183.

The election of 1946 ushered in the era of civilian control of electoral politics in a remarkably quiet way. The postwar political atmosphere temporarily short-circuited the plans of military candidates for presidential bids and allowed civilian bureaucrats surrounding Alemán the latitude they needed to reform the PRM into a more modern party, the PRI, officially sidelining the military as a group in the process. The consequences of this transformation were not widely understood until the election of 1952, when Henríquez ran for president in opposition to the PRI. As Gobernación argued in 1946, "With the political reform pursued by President Ávila Camacho a chapter in Mexican life characterized by violence has closed and another has opened, one in which our politics have been dignified and ennobled, restoring their true institutional character."[99] Padilla, for all of his political strengths and his widely acknowledged mental faculties, succumbed to the underlying nationalism of a country that could not stomach his close association with U.S. goals in the hemisphere. The election of 1946 elevated the idea of civilian government and the crucial importance of the intelligence services to new heights. During the Alemán administration, the project to remove the military from political influence accelerated alongside the professionalization of the intelligence services. In the end, by entrusting control of the new intelligence bureaucracy of the Dirección Federal de Seguridad (DFS) to the younger generation of military officers coming out of the military academies, Alemán succeeded in cementing three crucial goals pursued since the 1920s: removing the military from electoral politics while gaining its firm allegiance, professionalizing the intelligence services to defend the dominant elite from its opposition, and consolidating the electoral dominance of the PRI.

99. Secretaría de Gobernación, *Seis años de actividad nacional* (Mexico City: Secretaría de Gobernación, 1946), 37–38.

FOUR

OZTOMECA TO "JIMÉNEZ"

The Development of Mexican Intelligence

PRIOR TO WORLD WAR II, Mexico's domestic intelligence-gathering bureaucracy was a poorly organized and underfunded amalgamation of local police, regional informants, and federal agents. Intelligence memoranda based on conversations with gardeners were not uncommon.[1] By 1947, Mexico boasted an outwardly professional intelligence service modeled on the organization and techniques of the U.S. Federal Bureau of Investigation (FBI). This radical shift resulted from several factors: U.S.-Mexican cooperation during the war, growing fears in the United States about fascist and communist influence in Mexico, and the determined efforts of elements within the dominant political elite to create a force to control dissent.

Central to these efforts was Miguel Alemán in his successive positions as secretary of Gobernación (1940–45) and president of Mexico (1946–52). Through the early 1940s, Alemán was able to gain control of the existing intelligence services in Mexico and begin to shape them into a tool of the political elite. Once elected president, Alemán created the Dirección Federal de Seguridad (DFS) as a direct dependency of the president's office, apart from its sister agencies in Gobernación. This decision was emblematic of the transition of the intelligence services from indirect to overt agents of the

---

1. Report, Insp. 12 to DGIPS, Dec. 13, 1938, Archivo General de la Nación, Mexico City, Dirección General de Investigaciones Políticas y Sociales (DGIPS), Box 141, 2.1/310.1/7.

political agenda of the president and, by extension, the dominant Partido Revolucionario Institucional (PRI). This shift, accelerated by growing budgets and foreign training, made the intelligence community itself a prime tool for subverting, co-opting, or destroying electoral opposition to the political elite.

This chapter outlines the basic history of the Mexican intelligence services from 1918 to the present before discussing these services' original methods and how they changed over time. The focus then shifts to the issue of international interests in Mexico and the battle within the U.S. bureaucracy to control Latin American intelligence. Finally, the chapter examines the changes in techniques and funding in the Mexican services, utilizing the formation of the DFS in 1947 as a case study, to gauge the depth of the new professionalism in Mexican intelligence.

Examples from opposition presidential campaigns demonstrate the growing sophistication of Mexican agents as well as their changing responsibilities to the government. The Mexican services in the 1940s were more closely aligned with the increasingly consolidated political project of the dominant political party. Throughout, the interests of both the U.S. intelligence community and the PRM/PRI become very clear: a professional Mexican intelligence service would act as a brake on both international (i.e., fascists, communists) and domestic (i.e., opposition candidates, student movements) threats to the status quo. This newly trained intelligence bureaucracy became one of the PRI's crucial tools of political control throughout the twentieth century as the political elite used it to close avenues of dissent to reformist politicians and regular citizens alike.

Practically all societies created some variety of intelligence service at very early stages in their development, and this was certainly true for early Mesoamerican societies. The long-distance merchants of Aztec society, the *pochteca,* were often accompanied by *oztomeca* "who went disguised in the local garb and who spoke the local language [and] their task was to gather military intelligence as well as exotic goods." Further, Moctezuma was well apprised of Spanish landings at San Juan de Ulúa and elsewhere, and he sent agents to interview and spy upon Cortés and his followers.[2] These early examples of

---

2. "Disguised in the local garb": Michael D. Coe, *Mexico: From the Olmecs to the Aztecs,* 4th ed. (New York: Thames and Hudson, 1994), 168; well-apprised of Spanish landings: Bernal Díaz del Castillo, *The Discovery and Conquest of Mexico, 1517–1521,* trans. A. P. Maudslay (New York: Farrar, Straus, and Cudahy, 1956), 69–78.

simple surveillance demonstrated the facility of the Mexica for gathering intelligence. From that time forward, successive regimes organized intelligence operations to maintain control of local populations. In more recent times, for instance, the spy system of Porfirio Díaz was coordinated by Enrique Creel, governor of Chihuahua, who organized information from various private detective agencies and distributed it to officials in both Mexico City and Washington in the years leading up to the Mexican Revolution.[3]

The modern Mexican intelligence services began with the foundation of the Servicios Confidenciales in 1918. This bureaucratic entity changed names several times, becoming the Departamento Confidencial (DC) in 1924, the Oficina de Investigaciones Políticas y Sociales in 1925, the Departamento de Investigaciones Políticas y Sociales in 1938, and, in the late 1940s, the DGIPS.[4] In addition to the DGIPS, at least four other intelligence services had developed by 1941. These included the Mexican Army's general staff, the Office of the Attorney General, the Secret Service of the Chief of Police for Mexico City, and the special services of the president.[5] In January 1942, President Manuel Ávila Camacho created the Jefatura de Servicios de Vigilancia Policía within Gobernación to "coordinate espionage, sabotage and all other subversive activities" and instructed all domestic police forces to supply the group with information about Axis activities. Ávila Camacho appointed Demetrio Flores Fagoaga to lead this new agency, which the FBI called the

3. A detailed explanation of this system may be found in W. Dirk Raat, *Revoltosos: Mexico's Rebels in the United States* (College Station: Texas A&M University Press, 1981), 175–99. See also Friedrich Katz, *The Secret War in Mexico: Europe, the United States, and the Mexican Revolution* (Chicago: University of Chicago Press, 1981), 550–78.

4. Sergio Aguayo Quezada, ed., *El almanaque mexicano* (Mexico City: Grijalbo, 2000), 146. The homepage for the Centro de Investigación y Seguridad Nacional (CISEN), Mexico's central intelligence bureaucracy, states that the DGIPS was not renamed such until 1967, and outlines a different succession of agency names: Sección Primera (1918), Departamento Confidencial (1929), Oficina de Información Política (1938), Departamento de Investigación Política y Social (1942), and Dirección General de Investigaciones Políticas y Sociales (1967). I have been unable to definitively outline the proper succession of dates and names for this intelligence agency. Empirical evidence supports the shift to OIP in 1938. See AGN-DGIPS, Box 37, File 15, 2.1/100(014)/1, pp. 1–2. Agent Mena Alcocer reported the office as the Oficina Confidencial all year in 1927, then as the Departamento Confidencial again as of Jan. 1, 1928, ending with the Oficina de Departamento Confidencial in the 1930 budget. See "Resumen de los breves apuntes para la historia del Departamento Confidencial," by Jose de la Luz Mena Alcocer, [1934], AGN-DGIPS, Box 58, File 1, pp. 758–60.

5. Memo, Military Intelligence Division (MID), Sep. 15, 1941, National Archives and Records Administration, Washington, D.C. (NARA), Record Group 165, Box 2450. See also María Emilia Paz Salinas, *Strategy, Security, and Spies: Mexico and the U.S. as Allies in World War II* (University Park: Pennsylvania State University Press, 1997), 170–71. Paz Salinas cites Memo, Sep. 16, 1941, NARA, Record Group 226, Entry 168, N.Y-OSS-OP-5, Folder 656.

"Espionage Bureau of the Mexican Government."[6] Flores Fagoaga worked in this capacity for some time before reappearing as head of the DGIPS in 1952. This chapter will focus on the main service that became the DGIPS, as it was this agency that was most involved in the surveillance and subversion of political dissidence during the period from the 1930s to the early 1950s. Throughout, the intelligence services in Mexico were "indispensable . . . primarily for being the 'eyes and ears' where the *Superioridad* learns the truth of events."[7]

Owing to its genesis in the revolution, the DC in the 1920s was usually led by a military officer (see table 4.1). Intelligence was too important to be trusted to civilian chiefs, although agents could be—and often were—civilians. The army remained powerful enough to keep control of the intelligence services until the late 1930s, when a series of civilians circulated through the directorship. The leadership of the DGIPS became distinctly civilian in nature and was matched by a new trend toward longer tenures of service among agents, who no longer resigned en masse when the head of the department was replaced. The longer terms of service contributed to a growing sense of interdependence between the agents and the intelligence bureaucracy. Drawn from archival documents, the list of directors of the DGIPS in table 4.2 includes only one military officer.

The fact that civilian leadership dominated in this agency from the late 1930s offers a glimpse into its organizational and governmental requirements. When Venustiano Carranza began the DC in 1918, he needed information on his friends and enemies in order to maintain political control. This mission

Table 4.1 Chiefs of the Departamento Confidencial

Jan. 1, 1924–Jan. 11, 1925	Col. Martín Barcenas
Jan. 11, 1925–May 11, 1925	Lt. Col. and Prof. Eufrasio Ortega
May 11, 1925–May 6, 1930	Col. Francisco M. Delgado
May 6, 1930–Jun. 10, 1931	Pablo Meneses
Jun. 10, 1931–Sep. 6, 1932	Col. Adalberto Torres Estrada
Sep. 8, 1932–Jan. 9, 1934	Maj. Maximiliano Chávez Aldeco
Jan. 9, 1934–	Gen. Joaquín de la Peña

SOURCE: "Resumen de los breves apuntes para la historia del Departamento Confidencial," by Jose de la Luz Mena Alcocer, [1934], AGN-DGIPS, Box 58, File 1, pp. 750–82.

6. Report, "Totalitarian Activities: Mexico Today," Federal Bureau of Investigation (FBI), Sep. 1942, 436–437, NARA, Record Group 165, DOI, E188, Box 997.

7. Letter, Enrique Garza Garcia (chief of Departamento Confidencial) to Secretary of Gobernación, Dec. 12, 1934, AGN-DGIPS, Box 43, File 10, 128.1-"35." Emphasis added.

Table 4.2 Directors of the DGIPS

As of Apr. 12, 1938	Humberto M. Amaya
As of Dec. 21, 1938	Lic. Roberto Atwood
As of Jan. 17, 1939	Cipriano Arriola
As of Feb. 22, 1943	Lic. Jose Lelo de Larrea
As of Jul. 8, 1944	Lic. Eduardo Ampudia V.
As of Jul. 2, 1946	Gen. Emilio Baig Serra
As of May 28, 1947	Lamberto Ortega Peregrina
As of Jul. 25, 1952	Lic. Alejandro Romero Ortega
As of Oct. 4, 1952	Demetrio Flores Fagoaga

NOTE: This information was compiled in the course of reviewing the entire collection of documents in the AGN-DGIPS archive. The earliest occurrence of a subject who either signed as the director or was referred to as the director is presented here. While lacking in absolute precision, it approximates the terms of office of the succession of directors. It is likely that there were other directors interspersed in this succession, especially in the periods 1939–43 and 1947–52.

"of political information and administrative policing" was suited to a corps of government agents who may have begun their careers in the customs service or in a police department.[8] Intelligence agents used traditional methods of investigation that would have been a natural extension from previous work in police departments or similar fields. For instance, while researching the intentions of Henríquez after the election of 1952, agents found and interviewed men who had worked on one of his many highway construction jobs.[9] In short, the most qualified candidates for the task of political surveillance were the men and women who were already engaged in similar tasks in Mexican society.

Military officers, for all of their tactical skills and surveillance capabilities, were generally not suited to this mission as agents. While the early agent corps included a fair share of military veterans, this was a carryover effect from the expanding ranks of ambitious soldiers from the revolutionary period. As that generation grew older, the career path toward domestic intelligence work became mainly a civilian one. By the late 1930s, army officers maintained dominance in traditional military intelligence fields: monitoring ports and coastline, tracking arms shipments, identifying orders of battle, surveying national defense strategies, and so on. As has been argued for many Latin American nations, only when the threat of political opposition or unrest

8. CISEN, http://www.cisen.org.mx.

9. Memo, Insp. "R. C. M." and "T. G." to DGIPS, Oct. 27, 1952, AGN-DGIPS, Box 29, File 17, 2.1/061.8/15, Vol. 12.

became deeply associated with new doctrines of national security did the military take a leading role in domestic intelligence and operations.[10]

Another notable aspect of the list in table 4.2 is the short tenure of most directors of the DGIPS. It is unclear whether this was a bureaucratic safeguard against creating an intelligence fiefdom (like J. Edgar Hoover's FBI) or an indication that the position of director was a training ground for other, presumably more prestigious, assignments within the government. Lacking data representative of the tenure of later directors of the DGIPS, it is difficult to determine whether this pattern of rapid succession continued past 1952. There is reason to suggest that it became more regular since its sister agency, the DFS, maintained a pattern of succession more familiar to students of Mexico. The DFS maintained, for the most part, a succession that followed the pattern of the *sexenio,* the six-year presidential term of office. The DFS was also notable for the dominance of military officers in the position of director.

The DFS was created at a time of intense political conflict over the proper roles of civilians and soldiers in high political office.[11] Although the reformed military academies were producing a new generation of more highly skilled officers, the civilian bureaucrats surrounding President Alemán were intent on blocking their political ascent. Alemán recognized the necessity of calming the waters in the interest of political consolidation and determined a

Table 4.3   Directors of the DFS

1947–52	Gen. Marcelino Innureta de la Fuente
1952–58	Col. Leandro Castillo Venegas
1958–59	Lic. Gilberto Suárez Torres
1959–64	Col. Manuel Rangel Escamilla
1964–70	Cap. Fernando Gutiérrez Barrios
1970–76	Cap. Luis de la Barreda Moreno
1977–78	Javier García Paniagua
1978–82	Lt. Col. Miguel Nazar Haro
1982–85	Lic. José Antonio Zorrilla Pérez

SOURCE: Sergio Aguayo Quezada, ed., *El almanaque mexicano* (Mexico City: Grijalbo, 2000), 146.

10. For the Mexican case, see Bruce Michael Bagley and Sergio Aguayo Quezada, eds. *Mexico: In Search of Security* (Coral Gables: North-South Center, University of Miami; New Brunswick: Transaction Publishers, 1993); John Bailey and Sergio Aguayo Quezada, eds. *Strategy and Security in U.S.-Mexican Relations Beyond the Cold War* (San Diego: Center for U.S.-Mexican Studies, University of California at San Diego, 1996).

11. See chapter 2 for a discussion of the military's changing role in Mexican politics.

strategy that would effectively co-opt the emerging officer class of the military. Young officers identified as acquiescent and capable were invited to staff and lead the DFS, at once closing ranks with and defending the civilians who sought to dominate the armed forces politically. It is important to note that the young officers who chose the path of intelligence work did not, in the long term, achieve the kind of high-level posts within the defense establishment that their classmates from the Escuela Superior de Guerra did.[12]

The task of leading the domestic intelligence services, with all of their importance for the political stability of the country and the PRI, was congruent with officers' views of their role in Mexican society. As chapter 2 discussed, they had generally seen themselves as protectors of the institutions of the nation, a bulwark against both disorder and nefarious foreign influences. In the 1940s, the development of the intelligence services paralleled the political agenda of removing the military from electoral politics. This combination laid the foundation for PRI dominance over decades. However, it also provided a convenient, not to say risk-free, opportunity to shift the natural loyalties of the military from the realm of overt defense of the nation—including political campaigns, office holding, and the like—to a more covert defense of the nation involving surveillance of opposition groups, identifying and infiltrating subversive groups, and other intelligence activities.

Throughout this process, the military remained a crucial pillar of the state and a key factor in the longevity of the PRI in government. When the Partido Auténtico de la Revolución Mexicana (PARM) was formed in 1954, one of the key goals was to reiterate the social and political importance of the armed forces in Mexican society. This did not mean military dominance in politics, but rather a level of recognition of the vital role that soldiers played in the defense of the *patria*. It was this sense of duty and obligation that was transferred to the task of running the domestic intelligence services.

In 1985, the DFS and the DGIPS were fused into a single, national intelligence agency. This new agency, the Dirección de Investigación y Seguridad Nacional (DISEN) was itself transformed in 1989 into the Centro de Investigación y Seguridad Nacional (CISEN), which exists to this day. The stated mission of the present-day CISEN is "to develop and operate a system of investigation and analysis of strategic, tactical and operational intelligence to

---

12. Roderic Ai Camp, *Generals in the Palacio: The Military in Modern Mexico* (New York: Oxford University Press, 1992), 237–48; Roderic Ai Camp, *Mexico's Military on the Democratic Stage* (Westport, Conn.: Praeger Security International, 2005), 104–7.

aid in decision making."[13] It has returned to the convention of civilian directors with one notable exception. Jorge Carrillo Olea graduated first in his class at the Heroic Military College, became a professor at the Higher War College, served as a director of military intelligence, and was the only military subsecretary outside of the Secretariat of Defense in the mid-1980s.[14] In short, he possessed sufficient academic and professional credentials to be accepted in an organization geared toward civilian leadership.

Venustiano Carranza originally utilized the Servicios Confidenciales, an office of only twenty people, for surveillance of his political friends and foes.[15] After the revolution, the agency was charged with aiding the government in the "perfection . . . of the revolutionary government and the nation as a whole."[16] As secretary of Gobernación for Carranza, Manuel Aguirre Berlanga formed a corps of "Investigative Agents" who were paid out of the "Secret Expenses Account" of his department. The agents did not have office space, and all of their financial paperwork, assignments, and investigative reports were handled personally by the chief of staff of Gobernación.[17]

Subsecretary of Gobernación Gilberto Valenzuela, later a supporter of both Escobar and Almazán as well as a Supreme Court justice, started the

Table 4.4 Directors of the DISEN/CISEN

1985–89	Lic. Pedro Vázquez Colmenares
1989–90	Gen. y Lic. Jorge Carrillo Olea
1990–93	Lic. Fernando del Villar Moreno
1993–94	Lic. Eduardo Pontones Chico
1994–99	Ing. Jorge Enrique Tello Peón
1999–2000	Lic. Alejandro Alegre Rabiela
2000–2006	Lic. Eduardo Medina Mora Icaza
2006–7	Dr. Ing. Jaime Domingo López Buitrón
2007–	Lic. Guillermo Valdés Castellanos

SOURCE: Aguayo Quezada, *El almanaque mexicano*, 146; CISEN, e-mail message to author, Sep. 26, 2003.

13. "Desarrollar y operar un sistema de investigación y análisis de inteligencia estratégica, táctica y operativa para la toma de decisiones," CISEN, http://www.cisen.org.mx.

14. Roderic Ai Camp, *Mexican Political Biographies, 1935–1993*, 3rd ed. (Austin: University of Texas Press, 1995), 122–23; Humberto Musacchio, *Quién es quién en la política mexicana* (Mexico City: Plaza y Janés, 2002), 75–76.

15. Sergio Aguayo Quezada, *La charola: Una historia de los servicios de inteligencia en México* (Mexico City: Grijalbo, 2001), 37; also, CISEN, http://www.cisen.org.mx.

16. Mena Alcocer, "Resumen," AGN-DGIPS, Box 58, File 1, pp. 750–82. Also cited in Aguayo, *La charola*, 38.

17. Mena Alcocer, "Resumen," AGN-DGIPS, Box 58, File 1, pp. 753–54.

Oficina de Servicios Confidenciales in 1920 to further organize Carranza's 1918 creation.[18] At first, the agents dealt only with the subsecretary, a practice later amended so that they went directly to the head of Servicios Confidenciales. This position was held successively between 1920 and 1923 by Rafael Flores, Lamberto García, Jesus Moreno, Miguel Gutierrez, and Gral. Paulino Navarro, although the precise dates of their service are unclear. (Navarro was killed during operations to put down the de la Huerta rebellion in 1923.) By the early 1920s, the confidential agents had expanded their range to include investigations both within the city and outside of it.[19]

Plutarco Elías Calles shepherded the agency to department status through his years as secretary of Gobernación (1920–23) and as president (1924–28), realizing the advantages of timely and accurate political intelligence.[20] Col. Martín Barcenas undertook the task of converting the Servicios Confidenciales into the DC in 1924 and formalizing the procedures of the group of twenty agents. But because Barcenas spent most of his tenure in Jalisco, conducting operations against the de la Huerta rebellion, his deputy, Lt. Col. Ignacio Jiménez, "practically ran the Office until August 11 [1924] when his position was abolished by order of the Secretary [of Gobernación]."[21]

When Barcenas resigned to become inspector general of the Mexico City Police, Lt. Col. Eufrasio Ortega introduced new methods for the agents to follow, including signing into and out of the DC offices and writing draft reports at home. Importantly, he also oversaw the production of a set of political dossiers of all governors, congressmen, and senators. The practice of creating political profiles of all officeholders and candidates in elections extended across the twentieth-century history of these services and became the backbone of political analysis and strategy. Ortega also began a series of morning lectures for the benefit of the newer agents, run by agents Pastor Navarrete and Francisco M. Delgado (who succeeded Ortega as chief). In one lecture, Navarrete defined a confidential agent as "an element of security for the person who appointed the agent to his position."[22] This comment assigned agents a personal stake in the service they provided, while linking them deeply to the underlying mission of the intelligence group.

18. Roderic Ai Camp, *Mexican Political Biographies, 1884–1935* (Austin: University of Texas Press, 1991), 218–19.

19. Mena Alcocer, "Resumen," AGN-DGIPS, Box 58, File 1, pp. 754–55.

20. AGN-DGIPS, Box 43, File 10, 128.1-"35."

21. Mena Alcocer, "Resumen," AGN-DGIPS, Box 58, File 1, pp. 757–58.

22. Ibid.

Francisco M. Delgado, a lawyer from Guadalajara, rose to the rank of colonel during the revolution. He worked in Jalisco under the tutelage of Governor Basilio Vadillo before becoming a political information agent in Mexico City. He was promoted to head of the DC owing to the influence of Calles himself, who had appreciated Delgado's work during the de la Huerta rebellion. José de la Luz Mena Alcocer, a long-serving agent who wrote a detailed historical sketch of the early years of the Mexican secret police, viewed Delgado as the best leader the service had yet known given his treatment of the agents, "who did not see themselves as subordinates, but rather as collaborators" in the security of the nation. Further, "his efforts were not of *command* but rather of *coordination* of the activities of Agents and employees in service to the revolutionary institutions."[23]

Delgado oversaw a period of intense activity, including the Cristero crisis, the Serrano and Escobar rebellions, and other cases of political unrest. His success as head of the agency was due in part to his selection of "at least fifty percent of the agents from the ranks of former doctors, licenciados, professors, businessmen, [and] women." He carefully chose an appropriate agent for each investigation by attempting to match that person's particular character and qualities to the situation. Delgado's relatively long tenure brought a new level of prestige to the DC, and he was chosen to organize the secret service of the Secretariat of Finance and Auditing. The respect that Delgado engendered in the heads of government departments, such as War and Foreign Relations, ensured their cooperation in his investigations as well.[24]

Pablo Meneses was a trusted lieutenant of Emilio Portes Gil and became deputy head of the DC during his mentor's presidency. Agents delivered their intelligence reports personally to Portes Gil, along with Meneses, in the former's home and often at night. In his capacity as head of the DC, Meneses implemented his plan for making it a viable producer of political information, if not a professional one. The plan recognized the need for an expansion in the number of agents, political information from agents on the ground around the country, the surveillance of expatriates abroad (mainly in the United States), and the maintenance of strict secrecy for the handful of "confidential agents" that remained. More interesting was Meneses' proposal to create a "registry of political military officials and seditious elements" as well

23. Promoted to head of the DC: Mena Alcocer, "Resumen," AGN-DGIPS, Box 58, File 1, p. 762; "rather as collaborators" and "*coordination* of the activities": ibid., 757–58, emphasis added.
24. Mena Alcocer, "Resumen," AGN-DGIPS, Box 58, File 1, p. 762.

as an "impartial" commission that would judge the intentions of those on the list.[25] This registry marked the beginning of a long and voluminous tradition within the Mexican intelligence services.

Col. Adalberto Torres Estrada came to the DC from the office of the chief of staff for the president and was suggested for the job by Pascual Ortiz Rubio. Mena Alcocer saw this appointment as further proof of the "loss of principles" within the DC and a clear indicator that the mission of the group had changed: "[it now] had as its primary objective serving the President of the Republic." Torres Estrada retained strong ties to the president's office and, in fact, did not resign from the general staff of the president upon accepting the post in the DC. Instead, he simply delegated much of the administrative work to his deputy, Maj. Francisco Beas Mendoza, a "cultured military man" who had graduated from the Colegio Militar and began to "set rules for" (reglementar) the DC.[26]

Torres Estrada and his deputies resigned on September 6, 1932, when Ortiz Rubio left office. Maj. Maximiliano Chávez Aldeco took command of an organization that still had only fifteen agents to cover the entire country and special missions in the United States. These agents were given improbably large areas of surveillance. For example, Agent 4 was charged with keeping track of "elements and activities of Generals Cedillo and Almazán," while Agent 3 was assigned the "Confederación General de Trabajadores [CGT], public opinion, merchants, industrialists, professionals, news media, etc."[27] With such large areas of responsibility, it was all that agents could do to provide basic observations about the most important areas of activity within their portfolios.

The personnel of the DC were subject to high rates of turnover. Incredibly, when Delgado resigned from the DC in 1930, all of the inspectors of the department resigned alongside him, except for Mena Alcocer. Unfortunately, these agents could not be trusted by the new officials and "were spied upon and watched." The new agents hired were drawn from two groups: half were suggested by the new chief, Pablo Meneses, and had worked with him in the inspector's office of the Mexico City Police, and half were appointed by higher officials in Gobernación. As with Delgado and Torres Estrada, the

25. Delivered their intelligence reports: Mena Alcocer, "Resumen," AGN-DGIPS, Box 58, File 1, p. 759; "confidential agents" and "seditious elements": ibid., 766.

26. Mena Alcocer, "Resumen," AGN-DGIPS, Box 58, File 1, p. 769.

27. Resigned on September 6: Mena Alcocer, "Resumen," AGN-DGIPS, Box 58, File 1, p. 775; "elements and activities" and "merchants, industrialists, professionals": ibid., 777.

resignation of Meneses was complemented by the mass resignation of the entire corps of agents, except for Mena Alcocer.[28]

Staffing depended on financial considerations as well as personal loyalties. One measure of the importance of domestic intelligence in the early years was its relative level of federal funding and rates of pay for its agents. Although wages were decreasing, the overall budget increased slightly from 1932 to 1933 due to a growing group of inspectors (from five to nine) and smaller group of agents (from thirteen to eleven). The inspectors, who had more specialized training and were more adept at intelligence tasks, commanded higher wages than agents. Most remarkable was the relative stagnation of the formal intelligence budget in light of the major rebellions of Serrano (1927) and Escobar (1929) and the continuing violence associated with the Cristero movement.

The practice of paying an agent's expenses changed significantly during the 1920s. The old method was intended to relieve the agent of the need to sign his or her name on a receipt; the agent operated only in cash and was reimbursed by the chief from a strongbox full of money in his office. The agency's accounting department encountered predictable problems with this approach and by the late 1920s began requiring signed receipts and justification of expenses. The 1929 budget did not formally fund the DC, so Portes

Table 4.5 Departamento Confidencial (selected annual salaries, unadjusted)

Year	Jefe	Inspector de 2a	Agente de 1a	Total Budget
1927	10,220	5,475	4,380	133,812[i]
1928	10,248	5,490	3,660	120,973[ii]
1929	10,220	n/a	3,650	101,105[iii]
1930	10,220	5,475	3,650	98,185[iv]
1931	10,220	5,475	2,920	135,414[v]
1932	10,220	5,475	2,920	85,410[vi]
1933	7,665	4,243	2,336	88,605[vii]

[i] AGN-DGIPS, Box 43, File 14, 128.1-"27," p. 6. This is the only budget of those presented that allocated funds for the position of archivist ("Oficial Primero Archivero").
[ii] AGN-DGIPS, Box 43, File 11, 128.1-"28."
[iii] AGN-DGIPS, Box 43, File 12, 128.1-"29."
[iv] AGN-DGIPS, Box 43, File 3, 128.1-"30," p.5.
[v] AGN-DGIPS, Box 43, File 5, 128.1-"31," p.3.
[vi] AGN-DGIPS, Box 43, File 7, 128.1-"32," p.13.
[vii] AGN-DGIPS, Box 43, File 8, 128.1-"33," p.5.

28. Resigned alongside him: Mena Alcocer, "Resumen," AGN-DGIPS, Box 58, File 1, pp. 760, 762; "spied upon and watched": ibid., 762; drawn from two groups: ibid., 764; mass resignation of the entire corps: ibid., 769, 775.

Gil as president had to name supernumerary agents as a way to continue the work of gathering information. This was especially important given the activity of political and religious groups such as the Cristeros.[29]

In 1938, Gobernación circulated a list of regulations for all of its agencies, among them the Oficina de Información Política (OIP). This document neatly described the method and nature of the tasks set before agents of the OIP. The basic job of the OIP was "to conduct all manner of investigations relative to the political situation of the country and provide confidential services as directed by the senior officials of the Secretariat." The OIP would be staffed by "competent [*idóneos*] inspectors" who would be knowledgeable of the Constitution and laws of the nation, be capable with various types of vehicles, and be able to use diverse means of communication, including encrypted messages. Gobernación attempted to bind the agents quite tightly to the main office, requiring that they send notice of arrival in locations within an hour. The exception to this rule, comically, was that if it was past 8 P.M. the agent should call after 9 A.M. the next day. All of these regulations were meant to provide the framework for a professional and efficient intelligence service.[30]

Of course, problems existed with both the framework and methods of the Mexican services in the 1930s. The intelligence agencies were suspicious of requests for information from other government offices, even from within Gobernación. The head of the DC refused to release any information at all to the head of the legal section of Gobernación since "as much the nature as the variety of our tasks" precluded it. Yet, by September 1938, well after the Cedillo rebellion began, Gobernación gave explicit instructions to the OIP regarding the preparation of a daily intelligence briefing to be delivered to the president. The struggle to control information, familiar to any observer of bureaucracies, was present in Mexico. Before the development of the DFS within the president's office, the president already had, essentially, an in-house staff of intelligence advisors. This was evident in 1945 when the Transit Department in Mexico City denied agents of the DGIPS important data, as "it was [already] informing the President daily of the same information."[31]

29. Receipts and justification of expenses: Mena Alcocer, "Resumen," AGN-DGIPS, Box 58, File 1, p. 762; activity of political and religious groups: ibid., 759–60.

30. AGN-DGIPS, Box 36.

31. "Variety of our tasks": Memo, Torres Estrada to Díaz Escobar, Aug. 15, 1932, AGN-DGIPS, Box 37, File 11, 100–14; daily intelligence briefing: Memo, Agustín Rodríguez Ochoa to Director of OIP, Sep. 19, 1938, AGN-DGIPS, Box 132, 2.1/300(04)/1; "informing the President daily": Report, Insps. 13 and 16 to DGIPS, Sep. 5, 1945, AGN-DGIPS, Box 750, File 3, 2.1/A.G.D./818, Vol. 1.

Over the years, the policy and practice governing secrecy within the intelligence services varied. Under Berlanga, the identity of agents was such a strict secret that "only the Chief of Staff and his assistant knew the Agents, who entered and left his offices as if they were regular people seeking an audience with him." During the early 1920s, the agency "*sometimes* had the character of a true confidential service." In other situations, notably when working with the city police, the secrecy of agent identities was not maintained. During his tenure, Jiménez implemented many of the lasting reforms within the agency, including a rule that agents not identify themselves "even to the Authorities" without prior permission of the Department.[32] Ortega restated the policy of strict secrecy of agent identities, a fact to be kept even from all friends and family. Agents were given false identification cards and phony associations with existing companies, such as the Red Cross or news organizations. Under Delgado, the policy of strict secrecy was extended with the automatic denial of any information about an agent to, and a prohibition on making appointments with, anyone not of the agency.[33]

However, new rules meant to regulate the time each agent spent in the office, including announcing arrivals and departures by name, fomented a culture of carelessness in regard to the secrecy of identities. Agents often talked to outsiders about their jobs in intelligence gathering, and even those trying to maintain their cover were easily spotted as federal agents. This was more prevalent among those agents who had previously worked in the inspector's office of the Mexico City Police: "The indiscretion was so notorious that many times an agent would receive details of his new assignment from another agent before hearing it from the Chief." During the tenure of Chávez Aldeco as head of the DC, some agents "in their zeal to acquire documents, that often lack confidential value . . . present themselves as Confidential Agents to get the papers and rig them to their report."[34] The secrecy of agent identities, a mainstay of effective undercover investigation, was a goal that Mexican intelligence often missed.

A level of distrust pervaded even the president's office, which the agents provided with intelligence. "The functioning of the service was almost personalist, given that the agents often worked on security details of the President, a service that he disliked, such that they had to do their work discreetly

32. "Regular people seeking an audience": Mena Alcocer, "Resumen," AGN-DGIPS, Box 58, File 1, pp. 753–54; "true confidential service": ibid., 754–55, emphasis added; "even to the Authorities": ibid., 757–58.

33. Mena Alcocer, "Resumen," AGN-DGIPS, Box 58, File 1, pp. 757–58.

34. Previously worked in the Inspector's Office: Mena Alcocer, "Resumen," AGN-

around him, although many of the agents were perfectly well-known to the political groups."[35] The knowledge of who was an intelligence agent of the government produced a security problem, given that the agency was tasked with developing intelligence on friends and enemies of the administration. Anyone with sufficient power to have contact with and knowledge of the president's security detail was exactly the kind of person upon whom the intelligence agents would have been building a dossier.

Agents were divided into two groups: "political agents" (*agentes de información política*) and "confidential agents" (*agentes confidenciales*). Political agents concentrated on investigative assignments, while confidential agents worked on "executive" or police matters. Political agents were given three sets of identification documents, including credentials as both a travel agent and a public health official, and a press badge. When conducting investigations abroad, these agents were expected to maintain the secrecy of their identities.[36] It is difficult to understand how they accomplished this, considering the intermittent cooperation of Mexican agents with U.S. officials from the FBI, customs, or local police forces. Finally, all agents were provided with police badges, which could be used for train travel, entering venues, or requesting police assistance.[37]

The agents were divided into working groups to maximize productivity, but they were still understaffed for the nature of the task ahead of them. For example, Agents 1, 3, and 4 held the very large portfolio of covering "centers, alliances, parties, unions, daily press, transportation, buses [and] the Secretariat of Industry and Commerce."[38] The agents were instructed to submit a daily written report that would be abstracted in a briefing document for the president. This system clearly did not allow sufficient time or care to be taken in investigating real issues, and it forced the agents to produce written pages at times without regard for quality. In this way, intelligence reports often contained nothing more than hastily typed, random data gathered in the course of the day. The element of *analysis,* crucial to the production of useful intelligence, was sorely lacking.

DGIPS, Box 58, File 1, p. 764; "indiscretion was so notorious": ibid., 765; "zeal to acquire documents": ibid., 777.

35. Mena Alcocer, "Resumen," AGN-DGIPS, Box 58, File 1, p. 775.

36. Ibid., 761.

37. Intermittent cooperation of Mexican agents: Memo, Insp. 31 to DGIPS, Sep. 18, 1940, and Sep. 27, 1940, San Antonio, AGN-DGIPS, Box 191, 2.1/311.1/5, Vol. 19; provided with police badges: Mena Alcocer, "Resumen," AGN-DGIPS, Box 58, File 1, p. 761.

38. Mena Alcocer, "Resumen," AGN-DGIPS, Box 58, File 1, p. 770.

Agents of the DGIPS also took responsibility for relaying voting tallies from around the country during municipal, state, and federal elections.[39] Whether these totals were "official" is questionable, but they may have served to alert the managers at Gobernación to danger spots following a vote. At the very least, the early reports from agents in the field offered officials in Mexico City a glimpse of the national political situation on the ground.

In the early stages, the Mexican services performed basic surveillance and investigated cases of national interest. They also worked on security arrangements and basic questions of interest to the government. In few instances did these investigations go beyond the mundane. For example, from August 1924 through July 1925, the DC undertook forty-eight investigations in the category "Generalities." These included reports on matters such as the occupation and salary of a citizen named Lic. Carlos Salcedo, whether the film *Furia Desatada* was "denigrating" to the country, and which stores sold turquoise by the pound. There were forty investigations in the category "Political Matters," including reports on the "antecedents and political affiliations" of all electoral candidates at all levels, the municipal elections in Chiapas, Nayarit, and Puebla, and the "actions of the French Consul in Mexico against our country." The DC reported thirty cases in the category of "Localizations and Apprehensions," including incidents with Mexican, Spanish, and U.S. citizens. Ten cases of "Crimes" were reported, including episodes of fraud, the manufacture and sale of illicit drugs, and illegal gambling. The large category of "Antecedentes y Costumbres" recorded sixty-one investigations, mainly of public officials, foreign citizens in Mexico (U.S., Italian, Greek, and Spanish), and the odd army officer. Finally, the small sections of "Expulsions," "Work Stoppages and Strikes," and "Railroads" offered evidence that only eight persons had been expelled from Mexico during the year and that the political activity of the railroad workers was fast becoming an issue of deep concern for the government.[40] These reports, along with those filed for other years, provide a profile of the kind of work the early Mexican intelligence services were doing.

Specifically, these cases do not add much to the overall explanation of the history of the Mexican services. In general, however, they demonstrate that

39. See, for example, Report, Insp. 16 to DGIPS, Jul. 11, 1946; Memo, Baig Serra to Gobernación, Jul. 12, 1946; Report, Insp. 63 to DGIPS, Jul. 12, 1946 (all located in AGN-DGIPS, Box 750, File 1, 2.1/A.G.D./818, Vol. 2).

40. Report, "Informe de los trabajos desempeñados por el Departamento Confidencial de la Secretaría de Gobernación, de primero de agosto de 1924 al treinta y uno de julio del corriento año," Aug. 5, 1925, AGN-DGIPS, Box 38, File 1, 7/100(016)/4.

at the early stages, federal agents concentrated on relatively innocent tasks and basic investigations. In this sense, Sergio Aguayo's interpretation of an overly violent, intensely political domestic intelligence corps at this early stage is mistaken.[41] The intelligence agents of 1925 were not the Halcones of 1968. Mexican intelligence agents became increasingly politicized beginning in the late 1930s as they developed greater technical skill and their managers started to place more emphasis on strictly political tasks. This shift was not complete until after the election of 1952, when the military was effectively removed from electoral politics and the PRI had consolidated political control. Only then could the intelligence agents, armed with U.S. training and funds, dedicate themselves to political surveillance wholeheartedly. While the agencies that did such grievous harm to Mexican society during and after the 1960s had their roots in the old DC, the shift toward violent repression occurred over time and the new ethos was not fully entrenched until the early 1950s.

Changes in the Mexican intelligence agents occured through the 1940s. During this period, a new sense of politicization permeated their reports and activities. As the agents became more adept at professional intelligence collection and analysis, they also developed more lasting ties to the bureaucracy of the government and, more importantly, the dominant party. In the 1920s, agents were often political appointees or short-term replacements, not necessarily professional investigators. In the late 1930s and into the 1940s, the corps of agents began to stay longer in their positions, earning higher rank and pay and developing loyalty to the system that provided them with a living. In this process, the agents chose to align themselves with the ever more powerful political project of the PRM/PRI and became tools of political control for the party.

Already in 1934, Mena Alcocer criticized the nascent politicization of the intelligence services as a sign of their "decadence," evident in two processes. First was "the political importance that Gobernación has lost with the establishment of the Partido Nacional Revolucionario (PNR), which basically resolves conflicts before they appear in the official sphere." The second process was "the orientation that has been given to the confidential services, which at times have lost their basic footing, their discretion, and sometimes, the policy of principles." But not all agents were unscrupulous: in 1938 an agent opined that he "proceed[ed] with truth and professional rectitude in

41. Aguayo, *La charola,* 35–59.

the task because, since political problems are delicate, they should be treated with complete impartiality regardless of the persons involved."[42]

Claims to impartiality decreased in the late 1930s and early 1940s. One of the longest serving agents in the DGIPS was Manuel Ríos Thivol. His attention to detail and sometimes stunning ability to infiltrate organizations made his reports among the most consistently useful to his superiors. However, during the election of 1940, his apparently deep-seated contempt for elements of the conservative right in Mexico gushed forth in an ill-advised, and bluntly political, memorandum. He excoriated "those Organizations that operate under the political banner of *Almazanismo,* in order to hide what to my judgment are nothing more than Sinarquistas and Reactionaries, patent enemies of the present system of government of the Nation."[43] This outburst betrayed Thivol's personal politics as much as it demonstrated the creeping acceptability of such sentiments among the corps of agents and their superiors who read such reports.

Mexican intelligence agents often relied on simple presentation of information in their reports, although the memoranda could sometimes include prescriptive material. One such case occurred during the 1952 campaign, when the state governor was "disposed towards repressing the Henríquez rally that is being planned, using force if necessary." The reporting agent, however, suggested that "Mexico [i.e., the government] send precise instructions, since it is quite possible that it will provoke a bloody clash with fatal results, and in that case the state government could be blamed for the deaths."[44] It is clear that the agent was attempting to both interpret the political desires of the central government and provide cover for the state government authorities if the operation went badly. Intelligence agents did not often play the role of mediator in essentially political disputes, making this case an interesting exception.

A commonplace in any intelligence organization is what Allen Dulles called "overt intelligence."[45] Also known as open-source intelligence, this

---

42. "Political importance" and "lost their basic footing": Mena Alcocer, "Resumen," AGN-DGIPS, Box 58, File 1, p. 763; "truth and professional rectitude": Report, Insp. 4 to DGIPS, Jun. 14, 1938, AGN-DGIPS, Box 75, File 1, 130–606, p. 384.

43. Report, Insp. Thivol to DGIPS, Apr. 5, 1940, Tuxtla Gutiérrez, AGN-DGIPS, Box 30, File 4, 2.1/062.2(72)/2.

44. Memo, DGIPS, [Aug. 1951], AGN-DGIPS, Box 25, 2.1/061.8/15, Vol. 2, p. 105.

45. Allen Dulles, *The Craft of Intelligence* (New York: Harper and Row, 1963), 55. This book, written by the man who "made" the modern CIA, is a sort of primer on what intelligence is and how to obtain it.

category includes newspapers, press releases, radio programs, advertisements, books, and even theatrical presentations. It allows for the compilation of basic information on the status of governments, political and social groups, and other subjects of interest. The archival collections of the Mexican intelligence agencies are filled with newspaper and article clippings, book reviews, and loose flyers from political and cultural groups. These materials are often accompanied by a brief summary of the conditions surrounding whatever kernel of information is contained in the open source. Occasionally, a printed political announcement would spark an investigation of the signers, as was the case with railroad worker Leobardo Flores Vera after the publication of an advertisement critical of President Ávila Camacho.[46] In all, the foundation of Mexican intelligence efforts was a careful and thorough summary of daily press and other media sources.

Federal agents also maintained a time-honored and mostly ineffective simple surveillance of opposition figures. This typically involved posting a car outside of the subject's residence or office, noting the license plate information of visiting vehicles, commenting on any rumors heard in the mill of people outside the compounds, and so on. Following the election of 1952, Henríquez's Coyoacán home was monitored by officers of the Secret Service of the Mexico City Police, stationed in cars both in front and behind the house, as well as a carload of agents of the DFS.[47] This method concentrated on collection and not analysis. While there was no shortage of raw data in such an operation, "large numbers of trained personnel are required to cull it in order to find the grain of wheat in the mountains of chaff."[48] It was mainly in this area that the Mexican services through the early 1940s were found wanting: they did not have a regular and effective system in place to convert raw data into finished intelligence.

Moreover, before 1946 Mexican intelligence agents simply did not have a sense of the relative importance of information, sometimes privileging rumors or trifling matters over important developments. In one example, a sixteen-year-old informed the agency that while in a brewery, a group of men had gathered around a portrait of opposition presidential candidate Almazán and claimed that he would soon assume power. The DGIPS began to

46. Report, Insp. 29 to DGIPS, Jul. 21, 1946, Guadalajara, AGN-DGIPS, Box 750, File 1, 2.1/A.G.D./818, Vol. 2.

47. Report, Insp. Garay to DGIPS, Oct. 8, 1952, AGN-DGIPS, Box 29, File 17, 2.1/061.8/15, Vol. 12, p. 133.

48. Dulles, *Craft of Intelligence,* 56.

investigate the veracity of the matter to discover "if it is some kind of Committee." Another agent vowed to unravel a rumor that two high-level politicians had privately bet each other twenty thousand pesos as to whether Almazán would be appointed secretary of the national economy after his electoral defeat. In another case, an agent determined that the subject of his investigation was not at home by questioning "the boy who always comes to the door to see who is there."[49] This level of scrutiny, while admirable in the sense of being thorough, needlessly distracted agents and budgetary assets away from more useful veins of inquiry. Further, the Mexican intelligence services were "not coordinated in any systematic manner . . . [and were] limited to the Federal District of Mexico City, disregarding the rest of the interior and coastal points in the country."[50]

Financial and professional weaknesses aside, Mexican agents were at times able to provide timely and substantial intelligence. The case of the Cedillo rebellion demonstrated such capability. In February 1938, a month before the rebellion, a federal agent reported the quantity and quality of arms in the hands of *cedillistas* in San Luis Potosí, as well as their capacity for manufacturing ammunition.[51] Agents provided crucial intelligence again in the autumn of 1948 when a group of army generals led by Antonio Rios Zertuche and Juan Barragán began efforts to form a political party to challenge the growing hegemony of the PRI. This movement was a serious threat to the nascent tradition of civilian governance in Mexico and therefore worthy of intense surveillance. There were several instances that could have tipped off the news media, such as when Rios Zertuche conferred with Fernando Casas Alemán about his plans or when the army group held meetings with former presidents Ávila Camacho, Portes Gil, Abelardo Rodríguez, and Ortiz Rubio. Any of these figures could have broken the news to the morning papers that a political storm was brewing within military circles.[52] The fact that the government was able to keep this story out of public view long enough to begin dealing with the issue signaled an intelligence success.

49. "Some kind of Committee": Report, Insp. 1 to DGIPS, Apr. 16, 1942, AGN-DGIPS, Box 23, File 1, 2.1/061.7(725.1)/2, p. 73; unravel a rumor: Report, Insp. 19 to DGIPS, Oct. 29, 1940, AGN-DGIPS, Box 191, 2.1/311.1/5, File "General Juan Andrew Almazán, Candidato a la Presidencia de la República: Sus actividades después de las elecciones"; "boy who always comes to the door": Report, Insp. 1 to DGIPS, Mar. 19, 1942, AGN-DGIPS, Box 23, File 1, 2.1/061.7(725.1)/2, p. 62.

50. Memo, MID, Sep. 15, 1941, NARA, Record Group 165, Box 2450.

51. Report, Insp. 7 to DGIPS, Feb. 24, 1938, AGN-DGIPS, Box 134, 310(4.2)-"38."

52. Memo, DGIPS, Aug. 17, 1948; Memo, DGIPS, Aug. 19, 1948; Memo, Gobernación, Sep. 27, 1948 (all located in AGN-DGIPS, Box 24, File 3, 2.1/061.8/3).

Even though the intelligence bureaucracy was often used to consolidate particular political goals, it is important to emphasize that the political opposition was not the only target of government surveillance. Just as Carranza had used the DC to spy on his friends and enemies, the PRM/PRI utilized the intelligence services to keep track of internal feuds and external opposition threats. For example, in Sinaloa, the federal agent on the scene reported that the Henríquez campaign was gaining ground because the state government was divided between the president of the State Committee of the PRI and its secretary general.[53] This information was presumably taken to the national leaders of the PRI in an attempt to mediate the dispute.

The intelligence services kept track of all political activity, regardless of party affiliation, including the campaigns of the PRM/PRI candidates for president.[54] Agents were also employed to gather useful information about the intentions and activities of high military commanders. After the 1952 elections, a joint report among six agents described the movements and apparent tactics of federal troops in Mexico City.[55] Additional information flowed to Gobernación from a system of commissioned (*comisionado*) citizens of small towns and villages across the country who reported any local disturbances. While U.S. authorities viewed this information as "uncoordinated, scarcely legible and often unsupported," officials at Gobernación considered it a kind of grassroots early warning system for potential unrest.[56] The increasing use of the domestic intelligence service to monitor the activity of friends and enemies of the administration, while continuing a tradition begun well before Carranza, signaled a turning point in Mexican politics: the beginning of a more sophisticated age of surveillance.

Basic information on organizations and individuals formed the backbone of many intelligence reports. During the 1930s, monthly reports were compiled outlining the political situation in every Mexican state, including details of regional disputes, activity of foreign elements in the state, conflicts within and between political factions, results of elections, and local social issues. While not entirely political in nature, these reports served as briefing books

53. Memo, DGIPS, Feb. 15, 1952, AGN-DGIPS, Box 27, File 1, 2.1/061.8/15, Vol. 7, p. 99.

54. For the Ávila Camacho campaign of 1940, see AGN-DGIPS, Boxes 185–87, 2.1/311.1/2, Vols. 1–12.

55. Report, Insps. GTO, GMA, MPR, ACO, RBA, and JLP to DGIPS, Nov. 30, 1952, AGN-DGIPS, Box 29, File 17, 2.1/061.8/15, Vol. 12, pp. 528–29.

56. Report, "Nazi, Communist and Other Foreign Agents in Mexico," Consul Robert G. McGregor Jr., Jun. 28, 1940, p. 28, NARA, Record Group 165, Box 2463.

for high government officials who needed detailed information about re-gional issues.[57] Some reports were nothing more than lists of supporters of a particular campaign, such as the local directors of the Henríquez campaign in Oaxaca.[58] Other reports included extensive background on municipal and state elections and candidates.[59] Mexican agents also kept abreast of social movements during their political investigations. One agent working in Jalisco commented on the number of *corridos* and *versos circulantes* that focused on candidates Calderón, Padilla, and Henríquez in 1945 as a way of gauging public reaction to their campaigns.[60]

Because it is relatively easy to seed open-source materials with disinforma-tion, "clandestine intelligence (espionage) must remain an essential and basic activity of intelligence."[61] Although the Mexican services were ill equipped to conduct consistently useful open-source analyses, that weakness did not impugn their prowess in the field of infiltration, a form of domestic espio-nage. Given the often disorganized and underfunded nature of opposition candidacies and campaigns, volunteers and even intelligence agents were able to occupy important posts within the opposition, apparently undetected. This was the case when a DGIPS agent became a *delegado propagandista* for the Partido Autonomista Mexicano in 1942. In another instance, supporters of Nicolás Rodríguez offered to intervene to help their friend, an undercover federal agent, obtain a permit to stay in the United States as a "political refugee" in 1938. Inspector 87 gained the trust of a senior advisor to the Padilla campaign and thereby gleaned valuable information about the opposi-tion candidate. Finally, a DGIPS agent managed to insinuate himself into an executive session of the Federación de Partidos del Pueblo Mexicano (FPPM) in October 1952, although a party official eventually asked him to leave.[62]

57. For the period 1924–40, see AGN-DGIPS, Boxes 134–37 and 139–40.

58. Memo, DGIPS, [1952], AGN-DGIPS, Box 815, 2.1/52/528.

59. While this study focuses on the national level, the documents of the DGIPS archive are very rich in the field of local and state politics. See, for example, AGN-DGIPS, Boxes 761–70.

60. Report, Insp. 42 to DGIPS, Jul. 25, 1945, AGN-DGIPS, Box 750, File 3, 2.1/A.G.D./ 818, Vol. 1.

61. Dulles, *Craft of Intelligence*, 58.

62. Became a delegado propagandista: Report, Insp. 1 to DGIPS, Mar. 26, 1942, AGN-DGIPS, Box 23, File 1, 2.1/061.7(725.1)/2, p. 66; "political refugee": Report, Insp. 15 to DGIPS, Dec. 29, 1938, AGN-DGIPS, Box 141, 2.1/310.1/18; trust of a senior advisor: Report, Insp. 87 to DGIPS, Aug. 11, 1945, AGN-DGIPS, Box 750, File 3. 2.1/A.G.D./818, Vol. 1; executive session: Report, Insps. RMA and VRA to DGIPS, Oct. 7, 1952, AGN-DGIPS, Box 29, File 17, 2.1/061.8/15, Vol. 12, p. 124.

A very public case of infiltration was the tracking of Almazán's movements on his post-election trip from Veracruz to Havana and then to the U.S in 1940. An intelligence agent posing as a fellow passenger apparently befriended Almazán during the voyage and gathered information about his itinerary. Why Almazán trusted a stranger with details of his political plans is unclear. Nevertheless, on August 26, Almazán arrived in Mobile, Alabama, onboard the United Fruit Lines boat *Turrialba* traveling from Panama.[63] He was visibly agitated that his arrival, which he had planned to be secret, was so well known in advance that reporters from the local press (complete with bulb-popping photographers) awaited him on the dock, along with a group of his political advisors. The secrecy was intended to veil his movements to confuse the tactics of the Cárdenas administration as it sought to restrain the continuing opposition agitation. Almazán and his advisors promptly boarded a train headed to Baltimore.[64] The case of an agent penetrating the security measures of a serious opposition candidate only weeks after a hotly disputed election was a remarkable intelligence feat.

However, the concept of infiltration did not apply only to those agents who took positions within the opposition parties or managed to insinuate themselves into elite circles. Throughout the 1940s, agents of the DGIPS were able to regularly interview opposition aides and advisors in something akin to modern "background briefings." This technique fit the Dulles definition of espionage as "nothing more than a kind of well-concealed reconnaissance."[65] The usual tactic was for an agent to pose as a regular citizen interested in a given group who would then loiter at the party headquarters awaiting "orientaciones."[66] Although the nature of the collection method was rather basic, and prone to disinformation tactics, it also provided a decent gauge of the mood and preoccupations of the supporters of the group under surveillance. In all, the generalized openness of the organizational process in Mexican politics in the 1940s gave the upper hand to those who wished to either simply gather information or actually do real harm within opposition

---

63. Report, Insp. Ruiz Russek to DGIPS, Aug. 24, 1940, San Antonio, AGN-DGIPS, Box 191, 2.1/311.1/5, Vol. 17. Also, *Mobile Register,* Aug. 27, 1940; *Excélsior,* Aug. 27, 1940 (both located in AGN-DGIPS, Box 191, 2.1/311.1/5, Vol. 18).

64. Well known in advance: *Mobile Register,* Aug. 27, 1940; promptly boarded a train: *Excélsior,* Aug. 28, 1940 (both located in AGN-DGIPS, Box 191, 2.1/311.1/5, Vol. 18).

65. Dulles, *Craft of Intelligence,* 58.

66. This is very common in the intelligence files of the DGIPS archive. See, for example, Memo, Insp. Alemán Pérez to DGIPS, Nov. 21, 1940, AGN-DGIPS, Box 191, 2.1/311.1/5, Vol. 20; Report, Insp. 19 to DGIPS, Jun. 26, 1939, AGN-DGIPS, Box 188, 2.1/311.1/5, Vol. 2.

hierarchies. This process of infiltration was then, and has ever been, the most persistent and fruitful weapon in the arsenal of the Mexican intelligence services.

Due to the surveillance and infiltration sucesses of the DGIPS, the opposition elements aligned against the dominant political group understood the importance of counterintelligence methods. "Counterintelligence is an intelligence activity dedicated to undermining the effectiveness of hostile intelligence services" and aims "to both discern and deceive the plans and intentions of enemy intelligence services."[67] The political opposition sometimes relied on deception to thwart government surveillance. Henríquez employed a body double as a decoy when he needed to meet secretly with supporters or escape from federal scrutiny for other reasons, as was the case when he met with Pedro Rodríguez Triana outside Torreón in 1951. Disinformation could also be used to disorient official assessments of the national situation. In late 1952, rumors heralded a deal struck between Cárdenas, Alemán, and Henríquez that would limit Ruiz Cortines to one year in office before relinquishing power to Henríquez.[68] This rumor, coming on the heels of the Ruiz Cortines inauguration, aimed to embarrass or temporarily destabilize the incoming administration.

Just as federal agents could infiltrate the ranks of the opposition, elements within the government sometimes tried to aid the opposition with information or indirect support. During the unrest following the 1952 elections, a DGIPS agent became alarmed that the Henríquez group "has information of the actions the police are considering, such that it is quite possible that they have one or more sympathizers among the police chiefs or officers."[69]

After the election of 1940, the intelligence bureaucracy advocated an activist line against Almazán's supporters. Pointedly, when the DGIPS discovered that "the almazanistas have enough money to pay for spies," it argued, "All of our activities should tend toward not waiting for events to develop, but rather going out to meet them, to force the abortion of the almazanista preparations."[70] This escalation of the rhetoric and operations was a dual

67. Tyrus G. Fain, ed. *The Intelligence Community: History, Organization, and Issues* (New York: R. R. Bowker, 1977), 381.

68. Body double: Memo, DGIPS, Nov. 22, 1951, AGN-DGIPS, Box 25, File 3, 2.1/061.8/15, Vol. 4, pp. 152–53; rumors heralded a deal: Report, Insp. Delgado Garay to DGIPS, Dec. 2, 1952, AGN-DGIPS, Box 29, File 17, 2.1/061.8/15, Vol. 12, pp. 531–32.

69. Report, [unidentified agent] to DGIPS, Nov. 24, 1952, AGN-DGIPS, Box 29, File 17, 2.1/061.8/15, Vol. 12, p. 483.

70. Memo, DGIPS, Aug. 2, 1940, AGN-DGIPS, Box 191, 2.1/311.1/5, File "General

attempt to squelch the political opposition as well as halt the development of a group of opposition intelligence agents in Mexico. In part, the new activism was fueled by a nascent sense of impunity among the federal agents. One case of this was the warrantless search in November 1940 of the home of Héctor F. López, provisional president of the almazanista rump congress, by men claiming to be agents of the attorney general.[71] Such a combination of activism and impunity allowed the government agents to work consistently toward the degradation of the opposition's influence both in Mexico and abroad.

While most agents operated within Mexico, a small group of inspectors conducted surveillance and intelligence-gathering operations in the United States. English language classes were instituted in the DC on July 1, 1931, only to be cancelled three months later amid criticisms that the coursework took too much time away from investigations. These agents usually operated with the knowledge and consent of the U.S. authorities, most often the FBI and the customs service, and sometimes from within the diplomatic offices of Mexico in the United States. In May 1938, an agent of the DGIPS was conducting surveillance of Nicolás Rodríguez's movements in South Texas and his attempts to buy arms for a "revolutionary movement in Mexico." Interestingly, the U.S. War Department, while recognizing the limits of his influence, considered Rodríguez a candidate for recruitment as an agent.[72] In another instance, one Mexican agent worked in tandem with U.S. officials investigating a man identified only as Lebman, who was allegedly obtaining arms in San Antonio for the followers of Almazán after the presidential election of 1940.[73] Another coordinated Mexican efforts with the FBI to track Almazán's movements along the U.S.-Mexico border. A U.S. Secret Service agent relayed information to a DGIPS officer about connections between Almazán and U.S. presidential candidate Wendell Willkie. The DGIPS maintained an agent in San Antonio to keep watch on the elements of opposition,

Juan Andrew Almazán, Candidato a la Presidencia de la República: Sus actividades después de las elecciones"; Memo, DGIPS, Aug. 2, 1940, AGN-DGIPS, Box 191, 2.1/311.1/5, Vol. 18.

71. Telegram, McCombs to Thomas Krug (Time), Nov. 15, 1940, Holland McCombs Papers, Special Collections, University of Tennessee at Martin, Box 46, File 23.

72. English language classes: Mena Alcocer, "Resumen," AGN-DGIPS, Box 58, File 1, p. 772; "revolutionary movement in Mexico": Report, Insp. 4 to DGIPS, May 16, 1938, Laredo, AGN-DGIPS, Box 75, File 1, 130–606, p. 350; candidate for recruitment: Military Attaché Report 9163, McCoy to G-2, Aug. 31, 1939, Mexico City, NARA, Record Group 165, Box 2470.

73. Report, Insp. 31 to DGIPS, Sep. 18, 1940, San Antonio; Report, Insp. 31 to DGIPS, Sep. 27, 1940, San Antonio (both located in AGN-DGIPS, Box 191, 2.1/311.1/5, Vol. 19).

even conducting loose surveillance on the local head of the Almazán campaign, a funeral home director named Andrew Morales. Finally, an interesting case of cooperation occurred in 1940 as Mexican agents sent intelligence to Mexico City that they had gleaned from electronic surveillance of a New York apartment used by Almazán supporters.[74] This case was important, too, as evidence of a growing awareness among Mexican agents of the technological advances in intelligence gathering that U.S. agencies enjoyed. Such enhancements of traditional information gathering techniques were a key selling point in the postwar intelligence deal between Alemán and Truman.

The Mexican surveillance efforts within the United States were not without hazards and difficulties, however. Agents consistently ran out of money, time and again forcing a premature end to their intelligence gathering.[75] One agent complained that his efforts to cooperate with U.S. agents had led him to believe that "the American authorities are deceiving me by giving me certain information," a belief that was probably warranted.[76] The sometimes complicated relations between U.S. and Mexican agents could have been a result of lingering distrust from operations involving Francisco "Pancho" Villa in 1914–15, or simply a case of cultural and professional differences. Mexican agents in the United States faced the difficulties of language, cost, and institutional deception during their tours of duty across the northern border, although there was a certain level of identification with the U.S. agents in the Mexican services. Mexican agents adopted not only the methods of the U.S. agents, but their mode of dress as well. In a play on the term for U.S. government agents, "G-men," Mexican agents were colloquially referred to as "Jiménez."

74. Track Almazán's movements: Report, Insp. Gutiérrez to DGIPS, Oct. 16, 1940, Nogales, AGN-DGIPS, Box 191, 2.1/311.1/5, File "General Juan Andrew Almazán, Candidato a la Presidencia de la República: Sus actividades después de las elecciones"; U.S. presidential candidate Wendell Willkie: Report, Insp. 15 to DGIPS, Jun. 21, 1939, AGN-DGIPS, Box 188, 2.1/311.1/5, Vol. 2; conducting loose surveillance: Report, Insp. 1 to DGIPS, Sep. 18, 1939, Piedras Negras, AGN-DGIPS, Box 185, 2.1/311.1/2, Vol. 5; interesting case of cooperation: Report, Insp. 31 to DGIPS, Oct. 24, 1940, San Antonio, AGN-DGIPS, Box 191, 2.1/311.1/5, File "Juan Andrew Almazán, Candidato a la Presidencia de la República: Sus actividades después de las elecciones."

75. Letter, Jesús M. Costas S. [Inspector Jose M. Clavé] to Isidro Pérez Sánchez [IPS], Mar. 18, 1939, Monterrey, AGN-DGIPS, Box 187, 2.1/311.1/5, Vol. 1; Letter, Jesús M. Costas S. [Inspector Jose M. Clavé] to Isidro Pérez Sánchez [IPS], Mar. 25, 1939, Monterrey, AGN-DGIPS, Box 187, 2.1/311.1/5, Vol. 1; Report, Insp. 1 to DGIPS, Sep. 29, 1940, Ciudad Juárez, AGN-DGIPS, Box 191, 2.1/311.1/5, Vol. 19.

76. Report, Insp. 31 to DGIPS, Sep. 23, 1940, San Antonio, AGN-DGIPS, Box 191, 2.1/311.1/5, Vol. 19.

The congruence of technique and style did not necessaril extend to national interests, and the efforts of the Mexican intelligence bureaucracy during the period from 1939 to 1942 were deeply conflicted. On one hand, the Mexicans wanted to cooperate with U.S. priorities of watching and even deporting German spies operating Abwehr offices undercover in Mexico City. On the other hand, it was not until Pearl Harbor that Mexico decisively set itself in opposition to the German project and could safely begin to move against the German spy ring. Much of this had to do with earlier German oil purchases during the expropriation controversy and continuing diplomatic links. This conflictive situation, compounded by a natural Mexican distrust of U.S. intentions—especially when it involved U.S. agents operating on Mexican soil—so muddled the relations that Mexico appeared to be vacillating between alliance with the United States and with the Axis.[77]

Mexican intelligence officials were aware of Nazi activities in 1940 and took actions to thwart them. They had acquired a copy of German files listing all Mexican military commanders and their respective ideological interests "so as to know in what direction they should thrust their attempts at penetration." They also knew that the technical director of the Ericsson telephone network was actively engaged in intercepting calls for collection purposes.[78] These cases, and other examples, demonstrated "the existence of a political espionage net covering the entire Republic." However, Mexican agents were unable to effectively track the "Gold of Berlin" that was allegedly funding the Nazi activities. In fact, they concluded that "there is a Nazi service in Mexico which does not require subsidies from the Reich . . . [and] we should believe that the expenses of the Nazi service in Mexico are paid by the German Colony."[79] These findings provided ample grounds for expanding the surveillance of Germans and other Axis nationals in Mexico.

Although the links between Almazán and the Sinarquista base in "traditional intransigent Mexican ultra-reaction" were weak, they shared a common tie to the Spanish Falange movement. The Office of Strategic Services

77. Leslie B. Rout Jr, and John F. Bratzel, *The Shadow War: German Espionage and United States Counterespionage in Latin America During World War II* (Frederick, Md.: University Publications of America, 1986), 53–105.

78. The Mexican telephone system was dominated at this time by two large foreign companies: Ericsson and Mexicana, a division of ITT. Since all calls were placed through one exchange or the other, the presence of hostile agents in strategic positions in either company was a very serious security situation.

79. Translation of Report, "Nazism in Mexico," Heriberto Conrado Mieli (Gobernación) to Cárdenas, [Jun. 1940], Enclosure to Military Attaché Report 9379, McCoy to G-2, Jun. 4, 1940, Mexico City, NARA, Record Group 165, Box 2463.

(OSS) believed that the common appearance and language of the Spanish Falangistas allowed them to pass as Mexicans and funnel money, intelligence, and training to the Sinarquistas, even after Pearl Harbor.[80] Mexican agents interrogated Servicio Inteligencia Militar (SIM) agent Pedro Rodríguez Valiente in early 1942, and he confirmed that "the SIM was patterned completely after the German Gestapo service, and is taking over its functions in every Latin American country." He also disclosed that the "head of the SIM in Mexico is Alberto Mercado Flores, a very able man attached to the Spanish Embassy in Washington." Other reports intimated that the SIM was also directed by the German service. SIM agents were especially effective since they received "special training in the language and culture of the milieu where they are to work [and] are able to orient themselves at once, to deal with the masses . . . and to spend money liberally for information."[81] The existence of Spanish agents in Mexico provided a neat replacement for Gestapo requirements after the German agents were compelled to leave the country.[82]

German agents created a system to transmit detailed data through the mail via advanced microphotographic equipment, or "microdots." Mexican censors often overlooked invisible ink, another common medium. By August 1940, Mexican authorities were utilizing a "hit and skip" method of mail censorship "against any type of fifth column activity."[83] Nevertheless, "evasion of censorship in Mexico is relatively easy . . . [and] the Embassy and the local FBI representative concur in the view that this censorship is neither efficient nor dependable." At the end of December 1941, the Mexican government suspended telephone service to Japan, Germany, and territories under their control.[84] Understaffing and low budgets contributed to the weakness of Mexican efforts to hinder Axis agents. In 1940, U.S. reports indicated that Gobernación and the attorney general's office had a combined force of one hundred forty agents, and that twenty of those at Gobernación

80. Report, R&A No. 843, "The Sinarquista Movement in Mexico," Jun. 1943, v, 126–30, NARA, Record Group 226.

81. Report, "The Falange in the Other American Republics," Coordinator of Inter-American Affairs, Feb. 21, 1942, 6–7, NARA, Record Group 59, E451b, Box 15.

82. See chapter 3.

83. Mexican censors: Summary, "Axis Transmission of Information and Censorship—Mexico," MID, May 29, 1942, NARA, Record Group 165, Box 2453; "hit and skip" method: Memo, Hoover to Brig. Gen. Sherman Miles (G-2), Aug. 2, 1940, NARA, Record Group 165, Box 2463.

84. Summary, "Axis Transmission of Information and Censorship—Mexico," MID, May 29, 1942, NARA, Record Group 165, Box 2453.

were new hires working specifically on "subversive activity." The estimated intelligence budget of 285,000 pesos was considered insufficient for successful completion of the counterespionage mission.[85]

Compared to foreign-based fascist groups, "the UNS, with its emphasis on peasant support and its cautious infiltration of labor unions, proved to be better fitted to Mexican conditions."[86] This made it a perceived danger to U.S. aspirations for a secure southern border in the midst of World War II. The UNS was recognized as superior by its rivals in the quasi-fascist Camisas Doradas movement, who commented, "So complete is their organization that their command structure is secret, no one knows its true Chiefs and it already has 150,000 men, [and it] enjoys the sympathy and economic support of large sectors of society both here and abroad."[87] Public marches were key occasions to demonstrate the size of UNS influence, one example being the ten-thousand-strong group that walked into Querétaro's center despite a police ban in 1939.[88] By 1943, UNS membership was estimated at three hundred thousand in Mexico, with another two thousand members in the United States.[89] The UNS movement, organized along rigid hierarchical lines and reckoned to have fascist tendencies, was deemed a vital concern for U.S. policy makers and intelligence officials.[90]

However, more studied historical analysis disputes the view of the UNS as a pawn of international fascism, perhaps providing evidence of overreaction or paranoia within the U.S. intelligence community. Ortoll called the UNS "a Mexican movement that essentially responded to the national situation prior to the war" and "a *sui generis* nationalist movement that reflected its particular time and place."[91] Newcomer concurred that it "represented a

85. Report, "Nazi, Communist and Other Foreign Agents in Mexico," Consul Robert G. McGregor Jr., Jun. 28, 1940, 27–28, NARA, Record Group 165, Box 2463.

86. Report, R&A No. 843, "The Sinarquista Movement in Mexico," Jun. 1943, 143, NARA, Record Group 226.

87. Letter, Espiridión Rodríguez E. to Nicolás Rodríguez C., Apr. 19, 1940, Fideicomiso Archivos Plutarco Elías Calles y Fernando Torreblanca, Archivo Joaquín Amaro, Mexico City (FAPEC-AJA), Campaña Política, 1939–1940, File 020200, Acción Revolucionaria Mexicanista, "Los Dorados."

88. Report, R&A No. 843, "The Sinarquista Movement in Mexico," Jun. 1943, 14, NARA, Record Group 226.

89. Ibid., v, 21–22. Also, Jean Meyer, *El sinarquismo ¿Un fascismo mexicano? 1937–1947* (Mexico City: Editorial Joaquín Mortiz, 1979), 47. Meyer puts the number at 307,365 in Mexico and 3,000 in the United States in 1943.

90. Meyer, *El sinarquismo*; Report, R&A No. 843, "The Sinarquista Movement in Mexico," Jun. 1943, v, NARA, Record Group 226.

91. Servando Ortoll, "Catholic Organizations in Mexico's National Politics and International Diplomacy (1926–1942)" (PhD diss., Columbia University, 1987), 37. See also Albert L.

culture of elite, *criollo* conservatism based entirely in the Mexican context."[92] U.S. and Mexican officials working against the UNS were not alone in their misunderstanding of motives and strategies. The UNS was just as interested in plastering the Calles administration with the label of fascism and the Cárdenas group with that of communism as U.S. and Mexican agents were in defining the Sinarquistas as proto-fascists.[93] The fact of willful ignorance on all sides was difficult to dispute. For their part, UNS members eschewed the label of political or electoral party and instead described themselves as simply "a civic movement which seeks the restoration in Mexico of the Christian Social Order destroyed by anarchy." The UNS did not place faith in electoral institutions and declared on July 4, 1940, that the "farce of Democratic skirmishes is not worth the shedding of a single drop of Mexican blood."[94] Given the UNS ban on electoral activity by its membership, it refused to support any candidate in the 1940 presidential election.

Organizations like the UNS and the threat they seemed to pose made intelligence collection in Latin America crucial to hemispheric defense. The Latin American intelligence agencies were called upon to strengthen their counterespionage segments, maintain surveillance of German agents, and regularly exchange all related intelligence with U.S. agencies. Mexican cooperation came at the cost of U.S. arms provided under the Lend-Lease Act.[95] After the war, as the U.S. government feared a resurgence of European interests in the region, the U.S. War Department defined its intelligence objectives as "any activity which may influence our hemisphere defense plans either favorably or unfavorably, especially the latter."[96] The military emphatically supported a "program for furnishing arms and equipment to the Latin American countries and the eventual expansion of this program with a view

---

Michaels, "Fascism and Sinarquismo: Popular Nationalisms Against the Mexican Revolution," *Journal of Church and State* 8, no. 2 (1966): 234–50.

92. Daniel Newcomer, *Reconciling Modernity: Urban State Formation in 1940s León, Mexico* (Lincoln: University of Nebraska Press, 2004), 115.

93. For example, see Newcomer, *Reconciling Modernity*, 52, 55.

94. "Restoration in Mexico": Unión Nacional Sinarquista, Secretaría de Propaganda, *Sinarquismo: Summary of Its Program* (n.p.: UNS, Secretaría de Propaganda, [1942]), 14, quoted in Report, R&A No. 843, "The Sinarquista Movement in Mexico," Jun. 1943, 23, NARA, Record Group 226; "farce of Democratic skirmishes": Report, R&A No. 843, "The Sinarquista Movement in Mexico," Jun. 1943, 15, NARA, Record Group 226.

95. Rout and Bratzel, *Shadow War*, 29.

96. Report of Latin American Intelligence Conference, [held Jan. 13–17, 1947], Subsection "Intelligence Needs of the Pan American Branch," by Col. W. F. Hocker, Feb. 13, 1947, NARA, Record Group 59, E451b, Box 11.

to standardization of hemispheric military equipment and training *on American lines.*"[97] What was true for the armed forces was also true in the realm of intelligence, as U.S. agencies worked together to standardize U.S. intelligence efforts in the region and proffer training "on American lines."

Owing to its experience during World War I, the U.S. Military Intelligence Division (MID) dominated foreign intelligence operations through the 1930s, a role it ceded in Latin American affairs to the FBI after 1940.[98] During the period from 1917 to 1927, "the MID routinely conducted . . . espionage activities in Mexico."[99] But the MID was not particularly effective in the dispatch of its duties; one analysis concluded that it "was actually incapable at this time of truly educating American officials concerning the 'reality' of Mexico." Moreover, "regular army officers discovered that intelligence was not a viable career field [and] . . . G-2 became a kind of dumping ground for incompetents."[100] Finally, "the MID perspective was colored by cultural bias, ignorance, and misunderstanding . . . [and it] failed to grasp the reality of Mexico because it failed to ask the right questions."[101]

The FBI had staked a special claim on Latin America in general, and Mexico in particular, during the negotiations in 1939 and 1940 within the Joint Intelligence Committee (JIC). Roosevelt charged this group, consisting of the leaders of the FBI, the MID, and the Office of Naval Intelligence (ONI), with dividing intelligence responsibilities in Latin America. The talks were dominated by Hoover, who was able to parlay his connections to the Oval Office into a substantial role in Mexican affairs. Already in 1939 "Hoover and the FBI had established themselves permanently in Mexico," and as early as June 1940 they were advising Roosevelt that "Special Agents of the FBI

97. Report of Latin American Intelligence Conference, [held Jan. 13–17, 1947], Subsection "Report of Committee No. 1: Trends in Latin America," Feb. 13, 1947, NARA, Record Group 59, E451b, Box 11, emphasis added. See also John Child, *Unequal Alliance: The Inter-American Military System, 1938–1978* (Boulder: Westview, 1980), 72–74, 83–85.

98. W. Dirk Raat, "U.S. Intelligence Operations and Covert Action in Modern Mexico, 1900–1947," *Journal of Contemporary History* 22, no. 4 (Oct. 1987): 617.

99. Corbett S. Gottfried, "U.S. Military Intelligence in Mexico, 1917–1927: An Analysis" (master's thesis, Portland State University, 1995), 1. For background on early U.S. intelligence efforts in Mexico, see Carter Rila, "Army Intelligence Collection and the Mexican Revolution, 1913–1917" (master's thesis, Defense Intelligence College, 1991).

100. "Educating American officials": Gottfried, "U.S. Military Intelligence in Mexico," 5; "dumping ground for incompetents": Charles D. Ameringer, *U.S. Foreign Intelligence: The Secret Side of American History* (Lexington, Mass.: Lexington Books, 1990), 113. G-2 was another name for the military intelligence office within the War Department general staff.

101. Gottfried, "U.S. Military Intelligence in Mexico," 143.

have been established in Mexico and Cuba."[102] In 1943, Hoover instructed the U.S. agent in Mexico City to investigate whether the Partido Acción Nacional (PAN) was "controlled, infiltrated or financed by the Axis."[103] This agency, the Special Intelligence Service (SIS), solidified the bureaucratic supremacy of the FBI in intelligence efforts in Latin America.[104]

In the midst of this bureaucratic positioning was George Messersmith, who acted as coordinator of the JIC.[105] Messersmith had previously seen complicated diplomatic action in Vienna and Berlin from 1933 to 1937 and was a trusted advisor to Roosevelt. His role in the creation of the SIS, along with his distrust of Hoover, must have been complicating factors during his tenure as U.S. ambassador to Mexico (1942–46).

SIS operations in Latin America expanded during World War II. The initial 1940 budget of $900,000 grew to $5.4 million by 1945, reflecting the urgent wartime need for intelligence on Nazi maneuvers in the hemisphere. By funding the SIS activities in the hemisphere, "Roosevelt was indicating his belief that the Latin American nations were essentially incapable of taking effective counterintelligence action or indifferent to the threat that German espionage posed." In the postwar period, "U.S. training of Latin American police was explicitly designed to combat the perceived threat of left-wing subversion and armed guerrilla insurgency." The U.S. attempt to overcome the "inefficiency and lack of coordination of the Mexican couterespionage effort" obligated the United States to actively intervene in the training and arming of Mexican intelligence agents.[106]

Unfortunately, training agents for overseas assignments was not a strength of the FBI. "The desire to get agents rapidly into the field tended to obviate quality training." Further, "the FBI had no body of tradition or wealth of experience in foreign espionage and counterespionage to draw on. . . . It would be a case of on-the-job training." Rout and Bratzel concluded that

102. Friedrich E. Schuler, *Mexico Between Hitler and Roosevelt: Mexican Foreign Relations in the Age of Lázaro Cárdenas* (Albuquerque: University of New Mexico Press, 1998), 39. For quote from Memo, Hoover to White House, Jun. 2, 1940, see Rout and Bratzel, *Shadow War,* 33–37.

103. Memo, Hoover to [U.S. Civil Attaché, Mexico City], Dec. 4, 1943, cited in FBI file 6422553/15, Memo from Director of FBI to Department of State, Apr. 10, 1945.

104. Paz Salinas, *Strategy, Security, and Spies,* 192.

105. Rout and Bratzel, *Shadow War,* 37.

106. Urgent wartime need: Rout and Bratzel, *Shadow War,* 40; "effective counterintelligence action": ibid., 46; "threat of left-wing subversion": Martha Huggins, *Political Policing: The United States and Latin America* (Durham: Duke University Press, 1998), 3; "inefficiency and lack of coordination": Paz Salinas, *Strategy, Security, and Spies,* 170–71.

"this organization [SIS] was no better prepared for the spy-counterspy war in Latin America than either the Abwehr or SD."[107]

Gus T. Jones had been a Texas Ranger and FBI official before traveling to Mexico in 1939. Once there and "without official authorization, he instructed Mexican secret agents in the creation of a Mexican counterintelligence group."[108] He "had worked with Mexican security forces prior to September 1939 . . . and it was he who would organize and direct the U.S. counterespionage effort in Mexico in 1940–43." He was also a friend of Mexico City chief of police Miguel Z. Martínez, a former federal deputy from Nuevo Leon. This connection may have been of some assistance to Jones in setting up operations in Mexico, especially in the task of organizing surveillance in the northern states. "With the creation of an SIS group in Mexico . . . a secret surveillance agreement was quickly arranged with Mexican security forces." This compact was kept in a dangerous limbo, without a written agreement from August 1940 until December 1941, as Mexican officials negotiated an end to the oil expropriation crisis.[109] The reluctance of Mexican officials to formalize the intelligence agreement before settling the expropriation issue provided the push that the Roosevelt administration needed to force a settlement.

The DFS, built upon the groundwork of wartime intelligence cooperation, represented a major advance in the professionalization of Mexican intelligence. The function of the early DFS, according to a contemporary account, was "to provide the President with first-hand reports of events with the greatest public interest or that affect high national politics, all without the interference of the parties involved."[110] Formed in 1947 by presidential order, it was unique for its bureaucratic location and institutional ties. Unlike the DGIPS and other intelligence services that were based in Gobernación, the DFS operated directly under the supervision of the president's office.[111] The

---

107. "Obviate quality training": Rout and Bratzel, *Shadow War,* 42; "no body of tradition" and "spy-counterspy war": ibid., 43. The Abwehr was the German military intelligence agency. The SD, or Sicherheitdienst, was the intelligence service of the German Nazi party.

108. Schuler, *Mexico Between Hitler and Roosevelt,* 146.

109. "Worked with Mexican security forces": Rout and Bratzel, *Shadow War,* 72–73; friend of Mexico City chief of police: ibid., 73; "secret surveillance agreement": ibid., 55; dangerous limbo: ibid., 55–56.

110. *El Universal,* Jul. 17, 1948, AGN-DGIPS, Box 759, 2.1/A.G.D./1504.

111. Aguayo Quezada mistakenly asserts that the DFS was part of Gobernación and is surprised that it "really obeyed presidential orders and acted autonomously from Congress or the judicial system." See Sergio Aguayo Quezada, "The Uses, Abuses, and Challenges of Mexican National Security: 1946–1990," in *Mexico: In Search of Security,* ed. Bruce Michael Bagley

bureaucratic location of the DFS created various entanglements. For instance, when the DFS began to request files from the Población office, the secretary of Gobernación himself wrote a letter to the head of the DFS. He suggested that "not being subject to the usual practices, it creates an anomaly in the way of handling matters. . . . I recommend that in the future . . . you direct your requests to this Secretariat, so that we can determine what is appropriate."[112]

Alemán's efforts to expand and professionalize the secret police forces must be considered alongside his role in the process of "civilizing" politics. Alemán had been a popular and powerful governor of the state of Veracruz before agreeing to serve as campaign manager for Ávila Camacho in 1940. As secretary of Gobernación, he was able to solidify his connections to traditional power centers and mastermind a strategy for consolidating PRM influence, while simultaneously reducing military authority in political matters. It was Alemán who dealt with intelligence officials from the SIS and the FBI when the U.S. called upon Mexico to aid in hemispheric security during the war. And it was Alemán, the first civilian president of the new era, who created the DFS as a direct dependency of the president's office, apart from its secret brethren housed in Gobernación. Beginning with Alemán, four of the five presidents after Ávila Camacho came from Gobernación. This was due, in no small part, to the official purview of the Secretariat, including strong influence over the PRI machinery, elections, and the secret police.

One of the key figures in DFS training was Col. Rex Applegate. At the behest of OSS chief Col. William Donovan, in 1942 Applegate commenced study under William E. Fairbairn and E. A. Sykes, veterans of the British police in Shanghai and firearms experts. Fairbairn soon after began leading combat training for the OSS and became known as "the father of the modern SWAT team."[113] Applegate learned from these experiences the techniques of firearm usage and hand-to-hand combat. In 1943, he published *Kill or Get*

---

and Sergio Aguayo Quezada (Coral Gables: North-South Center, University of Miami; New Brunswick: Transaction, 1993), 105; also, Sergio Aguayo Quezada, "Intelligence Services and the Transition to Democracy in Mexico," in *Strategy and Security in U.S.-Mexican Relations Beyond the Cold War,* ed. John Bailey and Sergio Aguayo Quezada (San Diego: Center for U.S.-Mexican Studies, University of California at San Diego, 1996), 145. In fact, this was precisely how the new agency was intended to behave and how it operated until 1952 when it was formally subordinated to Gobernación.

112. Letter, Héctor Pérez Martínez to Director of DFS, Oct. 21, 1947, AGN-DGIPS, Box 759, 2.1/A.G.D./1504.

113. Obituary of Rex Applegate, http://www.clede.com.Memory/obitrexa.htm; see also *Law and Order,* Oct. 1996.

Killed, which explained his revolutionary new methods for close-quarters combat.[114] These credentials made Applegate valuable in training spies (and even President Roosevelt's bodyguards), as well as a luminary in the world of police training until his death in 1998.[115] After World War II, Applegate retired to Mexico City, where "he was involved in importing gun parts and assembling firearms . . . when Mexico imposed a 100 percent duty on imported forearms."[116] This activity, along with his training skills, made him a very valuable resource for the Mexican police and security services.

Soon after the DFS began receiving FBI training and support, Mexico City police chief Othón León Lobato proposed "to organize and train a riot squad." The prospect of a professional riot squad in the hands of the Mexican authorities did not please everyone. The U.S. army attaché worried that "the availability of such a trained unit might seem to the Mexican police mentality a 'quick and easy' way to 'solve' all manner of problems," a possibility exacerbated by the perceived pugnacity of the military man leading the force, León Lobato.[117] Applegate was selected to direct the riot squad's training program and accepted the assignment with the Mexico City Police, either as a convenient entrée to the world of Mexican security or as a cover for his other mission: training and equipping the DFS.

Applegate's mission was well known to the staff of the U.S. Embassy, with whom he was acquainted after he moved to Mexico City in the late 1940s. In June 1950, the head of the DFS, Marcelino Innureta de la Fuente, placed Applegate in charge of "the training of 26 new members of the secret police force." Applegate surmised that these officers were an expansion of the DFS rather than simply replacement agents, especially after Innureta told him that "his force was being called upon to provide more protection work." Innureta also made inquiries to Applegate about the purchase of "two more armored cars." This request, along with León Lobato's interest "about ordering more machine guns," pointed to Applegate's role as arms liaison for the Mexican security services.[118]

114. Rex Applegate, *Kill or Get Killed* (Harrisburg, Pa.: Military Service Publishing, 1943).

115. Thomas J. Nardi, "We Will Not See the Likes of Him Again: The Life and Times of Col. Rex Applegate," http://www.americancombatives.com/applegate.htm.

116. Obituary of Rex Applegate, http://www.clede.com.Memory/obitrexa.htm; see also *Law and Order,* Oct. 1996.

117. Memo, Army Attaché Raymond J. Barrett to Secretary of State, Feb. 15, 1950, Mexico City, NARA, Record Group 59. I thank Elisa Servín for alerting me to this document and providing me with a copy.

118. Memo, Burrows to U.S. Ambassador, Jun. 8, 1950, Mexico City, NARA, Record Group 59. I thank Elisa Servín for providing me with a copy of this document.

The DFS operated under the auspices of presidential authority and had the sole function of defending the political security of the nation. But, as Aguayo correctly noted, "the DFS was never a proper 'intelligence' service. . . . It served as an instrument for controlling the population." Since the U.S. trainers came from military, and not civilian police, backgrounds, "the policing and social control techniques taught were oriented toward military, not civilian, models of control." The use of this "political police force with the objective of analyzing and providing information about the security of the nation" afforded the political elite a valuable (and legal) tool for suppressing dissent: "Throughout its existence the DFS was seen by successive presidents as an instrument for doing dirty work and gathering raw information. . . . They kept very tight and personalized control over the DFS and other key organs of power, arguing that only they possessed a comprehensive understanding of security matters."[119]

Regarding the DFS, Aguayo argued that "violence was one of its favorite methods, and its main hiring criterion was personal loyalty to the chief, which in the absence of clear guidelines encouraged illegality and abuse of authority."[120] While this was certainly true of the DFS in the 1960s and 1970s, the period on which Aguayo has focused, it is not at all certain that this was the case in the late 1940s and early 1950s. Rather, in the early stages after its formation, the DFS reflected the still tenuous political consolidation of the PRI, a situation that required a more measured use of power than the DFS of later years. It would be wrong to assume that Mexican intelligence agencies have always operated with the level of violence and impunity of the 1960s and 1970s. That argument would negate the idea of historical change, and the Mexican agencies are nothing if not evolving.

The development of the DFS, with the technical assistance of the FBI, resulted in an intelligence organization that was able to dedicate its efforts to political surveillance in a modern and professional way. For the most part, the secret police were successful in disrupting the political opposition in Mexico using a range of methods from simple surveillance to a well-timed dirty trick. The opposition was at least partially aware of the extent of surveillance that they were under, although generally ineffective in combatting it.

119. "Instrument for controlling": Aguayo Quezada, "Intelligence Services and the Transition to Democracy," 146; "social control techniques": Huggins, *Political Policing*, 8; "political police force": Aguayo Quezada, "Uses, Abuses, and Challenges of Mexican National Security," 111; "instrument for doing dirty work": Aguayo Quezada, "Intelligence Services and the Transition to Democracy," 147.

120. Aguayo Quezada, "Intelligence Services and the Transition to Democracy," 146.

The combination of a newly consolidated political elite and a new intelligence service dedicated to defending it proved very successful, and it effectively short-circuited electoral opposition in Mexico. As the services were professionalized through the 1940s, they also became more politicized and established lasting ties to the bureaucratic and political agenda of the PRI leadership. This linkage formed the foundation of the PRI's electoral dominance over the decades after World War II.

The Mexican intelligence services began as a response to the political necessity of maintaining surveillance of revolutionary contenders in 1918. Through the 1920s and 1930s, the skills and tasks of the service were expanded to include the defense of the revolutionary state from both external and internal threats. The efforts of foreign countries (Japan, Germany, and Spain) to conduct intelligence operations in Mexico leading up to and during World War II forced a fundamental reevaluation of the Mexican services by Mexican officials and U.S. authorities alike. This led to heavy U.S. involvement in training and supplying the Mexican services in order to guarantee their reliability in protecting the common border. As the FBI gained ascendance in Latin American intelligence operations, it sought to professionalize Mexican agents and aided in the organization of the DFS. This agency, along with the DGIPS, became more closely associated with *priísta* political goals during the 1940s and 1950s, acting as a brake on domestic opposition movements. The repressive capabilities of the intelligence services combined with the political zeal of the PRI leadership provided the party with the means to dominate political life in Mexico for decades. In a prophetic warning of the mortal danger of this mechanism to opposition groups, the PAN stated in 1940, "Whenever the possibility of forming an independent party arises, all the official elements, direct or indirect, harass, threaten, and pursue it, until its existence becomes impossible."[121]

121. PAN statement, [1940], Archivo Manuel Gomez Morín, Mexico City, Fondo Acción Nacional, Vol. 6, File 60.

Plutarco Elías Calles (front row, center) began organizing the Partido Nacional Revolucionario (PNR) at this meeting of like-minded political elites on December 4, 1928. Courtesy of the Fideicomiso Archivos Plutarco Elías Calles y Fernando Torreblanca.

General Saturnino Cedillo, once a stalwart of the postrevolutionary state, rose in arms against the government of Lázaro Cárdenas in May 1938. His rebellion was the last such attempt by a revolutionary veteran to gain power through military force. Courtesy of the Fideicomiso Archivos Plutarco Elías Calles y Fernando Torreblanca.

General Joaquín Amaro was a former secretary of national defense and a close collaborator of former president Plutarco Elías Calles. Amaro aimed to pursue a more conservative line in Mexican
policy through his presidential candidacy in 1940. Courtesy of the Fideicomiso Archivos Plutarco
Elías Calles y Fernando Torreblanca.

As a former director of military education who had overseen major reforms in academy curricula, Amaro maintained ties to student groups that supported his candidacy through the Partido Revolucionario Anti-Comunista (PRAC). Courtesy of the Fideicomiso Archivos Plutarco Elías Calles y Fernando Torreblanca.

A man of many interests, General Juan Andreu Almazán was one of the most important contractors dealing in road construction, a longtime zone commander in Monterrey, and an eminent revolutionary veteran. A long revolutionary resumé and formidable presence were crucial to his attempt to attain dominance in the post-Cedillo arena of contestation: elections. Courtesy of the Fideicomiso Archivos Plutarco Elías Calles y Fernando Torreblanca.

Almazán (second from right) announced his candidacy for president on July 25, 1939. His platform represented a clarion call for the conservative elements that felt ill-served by the Lázaro Cárdenas administration. By riding the "conservative wave" in the election of 1940, Almazán demonstrated the power of the Right and forced the Partido de la Revolución Mexicana (PRM) to moderate the excesses of the previous term. Courtesy of the Fideicomiso Archivos Plutarco Elías Calles y Fernando Torreblanca.

Supporters of Almazán took to the streets on July 7, 1940, to press their case for a fair election. This effort produced numerous violent confrontations and underscored claims by the PRM that the almazanistas intended to provoke a rebellion. Courtesy of the Fideicomiso Archivos Plutarco Elías Calles y Fernando Torreblanca.

Federal forces moved to secure public areas in central Mexico City, including the plaza near the Bellas Artes theater, as supporters of Almazán protested the electoral results in July 1940. Courtesy of the Fideicomiso Archivos Plutarco Elías Calles y Fernando Torreblanca.

During his tenure as secretary of foreign relations from 1940 to 1945, Ezequiel Padilla earned the respect of the international diplomatic community, especially as a result of his efforts in organizing the Chapultepec Conference at the end of World War II. Padilla's presidential campaign in 1946 was hampered, however, by the perceived confluence of his platform and U.S. interests in the region. Courtesy of the Fideicomiso Archivos Plutarco Elías Calles y Fernando Torreblanca.

Political messages were presented visually during a campaign rally for Alemán in San Luis Potosí in 1946. In the foreground is the "political trashcan" of ideas associated with Padilla's candidacy, including his book *El hombre libre de América*. The placard following behind portrays Alemán as the Archangel Michael, his wings marked with the words "patriotism" and "popularity." He is slaying the allegorical devil of past excesses, a heavily freighted image in a deeply Catholic country like Mexico. Courtesy of the Fundación Miguel Alemán, A.C.

Alemán (third from left) built his political career in part on alliances with traditional power brokers like Gonzalo N. Santos of San Luis Potosí (fourth from left), who turned out massive support during campaign stops in 1946. Courtesy of the Fundación Miguel Alemán, A.C.

In office, Alemán walked a fine line in strengthening civilian control of the armed forces. At an awards ceremony at the Colegio Militar in 1947, he is flanked by his secretary of defense, General Gilberto Limón (left), and General Rafael Ávila Camacho (right). Courtesy of the Fideicomiso Archivos Plutarco Elías Calles y Fernando Torreblanca.

In March 1947, Harry S. Truman became the first sitting U.S. president to visit Mexico City. He took the opportunity to visit one of the great archaeological sites in the region, the Pyramid of the Sun at Teotihuacán. Courtesy of the Fundación Miguel Alemán, A.C.

Truman's tour of Mexico City aimed to take in a number of the public monuments and offer the Mexican public a chance to see the positive relationship between himself and Alemán. Note in the background the addition of Alemán's name to the list of illustrious Mexican leaders. Courtesy of the Fundación Miguel Alemán, A.C.

Truman's emotional visit to the monument to the Niños Heroes, Mexican cadets who leaped to their deaths from Chapultepec Castle rather than surrender to invading U.S. troops in 1847, symbolized the postwar effort to make amends for the past and forge a new bilateral relationship. Courtesy of the Fundación Miguel Alemán, A.C.

Alemán returned Truman's gesture by placing a wreath at the Tomb of the Unknown Soldier during his visit to Washington, D.C., in April 1947. By honoring each other's fallen soldiers, Alemán and Truman aimed to cleanse the animosities that drove the two nations to fight each other in the Mexican-American War of 1846–48. Courtesy of the Fundación Miguel Alemán, A.C.

Upon his arrival in Washington, D.C., Alemán was presented with the key to the city. He happily brandished it as he and Truman passed along the parade route filled with cheering spectators. National Park Service, Abbie Rowe, courtesy of Harry S. Truman Library.

On May 1, 1947, Alemán addressed a joint session of the U.S. Congress and offered his vision for a postwar bilateral framework. This was the first time that a Latin American head of state had addressed such a meeting, reinforcing the special relationship between the United States and Mexico. Courtesy of the Fundación Miguel Alemán, A.C.

General Miguel Henríquez Guzmán announced his presidential candidacy on January 8, 1951, saying it was his civic duty to lead the country in time of crisis. His efforts were centered on the Federación de Partidos del Pueblo Mexicano (FPPM) and offered a quasi-cardenista correction to the perceived excesses of the Alemán administration. Courtesy of the Fideicomiso Archivos Plutarco Elías Calles y Fernando Torreblanca.

The presidential campaign of 1952 was crowded with high-level candidates, including Cándido Aguilar, Vicente Lombardo Toledano, and Miguel Henríquez Guzmán (left to right). None was able to overcome the increasingly potent combination of police surveillance and official obstruction to defeat the electoral machine of the Partido Revolucionario Institucional (PRI). Courtesy of the Fideicomiso Archivos Plutarco Elías Calles y Fernando Torreblanca.

FIVE

ERASING DOUBTS
The Election of 1952

THE ELECTION OF 1952 presented a serious obstacle to the emerging dominance of the Partido Revolucionario Institucional (PRI). On one hand, the
political subjugation of the military within the party had been a success. The
elimination of the military sector of the PRI deprived soldiers of their privileged place at the table in 1946. Also, the PRI bureaucracy entrusted young
and ambitious officers coming out of the military academies with the crucial
supporting role of running the new intelligence apparatus. On the other
hand, the economic policies of the Miguel Alemán administration left a path
of inflation and poverty for many Mexicans, and the promise of prosperity for
all seemed hollow. Mexican labor lost pitched battles with the government, as
forcible interventions, or *charrazos,* limited the influence of the unions. Some
revolutionary veterans and former stalwarts of the PRI finally decided that
confrontation was necessary to rein in the exponential growth of the party's
dominance in national politics.

This chapter argues that the election of 1952 demonstrated the extent of
three crucial political transitions. First, the discipline of the PRI hardened as
more staunch leaders like Rodolfo Sánchez Taboada, an army general, took
the fore. To more tightly control the selection process, the party cracked
down on *futurismo,* the practice of hopeful candidates who publicly gauged
their political strength and angled for nomination. At the same time, President Alemán unsuccessfully attempted first to subvert the Constitution

through a reelection movement and then to impose his successor on the unwilling party. The contest to nominate a PRI candidate demonstrated both the constraints on presidential power and the continuing relevance of the party structure as the site of political negotiation. Second, the political and economic costs of opposing the PRI in elections became too high for any plausible candidate to bear. The formation of political parties and the attempt to take part in a democratic process, strategies of earlier opposition campaigns in 1940 and 1946, lost favor as methods for gaining political influence. After 1952, opposition elements usually worked within the PRI to effect change rather than risking their careers in an opposition campaign. Third, the military settled for a marginal role in electoral politics, even as it gained official representation in the Partido Auténtico de la Revolución Mexicana (PARM). The election of 1952 cemented the alliance between rising civilian bureaucrats in the Alemán administration and the ambitious group of officers from the military academies selected to run the domestic intelligence agencies.

By the time the waves of futurismo began in 1950, the political atmosphere in Mexico was already highly charged. The reformist policies of the Alemán administration produced severe criticisms that the rush to modernize the economy shunted aside the goals of the revolution. But the PRI leadership viewed the painful reforms as necessary for achieving the prosperity promised in revolutionary rhetoric. As early as March 1949, it claimed that "the battlegrounds are clearly defined: on one side, the enemies of the people, on the other the followers [partidarios] of the Revolution."[1] The question of whether Mexico was better off as a nation following the Alemán policies was the opening utilized by Miguel Henríquez Guzmán, who advocated a partial return to the populist policies of the Lázaro Cárdenas administration. The split on national policy was a main factor in Henríquez's decision to work outside the PRI and attempt to forge a truly national and popular organization in the Federación de Partidos del Pueblo Mexicano (FPPM).

The role of the military in politics remained a contentious issue in the election of 1952. As the case of Véjar Vázquez in chapter 2 demonstrated, the PRI tightly circumscribed the political rights of soldiers in the postwar period to discourage autonomous organizations outside of the party. Soldiers could vote and serve the government, notably through increased military staffing of the intelligence services, but any overt political activity or electoral participation required government permission. As chapter 2 also demonstrated, the

---

1. *La Prensa,* Mar. 2, 1949, Archivo General de la Nación, Mexico City, Dirección General de Investigaciones Políticas y Sociales (AGN-DGIPS), Box 19, File 2, 2.1/061.3/10.

process for soliciting *licencia* was both much politicized and quite risky. PRI officials shifted their rationale through the late 1940s, arguing that ordinary (i.e., temporary) licencia was no longer a sufficient requirement for political activity. Rather, soldiers interested in pursuing political goals were forced to take *licencia ilimitada* or, worse, voluntarily retire from the army. This change in military policy raised the stakes for opposition-minded soldiers, either stifling dissent from within the armed forces or driving those dissenters out of the institution entirely.

Ezequiel Padilla's shadow cast a pall over the campaign in 1952, as well. As the events of 1946 demonstrated, large elements of the public were disaffected with the increasingly conservative policies of the Manuel Ávila Camacho administration and the growing consolidation of the Partido de la Revolución Mexicana (PRM). The conduct of the Alemán administration could not have assuaged the concerns of this segment of the population. In short, the issues of increasing conservatism in the government and the strengthening of single party dominance in politics still had resonance in 1952. One editorial asserted that Padilla made a critical mistake in leaving the country after his electoral defeat in 1946 since "if he had stayed, now there would exist another strong political party that would be an important factor in these new presidential elections."[2] Padilla's followers, while not necessarily allying themselves with Henríquez or the opposition in general, maintained a certain unity in the demands that they placed on the political system, some of which had been simmering since at least 1946.

The presidency was the site of the most concentrated—though not unlimited—political power in Mexico, making the question of succession a thorny and crucial one. As early as 1947, Jesús González Gallo was positioning himself to succeed Alemán, an extreme case of futurismo that was resolved when he was elected governor of Jalisco in the same year.[3] But the main problem with futurismo was the way that it undercut the authority of PRI officials to make decisions regarding candidacies and, ultimately, balances of political power.

The most dangerous case of futurismo leading up to the election of 1952 was that of Miguel Henríquez Guzmán. Henríquez, a stalwart of the dominant party since the Cárdenas administration, boasted a long history of loyalty

---

2. *Excélsior,* Jan. 11, 1951, AGN-DGIPS, Box 807, Campaña Presidencial, Jan. 1951.

3. Roderic Ai Camp, *Mexican Political Biographies, 1935–1993,* 3rd ed. (Austin: University of Texas Press, 1995), 949.

to the government. He began his military career when he enrolled at the Colegio Militar in 1913 to study engineering.[4] He was one of the cadets who escorted Francisco Madero during the Félix Diaz revolt of 1913, and after Venustiano Carranza closed the Colegio Militar, he joined the Consitutionalist Army in his native state of Coahuila.[5] During the revolution, Henríquez fought alongside and was promoted through the ranks by Pablo González and Vicente González.[6] He fought in no less than forty-one battles against *zapatistas* and *villistas* and thirty-five battles against *delahuertistas*. Through the early 1920s, he served in various midlevel capacities and was recognized for his organizational talents.[7] His aptitude for military operations and charismatic leadership qualities earned him positions of increasing trust and authority in the army.

As he ascended through the ranks, Henríquez went from being a common soldier to an officer and a manager. He served as chief of staff (*jefe del estado mayor*) in Iguala and Morelia before leading a succession of cavalry regiments, all the while learning the methods of successful management.[8] When General Evaristo Pérez died in 1935, Cárdenas appointed Henríquez to his first position as zone commander, in the Eighteenth Military Zone. Up to 1940, Henríquez led the military zones at Villahermosa, Tepic, Durango, Hermosillo, Torreón, San Luis Potosí, and Monterrey. Throughout his career, Henríquez exhibited a sense of loyalty that civilian and military superiors prized. Indeed, in 1932, Anacleto López classified his civil and military conduct in the highest category: irreproachable (*intachable*).[9]

4. Ibid., 341.

5. Memo, Lázaro Cárdenas to Secretaría de Defensa Nacional (SDN), Jan. 31, 1939, Archivo Histórico de la Secretaría de la Defensa Nacional, Mexico City (AHSDN), Cancelados, General de División Miguel Henríquez Guzmán, 13 vols., XI/III/1–189, pp. 1611–14.

6. Memo, Gral. Ignacio L. Pesqueira, Feb. 28, 1916, AHSDN, Cancelados, General de División Miguel Henríquez Guzmán, 13 vols., XI/III/1–189, p. 3; Letter, Gral. Brig. Vicente González to Srio. de Guerra, Jun. 15, 1922, Tapachula, Chiapas, AHSDN, Cancelados, General de División Miguel Henríquez Guzmán, 13 vols., XI/III/1–189, p. 64; Letter, Gral. de Brig. Vicente González to Sub-Srio de Guerra, Jan. 7, 1925, AHSDN, Cancelados, General de División Miguel Henríquez Guzmán, 13 vols., XI/III/1–189, p. 240.

7. Forty-one battles: Study of Service Record, Jan. 19, 1932, AHSDN, Cancelados, General de División Miguel Henríquez Guzmán, 13 vols., XI/III/1–189, p. 625–26; various midlevel capacities: Various reports, Sep. 1921–Sep. 1925, AHSDN, Cancelados, General de División Miguel Henríquez Guzmán, 13 vols., XI/III/1–189, pp. 134–42.

8. Service Record, May 20, 1940, AHSDN, Cancelados, General de División Miguel Henríquez Guzmán, 13 vols., XI/III/1–189, pp. 1678–85. Between 1929 and 1935, Henríquez Guzmán had exercised command of the Fourth, Tenth, Thirty-sixth, Sixty-fourth, and Seventy-ninth Cavalry Regiments.

9. Henríquez led the military zones: Service Record, May 20, 1940, AHSDN, Cancelados, General de División Miguel Henríquez Guzmán, 13 vols., XI/III/1–189, pp. 1678–85;

Henríquez derived political and business connections from his service in the military. In fact, one of the witnesses at his wedding in Villahermosa in 1925 was Tomás Garrido Canabal, then the governor of Tabasco.[10] When Henríquez was appointed zone commander in Villahermosa in 1935, Alfonso Pedrero, a local activist who opposed Garrido Canabal, protested to the secretary of national defense. Pedrero wrote that due to his marriage to "a distinguished Tabascan woman" Henríquez was deeply involved in state politics, to the point of "organizing, arming, sponsoring and even supplying political plans" to the pro-Garrido groups. Pedrero found this behavior unsatisfactory since it prejudiced political activity in the state at the whim of a military commander who was supposed to remain apolitical.[11] Another citizen blamed Henríquez for the deaths of two of his brothers, accused him of "becoming the servant [mozo]" of Garrido Canabal, and demanded that he be removed from his post as zone commander. In February 1936, perhaps due to popular pressure for his removal, Henríquez was transferred to the military zone at Nayarit.[12]

Like Almazán before him, Henríquez became a trusted "fixer" for the central government, which assigned him the most important commands at key moments. For example, Cárdenas named Henríquez to lead military operations in San Luis Potosí in November 1938, when the Cedillo rebellion had been under way for eight months.[13] Being entrusted with the task of suffocating the Cedillo rebellion was what one scholar marked as "the highest point of his career."[14] Henríquez's success in quelling the rebellion and killing Cedillo earned him a place of honor in national politics and provided further

military conduct in the highest category: Report, Gral. de Div. Anacleto López, Dec. 31, 1932, Toluca, AHSDN, Cancelados, General de División Miguel Henríquez Guzmán, 13 vols., XI/III/1–189, p. 650.

10. Copy of wedding certificate, Mar. 14, 1925, AHSDN, Cancelados, General de División Miguel Henríquez Guzmán, 13 vols., XI/III/1–189, p. 552.

11. Letter, Lic. Alfonso Pedrero G. to Gen. Andrés Figueroa (SDN), Dec. 11, 1935, AHSDN, Cancelados, General de División Miguel Henríquez Guzmán, 13 vols., XI/III/1–189, pp. 1411–13.

12. "Becoming the servant": Letter, Ezequiel Hernández Martínez to SDN, Dec. 27, 1935, Villahermosa, AHSDN, Cancelados, General de División Miguel Henríquez Guzmán, 13 vols., XI/III/1–189, p. 1423; popular pressure for his removal: Decree, Deputy Secretary of Defense Manuel Ávila Camacho, Feb. 24, 1936, AHSDN, Cancelados, General de División Miguel Henríquez Guzmán, 13 vols., XI/III/1–189, p. 1448.

13. Decree, Secretary of Defense Manuel Ávila Camacho, Nov. 12, 1938, AHSDN, Cancelados, General de División Miguel Henríquez Guzmán, 13 vols., XI/III/1–189, p. 1083.

14. Arturo Sánchez Gutiérrez, "Los militares en la década de los cincuenta," Revista Mexicana de Sociología 50, no. 3 (1988): 286.

opportunities to enhance his military and economic prestige. It also earned him the lasting enmity of the Cedillo family. During the election of 1952, Elena Cedillo reminded the country that Henríquez had "a grave responsibility in the death of [her] brother."[15] Promoted to brigadier general only in April 1938, Henríquez moved up to brigade general in October 1939 for reasons of "seniority and special merits."[16] Such a rapid ascent violated the established procedure for military promotions, as he skipped ahead of more senior officers, but it demonstrated his value to the government as well as his close alliance with Cárdenas.

After Henríquez served in San Luis Potosí, Cárdenas moved him to Monterrey to defang *almazanismo* on its home turf during the election of 1940. Following Almazán's resignation, Henríquez assumed command of the Seventh Military Zone, demonstrating "his unquestioned fidelity to the government."[17] His tenure there allowed him to cement his ties to U.S. businessmen and take over the network of highway and construction contracts that had made Almazán so rich before him. Only three months into the assignment, Henríquez facilitated the visit of a group of officials and businessmen from the Texas border region.[18] These types of contacts raised Henríquez's visibility among U.S. observers and positioned him to develop business relationships stretching northward. In late 1941, he was transferred to the military zone at Guadalajara.[19] And in August 1942, Henríquez attained the highest rank possible in the army—division general. As a *divisionario,* he joined the small group of elite officers who in the early 1940s still participated in both military and political matters.

Henríquez's growing power prompted Ávila Camacho to send him to South America in 1944 to represent Mexico at the Chilean national celebrations held in Santiago. The following year, Henríquez received two international recognitions that forced him to leave the country for an additional

15. *El Nacional,* Feb. 15, 1952, AGN-DGIPS, Box 811, 2.1/52/54.

16. Decree, Lázaro Cárdenas, Mar. 28, 1938, AHSDN, Cancelados, General de División Miguel Henríquez Guzmán, 13 vols., XI/III/1–189, p. 1506; Patente, Lázaro Cárdenas, Oct. 20, 1939, AHSDN, Cancelados, General de División Miguel Henríquez Guzmán, 13 vols., XI/III/1–189, p. 1667.

17. McCombs report of the death of Zarzosa, [Oct. 3, 1940], Holland McCombs Papers, University of Tennessee at Martin, Special Collections, Box 46, File 22.

18. Memo, Oficial Mayor Ernesto Hidalgo to SDN, Oct. 10, 1940, AHSDN, Cancelados, General de División Miguel Henríquez Guzmán, 13 vols., XI/III/1–189, p. 2094.

19. Decree, President Manuel Ávila Camacho, Dec. 27, 1941, AHSDN, Cancelados, General de División Miguel Henríquez Guzmán, 13 vols., XI/III/1–189, p. 2135; Memo, Gral. de Brig. Mariano Garay Olguin, Dec. 26, 1941, AHSDN, Cancelados, General de División Miguel Henríquez Guzmán, 13 vols., XI/III/1–189, p. 1769.

period of time. He accepted the Condecoración de la Orden Nacional del Cruzeiro do Sul from the president of Brazil in April 1945. The nation of Paraguay accorded him the second honor, the Orden Nacional de Mérito, in November 1945.[20] When he returned to Mexico, speculation was rife that Henríquez might be a candidate for the presidency in the election of 1946, fueled by his successful request for licencia ilimitada to participate in political affairs.[21] To that point, the real battle in 1946 had been between the two candidates vying for the PRM endorsement, Alemán and Padilla.[22] When the dominant party chose Alemán, Padilla became the candidate of the Partido Democrático Mexicano (PDM). The Comité Nacional Pro-Henríquez Guzmán formed thereafter, awaiting Henríquez's decision about whether to run in 1946.

On October 31, 1945, the henriquistas formed the FPPM as a support organization for Henríquez's political aspirations. Although early support seemed to be forthcoming from the Confederación Nacional Campesina (CNC) and the Confederación de Trabajadores de México (CTM), these organizations finally opted for Alemán's program. (This support would be crucial again in the election of 1952.) A federal agent reported in 1950 that leading up to the 1946 election, Henríquez asked Ávila Camacho for support in a presidential bid. When Ávila Camacho declined, Henríquez reportedly replied with "insulting words" (palabras injuriosas).[23] Eutimio Rodríguez, senator from Tamaulipas, averred that "they gave Henríquez the madrugón in the last campaign."[24] Henríquez claimed that he had not participated in the 1946

20. Chilean national celebrations: Memo, Subsecretary of Foreign Relations Manuel Tello to SDN, Nov. 22, 1944, AHSDN, Cancelados, General de División Miguel Henríquez Guzmán, 13 vols., XI/III/1–189, pp. 2380–81; president of Brazil: Henríquez Guzmán to SDN, Apr. 20, 1945, Guadalajara, AHSDN, Cancelados, General de División Miguel Henríquez Guzmán, 13 vols., XI/III/1–189, p. 2364; second honor: Memo, Diputados José de Jesús Lima and Juan Fernández Albarrán to SDN, Nov. 23, 1945, AHSDN, Cancelados, General de División Miguel Henríquez Guzmán, 13 vols., XI/III/1–189, p. 2366.

21. Decree, Francisco L. Urquizo (SDN), Sep. 3, 1945, AHSDN, Cancelados, General de División Miguel Henríquez Guzmán, 13 vols., XI/III/1–189, p. 2375. The original request may be found in Letter, Henríquez Guzmán to SDN, Aug. 25, 1945, AHSDN, Cancelados, General de División Miguel Henríquez Guzmán, 13 vols., XI/III/1–189, p. 2376.

22. The election of 1946 is treated in detail in chapter 3.

23. Report, Insp. 16 to DGIPS, May 8, 1950, AGN-DGIPS, Box 803, Futurismo Político, Campaña Presidencial, 1952–1958, Vol. 2. Ezequiel Padilla retold this story on behalf of the UNS in 1951. See Excélsior, Jul. 4, 1951, AGN-DGIPS, Box 808, File 7, 2.1/51/371.

24. Excélsior, Jan. 10, 1951, AGN-DGIPS, Box 807, Campaña Presidencial, Jan. 1951. The verb madrugar means to rise early, and the term madrugón refers to a situation in which a political opponent "gets up earlier" and thereby achieves an insuperable advantage. It is a variation on the English-language saying "The early bird gets the worm."

elections due to the country's needs during and after the war and his role as a soldier, which precluded his separation from the army to join the political contest.[25] Because of the postwar sentiment in favor of a civilian president, coupled with the decreasing political leverage of the military vis-à-vis the civilian bureaucrats, 1946 was not an opportune moment for Henríquez.

PRI officials faced a difficult challenge ending Henríquez's futurismo. Rumors circulated as early as January 1950 that thirty army generals had pledged to support Henríquez if he decided to run in 1952. The prospect of an Henríquez campaign offered the military a chance to reclaim its position in national politics, according to some of the henriquista faithful. Some even claimed that the participation of Mexico during the war, and its situation afterward, "cries out for a soldier in the presidency." In April 1950, PRI members across the nation were founding "comités de tendencias electorales," a practice that the national leaders of the party strictly renounced but could barely contain. That same month, the PRI leadership again warned army officers of the "necessity of stopping all futurista political agitation."[26]

The crackdown against those who were looking forward to 1952 was not specifically directed at the opposition. In Jalisco in May 1950, the PRI had to intervene to halt the "futurista outbreak" in favor of Henríquez, "not precisely because the PRI has already discarded the possibility that the General could be the party's candidate . . . but because it judges that the agitation is premature." Soon after, PRI officials announced that they had "prohibited General Miguel Henríquez Guzmán . . . from continuing to dedicate himself to futurista activities with a view toward the presidential succession" and that, as a member of the party, "he should discipline himself."[27] Party leaders were adamant that Henríquez had every right to seek the candidacy, but that as a member of the party "he should proceed within the Statutes and norms

25. *Excélsior,* Jan. 11, 1951, AGN-DGIPS, Box 807, Campaña Presidencial, Jan. 1951.

26. Thirty army generals: *Excélsior,* Jan. 28, 1950, AGN-DGIPS, Box 803, Campaña Presidencial, Futurismo, 1950–1952, Vol. 1; "cries out for a soldier": *El Universal Gráfico,* Jun. 8, 1950, AGN-DGIPS, Box 803, Futurismo Político, Campaña Presidencial, 1952–1958, Vol. 2; "comités de tendencias electorales": *Excélsior,* Apr. 27, 1950, AGN-DGIPS, Box 803, Campaña Presidencial, Futurismo, 1950–1952, Vol. 1; "necessity of stopping": *El Universal,* Apr. 11, 1951, AGN-DGIPS, Box 807, Campaña Presidencial, Apr.–Jun. 1951.

27. "Futurista outbreak" and "agitation is premature": *Excélsior,* May 27, 1950; "dedicate himself to futurista activities" and "discipline himself": *El Universal Gráfico,* May 4, 1950 (both located in AGN-DGIPS, Box 803, Futurismo Político, Campaña Presidencial, 1952–1958, Vol. 2). The phrase *debe disciplinarse* is literally translated here, but could also be read as "follow the rules" or even, ecclesiastically, as "scourge oneself in penance."

of that political party, and at the proper time."[28] The inherent criticism of Henríquez's actions was that he was not following the established rules of the party for nomination and candidate selection. His lack of "discipline" invited attack for both challenging the power of the party's committee mandarins and forgetting the rigid structure of his military life. In short, Henríquez was denounced as both a bad politician and a bad soldier.

When Henríquez began his campaign in 1950 with efforts at *auscultación* (literally, to listen carefully or auscultate), the PRI leadership feared the worst. In Henríquez, the PRI bureaucracy faced a challenger with intimate knowledge of the inner workings of the government, the military, and the party, and with long connections to each of these sectors. Henríquez was one of the nation's richest contractors, best-connected military officers, and most competent party in-fighters. His withdrawal from the presidential race in 1946 had made the Alemán period possible, but it came with the expectation of future considerations. Henríquez's initial strategy in 1950 was to claim the nomination of the PRI for the presidency. Other reports, according to "preeminent henriquistas," indicated that Henríquez intended to run with the support of the FPPM instead of trying to gain the PRI nomination.[29] Either way, the prospect of Henríquez disrupting the process of the PRI candidate selection provoked a visceral reaction from his enemies within the party. In conducting his "listening campaign" in 1950, Henríquez clearly signaled to the PRI that he did not intend to sit out another presidential election.

By July 1950, reports indicated that even Cárdenas and Ávila Camacho were meeting to discuss the presidential succession, a situation in which the party could not reasonably interfere.[30] At the same time, Henríquez began to establish state and local committees to adhere to his national organization, as well as line up support from state governors.[31] Henríquez met with Alemán at Los Pinos on July 1, 1950, presumably to discuss the question of the presidential succession. On July 4, 1950, the Comité Central de Auscultación Nacional pro-Miguel Henríquez Guzmán was founded in Mexico City, led

28. *El Universal*, May 27, 1950, AGN-DGIPS, Box 803, Futurismo Político, Campaña Presidencial, 1952–1958, Vol. 2.

29. Claim the nomination of the PRI: *El Universal*, Jul. 9, 1950; "preeminent henriquistas": *Excélsior*, Jul. 10, 1950 (both located in AGN-DGIPS, Box 999, File 2).

30. Report, Insp. FLP to DGIPS, Jul. 3, 1950, Morelia, AGN-DGIPS, Box 999, File 2.

31. *Prensa Gráfica*, Jul. 12, 1950; *El Universal*, Jul. 12, 1950 (both located in AGN-DGIPS, Box 999, File 2). Henríquez was said to have the support of the governors of Jalisco, Michoacán, Nayarit, Sinaloa, and Sonora.

by former head of the Distrito Federal Raúl Castellano. Castellano was important for another reason: he was a close collaborator of Cárdenas who had only recently been taken back into the PRI through the interventions of party heavyweights such as Cesar Martino, Wenceslao Labra, and Silvano Barba González. Therefore, "it seemed natural to suppose that the *cardenistas* had unified to aid [Henríquez] in the next race for President and that, moreover, his candidacy will be within the national revolutionary groups."[32]

Sánchez Taboada, president of the PRI, rejected Henríquez's *futurista* efforts out of hand, stating, "It has been the norm in our Party that no member carries out activities of presidential *futurismo* before the respective *convocatoria* is issued." PRI officials also rejected the efforts of the henriquistas owing to what it termed their "doble militancia." On one hand, the henriquistas were exercising their rights as citizens to support a political candidate through the auscultación group and the FPPM, both entities outside the PRI. On the other hand, they were also still members of the PRI and thus bound by its rules, practices, and judgments.[33] The PRI leadership saw this as contradictory and dangerous, as it suggested the possibility that the party could be shot through with activists working for the opposition.

On January 8, 1951, Henríquez announced his candidacy to a small gathering of friends and reporters in his home. He declared that having received "significant manifestations of support" from all sectors of Mexican society, he had decided that it was his civic duty to run for president. Henríquez then offered a toast to prosperity over a glass of 1802 Napoleon cognac.[34] Henríquez had reason to be hopeful for future good fortune, not least because of the support that he enjoyed from powerful political figures. The DGIPS reported that several days prior to Henríquez's announcement, Labra hosted a dinner at his home for guests including Cárdenas, Marcelino García Barragán, Cosme Hinojosa, and Henríquez. García Barragán had accepted the presidency of the FPPM in 1950. This and other developments suggested a hunger for the Henríquez candidacy within the military ranks. Just one day after the

32. *La Prensa,* Jul. 3, 1950. Also, *Excélsior,* Jul. 5, 1950, AGN-DGIPS, Box 999, File 2.

33. "Norm in our Party": *El Nacional,* Jul. 15, 1950, AGN-DGIPS, Box 999, File 2; "doble militancia": *Excélsior,* Jan. 4, 1951, AGN-DGIPS, Box 807, Campaña Presidencial, Jan. 1951.

34. *Excélsior,* Jan. 9, 1951; *El Universal,* Jan. 9, 1951; *La Prensa,* Jan. 9, 1951 (all located in AGN-DGIPS, Box 807, Campaña Presidencial, Jan. 1951). In the printed announcement distributed to those gathered, Henríquez signed his name without the use of his military title, general de división, a fact that suggests his reluctance to make the issue of the military in politics a central theme in his campaign.

announcement, reports began appearing about the formation of groups of officers uniting to support Henríquez in his bid.[35]

That same day, Sánchez Taboada went on the attack, arguing that "with his [Henríquez's] attitude of not respecting the arrangements, he has been placed on the fringe of our party." When asked whether that meant that the henriquistas were "outside it [fuera]," he said that it did. Ernesto Soto Reyes retorted that Sánchez Taboada had no authority to expel anyone from the party, that such decisions had to come from the Gran Comisión of the PRI, and that to date the henriquistas had received no communication from such authorities. Sánchez Taboada again accused Henríquez of "breaking the discipline of the party" in June 1951, declaring that "the party does not fear, or want within its ranks dissidents or those who call themselves oppositionists." The FPPM was granted its registro on June 14, 1951.[36] Just two weeks later, Henríquez supporters were expelled from the PRI "in view of their systematic opposition to the work of the [Alemán] administration."[37] As with Almazán supporters, so were the henriquistas expelled from the party for their political beliefs.

Beyond the problem of Henríquez's futurismo and eventual expulsion from the PRI was the continuing internal negotiation over the presidential succession and the need to select the party's candidate. The same issues that drove the opposition candidacy of Henríquez sparked wide-ranging activity within the PRI after his expulsion. As one scholar has correctly noted, "Alemán's succession was the arena where the political groups who were dissatisfied with the regime made their strength felt."[38] Further, PRI officials announced in January 1951 that the party would not select a candidate until January 1952, leaving Henríquez open to attack for an entire year without a specific opponent to respond to, except the party itself. In May 1951, PRI spokesmen reiterated the party's intention to slow the process of candidate

35. Dinner at his home: Memo, DGIPS, Jan. 19, 1951; formation of groups of officers: see, for example, *La Prensa,* Jan. 10, 1951 (both located in AGN-DGIPS, Box 807, Campaña Presidencial, Jan. 1951).

36. "Fringe of our party" and "outside it": *Excélsior,* Jan. 10, 1951; no authority to expel anyone: *El Universal,* Jan. 11, 1951 (both located in AGN-DGIPS, Box 807, Campaña Presidencial, Jan. 1951); "party does not fear": *Excélsior,* Jun. 15, 1951, AGN-DGIPS, Box 19, File 2, 2.1/061.3/10; granted its *registro*: La *Prensa,* Jun. 15, 1951, AGN-DGIPS, Box 24, File 15, 2.1/061.8/15, Vol. 1, p. 35. A registro recognized the national scope of a party and allowed a party to field candidates in elections across the spectrum of open offices. Gobernación required that a sufficient number of signatures or supporters be verified before such a registro could be issued.

37. *El Popular,* Jul. 2, 1951, AGN-DGIPS, Box 24, File 15, 2.1/061.8/15, Vol. 1, p. 51.

38. Sánchez Gutiérrez, "Los militares en la década de los cincuenta," 285.

selection by waiting for the November and December 1951 regional caucuses before making further decisions.[39]

The movement to reelect Alemán complicated the election of 1952. Despite the economic turbulence of his term in office, Alemán had strong supporters who viewed his policies as crucial to the continuing modernization of the country. These supporters outlined the need for the continuity and steady leadership that Alemán could provide. The efforts of the party that thus formed for the explicit purpose of facilitating the extension of his term of office supported the idea of reelection, or *prórroga*.[40] In June 1950, an architect named Guillermo Zárraga established the Partido Artículo 39 Constitucional (PA39C), which sought to reform the Constitution to allow Alemán to be reelected. Licenciado Guillermo Ostos then took charge and argued that the party was neither for nor against reelection, but rather was defending the idea that Mexicans were capable of "choosing their own paths."[41] The possibility that Alemán would extend his term of office swirled throughout the campaign season, from 1950 until the early months of 1952.

Within army installations, several military officers set about collecting signatures in support of a constitutional amendment to permit reelection.[42] Juan Barragán, later a cofounder and head of the PARM, argued that he was in favor of *prorroguismo* because Carranza himself had been a proponent of the idea when Barragán served as his chief of staff in 1920.[43] For his part, Alemán responded "categorically" to the prórroga debate in July 1950: "Under no circumstances will I accept re-election."[44] But the flurry of activity in favor of reelection, combined with Alemán's reticence in naming a successor, fanned the flames of the opposition.

39. Leaving Henríquez open to attack: *Excélsior,* Jan. 25, 1951, AGN-DGIPS, Box 807, Campaña Presidencial, Jan. 1951; party's intention to slow the process: *El Universal,* May 17, 1951, AGN-DGIPS, Box 19, File 2, 2.1/061.3/10.

40. The word *prórroga* literally means "deferment" or "extension of time." However, I have translated it here as "reelection" because that was what the supporters of *prorroguismo* were actually propounding. The memory of Porfirio Díaz's several reelections and the ideological weight of revolutionary slogans ("No reelección!") precluded Mexicans in the 1940s from using such terminology, but modern authors suffer from no such obstacles.

41. Reform the Constitution: *Excélsior,* Jun. 10, 1950; "choosing their own paths": *El Universal,* Jun. 22, 1950 (both located in AGN-DGIPS, Box 803, Futurismo Político, Campaña Presidencial, 1952–1958, Vol. 2).

42. *La Prensa,* Jul. 11, 1950, AGN-DGIPS, Box 999, File 2.

43. *La Prensa,* Aug. 9, 1951, AGN-DGIPS, Box 998, File 2. See also Camp, *Mexican Political Biographies, 1935–1993,* 60–61.

44. *Excélsior,* Jul. 26, 1950, AGN-DGIPS, Box 999, File 2.

Opponents of prórroga were numerous among opposition groups. Pedro Tornel of the FPPM claimed that it was antidemocratic and that it would mark Alemán as a "dictator" and an "autocrat." The Partido Acción Nacional (PAN), through Central Committee chairman Juan Gutiérrez Lascuráin, had a distinctly acid viewpoint: "Given electoral fraud, it is useless to discuss re-election, which would only be the imposition of oneself rather than an heir."[45] García Barragán, a committed henriquista and head of the FPPM, told a U.S. consulate staff member that he viewed Alemán's reelection as unlikely "because Alemán is too intelligent *and understands that he might get killed.*"[46] The threatening tone of this message signaled the depth of opposition to the idea of a second Alemán term.

In all, the reelection movement may have purposely obscured Alemán's political maneuvering as much as it advanced the possibilities of a second term. Notably, U.S. Embassy staff argued that *"re-eleccionismo* has served as a brake upon futurismo, and it seems quite possible that this braking action was Alemán's real purpose in his hints, his ambiguous statements, and his failure to silence talk of re-election among some of his henchmen."[47] Indeed, Alemán skillfully avoided engaging in the prórroga debate while permitting it to continue throughout political circles in the capital. Cándido Aguilar argued that the idea of prorroguismo was just a "smoke screen to aid the imposition of the candidate already selected . . . betting that the people will accept him without resistance given the choice between him and the hated prórroga."[48] Alemán seemed to have successfully controlled the timeline of the succession debate.

The dispute over the prospect of Alemán's reelection was accompanied by the possibility that he could impose his own candidate over the objections of elements within the PRI. Fernando Casas Alemán directed Miguel Alemán's presidential campaign in 1946 and served as the head of the Distrito Federal from 1946 to 1952.[49] Conventional wisdom held that he was the preferred choice of the president, as well as a close friend and distant relation.

45. "Dictator" and "autocrat": *Excélsior,* Aug. 4, 1951, AGN-DGIPS, Box 998, File 2; "useless to discuss re-election": *Excélsior,* Jul. 22, 1950, AGN-DGIPS, Box 999, File 2.

46. Memo, Mario Rauche Garciadiego to Consul Richard Johnson, Sep. 5, 1951, Guadalajara, National Archives and Records Administration, Washington, D.C. (NARA), Record Group 84, Box 130. Emphasis added.

47. Report, "Political Conditions in Mexico from May 16 through June 15, 1950," First Secretary of Embassy Charles R. Burrows, Jun. 23, 1950, NARA, Record Group 84, Box 129.

48. *El Popular,* Aug. 10, 1951, AGN-DGIPS, Box 998, File 2.

49. Camp, *Mexican Political Biographies, 1935–1993,* 126.

The precandidacy of Casas Alemán presented a troubling scenario to the stalwarts of the PRI. In September 1951, the nomination of the party was still undecided, with Casas Alemán carrying the support of the Confederación Nacional de Organizaciones Populares (CNOP) and Adolfo Ruiz Cortines that of the CTM. Casas Alemán also reportedly had the support of "los dioses mayores de la política," including regional power brokers Antonio Taracena, Antonio Canale, Jose Gómez Esparza, Donato Miranda Fonseca, and Alfonso Corona del Rosal, in his quest to lead the "moral reconstruction of the country."[50]

Yet, by the end of September 1951, Casas Alemán recognized the weakness of his precandidacy and withdrew from the electoral contest, thus avoiding an internal struggle within the PRI for the nomination.[51] Casas Alemán was "cast aside in favor of Ruiz Cortines when [he] showed too great independence on his own behalf and disregard for the President and his entourage." The PAN congressman Jaime Robles reported that the common belief among his congressional colleagues was that "Casas Alemán was used by President Alemán to distract attention from the campaign to re-elect him." In Tijuana, "local politicians and the general public were puzzled over the inexplicable turn events had taken in the choice of Ruiz Cortines to succeed President Alemán when the cards had already been stacked in favor of Licenciado Casas Alemán."[52]

The good people of Tijuana need not have been puzzled. The rise and fall of Casas Alemán highlighted both the limits of presidential power in selecting a successor and the burden on the successor to unify the disparate factions of the party. Casas Alemán failed in his bid to be the PRI candidate because he was too closely associated with Alemán and because he did not properly negotiate with the traditional sectors of PRI influence. A contemporary analysis suggested that "President Alemán appears to have nominated his successor through skillful use of a now perfected political machine."[53]

50. Nomination of the party was still undecided: *La Prensa,* Sep. 13, 1951; *Excélsior,* Sep. 13, 1951 (both located in AGN-DGIPS, Box 998, File 3); "los dioses mayores de la política": Memo, DGIPS, [1951], AGN-DGIPS, Box 131, 2.1/290/157.

51. *La Prensa,* Sep. 22, 1951, AGN-DGIPS, Box 131, 2.1/290/157.

52. "Cast aside": Despach 1900, Robert S. Folsom to Dept. of State, Feb. 12, 1952; "distract attention from the campaign": Memo, Mario Rauche Garciadiego to Consul Richard Johnson, Nov. 17, 1950, Guadalajara (both located in NARA, Record Group 84, Box 130); "puzzled over the inexplicable turn": Memo, Consul Louis F. Blanchard to Ambassador William O'Dwyer, Dec. 11, 1951, Tijuana, NARA, Record Group 84, Box 133.

53. Despach 1900, Robert S. Folsom to Dept. of State, Feb. 12, 1952, NARA, Record Group 84, Box 130.

That is, it seemed that Alemán got the candidate he wanted while appearing to accept a compromise. In "losing" the succession battles over prórroga and Casas Alemán, Alemán had actually won.

Ruiz Cortines presented an interesting figure to succeed Alemán. In the succession, Alemán had a very delicate balance to strike: he wanted to maintain his influence and guarantee the continuation of his policies, but he could not ignore the antipathy that his name and associates drew from various sectors of the political class. Ruiz Cortines was a good consensus candidate for several reasons. As a civilian, he could continue to marginalize the political authority of the military. Like Alemán, he was a native of Veracruz who had experience in presidential campaigns and party bureaucracy.[54] Moreover, he understood the nature and practice of political control, having headed Gobernación and its intelligence divisions from 1948 to 1951. Finally, his bland personality worked to Alemán's advantage. Alemán was known for his flamboyance and youthful vigor, and Ruiz Cortines could not possibly threaten the bases of his popularity in these aspects. Within the PRI, Ruiz Cortines evoked no strong feelings of either positive or negative persuasion. His image was that of a caretaker, one who would continue Alemán's economic policies with a sort of paternal moderation. Even after Ruiz Cortines's inauguration, Alemán continued to wield influence over the federal bureaucracy through high-level staff carryovers from his administration, principally within the cabinet offices.[55]

Ruiz Cortines fulfilled the needs of the Alemán group, which, failing to maintain itself in the presidency, succeeded in appointing a candidate that would be supportive of its future aspirations. As one observer noted, "Ruiz Cortines accepted the nomination, but apparently did not seek it and certainly did not intrigue to secure it."[56] But by September 1951, Ruiz Cortines had acquired numerous and powerful supporters within the party, including senators Fernando Moctezuma, Gustavo A. Uruchurtu, Gustavo Díaz Ordaz, and Adolfo López Mateos.[57] In a speech in Mérida, Ruiz Cortines set the

54. Ruiz Cortines was campaign manager for Alemán in 1946 and had been treasurer for Manuel Ávila Camacho's campaign in 1940. See Camp, *Mexican Political Biographies, 1935–1993,* 628.

55. Monthly Operations Report, U.S. Embassy to Dept. of State, Dec. 9, 1952, NARA, Record Group 59, Institute for Inter-American Affairs, Administrative Office, Country Files (Central Files), 1942–1953, Box 86.

56. Despatch 1900, Robert S. Folsom to Dept. of State, Feb. 12, 1952, NARA, Record Group 84, Box 130.

57. Memo, DGIPS, [Sep. 1951], AGN-DGIPS, Box 131, 2.1/290/156.

tone for his campaign: "Above the divergence of opinions and the variety of interests, we will impose human dignity, collective security and progress for the nation." The shapeless agenda presented by Ruiz Cortines was short on specifics but long on the type of platitudes that engendered the belief that his paternalistic style would translate into reasonable and steady leadership. Unlike his predecessor, who was often criticized for his charm and dalliances, Ruiz Cortines was a trustworthy (if colorless) bureaucrat who inspired a sense of stability in his countrymen. One journalist provided the unintentionally laughable assessment that "if don Adolfo were a bullfighter, he would cut both ear and tail."[58] In contrast to the violence of some opposition elements, Ruiz Cortines's campaign was "inspired by the feelings and needs of the people, who do not want violence."[59] His paternalistic image assuaged concerns about a radical shift in government policy after Alemán's term of office.

A cross-section of prominent groups backed the Ruiz Cortines candidacy. Ruiz Cortines enjoyed the support of the Legión de Honor Mexicana, a group that included "*villistas, zapatistas, carrancistas* and *obregonistas* . . . members of armies that in other times would have been the most bitter enemies."[60] The Legión de Honor had been created in 1917 by President Venustiano Carranza to provide an "honorable location for excess officers of the Constitutionalist Army." In addition to forming a reserve of veteran officers in case of a military emergency, the Legión de Honor members also provided instruction to military cadets, thereby strengthening institutional continuity. As members of the revolutionary generation aged and were marginalized in political life, the Legión de Honor became a symbol of lasting status for the officer corps, especially after its reorganization in 1949 by President Alemán. Under the new rules, military elites who had "forged our nationality, defended the Republic against foreign aggressions . . . meritoriously served the State," or completed at least thirty years of active duty were eligible for membership.[61] The support of the Legión de Honor thus represented

58. "Impose human dignity": *Excélsior,* Jan. 17, 1952; "cut both ear and tail": *Excélsior,* Jan. 1, 1952. In bullfighting, the *matador* is rewarded for valorous behavior and a graceful kill with the freshly cut ear(s) of the bull. If the spectacle is especially sublime—an increasingly rare occurrence in Mexico today—the tail is also cut off and awarded.

59. *Excélsior,* Jan. 24, 1952.

60. José Luis Piñeyro, "Las fuerzas armadas en la transición política de México," *Revista Mexicana de Sociología* 59, no. 1 (1997): 170. See also José Luis Piñeyro, *Ejército y sociedad en México: Pasado y presente* (Puebla: Universidad Autónoma de Puebla, 1985), 67.

61. Secretaría de Defensa Nacional, http://www.sedena.gob.mx/leg_hon/cont.htm (accessed February 10, 2008).

the formal approval of Ruiz Cortines by the remaining revolutionary veterans and the retired military elite. Furthermore, the Grupo México, consisting of members of the Guardias Presidenciales and the Estado Mayor Presidencial, pledged to support whomever the PRI selected as its presidential candidate.[62] And Ruiz Cortines enjoyed the approval of the press. The newspaper *Excélsior* printed an article titled "Contrast in the Positions of the Candidates," but the article exclusively discussed the viewpoints of Ruiz Cortines, the other candidates not being mentioned even once.[63] These groups accentuated the wide institutional support already in the hands of the Ruiz Cortines campaign.

Ruiz Cortines, though lacking the military background of Henríquez or Aguilar, recognized the importance of keeping the military in his corner, or at least neutralizing its influence. He declared in October 1951 that "the people's military, which has been taking in technicians from the glorious Colegio Militar, the glorious Escuela Naval Militar and from all the centers of military education, has been and will continue being one of the most solid supports of our institutions."[64] This statement also affirmed the growing importance of the reformed military academies in the formation of a new elite within the armed services.[65]

To solidify his backing within the PRI, Ruiz Cortines still had to deal with the supporters of Casas Alemán. After a formal meeting with Casas Alemán in early January 1952, Ruiz Cortines accompanied him on a long automobile ride around Chapúltepec Park and "a large area of the city." This trip allowed them time to negotiate a political settlement that was mutually useful, and it was no coincidence that the trip ended at PRI headquarters in San Cosme, "where both said goodbye with a hug [*abrazo*]." As a result of their conference, friends and supporters of Casas Alemán received high posts within the PRI and the Ruiz Cortines campaign. For instance, Alfonso Corona del Rosal was named head of the Regional Committee of the PRI for the Distrito Federal, while Cesar Cervantes became Ruiz Cortines's personal representative in Mexico City.[66] This deal allowed Casas Alemán to maintain his political clout in a new accommodation and permitted Ruiz Cortines to proceed with the campaign, confident in the unity of the PRI behind him.

62. Report, DGIPS, [Sep. 1951], AGN-DGIPS, Box 808, File 4, 2.1/51/373.

63. *Excélsior*, Jan. 24, 1952.

64. *Discursos de Ruiz Cortines,* Vol. 1, Speech at the Estadio Olímpico, Mexico City, Oct. 14, 1951, AGN-DGIPS, Box 811, File 1, 2.1/52/54.

65. See chapter 2 for further detail on this process.

66. *La Prensa,* Jan. 12, 1952, AGN-DGIPS, Box 815, Campaña Presidencial, Jan. 1952.

PRI officials also acted to smooth over regional political disputes to facilitate the presidential campaign. The party negotiated an apparent political truce among the warring factions of Guerrero in preparation for the 1952 election. Reportedly, Ruiz Cortines personally brokered the deal that allowed such enemies as Gabriel R. Guevara and Adrian Castrejón to "give each other a hug and their word as gentlemen that they would form a single group."[67] Ruiz Cortines tasked Gonzalo N. Santos with mediating the political differences between the three factions in Tamaulipas, centered on Governor Horacio Terán, General Raúl Gárate, and former president Emilio Portes Gil, "to assure that the support of the PRI in this area will not be weakened in the forthcoming elections through internal disagreement."[68] PRI officials' ability to negotiate such regional political truces for the sake of the greater good of the party demonstrated how much leverage it had developed since the 1930s and the level of discipline expected of the high-level politicians who fed at its trough.

The selection of Ruiz Cortines did not provoke an outcry from within the party. As one observer overstated, "The solidity of the present administration and of the PRI obliges *instant obedience* of their wishes."[69] Although this comment no doubt overestimated the latitude of the administration in making such decisions, it was clear that once the PRI leadership decided on Ruiz Cortines, he would face no subversion or organized dissent from within the party.

A key figure in managing the PRI's support for Ruiz Cortines was the party president, General Rodolfo Sánchez Taboada, who served as campaign director.[70] Sánchez Taboada, known colloquially as "the gravedigger," was something of an odd choice for a position that required heavy doses of public relations and political maneuver.[71] Sánchez Taboada's term as governor of the Territory of Baja California del Norte (1937–44) ended when he was "removed by the Central Government apparently because of considerable irregularities in office."[72] Graciano Sánchez accused him of being a culprit in

67. *Excélsior*, Mar. 13, 1952, AGN-DGIPS, Box 811, File 2, 2.1/52/55.

68. Memo, Consul Kennedy M. Crockett to Ambassador William O'Dwyer, Jun. 3, 1952, Tampico, NARA, Record Group 84, Box 133.

69. Memo, Consul Louis F. Blanchard to Ambassador William O'Dwyer, Dec. 11, 1951, Tijuana, NARA, Record Group 84, Box 133. Emphasis added.

70. Sánchez Taboada was president of the Comité Ejecutivo Nacional of the PRI for the entirety of Alemán's term, from Dec. 5, 1946, to Dec. 1, 1952. See Camp, *Mexican Political Biographies, 1935–1993*, 654–55.

71. *El Universal*, Jun. 4, 1951, AGN-DGIPS, Box 19, File 2, 2.1/061.3/10.

72. Memo, Consul Louis F. Blanchard to Ambassador William O'Dwyer, Jan. 29, 1952, Tijuana, NARA, Record Group 84, Box 133.

the murder of Emiliano Zapata.[73] Subsequently, from 1946 to 1952, Sánchez Taboada's main attribute was his willingness to freely brandish the increasing power brought about through the consolidation of the PRI.

Sánchez Taboada provoked an outcry from the opposition when he labeled himself, perhaps jokingly, the "Grand Inquisitor and Supreme Judge of all the revolutionaries." Antonio Espinosa de los Monteros, a founder of Nacional Financiera, S. A. (NAFINSA) and senior advisor to the Henríquez campaign, excoriated him the next day in the press: "While President Alemán, with his usual prudence only counsels and recommends, the head of the sole [único] party prohibits, commands and orders with a thunderous voice. . . . Who authorized him to treat free Mexicans, and the true revolutionaries, as if they were a platoon of beardless and docile recruits? Is it possible that the head of the PRI has not yet been informed that the free world, of which Mexico is a part, is fighting to defend effective suffrage and respect for the vote, and to end the totalitarian and single party systems, whether they are called fascist, communist or institutionalist?"[74] The UNS later referred to Sánchez Taboada as the "Gran Elector" in their effort to discredit him. His crude style elicited harsh criticisms from the FPPM: "Unknown in the political history of Mexico is any case in which impositionist cynicism has gone to the extreme like today, when they boast of the disdain that the people should receive."[75]

Sánchez Taboada feigned indifference to the charges made against him and characterized the verbal attacks of the FPPM as a "direct product of evil, impotence and failure." But his insistence on utilizing the considerable political leverage of the party did little to assuage his critics. The press criticized his imperious and egotistical attitude and his apparent assumption that "the Patria is the PRI and the PRI is Rodolfo Sánchez Taboada." In a physical manifestation of his psychological self-importance, the PRI made use of three airplanes during campaign trips: one for Ruiz Cortines and his staff, one for the press, and one for Sánchez Taboada and his guests.[76] Throughout the

73. *Excélsior,* Jan. 24, 1952.

74. *Últimas Noticias,* Jan. 2, 1951; *Excélsior,* Jan. 3, 1951 (both located in AGN-DGIPS, Box 807, Campaña Presidencial, Jan. 1951).

75. "Gran Elector": *La Prensa,* Apr. 28, 1951, AGN-DGIPS, Box 807, Campaña Presidencial, Apr.-Jun. 1951; "boast of the disdain": *La Prensa,* Dec. 20, 1951, AGN-DGIPS, Box 808, File 6, 2.1/51/372.

76. "Direct product of evil": *Excélsior,* Oct. 2, 1951; "*Patria* is the PRI": *Atisbos,* Oct. 18, 1951 (both located in AGN-DGIPS, Box 998, File 1); made use of three airplanes: *Excélsior,* Nov. 23, 1951, AGN-DGIPS, Box 999, File 1.

campaign, the attacks leveled against Sánchez Taboada allowed the opposition to score points versus the PRI as an institution, but left Ruiz Cortines, the actual candidate, relatively unscathed.

Personality and public perceptions aside, Sánchez Taboada was adept as the leader of the PRI. His efforts focused on both protection of Alemán and the election of Ruiz Cortines. In September 1951, as the PRI nominating congress approached, he lined up the main industrial unions, giving him tremendous leverage.[77] When he added four more unions to his alliance the next day, Sánchez Taboada declared, "We are going to demonstrate in a palpable way the power of the Revolution gathered in our party, in contrast to what the sometime parties [partidos de ocasión] are trying to display."[78] The CNC and Confederación Regional Obrera Mexicana (CROM) joined with Sánchez Taboada just a day after that, and the Confederación General de Trabajadores (CGT) agreed to support the PRI candidate on October 1.[79]

One of the crucial issues of the election of 1952 was the direction of Mexico's development. If Ruiz Cortines represented a continuation, and perhaps moderation, of Alemán's policies, the candidacy of Henríquez offered the prospect of a return to the idealized past of the Cárdenas administration. Henríquez attempted to bridge the gap between the political situation deriving from Alemán's tenure and the disaffection of elements of the Cárdenas and Ávila Camacho administrations, drawing support from those who disliked the Alemán policies and those who wished for a return to the past.[80] He also counted on a generalized movement supporting a change in the way Mexico was governed. In August 1951, the American consul in Tijuana noted the prevalent opinion among local editorialists and media outlets "that conditions are approaching the point of a propitious atmosphere for a capable

77. Excélsior, Sep. 18, 1951, AGN-DGIPS, Box 998, File 3. The main industrial unions included the Sindicato Nacional de Trabajadores Mineros, Metalúrgicos y Similares de la República Mexicana (SNTMMSRM), the Sindicato de Trabajadores Ferrocarrileros de la República Mexicana (STFRM), and the Sindicato de Trabajadores Petroleros de la República Mexicana (STPRM).

78. Novedades, Sep. 19, 1951, AGN-DGIPS, Box 998, File 3. The unions included were the Confederación Nacional Proletaria (CNP), the Confederación de Obreros y Campesinos de México (COCM), the Confederación Nacional de Trabajadores (CNT), and the Confederación Única de Trabajadores (CUT).

79. La Prensa, Sep. 20, 1951, AGN-DGIPS, Box 998, File 3. Also, La Prensa, Oct. 2, 1951, AGN-DGIPS, Box 998, File 1.

80. See, for example, Últimas Noticias, May 4, 1950, AGN-DGIPS, Box 803, Futurismo Político, Campaña Presidencial, 1952–1958, Vol. 2. Also, Gabriela Urquiza Ruiz, "El movimiento henriquista: La sucesión presidencial de 1952" (licenciatura thesis, Universidad Autónoma Metropolitana [Mexico City], 1978), 30.

opposition candidate."[81] Henríquez aimed to take advantage of this atmosphere in a way that he could not in 1946.

As noted earlier, the FPPM was formed in 1945 within the PRM to "act as a political platform for the presidential aspirations of General Henríquez."[82] When Henríquez did not run in 1946, although he had requested and gained licencia ilimitada, the FPPM remained in existence as a sort of small political action committee, working to advance the prestige of its founder and beginning to build support for his campaign in 1952. The FPPM's statement of May 30, 1951, that "the group was formed *in order to offer him its candidacy*" squelched rumors that the party might present a candidate for president other than Henríquez.[83] By the time the FPPM received its registro from the government in June 1951, marking it as a national political party, it had constructed a wide alliance of interests in support of Henríquez.[84] Throughout the campaign, the FPPM endeavored to align supporters in the creation of a truly national opponent to PRI candidates.

The country knew well of Henríquez's accomplishments in public service, as well as his political aspirations. Yet *El Universal* sourly opined that "he did not understand in 1945 that the national tendency was different, favoring civilians, and that power was no longer plunder for military men."[85] To this end, though he could not hide his military background—which was, after all, a main source of his political connections—Henríquez attempted to style himself as a civilian leader. Because he was granted licencia ilimitada in 1945, he was more comfortable wearing his trademark double-breasted suits and darkened spectacles than a military uniform, and he seemed every bit the modern businessman and executive. This sartorial change suggested a tacit recognition that the political influence of the military was faltering.

Yet chief among his supporters, and of great interest to both U.S. observers and the civilian leaders of the PRI, were military officers. Henríquez claimed that "the most painful moment of my life was when I decided to request

81. Memo, Consul Louis F. Blanchard to Ambassador William O'Dwyer, Aug. 10, 1951, Tijuana, NARA, Record Group 84, Box 133.

82. Urquiza Ruiz, "El movimiento henriquista," 37.

83. *Excélsior,* May 30, 1951, emphasis added. For reports of the rumor itself, see *Novedades,* May 29, 1951; and *Excélsior,* May 29, 1951 (both located in AGN-DGIPS, Box 24, File 15, 2.1/061.8/15, Vol. 1, pp. 20–23).

84. *El Universal,* Jun. 15, 1951, AGN-DGIPS, Box 807, Campaña Presidencial, Apr.–Jun. 1951.

85. *El Universal,* Feb. 27, 1950, AGN-DGIPS, Box 803, Campaña Presidencial, Futurismo, 1950–1952, Vol. 1.

licencia ilimitada to separate myself from the Army, to which I had devoted the best years of my life." In 1945, Henríquez reportedly had a substantial following among the military leaders in the state of Veracruz. Another report from Puebla indicated that Henríquez had hosted a political meeting at his home in Mexico City with a "very large [*nutrido*] group of soldiers" and promised to "risk his fortune, and even his life if necessary, to ensure that he would not be a second Almazán."[86] As Sánchez Gutierrez correctly noted, perhaps of most interest to U.S. and Mexican observers was that "from a military standpoint the importance of the henriquista campaign resided in the number of revolutionary generals who supported the movement and in the capacity of the FPPM to mobilize different sectors of society in its cause."[87]

Henríquez drew upon his revolutionary credentials for political credibility. In a typical campaign speech, he commented on the revolutionary legacy by saying, "We have walked up and down paths all under the banner of *revolucionarismo*. . . . The central goal of the Revolution, we must remember, was to better the standard of living of the people through an honest and effective democracy in which the people themselves could choose the men best suited to achieve the common good."[88]

Henríquez attempted a political campaign that would appeal to both poor and working class voters while conforming to the pro-business philosophy necessary in Mexico during those years. Organized labor never did join his crusade in large numbers, though notable exceptions occurred. When the CNC endorsed the PRI in the 1952 elections, the CNC president, Salvador Camelo Soler, broke away from the organization and formed the pro-Henríquez Guzmán Comité Nacional de Defensa de Derechos Agrarios.[89] The FPPM worked diligently to create a grassroots base among campesinos throughout Mexico as part of its national strategy. It founded state-level organizations from late 1950s onward, providing a basis for later campaigning.[90]

---

86. "Most painful moment of my life": *La Prensa,* Apr. 17, 1950, AGN-DGIPS, Box 803, Campaña Presidencial, Futurismo, 1950–1952, Vol. 1; substantial following among the military leaders: Report, Insp. Migoni to DGIPS, Oct. 7, 1945, Veracruz, AGN-DGIPS, Box 787, 2.1/45/282; "risk his fortune": Report, Insp. 42 to DGIPS, Sep. 10, 1945, Puebla, AGN-DGIPS, Box 787, 2.1/45/289.

87. Sánchez Gutiérrez, "Los militares en la década de los cincuenta," 286.

88. *Excélsior,* Jan. 4, 1952.

89. *Excélsior,* Feb. 27, 1952.

90. The founding dates of some of the campesino organizations were: Toluca, Dec. 3, 1950; Aguascalientes, Dec. 16, 1950; Tepic, Dec. 22, 1950; Guadalajara, Dec. 23, 1950; Tlaxcala, Dec. 26, 1950; Guadalupe Victoria, Jan. 6, 1951; Torreón, Jan. 8, 1951; Colima, Jan. 21, 1951; Puebla, Jan. 21, 1951; Chihuahua, Jan. 28, 1951; Iguala, Feb. 10, 1951; Cuautla, Feb. 11, 1951;

By May 1951, only five states still lacked an henriquista campesino organization.[91] By far, the Unión de Federaciones Campesinas de México (UFCM) was the primary foundation of FPPM support, claiming membership of over one million by April 1951.[92] Indeed, the message of the Henríquez campaign was clear from the beginning, even if his plans for the government were not. In a full-page ad, the candidate declared, "Estoy a los órdenes del pueblo, en esta lucha por México y para México."[93] This theme, repeated throughout the campaign season, came to symbolize Henríquez's political efforts.

Like Almazán in 1940, Henríquez derived political strength from the support of railroad workers, "the sector of the labor movement that supported henriquismo until the end."[94] The leader of FPPM efforts among railroad workers was Juan Gutiérrez, who had occupied the posts of general secretary of the Sindicato de Trabajadores Ferrocarrileros de la República Mexicana (STFRM), director of Ferrocarriles Nacionales de México (FNM), and buying agent for the FNM in New York.[95] Intelligence gathered in January 1951 by the DGIPS pointed to growing support among railroad workers for Henríquez, a fact seemingly confirmed in the full-page ad that the Trabajadores Ferrocarrileros de México took out in *La Prensa*.[96] By July 1952, reports indicated that upwards of 90 percent of railroad workers around Mazatlán had supported Henríquez at the polls.[97] This level of enthusiasm for the Henríquez candidacy sparked concern among the PRI leaders, who had just brought the railroad union to heel in the late 1940s.

The support of the campesino organizations and the railroad workers aided in the FPPM's national strategy. By February 1951, twenty-six states

Querétaro, Feb. 25, 1951; Irapuato, Mar. 11, 1951; Huichipán, Mar. 15, 1951; Linares, Mar. 17, 1951; San Luis Potosí, Mar. 18, 1951; Oaxaca, Apr. 1, 1951; Culiacán, Apr. 8, 1951; Motul, Apr. 29, 1951; Fresnillo, May 9, 1951; Mexicali, May 13, 1951; Campeche, May 19, 1951; Villahermosa, May 20, 1951; Tuxtla Gutiérrez, May 27, 1951. See *La Prensa*, Jun. 7, 1951, AGN-DGIPS, Box 24, File 15, 2.1/061.8/15, Vol. 1, p. 10.

91. *El Universal*, May 4, 1951, AGN-DGIPS, Box 807, Campaña Presidencial, Apr.–Jun. 1951.

92. Memo, R. Smith Simpson to Ambassador, Apr. 9, 1951, NARA, Record Group 84, Box 130.

93. "I am at the orders of the people, in this struggle by Mexico and for Mexico." *Excélsior*, Jan. 17, 1952.

94. Urquiza Ruiz, "El movimiento henriquista," 28–29.

95. *Excélsior*, Feb. 1, 1951, AGN-DGIPS, Box 807, Campaña Presidencial, Jan. 1951.

96. Report, Insp. 20 to DGIPS, Jan. 4, 1951, AGN-DGIPS, Box 807, Campaña Presidencial, Jan. 1951. Also, *La Prensa*, Jan. 4, 1951.

97. Memo, Josefina V. de Llausás (Consulate) to Embassy, Jul. 18, 1952, Mazatlán, NARA, Record Group 84, Box 131.

had established pro-Henríquez committees.[98] Overall, the U.S. Embassy reckoned the centers of FPPM strength to be Chihuahua, the Distrito Federal, Michoacán, Morelia, and Sonora.[99] However, problems arose in some states where Henríquez and the FPPM did not have the leverage to mediate regional disputes the way that Ruiz Cortines and the PRI could. For example, personal rivalries divided the FPPM organization in the state of Yucatán, and its infiltration by the Mérida police made it incapable of battling the heavily clientelist campaign of Ruiz Cortines in the state.[100] And some regions did not respond to Henríquez's cause, as in Mexicali, where various FPPM rallies drew only "negligible" attendance. Finally, the relative newness of the party meant that Henríquez received greater support in Culiacán, the capital city of Sinaloa, than in the rural areas of the state.[101]

Prominent political leaders and members of the Alemán government aligned themselves with the Henríquez campaign. Former secretary of agriculture Marte Gómez took over as head of the campaign in July 1950. In April 1951, Excélsior reported that up to 17,500 members of the government bureaucracy backed Henríquez.[102] But the support of high-level politicians and bureaucrats was a double-edged sword for Henríquez, who had always faced criticism that he perpetuated cronyism and graft in government contracts. Several leading supporters of his candidacy reportedly received lucrative salaries from the FPPM. Monthly totals included five thousand pesos for José Muñoz Cota, ten thousand pesos for Cesar Martino, and ten thousand pesos for Ernesto Soto Reyes. The Henríquez campaign was also perceived

98. Memo, DGIPS, Feb. 1, 1951, AGN-DGIPS, Box 807, Futurismo Presidencial, Feb. 1951. States included were Aguascalientes, Baja California Norte, Campeche, Chiapas, Chihuahua, Coahuila, Colima, Durango, Guerrero, Hidalgo, Jalisco, Mexico, Michoacán, Morelos, Nayarit, Nuevo León, Oaxaca, Puebla, San Luis Potosí, Sinaloa, Sonora, Tabasco, Tamaulipas, Veracruz, Yucatán, and Zacatecas.

99. Memo, R. Smith Simpson to Ambassador, Apr. 9, 1951, NARA, Record Group 84, Box 130.

100. Memo, Vice Consul Abraham Katz to Ambassador O'Dwyer, Jul. 2, 1952, Mérida; Telegram, Vice Consul Abraham Katz to Ambassador O'Dwyer, Jul. 4, 1952, Mérida (both located in NARA, Record Group 84, Box 131).

101. "Negligible" attendance: Memo, Consul Antonio Certosimo to Ambassador O'Dwyer, Mar. 28, 1952, Mexicali; relative newness of the party: Memo, Josefina V. de Llausás (Consulate) to Embassy, Mar. 20, 1952, Mazatlán (both located in NARA, Record Group 84, Box 131).

102. Head of the campaign: El Universal, Jul. 8, 1950, AGN-DGIPS, Box 999, File 2; 17,500 members of the government bureaucracy: Excélsior, Apr. 2, 1951, AGN-DGIPS, Box 807, Campaña Presidencial, Mar.-Apr. 1951. As the total number of bureaucrats was roughly two hundred fifty thousand, approximately 7 percent of the entire group was considered henriquista, according to this report.

as a vehicle for new abuses by old politicians, as one newspaper suggested: "Henriquismo is not an ideological current, but rather a group of discredited politicians, who have now killed enough time and are dreaming of regaining positions that they used to enjoy."[103] Yet the FPPM maintained a general sense of unity despite the charges against it and attempted to turn public debate toward issues that were favorable to its candidate.

Evidence of revolutionary credentials had been a very valuable political asset since the late 1910s and was again important in the electoral contest of 1952. Henríquez, along with many other critics from across the nation, accused Ruiz Cortines of lying about his presence and action in Veracruz during the U.S. invasion in 1914.[104] At the Partido Constitucionalista Mexicano (PConstM) assembly in October 1951, Francisco Múgica savaged Ruiz Cortines's actions during the U.S. invasion, in which Múgica personally fought, saying, "I cannot attack Ruiz Cortines [now] because I already attacked him in 1914." After apparently eluding federal police surveillance in Torreón, Henríquez attended a secret meeting with General Rafael Clamont, who offered financial support and promised decisive proof of Ruiz Cortines's "services to the Americans" in 1914 at Veracruz.[105] In June 1952, Ruiz Cortines was publicly exonerated when he was officially claimed "favorite son" of the city of Veracruz, which provided papers documenting his valor in the Mexican efforts of 1914.[106] This did little to settle the controversy but provided some official political cover from an issue that was all but impossible for the PRI to ignore.

Sánchez Taboada made the case that the PRI also had revolutionary credentials, even if its candidate did not. According to him, there were only three sectors in the political spectrum of Mexico. First was the Right, conservative without being reactionary, which could not return to power because the populace recognized it as the old guard of Porfirian Mexico and did not wish to return to the ways of the past. Second was the Left, infused with revolutionary ideology but too far removed from the realities of postrevolutionary Mexico, such as the suffering of the campesinos. Finally, the "revolutionary" group, linked to the PRI, was full of revolutionary ideals yet able

103. Monthly totals: *Novedades,* Nov. 28, 1951, AGN-DGIPS, Box 25, File 3, 2.1/061.8/ 15, Vol. 4, p. 310; "dreaming of regaining positions": *La Voz del Sureste,* Dec. 4, 1951, quoted in *Excélsior,* Dec. 5, 1951, AGN-DGIPS, Box 808, File 6, 2.1/51/372.

104. *Excélsior,* Feb. 4, 1952.

105. "I already attacked him": *El Popular,* Oct. 8, 1951, AGN-DGIPS, Box 24, File 10, 2.1/061.8/10, p. 80; "services to the Americans": Internal memo, DGIPS, Nov. 22, 1951, AGN-DGIPS, Box 25, File 3, 2.1/061.8/15, Vol. 4, p. 155.

106. *Excélsior,* Jun. 8, 1952.

to provide material benefits like growth of industry and advancement in agriculture "as factors of progress that the people could never forget."[107] Sánchez Taboada's national political scheme predictably ascribed the economic success of the nation to the direct involvement of the PRI, and conveniently removed the weaknesses of the PRI's candidate from the table since Ruiz Cortines was "revolutionary" by association.

Beyond the specific case of Ruiz Cortines, the question of revolutionary credentials as a prerequisite for high political office underwent a reexamination. The newspaper *El Mexicano* argued against the necessity of such experience for high-level politicians, since "there are others who, while not engaged in the revolutionary struggle . . . have faithfully interpreted the ideals of the revolution *as if they had borne arms.*"[108] This shift in thinking began to blur the once clear line that separated those who fought in the revolution from those who did not, or from those who fought on the wrong side. It also fit well with a PRI spokesman's assertion that "the people will not permit the triumph of any candidate who is not firmly established in the principles of the Mexican Revolution."[109] This transition, as chapter 2 demonstrated, destroyed the political monopoly once enjoyed by the revolutionary (military) elite and provided the window of opportunity for younger politicians and more highly skilled technocrats to enter and dominate political life.

There were three other notable candidates in 1952: Vicente Lombardo Toledano, Cándido Aguilar, and Efraín González Luna. Lombardo had been the mastermind of the CTM in the 1930s and was a stalwart of the PRM during the Cárdenas and Ávila Camacho administrations. His appeal waned during the Alemán years, however, and the U.S. State Department reckoned that "by 1951 Lombardo had lost most of his political influence."[110] Still, Manuel Gómez Morín commented in 1952 that, aside from the PAN candidate, only Lombardo had a true ideological position: "the rest are just degenerations of the regime."[111] Lombardo's burgeoning ideological quarrels with the government began to pose a threat, especially when he suggested in a "somewhat sensational" speech at Aguascalientes in 1950 that the PRI's failure to address political and economic problems "might degenerate into civil

107. *Excélsior*, Jan. 3, 1952.
108. Memo, Consul Stephen E. Aguirre to Ambassador Walter Thurston, Sep. 27, 1951, Ciudad Juarez, NARA, Record Group 84, Box 129. Emphasis added.
109. *Excélsior*, Jan. 3, 1952.
110. Despatch 1900, Robert S. Folsom to Dept. of State, Feb. 12, 1952, NARA, Record Group 84, Box 130.
111. *Excélsior*, Jan. 5, 1952.

war." His rhetoric in public speeches also inflamed U.S. diplomatic opinion against him. In Tampico, "he attempted to show a parallel between Hitler's dream of world conquest and . . . the preparations of the giant monopolies of the colossus of the north for a new world war."[112] Lombardo's programs and ideas garnered support among the more energetic sectors of society, mainly student activists. In late January, Lombardo's Partido Popular (PP) sponsored a convention for urban youths in Mexico City, the Movimiento de la Juventud Popular.[113] Yet, for all of his activity and vigor, Lombardo's efforts in 1952 were largely without focus. Only when the opposition attempted to form a coalition (explained below) did Lombardo seriously affect the presidential campaign.

Another military officer who attempted to exercise political influence in the election of 1952 was Cándido Aguilar. Aguilar had been active in the revolution and was a staunch supporter (and son-in-law) of Venustiano Carranza. Though exiled after supporting the de la Huerta rebellion in 1923, Aguilar rehabilitated himself and became a senator from Veracruz during the Cárdenas administration.[114] The Partido de la Revolución (PR), founded in 1951, was his vehicle for electoral activities and included among its members several high-ranking officers.[115] As Sánchez Gutiérrez argued, "Aguilar's followers did not have a defined ideology and his program was unclear, however, he represented a group of revolutionary veterans who felt excluded by the official party."[116] His connections to the armed forces made Aguilar a source of concern for PRI officials, a situation compounded by his fiery rhetoric.

Aguilar cautioned against deepening relations with the United States too quickly, arguing that Mexico should be friends with its neighbor "but never in any way unworthy satellites." He did not reserve his vitriol for the United States alone, as he was also severe in his appraisal of the Mexican political

112. "Somewhat sensational" and "degenerate into civil war": Report, "Political Conditions in Mexico from May 16 through June 15, 1950," First Secretary of Embassy Charles R. Burrows, Jun. 23, 1950, NARA, Record Group 84, Box 129; "Hitler's dream of world conquest": Memo, Consul Kennedy M. Crockett to Ambassador William O'Dwyer, Mar. 25, 1952, Tampico, NARA, Record Group 84, Box 133.

113. *Excélsior*, Jan. 24, 1952.

114. Camp, *Mexican Political Biographies, 1935–1993*, 10.

115. AGN-DGIPS, Box 19, File 13, 2.1/061.3/21. The PR counted among its members Generals Luis Alamillo Flores, Everardo Martínez Portillo, Juan Barragán, Lorenzo Merino Fernández, Donato Bravo Izquierdo, and Jorge A. Grajales, along with Colonels Porfirio del Castillo and Octavio Magaña Cerda.

116. Sánchez Gutiérrez, "Los militares en la década de los cincuenta," 287.

landscape: "It is more forgivable when Perón closes a periodical in Argentina by force, than the counter-revolutionary attitude brought on by bribes, money, and fear. Freedom of expression, the freedoms to write, think and create, shut down by force as embarrassments, is less censurable since the dictator bravely assumes his responsibilities. In our Mexico, those who have trampled such sacred liberties in these last years, assume nothing."[117]

Aguilar viewed the task before him with both cynical realism and idealistic hope: "we are part of a legal and clear opposition, which we have a right to as citizens . . . but we patiently await the arbitrariness, the persecution and the violence that has always characterized dictatorships and tyrannies, which are always transitory." The day after this statement appeared, Gobernación rejected the PR's application for registro, citing a failure to collect sufficient signatures.[118] Although Aguilar and the PR were denied official recognition, they continued to work against the interests of the PRI in the campaign and took part in the efforts to unify the opposition in early 1952.

Efraín González Luna stood as the presidential candidate of the PAN after Gómez Morín refused the position, despite attempts by young members of the party to convince the latter otherwise. González Luna, who had founded the PAN with Gómez Morín in 1939, suffered from the beginning of the campaign from a poorly defined message and a lackluster personality. He even received criticism for campaigning with an "unsportsmanlike" (*antideportiva*) attitude, assuming that he would lose the election and therefore not competing very hard.[119] This criticism was all the more sharp coming as it did from Monterrey, one of the centers of PAN activity and support. Indeed, González Luna's only important rally took place in Mexico City at the statue of Carlos IV in June 1952, drawing an estimated one hundred fifty thousand people.[120] Ultimately, the main contribution of the PAN's campaign in 1952 was to document and protest some of the wide-ranging electoral abuses of the PRI.

117. "Unworthy satellites": *El Universal,* Feb. 8, 1952, AGN-DGIPS, Box 27, 2.1/061.8/15, Vol. 7, p. 51; "trampled such sacred liberties": *El Universal,* Apr. 24, 1951, AGN-DGIPS, Box 807, Campaña Presidencial, Apr.–Jun. 1951.

118. "Legal and clear opposition": *La Prensa,* Jul. 12, 1951; failure to collect sufficient signatures: *La Prensa,* Jul. 13, 1951 (both located in AGN-DGIPS, Box 19, File 13, 2.1/061.3/21). Thirty thousand signatures were required to demonstrate sufficient popular appeal and obtain the registro.

119. González Luna stood as the presidential candidate: *Excélsior,* Sep. 28, 1951, AGN-DGIPS, Box 808, File 7, 2.1/51/37; not competing very hard: *El Tiempo* (Monterrey), Dec. 10, 1951, quoted in *Excélsior,* Dec. 11, 1951, AGN-DGIPS, Box 808, File 6, 2.1/51/372.

120. *Excélsior,* Jun. 15, 1952.

The last major group, the Unión Nacional Sinarquista (UNS), wielded some political authority given the size of its membership, although it was not a political party. The UNS had a long record of supporting the moral and economic strength and development of Mexico.[121] The UNS colonists in Baja California Sur, for instance, believed that Alemán was "the best sinarquista in Mexico" since his construction and public works projects fomented national development and job creation. But the UNS sharply criticized Sánchez Taboada and the increasingly heavy-handed political maneuvers of the PRI, arguing that "the president of a governing party whose very existence is the most complete negation of democracy and civic liberties lacks any moral authority to speak to us about freedoms."[122]

The UNS described itself as "a group whose goal is to facilitate the moral, cultural and material elevation of its members . . . and the betterment of Mexicans through the application of the doctrines of the Church." Alongside its rhetoric about morality and personal growth, the UNS left room for unpalatable interpretations, as in its rallying cry, "Civic insurgency, not revolution!"[123] For the UNS, the González Luna effort offered the hope that "Mexican Catholics would have the opportunity to join a non-revolutionary candidacy."[124] In early January 1952, the UNS officially announced its support of González Luna, in large part due to his "solid Catholic formation." However, it was quick to note that the endorsement did not signal a union of the PAN and UNS organizations and that the UNS would retain its "political independence." The UNS also explained its rejection of Henríquez, contending that his links to the "extreme left" and the prospect of a "government of soldiers" would not serve the Mexican public best.[125] In all, as in 1940, the UNS added to the political debate by unifying a section of conservative Mexicans, but it did so in a way that eschewed associations with political parties and elections that would hinder its higher spiritual goals.

The conduct of the presidential campaign in 1952 hinged on two key concepts: the rhetoric of democratic participation and the rhetoric of violence. The PRI leadership sought to portray the party as a participant in a

---

121. The UNS is treated in greater depth in chapters 1 and 4.

122. "Best sinarquista in Mexico": *Novedades,* Apr. 20, 1951; "complete negation of democracy": *Últimas Noticias,* Jun. 22, 1951 (both located in AGN-DGIPS, Box 808, File 7, 2.1/ 51/37).

123. "Betterment of Mexicans": *Novedades,* Dec. 10, 1951, AGN-DGIPS, Box 808, File 6, 2.1/51/372; "civic insurgency, not revolution": *La Prensa,* May 29, 1952, AGN-DGIPS, Box 810, File 1, 2.1/52/53. "¡Insurgencia cívica, no revolución!"

124. *Excélsior,* Nov. 26, 1951, AGN-DGIPS, Box 808, File 7, 2.1/51/37.

125. *Excélsior,* Jan. 11, 1952, AGN-DGIPS, Box 808, File 7, 2.1/51/37.

multiparty electoral system, intent on following legal norms and guaranteeing fair play for all contenders. In a June 1951 editorial, Sánchez Taboada argued that "the PRI in no way opposes that there are other parties . . . [since] it is not its goal to be the only political party in the country." He later claimed that "it has never been [the PRI's] goal to impose iron discipline or cut off the freedom of expression of its members."[126]

However, Sánchez Taboada found fault with the opposition candidates and parties who, he suggested, "have been abusing the freedom that we enjoy in Mexico."[127] He took issue with the efforts of the FPPM as a national political contender, saying, "It is neither a federation nor a party, and it has no people."[128] And Sánchez Taboada took every opportunity to heap scorn on Henríquez's party, offering that "henriquismo is a movement that does not obey the laws of nature: be born, grow and die, since it skipped the second stage and only was born and died."[129]

The peasant sector of the FPPM retorted, "If henriquismo is dead, what is the point of the brutal repression that the civil and, in some cases, the military authorities carry out?" The henriquistas repeated similar responses throughout the campaign, as they continued to portray Sánchez Taboada as dictatorial, authoritarian, and insensitive to the political rights granted to Mexican citizens under the Constitution of 1917.[130] Múgica, too, excoriated the leaders of the PRI for "uselessly trying to silence the will of the people [and] to provide government only as it wishes."[131]

Henríquez sought the full and informed participation of the public at large as he took up the battle against the undemocratic political tendencies of PRI officials. Speaking at Hermosillo, he argued that "the authorities should guarantee to citizens, as is their duty, unrestricted liberty in the use of their rights, without trying to cancel them through the functioning of an official party that is the instrument for denying the sovereignty of the people." In a speech

126. "Only political party in the country": El Universal, Jun. 4, 1951; "impose iron discipline": Excélsior, Aug. 3, 1951 (both located in AGN-DGIPS, Box 19, File 2, 2.1/061.3/10).

127. La Prensa, Jan. 3, 1952, AGN-DGIPS, Box 815, 2.1/52/377, Campaña Presidencial, Jan. 1952.

128. Excélsior, Jul. 2, 1952. The play on words is more evident in Spanish. The Federación de Partidos del Pueblo Mexicano (FPPM), according to Sánchez Taboada, "ni es federación, ni partido, ni tiene pueblo."

129. La Prensa, Mar. 14, 1951, AGN-DGIPS, Box 807, Futurismo Presidencial, Feb. 1951.

130. "Point of the brutal repression": La Prensa, Dec. 20, 1951, AGN-DGIPS, Box 808, File 6, 2.1/51/372; similar responses: see, for example, Excélsior, Mar. 16, 1951, AGN-DGIPS, Box 807, Campaña Presidencial, Mar.–Apr. 1951.

131. Excélsior, Jan. 17, 1952.

given in Los Mochis, Sinaloa, he continued on the theme of electoral politics in Mexico: "The rescue of popular sovereignty is an historical imperative that Mexicans of today cannot scorn, given that the indifference of the citizenry will facilitate the impositionism of the PRI. . . . The people are ready to fight to assert their rights and fundamental liberties."[132] The FPPM waged a constant battle with the PRI over substantial and rhetorical facets of basic political rights. Throughout, the FPPM called for a system of political conflict that allowed for "the free and open competition between parties, the comparison and clash of their different programs, and the establishment of a climate of truly democratic liberty that will facilitate each effort." The FPPM also urged the need to "put an end to the era of phony elections, of voting regimes that only reflect fraud and brash actions." This process of "indispensable cleansing of our electoral system" was a priority for the leadership of the FPPM in formulating its strategy for the presidential campaign.[133] These ideas of a functioning multiparty system of politics and elections had been a hallmark of the Almazán and Amaro campaigns in 1940, a fact not lost on the PRI bureaucracy.

Still, Henríquez realized the difficulty of the opposition campaign he was leading. At Tlaxcala, he argued that the PRI "constitutes a true electoral monopoly" and acknowledged that skeptics viewed opponents of the regime as "condemned to martyrdom or ruin." In the Comisión Federal Electoral (CFE), FPPM representative Ezequiel Burguete raised the issue of the "series of obstacles" placed before soldiers wishing to work in support of the Henríquez campaign. He also filed a complaint that functionaries of the PRI, including many who had made public statements of support for the Ruiz Cortines campaign, staffed most of the state elections committees. Despite the difficulties, Henríquez consistently argued for the power of the people to express their will in a unified manner. Henríquez was emphatic in his belief that the concerted efforts of citizens could overturn the increasingly authoritarian electoral maneuvers of the PRI. In a speech at Nuevo Laredo, he contended, "This campaign is unlike any before. Today there are signs of political maturity in the citizenry and an implacable popular demand to put an end to misery and the corruption that fill the lives of the great majority of anguished citizens. Therefore, in the face of impositionist tactics, in the face

132. "Unrestricted liberty": *Excélsior*, Feb. 4, 1952; "rescue of popular sovereignty": *Excélsior*, Feb. 15, 1952.
133. *La Prensa*, Mar. 30, 1951, AGN-DGIPS, Box 807, Campaña Presidencial, Mar.–Apr. 1951.

of the abuses of the authorities, and in the face of the antidemocratic system of the PRI, we affirm, always more convinced of it, that this time the elections will be made and decided by the people." And at a rally in Puruándiro, Michoacán, he declared that "whoever, upon seeing the coalition of forces arrayed against the free political expression of the citizenry, think that the battle is fruitless, do not understand that the people are invincible."[134]

Beyond the general issue of citizen's rights in a democracy was the more specific case of women's political rights. Like Almazán, Henríquez supported voting rights for women in elections at all levels.[135] Ruiz Cortines, on the other hand, was circumspect, saying that women "will receive all of the stimulus and aid for their growing participation in the political life of Mexico." His rhetoric portrayed women as the maternal guardians of the national spirit since "she is the one that infuses us since the womb with the sentiment of *mexicanidad*." By March of 1952, PRI officials began to shift their position and women were given the right to make presentations in meetings of the Ruiz Cortines campaign. By April 1952, Ruiz Cortines promised that as president he would "initiate before Congress the legal reforms in order for women to enjoy the same political rights [as men] . . . since the participation of women in national life is necessary for the prosperity of the country."[136] The goal of full voting rights for women was achieved after the election, thanks in large part to the continuing support that women received from the FPPM, a situation that pressured the PRI to change its position.

Henríquez played upon the theme of citizen's rights and democratic procedure because concerns about the impositionist and undemocratic tendencies of PRI functionaries were already current in the popular imagination.

134. "True electoral monopoly": Transcript of Henríquez speech, Tlaxcala, Sep. 30, 1951, AGN-DGIPS, Box 25, File 2, 2.1/061.8/15, Vol. 3, pp. 151–52; "series of obstacles": *Excélsior,* Feb. 2, 1952, AGN-DGIPS, Box 815, 2.1/52/375, Campaña Presidencial, Feb. 1952; filed a complaint: *El Universal,* Jan. 10, 1952, AGN-DGIPS, Box 815, 2.1/52/377, Campaña Presidencial, Jan. 1952; "political maturity in the citizenry": *El Universal,* Apr. 22, 1952, AGN-DGIPS, Box 814, File 1, 2.1/52/374; "people are invincible": *Novedades,* Dec. 6, 1951, AGN-DGIPS, Box 808, File 6, 2.1/51/372.

135. Since the 1920s, women had been gaining voting rights in a piecemeal fashion that varied greatly by town and state. Typically, the first voting rights were the smallest, at the level of the town council, and were then graduated upward to state and regional authorities. In 1952, women still did not have the right to vote in presidential elections.

136. "Stimulus and aid": *Discursos de Ruiz Cortines,* Vol. 1, Speech at the Estadio Olímpico, Mexico City, Oct. 14, 1951; "infuses us since the womb": *Discursos de Ruiz Cortines,* Vol. 3, Speech at Hermosillo, Nov. 28, 1951 (both located in AGN-DGIPS, Box 811, File 1, 2.1/52/54); right to make presentations: *El Nacional,* Mar. 4, 1952, AGN-DGIPS, Box 811, File 2, 2.1/52/55; "enjoy the same political rights": *Excélsior,* Apr. 3, 1952, AGN-DGIPS, Box 812, 2.1/"52"/63.

An editorial in January 1951 outlined the role of the PRI and the rules of the electoral game: "Everyone knows that the key function of the PRI is to manipulate electoral schemes. . . . No one connected in some way to the administration can hope to succeed by campaigning outside the official party. Even little children know this."[137] Diplomats perceived the obvious as well, and the American consul in Agua Prieta predicted a "clean sweep" for the PRI in the 1952 elections. The perception of an undemocratic PRI did not convey a position of strength for the party or redound to its benefit. Some crowds in Veracruz were unenthusiastic in their reception of Ruiz Cortines "not as much from opposition to the candidate as from a reluctance to waste time on what is taken to be a *lead-pipe cinch.*"[138] In the debate over democratic procedure and citizen's participatory rights in Mexico, the opposition clearly held the advantage.

The second key concept in the conduct of the presidential campaign in 1952 was the rhetoric of violence. The FPPM, along with the other opposition parties, claimed that a large measure of the PRI's success in elections depended on the violent repression of opponents. From the beginning of the campaign, police were organized against the Henríquez effort. The CFE strongly reproached General Othón León Lobato, chief of police in the Distrito Federal, for jailing FPPM activists who were posting political propaganda that he found offensive to "national dignity." This, claimed the CFE, violated the rights extended to all parties under the Federal Elections Law.[139] Burguete also denounced León Lobato to the CFE for "protecting the Ruiz Cortines candidacy through the persecution of the opposition groups." He outlined charges that the local police forces were harassing opposition supporters, covering or taking down opposition posters and on occasion beating or jailing opponents of the PRI.[140] Martínez Tornel of the FPPM went so far as to file charges against León Lobato before the attorney general of the Distrito Federal for "constitutional violations" in November 1951.[141]

The FPPM further claimed that PRI functionaries intentionally damaged roadways in Nayarit, made *federales* hostile to the Henríquez campaign in

137. "Infantilismo Político," by Dr. Luis Lara Pardo, *Excélsior,* Jan. 3, 1951, AGN-DGIPS, Box 807, Campaña Presidencial, Jan. 1951.

138. "Clean sweep": Memo, Consul Arthur R. Williams to Ambassador William O'Dwyer, Jul. 2, 1952, Agua Prieta, NARA, Record Group 84, Box 129; "taken to be a *lead-pipe cinch*": Memo, Consul Warren C. Stewart to Ambassador William O'Dwyer, Jun. 10, 1952, Veracruz, NARA, Record Group 84, Box 133, emphasis added.

139. *Excélsior,* Jan. 17, 1952.

140. *La Prensa,* Apr. 24, 1952, AGN-DGIPS, Box 814, File 1, 2.1/52/374.

141. *Novedades,* Nov. 30, 1951, AGN-DGIPS, Box 999, File 1.

Guanajuato, ordered police forces in Coahuila to obstruct the movements of henriquistas in the state, and supported the efforts of local leaders in Fresnillo, Zacatecas, who shouted insults throughout Henríquez rallies in the area. On January 27, a rally in Mexicali became chaotic when federal soldiers fired over the crowd. The henriquistas denounced the action as a "deplorable intervention" and petitioned the government to severely restrict military participation in any electoral demonstrations or gatherings.[142] In one of the most odd and creative cases of official interference, the FPPM claimed that serious economic damage had been inflicted upon Mexicali smallholders owing to the "intentional flooding caused by the local authorities, who opened the sluice-gates of some irrigation canals" in order to prevent campesinos from attending an Henríquez rally. The FPPM complained that in advance of a rally in Culiacán that drew forty thousand people, local police and prison inmates removed henriquista posters and used large tractors to destroy the roads leading into the city, all to impede the efforts of the opposition.[143] Finally, a group of PRI activists blocked the passage of the Henríquez caravan into Acapulco by dynamiting the mountainside along the road to cause a landslide, thus obstructing the road.[144]

Campaign stops in Tampico and Ciudad Madero demonstrated the awareness of U.S. diplomats of repressive or obstructionist tactics by the PRI and local authorities loyal to the party. The American consul in Tampico, Kennedy M. Crockett, reported that the Henríquez rallies "did not result in any unusual disorder, *contrary to expectations*." Even when henriquistas destroyed or covered all Ruiz Cortines propaganda, the local authorities "ensure[d] that no conflicts developed." The large trucks that brought supporters to the rally passed freely to the venue since "the officials concerned were under orders not to take any action which might result in a clash with Henríquez's supporters." Local policemen worked to direct traffic but were "conspicuously disarmed" and offered the henriquistas a chance to operate freely in the city. Crockett concluded, "The fact that the local authorities cloistered themselves for the day unquestionably . . . gave them [henriquistas] the feeling that they constitute a strong enough force to be feared." Since Crockett described the

142. Intentionally damaged roadways: *Excélsior*, Jan. 24, 1952; "deplorable intervention": *Excélsior*, Jan. 30, 1952.

143. "Opened the sluice-gates": *El Popular*, Jan. 29, 1952, AGN-DGIPS, Box 26, File 2, 2.1/061.8/15, Vol. 6, p. 157; local police and prison inmates: *El Universal*, Feb. 18, 1952, AGN-DGIPS, Box 815, 2.1/52/375, Campaña Presidencial, February 1952.

144. *Excélsior*, Jun. 7, 1952.

success of the authorities' tactics in the negative—by what could have happened but did not—he suggested the lengths to which the PRI would go to stamp out the opposition or obstruct its activities.[145]

For all the criticism that the PRI received for its tactics, Henríquez constantly faced accusations of his own violent nature and the untoward activities pursued by members of the FPPM. His detractors accused him of being the assassin of one Silvestre Castro during the years of the revolution. Only a few days before the voting, a group in Atlixco published a half-page message to the nation regarding the killing of Bernardo Cid de León, a revolutionary leader of the area. The text alleged that Henríquez had murdered Cid de León outright, for the sole purpose of "earning points."[146] These accusations, never adequately proven, portrayed Henríquez as a cold-blooded killer who solved problems with gunfire and violence. Such images provided a useful point of contrast to the reputation of law and order that PRI strategists strove to project.

During the campaign, rumors began to circulate that the family of Saturnino Cedillo supported Henríquez and his progressive platform despite his role in quelling Cedillo's rebellion in 1939. The Cedillo family rejected this notion and denounced the FPPM candidate in a half-page advertisement. They accused Henríquez of being "the intellectual author" of Saturnino Cedillo's "assassination," arguing further that since their brother was suffering dire illness at the time he was killed that Henríquez "demonstrated his lack of respect for the Armed Forces to which he unduly belongs." For this reason, the Cedillo family made it clear that they could never support Henríquez's attempt to gain "the power that he does not deserve for moral, political, or revolutionary reasons."[147]

Before the CFE, the henriquistas were officially reprimanded for violent events and overt use of force in the early weeks of 1952. Among the occurrences were the fracas that left three dead in Tlacotepec, Puebla, the assaults on PRI offices in Monclova and Morelia, and the machine gun attacks on posted PRI propaganda in Querétaro. Tito Ortega, representing the PRI

145. Memo, Consul Kennedy M. Crockett to Ambassador William O'Dwyer, Apr. 30, 1952, Tampico, NARA, Record Group 84, Box 133. Emphasis added.

146. *Excélsior,* Jul. 3, 1952.

147. The open letter was signed by Elena Cedillo, Engracia Cedillo de Luna, Cleofas González Cedillo, Efrén González Cedillo, Régulo Salas Cedillo, J. Reyes Cedillo, Nicolás Cedillo, Emma Salas Cedillo, Francisco Cedillo, Celia Cedillo, and Leopoldo Palencia Jr. See Advertisement, *El Nacional,* Jan. 21, 1952, DGIPS, Box 815, Campaña Presidencial, Enero de 1952.

before the CFE, argued that "since the beginning of their campaign . . . the henriquistas have been carrying out a great deployment of weapons."[148] The PRI was thereby able to utilize existing laws against delinquency to shutter any kind of henriquista agitation that approached the line of violent confrontation.

Supporters and officials of the PRI were prime targets for henriquista violence. In February 1952, as PRI propagandist Ángel Sánchez Pacheco was en route to a conference in Mexico City, henriquistas fired at his car. In March of the same year, a van equipped with loudspeakers was making its way through the streets announcing a PRI rally when it was met with gunfire from henriquistas attempting to stop its progress. Sixty armed henriquistas attacked an office of the PRI in Mexico City, destroying furniture, files, and anything else they could find. In April, the FPPM was implicated in the shooting death of a PRI activist following the attempted assassination of a PRI director in Mexico City. Two days later, henriquistas attempted to assassinate Salvador Ríos Sánchez, Francisco H. Navarro, and José Muñetón Flores, all PRI candidates for Congress. In June, Dr. Efrén Bermúdez, nephew of the director of PEMEX, died in a shooting incident that involved supporters of the FPPM. Local citizens did not always tolerate this kind of activity. In Tampico, Tamaulipas, the assassination of Pedro M. Gallegos, a prominent leader associated with the Ruiz Cortines campaign, sparked a popular reaction. Six hours after Gallegos's death, a group of nearly three hundred campesinos attacked the local Henríquez campaign office and blamed the party for the crime.[149]

Along with the actual use of violence by the FPPM on the campaign trail was the threat that more serious conflict could follow election day. The FPPM, aware of the Almazán precedent, was careful in the early part of the campaign not to openly advocate rebellion if the vote was not respected. Rather, henriquistas utilized a system of veiled warnings to express their intentions without actually threatening armed rebellion. When a rumor of armed insurrection by the henriquistas circulated—supposedly based in the states of Sinaloa and Sonora—Corona del Rosal claimed that the federal government would require no more than eight days to completely quell such an

148. *Excélsior,* Jan. 24, 1952.

149. Fired at his car: *Excélsior,* Feb. 19, 1952; van equipped with loudspeakers: *Excélsior,* Mar. 4, 1952; sixty armed henriquistas: *Excélsior,* Mar. 8, 1952; shooting death of a PRI activist: *Excélsior,* Apr. 24, 1952; attempted to assassinate: *Excélsior,* Apr. 26, 1952; died in a shooting incident: *Excélsior,* Jun. 15, 1952; three hundred campesinos: *Excélsior,* Jun. 20, 1952.

uprising. The FPPM responded that since Alemán claimed he would relinquish power to whoever was freely elected, "the people do not need to rise in arms to ensure that their civic rights are respected."[150] And vaguely, FPPM director García Barragán told consular staff in Guadalajara that if the election was not free and fair "we will make them respect it."[151]

As election day neared, the rhetoric of the FPPM became more pugnacious. Graciano Sánchez claimed at El Mante that "we will prevail even if it is necessary to shed our blood for the salvation of Mexico."[152] Ernesto Soto Reyes, speaking in Pachuca, exhorted the crowd with the words, "We will raise up our clenched fist and swear by the heroes of our Revolution that on December 1 we will carry Miguel Henríquez Guzmán, wearing the national insignia, to the National Palace." Aguilar, having swung his support to Henríquez, argued that during the revolution "we did not sacrifice 600,000 men in the battlefield in vain, or sacrifice our youth in vain." Further, he warned anyone who opposed henriquismo that "the people will roll over every obstacle."[153] The kind of rhetoric that pervaded the election of 1952 demonstrated that violence was a commonplace on the campaign trail. While the last armed rebellion had occurred in 1938, still "politicians [went] to public meetings surrounded by gunmen, as if it were a war expedition and not a civic act."[154] Evidently, the prospect of violence was still a current in Mexican politics, even if its actual use did not rise to the pervasive level that it had in the immediate postrevolutionary period.

Beyond the question of democratic norms and the use of violence, Henríquez had to nurture the political sympathies of his mentor: Lázaro Cárdenas. Though he left office in 1940, Cárdenas remained one of the most influential political figures in Mexico. The U.S. Embassy referred to Henríquez in 1945 as "the choice of ex-President Cárdenas." By 1950, U.S. observers reported the conventional wisdom that "Cardenista elements," and potentially Ávila Camacho and Cárdenas himself, would support Henríquez.[155] In 1951, García

150. Rumor of armed insurrection: *Excélsior,* Feb. 13, 1952; "need to rise in arms": *Excélsior,* Feb. 23, 1952.

151. Memo, Mario Rauche Garciadiego to Consul Richard Johnson, Sep. 5, 1951, Guadalajara, NARA, Record Group 84, Box 130.

152. Memo, Consul Kennedy M. Crockett to Ambassador William O'Dwyer, Jun. 3, 1952, Tampico, NARA, Record Group 84, Box 133.

153. "Raise up our clenched fist": *Excélsior,* Jun. 24, 1952; "sacrifice our youth in vain": *Excélsior,* Jun. 27, 1952.

154. Editorial, "El Camino de la Violencia," *Excélsior,* Apr. 22, 1952, AGN-DGIPS, Box 814, File 1, 2.1/52/374.

155. "Choice of ex-President Cárdenas": Despatch 1900, Robert S. Folsom to Dept. of State, Feb. 12, 1952, NARA, Record Group 84, Box 130; "Cardenista elements": Report,

Barragán confided to U.S. consular staff in Guadalajara that Henríquez "enjoys the support" of Cárdenas. Moreover, Henríquez reportedly had plans for a secret meeting with Cárdenas on December 2, 1951, "to complete arrangements for the adhesion of ex-President Cárdenas to the Henríquez party."[156]

All of the stir surrounding the potential endorsement of Cárdenas gave extra impetus to the efforts of the FPPM. Not least, it enabled Henríquez to magnify the aspects of his political program that echoed old cardenista goals. As one scholar has noted, a direct (or even implied) link to Cárdenas attracted many campesinos to the regional FPPM organizations "with the hope of returning to something like the cardenista agrarian regime."[157] This hope, vague as it may have been, held out the possibility that the FPPM could make political inroads with the masses of rural poor who formed the basis of PRI electoral strength. As Elisa Servín has argued, the agrarian leagues of the FPPM were the lasting achievement of the 1952 campaign.

But the political inclinations of Cárdenas were, at best, unclear. While it was certain that he had aided the rise of Henríquez in the military and in business dealings with the government, Cárdenas remained reluctant to disclose his political calculations openly. In Morelia in March 1952, at a rally of one hundred fifty thousand people, enormous placards bearing the images of Ruiz Cortines and Lázaro Cárdenas were circulated. Three ministers of the Cárdenas administration attended the rally, though Cárdenas himself was absent. Dámaso Cárdenas, governor of Michoacán, denied that the former president supported any particular candidate for the presidency, saying, "It does not matter to my brother whether Henríquez Guzmán figures as a candidate or not."[158] Lázaro Cárdenas argued in an open letter to the nation that he was simply following the path he always had since leaving political life—that "of not participating in the country's political activities or decisions."[159] Cárdenas, ever the strategist, was guarding his options closely.

"Political Conditions in Mexico from May 16 through June 15, 1950," First Secretary of Embassy Charles R. Burrows, Jun. 23, 1950, NARA, Record Group 84, Box 129.

156. "Enjoys the support": Memo, Mario Rauche Garciadiego to Consul Richard Johnson, Sep. 5, 1951, Guadalajara; "arrangements for the adhesion": Memo, Consul Richard A. Johnson to Ambassador O'Dwyer, Nov. 21, 1951, Guadalajara (both located in NARA, Record Group 84, Box 130).

157. Urquiza Ruiz, "El movimiento henriquista," 41.

158. Three ministers: Excélsior, Mar. 3, 1952; "figures as a candidate or not": Excélsior, Mar. 6, 1952.

159. Excélsior, Mar. 10, 1952, AGN-DGIPS, Box 27, File 2, 2.1/061.8/15, Vol. 8, p. 43.

In early April 1952, a rumor circulated regarding the tacit support of Cárdenas for the Henríquez campaign. There was certainly ample evidence for such a claim, though much of it could not be substantiated. According to henriquista Enrique Quiles Ponce, when Henríquez was campaigning in Michoacán, Raymundo Cárdenas, father of the former president, granted an interview to the press in which he supposedly confirmed the sympathies of the Cárdenas family for the candidacy of Henríquez. It was impossible to corroborate the story because that evening, after a long discussion between Don Raymundo and Henríquez in the back of a car, the elder Cárdenas pleaded with the reporter to intercept the interview material and prevent its publication the next day at all costs.[160]

In his personal journals, Lázaro Cárdenas claimed that he was simply trying to "keep a calm attitude waiting to see the national feeling develop, attempting to maintain revolutionary unity for the good of national social interests." Nevertheless, when Henríquez founded the FPPM, he attracted old cardenistas like Generals Marcelino García Barragán and Celestino Gasca, as well as civilians like CNC founder Graciano Sánchez. But the new henriquismo was not the heir of the old cardenismo, as some claimed. Indeed, Cárdenas denied the existence of cardenismo as such, relying instead on the simpler program of fulfilling the promises of the revolution. Amalia Solórzano de Cárdenas, wife of the former president, later in life confided that "the presence of these people in the henriquista campaign allowed some to see a link between Cárdenas and Henríquez."[161] This reticence belied the unusually open support that Amalia Solórzano and Cuauhtémoc Cárdenas gave the henriquista movement during the campaign.[162]

Considering that the idea of henriquismo was basically an extension of cardenismo, Cárdenas's silence essentially destroyed any claim Henríquez might have had to his revolutionary inheritance. In his journal, Cárdenas made the issue very brief and clear: "Why didn't Henríquez win the election? Among other reasons, because many of his friends and supporters used my

160. Carlos R. Martínez Assad, *El henriquismo, una piedra en el camino* (Mexico City: Martín Casillas Editores, 1982), 35–37. See also Enrique Quiles Ponce, *Henríquez y Cárdenas ¡Presentes! Hechos y realidades de la campaña henriquista* (Mexico City: Costa Amic Editores, 1980).

161. "Keep a calm attitude": Luis Suárez, *Cárdenas, retrato inédito testimonios de Amalia Solórzano de Cárdenas y nuevos documentos,* 2nd ed. (Mexico City: Grijalbo, 1988), 191; fulfilling the promises of the revolution: ibid., 195; "link between Cárdenas and Henríquez": ibid., 197.

162. Urquiza Ruiz, "El movimiento henriquista," 34. For Cuauhtémoc Cárdenas, see Camp, *Mexican Political Biographies, 1935–1993,* 115. Also, Roderic Ai Camp, *Generals in the Palacio: The Military in Modern Mexico* (New York: Oxford University Press, 1992), 81.

name to buoy his candidacy, without realizing that they would stir the opposition of numerous sectors that felt harmed by my administration."[163] He reiterated his distance from political struggles after the election: "I am not a political banner. . . . Personally, I never authorized anyone to involve me in politics." In the end, Cárdenas may have made the canniest political calculation of all. As the San Luis Potosí paper posited, "Now we see that it was not Henríquez who used Lázaro, but Lázaro who used Henríquez. His potential support of Henríquez, announced by the henriquistas, reinforced the eminently political position of Lázaro."[164]

Cárdenas's public disavowal of support for Henríquez seriously weakened the efforts of the FPPM to build a national organization. But throughout the campaign, rumors of and plans for a coalition of the opposition candidates continued to circulate. All sides seemed to realize the potential strength of a unified opposition and the obvious weakness of a "disoriented and anemic" one.[165] Not least, political observers must have recognized the missed opportunity of such a coalition from the 1940 election.[166] As one newspaper opined, "For the Government, the situation could not be better, after all it has always been much easier to fight against a dispersed opposition than a compact and homogenous front."[167] The prospect of an opposition coalition was a difficult undertaking at best. A contemporary headline summed it up this way: "Difícil Coalición de los Partidos Oposicionistas: No hay Afinidad ni Política, ni Social, ni Económica." In the rumor mill, too, was "the certainty that there will be no coalition of the independent parties."[168] But the potential advantages of such a coalition kept alive the hope that a union could be forged.

The relations between Henríquez and Aguilar were not always smooth. Aguilar said in June 1950, rather unbelievably, that he had never even met

163. Suárez, Cárdenas, retrato inédito, 199.

164. "Political banner": Excélsior, Nov. 8, 1952, AGN-DGIPS, Box 29, File 17, 2.1/061.8/ 15, Vol. 12, p. 483; "eminently political position of Lázaro": El Heraldo (San Luis Potosí), Sep. 7, 1952, quoted in Excélsior, Sep. 8, 1952, AGN-DGIPS, Box 815, 2.1/52/375, Campaña Presidencial, Feb. 1952.

165. "Una Oposición Dividida," Excélsior, Feb. 16, 1952, AGN-DGIPS, Box 815, 2.1/52/ 375, Campaña Presidencial, February 1952.

166. See chapter 1 for a more detailed discussion of the failed Almazán-Amaro coalition.

167. El Imparcial (Hermosillo), Nov. 25, 1951, quoted in Excélsior, Nov. 26, 1951, AGN-DGIPS, Box 999, File 1.

168. Contemporary headline: "Difficult Coalition of Opposition Parties: There Is No Affinity: Neither Political, Nor Social, Nor Economic," in Excélsior, Jul. 13, 1951; "no coalition of the independent parties": La Prensa, Jul. 13, 1951 (both located in AGN-DGIPS, Box 803, Campaña Presidencial, Jun.-Jul. 1952).

Henríquez, much less supported him. In October 1951, he reiterated that the PR did not have any deal with either Ruiz Cortines or Henríquez, "only having an honorable commitment with the Mexican people." Moreover, Aguilar was critical of Henríquez, claiming that he had no support among campesinos, organized labor, or the middle class, and that he had only "dedicated his life to the exploitation of huge industrial business deals."[169] Yet, as the campaign progressed, Aguilar managed to find common ground with Lombardo and the PP. By November 1951, Aguilar had steered the PR toward the Left, claiming that it was the "party of the poor" and forming a "political pact" with Lombardo.[170] Aguilar and Lombardo met in Tehuacán, Puebla, on December 28, 1951, and agreed to join the forces of their PR and PP supporters in the election campaign.[171] With this, part of the opposition coalition was in place.

In late February, preliminary talks took place between the PP and the FPPM regarding a possible unification of the Lombardo and Henríquez campaigns. Reportedly, Lombardo agreed with the platform and political stance of the FPPM, though Henríquez was still studying the documents of the PP. Such a union would not necessarily lead to a Lombardo or Henríquez candidacy, reports indicated, but a third candidate was possible. General Luis Alamillo Flores, speaking for the FPPM, dismissed the rumors of a coalition, claiming that Henríquez did not agree with the platform of the PP and that Lombardo, rather than the FPPM, should be willing to compromise on the issues.[172] But Lombardo announced that "it is not precisely a fusion, rather the adoption of the same political platform, which will be that of the Partido Popular, since it is the only one that properly speaking has a political platform."[173] The United States was wary of any union between Henríquez and Lombardo, arguing, "Henríquez's position relative to the United States is at least equivocable [sic], while Lombardo is openly hostile. Thus any coalition

169. Never even met Henríquez: El Universal, Jun. 30, 1950, AGN-DGIPS, Box 803, Futurismo Político, Campaña Presidencial, 1952–1958, Vol. 2; "honorable commitment": La Prensa, Oct. 20, 1951, AGN-DGIPS, Box 809, 2.1/51/515; "huge industrial business deals": El Universal, Nov. 22, 1951, AGN-DGIPS, Box 19, File 13, 2.1/061.3/21.

170. El Universal, Nov. 22, 1951; La Prensa, Jan. 2, 1952 (both located in AGN-DGIPS, Box 19, File 13, 2.1/061.3/21).

171. Novedades, Jan. 2, 1952, AGN-DGIPS, Box 815, 2.1/52/377, Campaña Presidencial, Jan. 1952.

172. Third candidate was possible: Excélsior, Feb. 23, 1952; dismissed the rumors: Excélsior, Feb. 24, 1952.

173. La Prensa, Feb. 14, 1952, AGN-DGIPS, Box 815, 2.1/52/375, Campaña Presidencial, February 1952.

of Henríquez–Lombardo strength would pose a candidate probably hostile to the United States."[174]

Although the efforts in February 1952 did not achieve the goal of unifying all of the opposition parties, they provided the framework for some cooperation and future collaboration. The Partido Nacionalista de México (PNM) remained outside of the potential union, claiming that the parties involved would have co-opted its program. The FPPM, PP, PR, Partido Constitucionalista Mexicano (PConstM), PC, and the Partido del Obrero y Campesino Mexicano (POCM) met, despite the breakdown of the coalition, to discuss zones of influence in the nation. According to these discussions, each party could effectively budget its time and resources without interfering unnecessarily with the other opposition parties.[175]

The FPPM did succeed in uniting with the PR and the PConstM in early March.[176] The common enemy of the policies of the Alemán administration helped to soothe the old political rivalry between Aguilar and Henríquez.[177] With the PR aligned with the Henríquez campaign, Aguilar became a major figure in the alleged seditious plans of the opposition after the election. The prospects engendered by this alliance prompted Lombardo to remark that it was "a new type of politics and the beginning of a new phase in the life of the nation."[178] Still, Lombardo and the PP remained aloof.

It was in April 1952, however, that the coalition movement blossomed. In their "Manifiesto a la Nación," Henríquez, Lombardo, and Aguilar outlined the basis of the new union. The candidates declared their "common goal of contributing to a democratic and peaceful resolution to the problem of the presidential succession." For his part, PRI chief Sánchez Taboada claimed that the union of the parties would be as fruitless as their independent efforts, commenting coolly that "zero plus zero equals zero." In a long meeting, the parties agreed that two of the candidates must withdraw from the contest, in order to present a unified front and the strongest possible challenge to the PRI.[179]

174. Despatch 1900, Robert S. Folsom to Dept. of State, Feb. 12, 1952, NARA, Record Group 84, Box 130.

175. Co-opted its program: *Excélsior,* Feb. 27, 1952; effectively budget its time: *Excélsior,* Mar. 1, 1952.

176. *Excélsior,* Mar. 8, 1952.

177. Sánchez Gutiérrez, "Los militares en la década de los cincuenta," 287.

178. *Novedades,* Apr. 7, 1952, AGN-DGIPS, Box 814, File 1, 2.1/52/374.

179. "Democratic and peaceful resolution": *Excélsior,* Apr. 3, 1952; "zero plus zero": *Excélsior,* Apr. 1, 1952; withdraw from the contest: *Excélsior,* Apr. 3, 1952.

However, from the beginning there were problems inherent in the coalition. The personalities of Henríquez and Lombardo did not allow for the level of compromise and discussion required for a successful union. Moreover, neither candidate wanted to relinquish his place on the ballot. Finally, the PP split over whether to support the union, since Lombardo had not consulted the general membership of the party before forming the alliance with Henríquez and Aguilar.[180] Lombardo knew well the difficulty of attempting to hold together an opposition coalition, saying, "This is not an arithmetical calculation but a political one. . . . It is a problem of quality and not quantity."[181]

On May 9, the coalition officially fractured, leaving Henríquez and Aguilar on one side and Lombardo alone on the other. This event, critically detrimental in terms of dissident victory at the polls, delighted PRI officials, who once again had a divided opposition. One rather alarmist editorial held that a coalition of the FPPM and the PP would have "caused such disorganization in the PRI that it would have provided a crushing defeat and a decomposition and dissolution that would signal its ultimate disappearance."[182] In June 1952, the POCM sent a missive to the parties asking them to renew their alliance on the following grounds: a single candidate, Lombardo, with a single unified platform of "peace, bread, national independence and democratic rights," and coalition government; single candidacies for senators and deputies; and action as a unified group, regardless of the electoral outcome.[183] All parties involved brusquely refused this suggestion, though it demonstrated the impact that such a movement could have had on the national political scene. In 1952, as in 1940, the uncompromising attitudes of the candidates, along with their outsized political egos, conspired to destroy the opportunity for electoral victory over the PRI. In both elections the dominant party was vulnerable, but the opposition leaders were too shortsighted, even selfish, to grasp the moment before them.

Through the spring of 1952, the major political parties worked in the CFE to interpret and fairly apply the new Federal Elections Law passed in December 1951. The FPPM selected Ezequiel Burguete, a law professor at the Universidad Nacional Autónoma de México (UNAM), as its representative to

180. *Excélsior*, Apr. 17, 1952.
181. *Tiempo*, May 9, 1952, cited in Urquiza Ruiz, "El movimiento henriquista," 85.
182. "Admonitorias," by Mateo Podán, *La Prensa*, May 11, 1951, AGN-DGIPS, Box 807, Campaña Presidencial, Apr.–Jun. 1951.
183. *Excélsior*, Jun. 3, 1952.

the CFE on December 7, 1951.[184] He advanced the FPPM criticism that the electoral law was an attempt at "perfecting the electoral apparatus in order to legalize fraud in the next elections."[185] But as Burguete soon discovered, "decisions favoring the opposition [in the CFE] are only rare tokens of democratic impartiality."[186] Within that climate as the election neared, Burguete was about to seriously mishandle a potentially explosive situation.

In one of the most startling events of the election, on Friday, July 4—just two days before the voting—Burguete revealed spontaneously to the CFE that the FPPM had manufactured nearly one million extra ballots in the printing house La Carpeta during the preceding weeks. The CFE received samples of the counterfeit ballots, complete with the emblem of the nation, for examination. In attempting to justify the party's action, Burguete said that "the only goal was to foresee those cases in which voting booths might not be installed due to a lack of proper officials, and with these ballots all of the registered voters could submit their ballots." This was in accordance with Article 80 of the Federal Elections Law, which allowed blank sheets to be used so that every registered voter might vote if appropriate ballots were not available or were insufficient in number.[187]

However, in a crucial exchange before the CFE, Adolfo López Mateos cornered Burguete.

LÓPEZ MATEOS: Is it true that [the FPPM] ordered 15 million ballots printed?

BURGUETE: It is not true, only one million were ordered! We were not going to supplant all of them!

LÓPEZ MATEOS: So then, you were only going to supplant *some* of the votes![188]

The PAN accused the FPPM of attempting to defraud the nation and of violating various provisions of the Federal Elections Law. According to the panistas, the FPPM did not have the authority to print the ballots and could

184. *Novedades,* Dec. 8, 1951, AGN-DGIPS, Box 808, File 6, 2.1/51/372. Other members included Ernesto Uruchurtu (president), Dip. Alfonso Pérez Gasca and Sen. Gustavo Diaz Ordaz (congressional representatives), Francisco Hernandez y Hernandez (PRI), and Lic. Roberto Cossío Cossío (PAN). None of the other parties had sufficient membership to gain inclusion in this national commission.

185. *Excélsior,* Dec. 10, 1951, AGN-DGIPS, Box 808, File 6, 2.1/51/372.

186. CIA Report SR-18, "Mexico," Jan. 24, 1951, p. 7, NARA, Record Group 84, Box 130.

187. *Excélsior,* Jul. 5, 1952.

188. Ibid. Emphasis in original.

only be planning "the most abominable fraud." The PAN argued that the FPPM members responsible should be punished under Article 141 of the Federal Elections Law, which called for a prison term of one month to a year and the suspension of "political rights" for two to six years.[189]

The consequences for the FPPM were grave. The CFE reprimanded the party and ruled that any false ballots found in voting boxes would be completely void. In real terms, this signaled an opportunity for PRI functionaries to use the FPPM's mistake against them. Any votes for Henríquez could be declared void since the entire nation was cognizant of the suspicious actions of the henriquistas. The PRI published a statement the day before the election that turned the FPPM's criticisms of PRI misconduct and impositionism on its head: "The citizenry should not be surprised. . . . The revelation of Burguete constitutes another clear piece of evidence of the fraudulent actions that the henriquistas have employed during the entire electoral campaign. Their only weapons have been calumny, insult, deception and the incitation to violence. What Burguete said in the CFE coincided with the last statement of General Henríquez Guzmán, that the voting 'is already done.' Done, of course, anticipating the results of the election, by way of their failed plan to supplant more than a million votes." Sánchez Taboada could not resist revisiting his assertion that "henriquismo was stillborn," adding that Burguete had succeeded in "throwing the last few shovels of dirt [in the grave]."[190]

González Luna of the PAN made a final plea to voters in the days before the election, declaring that "the vote is not a mere formality or simple accident of a determined electoral decision" and urging them "not to let the people be robbed of their victory."[191] He also admitted that he believed the PRI was "preparing very considerable frauds." Lombardo flatly expected "a multitude of frauds by the official party and the authorities." Henríquez stated his consciousness "of the fraud that the PRI intends to commit," but he was "also aware of our force and the support of the people."[192] Accusations of fraud and irregularities resounded from all sides during and after the voting on July 6.

189. *Excélsior*, Jul. 6, 1952.

190. Reprimanded the party: *Excélsior*, Jul. 5, 1952; "evidence of the fraudulent actions" and "last few shovels of dirt": *Excélsior*, Jul. 6, 1952.

191. *Novedades*, Jul. 4, 1952, AGN-DGIPS, Box 815, 2.1/52/376, Partido Acción Nacional, 1952.

192. "Considerable frauds" and "multitude of frauds": *Excélsior*, Jul. 6, 1952; "aware of our force": *Excélsior*, Jul. 5, 1952.

PRI spokesmen claimed that at Tecamalucan, Veracruz, Cándido Aguilar and fifteen armed men passed out guns to a group of henriquistas who had arrived to vote and attempted to steal the ballot box. The supervisor of the voting station (*casilla*) fled with the ballot box, and protesters shot at and stoned his car during the trip to the nearest police station.[193] In the hinterlands around Guadalajara, there were "reports of army interference, violence, and stealing of ballot boxes."[194] The PAN claimed that "runaway theft of ballot boxes and a string of assaults" were taking place across the nation. Among the specific complaints, the robbery of sixty-seven of seventy ballot boxes in Torreón stopped only when federal forces arrived to dislodge the PRI activists. Robberies of ballot boxes occurred in Tulyehualco, Cuautitlán, and Huejotzingo. In Matamoros, *agraristas* threw stones at the casillas and impeded the free voting of the community. The false ballots of the FPPM appeared throughout the nation with notable totals in Jalisco (86,500 recovered) and Tampico (14,000 recovered). PRI supporters in Villahermosa, Michoacán, marched about the city displaying the false ballots as a sort of electoral trophy.[195]

The FPPM, in formal complaints before the CFE, cited the following cases of electoral irregularities in the Mexico City area. In the Calzada de Madereros, workers from a glass factory voted en masse for the PRI against their will. Likewise, workers of the Departamento de Parques y Jardínes voted for the PRI in District 17 under official pressure. In Districts 4, 7, 8, 12, 16, and 17, voting officials denied representatives of the FPPM positions as observers at the polls. In District 16, casilla 13, people voted with blank sheets marked for the PRI. In the *colonia* Gabriel Hernández, voters received voting sheets without the district or casilla information as required. In the school "Ignacio López Rayón," District 17, three thousand men from the Departamento de Limpia y Transportes congregated after having gone in various busloads to vote for the PRI at La Morena. A false casilla operated at the Cooperativa Materiales de Guerra. In District 8, there was another concentration of workers from the Bombas de la Condesa. In District 14, unknown assailants kidnapped José Fortunato Colunga, president of the henriquista petroleum workers committee, and his wife. In Tenancingo, henriquistas could not vote because of what officials called "altered" credentials.

193. *Excélsior*, Jul. 7, 1952.

194. Memo, Consul J. W. Wilson to Ambassador O'Dwyer, Jul. 8, 1952, Guadalajara, NARA, Record Group 84, Box 130.

195. *Excélsior*, Jul. 7, 1952.

In Ixtlahuaca, all of the henriquista representatives ended up in jail, as occurred in San Cristóbal Ecatepec. In District 10, casilla 16, various campesinos voted for the PRI under duress. Ballots for the FPPM were not available in District 11, casillas 13, 17, 25, 26, and 36. In District 17, election officials distributed false ballots, as occurred in District 19, casillas 13 and 25. All parties except the PRI complained that in Districts 3, 13, and 17, serious irregularities occurred in all of the casillas, due to the fact that officials made no comparison between voters and the registration records. Beyond these incidents, the CFE dealt with "many other complaints that were received about a countless number of irregularities."[196]

After the election, González Luna of the PAN harshly criticized the conduct of the PRI throughout the process: "One cannot speak of electoral victories or defeats in a country where there are no free and honest elections. . . . The regime showed how to be perfectly undemocratic and the elections of July 6 constituted a new fraudulent imposition."[197] Lombardo correctly placed the blame for the fraud on the Federal Elections Law of 1951, which left the task of running and verifying the elections to the party in power alone. In his post-electoral statement, he remarked that "the organization of Mexico, in political terms, corresponds to feudal times."[198] Both were correct that the very structure of the electoral process militated against the formation or even marginal success of a true opposition party. By 1952, civilian leaders within the PRI had managed to cobble together a system, codified in the Federal Elections Law of 1951, that virtually assured its perpetuation in power.

The U.S. Embassy seemed to misunderstand the political situation in Mexico almost completely in 1952. In analyzing the political changes between 1946 and 1952, embassy staff concluded that "there has been a not inconsiderable growth of domestic political democracy, a move from complete one party government towards a willingness to allow political opposition to exist." To support this argument, the report referred to the fact that Aguilar and Henríquez "did not consider it worthwhile to run for office" in 1946 but were active candidates of the opposition in 1952.[199] This viewpoint

196. Ibid.

197. *Excélsior,* Jul. 30, 1952, AGN-DGIPS, Box 815, 2.1/52/376, Partido Acción Nacional, 1952.

198. *Excélsior,* Jul. 7, 1952.

199. Despatch 1900, R. Smith Simpson to Dept. of State, Feb. 12, 1952, NARA, Record Group 84, Box 130.

ignored two crucial aspects of the situation. First, the election of 1946 had as much to do with the new postwar realities (i.e., equating civilian government with democratic development) as it did with the growing strength of Alemán himself at the head of the intelligence services in Gobernación. Second, Aguilar and Henríquez did not run in 1946 because they were still optimistic that their aspirations could be accommodated within the PRI. By 1952, it was clear that this was impossible and that the only real option for the redress of their grievances was an opposition campaign, by definition outside the structure of the PRI.

The bias of U.S. observers could sometimes be painfully clear. The American consul in Agua Prieta reported on the activities of "the Partido Popular and their Commie playmates" and how their speeches "followed the Commie line" of criticizing Truman's foreign policy. He went further, relating with evident glee that "the local PRI administration kindly serenaded the speakers with phonograph records played over a powerful loudspeaker, so that only those of the audience who were very close to the [PP] speakers could hear what they had to say." When Lombardo polled 35 percent of the vote in the mining town of Cananea, the same consul reported his certainty that the PP's success was masterminded in "the headquarters of the Partido Comunista or in the Soviet mission." This he wrote despite a report by U.S. diplomatic staff citing the CIA that communism "[did] not constitute a serious threat to the administration" in 1951 and that only Sinarquismo was a potential problem for U.S. interests.[200] As the United States nevertheless continued to focus on the threat of communist influence in Mexico, it missed the opportunity to understand the deep transition the country was making from a system with space for opposition movements to one that fostered a unique pluralism within a single overwhelmingly dominant party.

The rhetoric of violence surrounding the Henríquez campaign provided the backdrop for events following the election. Henríquez himself was aware of the precedent of the 1940 election and how it might affect his supporters. At a rally in Parral, someone in the crowd shouted, "Just as long as you don't do it to us like Almazán did." The FPPM candidate aggressively responded, "My name is not Almazán; I am Miguel Henríquez Guzmán and I have

200. "Commie line" and "serenaded the speakers": Memo, Consul Arthur R. Williams to Ambassador William O'Dwyer, Jul. 2, 1952, Agua Prieta; "headquarters of the Partido Comunista": Memo, Consul Arthur R. Williams to Ambassador William O'Dwyer, Jul. 16, 1952, Agua Prieta (both located in NARA, Record Group 84, Box 129); "constitute a serious threat": CIA Report SR-18, "Mexico," Jan. 24, 1951, p. 1, NARA, Record Group 84, Box 130.

never backed away from anything in my life."[201] This declaration reinforced the belief that Henríquez, unlike Almazán, was willing to fight to defend his victory at the polls. López Mateos took this kind of rhetoric to mean that "the FPPM is deliberately trying to provoke disorder."[202]

The day after the voting, the FPPM placed an advertisement in the Mexico City newspapers announcing the "clamorous triumph of the people" and the election of Henríquez to the presidency. The party invited all citizens to gather that evening in front of the offices of the Partido Constitucionalista Mexicano (PConstM) on Avenida Juárez for a "Fiesta de la Victoria."[203] This rally, in the very heart of the city along the Alameda Central, became at once the outlet for the accumulated frustration of the henriquistas and the manifestation of the simmering violence everyone feared.

Throughout the afternoon of July 7, FPPM supporters began gathering around the Alameda Central. The Federal District chief of police, General Leandro Sánchez Salazar, sent agents to meet with the henriquistas and attempt to dissuade them from holding the rally, but the entreaties were unsuccessful. As the afternoon wore on, FPPM supporters arrived from outside the city, and the crowd began to jeer and insult the police forces arrayed to maintain order. When a hail of the protesters' stones hit the police lines, a contingent of riot police (granaderos) were called in and fired tear gas into the crowd. As the newspaper reporter on the scene noted, "This seemed to be the only thing the henriquistas were waiting for, and they threw themselves at the police and started to beat some of the riot police."[204] The situation had gotten far out of hand.

As ambulances arrived on the scene, Sánchez Salazar ordered mounted police and more riot police into the area to subdue the henriquistas. The hundreds of protesters escalated the violence by using firearms and Molotov cocktails against the police forces. As the situation deteriorated, it also spread, soon involving action on a number of downtown streets: Hidalgo, Juárez, Madero, and 5 de Mayo. Protesters fled down Reforma toward the FPPM offices, which were "hermetically sealed," and found that two army transports had already arrived to prevent disturbances there. Mounted police arrived and beat the protesters, who fled back toward the Alameda. As the

201. *El Universal,* Apr. 17, 1952, AGN-DGIPS, Box 27, File 2, 2.1/061.8/15, Vol. 8, p. 208.
202. *Excélsior,* Jul. 2, 1952.
203. *Excélsior,* Jul. 7, 1952.
204. *Excélsior,* Jul. 8, 1952.

groups of protesters and police circled one another through the streets, tear gas hung heavy in the air and sporadic gunfire and explosions continued to rock the city. When it became obvious that the tear gas would not quell the riot, policemen fired into the air, "not intending to hurt anyone, just to scare them." Protesters lit fires to block the movement of federal troops while others climbed into the bell towers of the cathedral to continue shooting at the police in the Zócalo. By midnight, seven hours after the riot began, the overwhelming number of police and federal troops and the fact that the protesters had run out of ammunition combined to end the bloody fracas.[205]

The police began arresting the protesters en masse at the points of concentration around the downtown area: the FPPM offices, the Alameda Central, the cathedral, and the Teatro Follies. Reports indicated that over three hundred people were in custody. Agents of the Secret Service arrested Partido Comunista Mexicano (PCM) officials Ignacio Ramos Praslow, Juan Martínez Barranco, and Hermilio Petricioli, who were in the party headquarters when the whole affair began. In all, the granaderos used over two hundred tear gas canisters.[206] The fighting during this "Fiesta de la Victoria" provided all the evidence that PRI strategists required to support their claim that Henríquez was a destabilizing and dangerous force, willing to use violence to achieve his political goals. It was an echo of the speeches of Sánchez Taboada, who warned throughout the campaign that the FPPM would stop at nothing to acquire power. The night of July 7 seemed to prove him right.

But there was another facet of that night that went largely unexplored in the press. The *Excélsior* account of the riot on July 7 may have unintentionally reflected a different aspect of the episode. Lacking other accounts, it was unclear whether the police and security forces restrained themselves from being more aggressive in battling the protesters—firing their sidearms, for instance. Throughout the account in *Excélsior,* the protesters were portrayed with a number of negative attributes: drunk, communist, violent. But there was no comparable account that could corroborate what may have been a true battle between unlikely foes: under-equipped student activists and the full strength of the city police and federal troops. After all, the city and federal authorities had been preparing for such a conflagration since at least 1950, training a proper riot squad and arming themselves appropriately.[207] It remains

205. Ibid.
206. Ibid.
207. See chapter 4 for further detail.

unclear whether more traditional forms of persuasion reinforced Sánchez Taboada's claim that the PRI would "fight with the law in our hand."[208] The rally, supposedly intended to honor Henríquez's clean victory in the presidential election, had degenerated into a violent and bloody fracas. Oddly, this embarrassing contest of guns and tear gas in the heart of Mexico City was a fitting epitaph for the electoral season of 1952. Henríquez had lost the election by over two million votes.[209]

Following the riot of July 7, federal authorities revisited the possibility that Henríquez would foment an armed rebellion. The rhetorical vehemence at Henríquez rallies, in combination with intelligence reports, led Mexican agents to the troubling conclusion "that [Rubén] Jaramillo has already come up with a plan, in agreement with General Miguel Henríquez Guzmán, to rise up in rebellion, when circumstances require."[210] In July, the henriquistas reportedly had two thousand rifles in their possession in Mérida and surrounding areas.[211] Electronic surveillance by Mexican intelligence agents supported the beliefs within the government that Henríquez and Aguilar intended to lead a "subversive movement" centered at Coatepec, Veracruz, in July 1952.[212]

Given Aguilar's connections to Veracruz, this situation demanded quick action. When the news broke, Aguilar faced arrest on charges of "creating an atmosphere propitious for violence and subversion, having contravened in a flagrant manner the electoral rules . . . [and] having insulted the President of the Republic who is Chief of the Mexican Army."[213] The offense carried a penalty of fifteen years in prison, which Aguilar rebuked as "plain old

208. *Excélsior,* Jul. 2, 1952.

209. Martínez Assad, *El henriquismo,* 56. The final vote total was Ruiz Cortines, 2,713,745; Henríquez Guzmán, 579,745; González Luna, 285,555; and Lombardo, 72,482.

210. Memo, DGIPS, May 16, 1952, AGN-DGIPS, Box 27, File 3, 2.1/061.8/15, Vol. 9, pp. 85–86.

211. Telegram, Vice Consul Abraham Katz to Ambassador O'Dwyer, Jul. 4, 1952, Mérida, NARA, Record Group 84, Box 131.

212. *Novedades,* Jul. 11, 1952, AGN-DGIPS, Box 19, File 13, 2.1/061.3/21. The article notes that the information about the supposed revolt was derived from a telephone call between Henríquez and Aguilar, which suggests domestic use of the electronic techniques that Mexican agents may have learned in New York from U.S. police during their surveillance of Almazán after the 1940 election. See chapter 1, n. 147. The American consul in Veracruz took this report seriously enough to forward it to the U.S. ambassador in Mexico City. See Memo, Consul Warren C. Stewart to Ambassador William O'Dwyer, Jul. 16, 1952, Veracruz, NARA, Record Group 84, Box 133.

213. Memo, Consul Warren C. Stewart to Ambassador William O'Dwyer, Jul. 16, 1952, Veracruz, NARA, Record Group 84, Box 133.

porfirismo." His statement was accurate in that porfirismo depended on both the promise of force and the hope of negotiation. After a meeting that reportedly lasted seventy-two hours straight, the *aguilaristas* accepted a compromise that allowed them to rejoin the political fold and align themselves with the outgoing Alemán administration and, implicitly, the political line of the PRI.[214]

After federal authorities discovered and shut down the Aguilar plot, Henríquez's activities came under even closer scrutiny. U.S. Embassy staff in Mexico City continued to receive evidence that Henríquez was planning some sort of armed uprising that would rely on army support. In the Mazatlán district, rumors were current in the autumn of 1952 that "the least that could happen would be the overthrowing of the Mexican Government by means of a 'Cuban type coup.'"[215] In October 1952, authorities obliquely accused Henríquez of using clandestine airfields in Chiapas to smuggle weapons into Mexico.[216] By November, U.S. diplomats discounted apparent henriquista plans to attack the National Palace as improbable, even suicidal: "We figure that, if they try it, the troops would mow them down and all they would need to do is take the bodies across to the Cathedral and have a mass ceremony all at once."[217] A headline in late November further sensationalized the FPPM struggle: "Police Frustrate Another July 7, Seize a Real Arsenal from Henriquistas About to Cause Disturbances."[218] The continual discovery of alleged or actual weapons in the possession of FPPM loyalists supplied the PRI with a rationale for maintaining pressure on them to withdraw from the political struggle. In the end, like Almazán, Henríquez did not attempt an armed rebellion in defense of his election totals.

For Henríquez, the loss at the polls had serious repercussions. Since at least the mid-1930s, Henríquez and his brother Jorge had presided over an increasingly lucrative construction business that thrived on government contracts. When Almazán resigned his post as zone commander at Monterrey,

214. "Plain old porfirismo": *Excélsior,* Jul. 12, 1952; seventy-two hours straight: *Novedades,* Jul. 12, 1952 (both located in AGN-DGIPS, Box 19, File 13, 2.1/061.3/21).

215. Some sort of armed uprising: Telegram, Paul T. Culbertson to Secretary of State, Oct. 2, 1952, NARA, Record Group 84, Box 130; "Cuban type coup": Memo, Josefina V. de Llausás (Consulate) to Embassy, Oct. 10, 1952, Mazatlán, NARA, Record Group 84, Box 131.

216. *Excélsior,* Oct. 24, 1952, AGN-DGIPS, Box 29, File 17, 2.1/061.8/15, Vol. 12, p. 259.

217. Memo, Paul T. Culbertson to R. R. Rubottom (ARA), Nov. 7, 1952, NARA, Record Group 84, Box 130.

218. *Excélsior,* Nov. 26, 1952, AGN-DGIPS, Box 29, File 17, 2.1/061.8/15, Vol. 12, p. 491. Emphasis added.

Cárdenas installed Henríquez, who quickly commandeered the road construction contracts that had made Almazán so wealthy. In 1951, one observer criticized Henríquez for such deals with the government given "the difference between being a *militar de carrera* and just being one *de carretera.*"[219] As late as August 1952, the DGIPS reported the "constant intervention of the Henríquez Guzmán brothers in the construction projects of the government." Jorge Henríquez provided political cover for his brother Miguel, who claimed that he had "never signed a single contract or received any concession, not only from the current government but from any previous one either." This apparent word game only barely hid the vast resources Miguel Henríquez had invested in "no less than 75 private companies where in each case the company is him alone, behind the financial screen of his brother Jorge Henríquez Guzmán."[220] The wealth of Miguel Henríquez provided the footing for his presidential bid, but it also exposed him to the potential for great loss.

In the last month of the campaign, the federal authorities began to seriously threaten the security of Henríquez's companies and wealth. Three large companies owned by the Henríquez brothers were "embargoed" by the Secretaría de Hacienda in June 1952, an action that the Henríquez family attorney, Ezequiel Burguete, challenged in court. The judge in the case, Ignacio Burgoa, effectively froze the assets of the companies until a decision could be reached, a date he set at no later than September 26. Given that two of the companies, Compañía de Construcciones, S.A., and Urbanizaciones, S.A., were among the largest in the Henríquez portfolio, "the losses incurred by this situation [were] substantial."[221] As part of the provisional judgment, the

219. Letter to the editor from Gral. Gustavo A. Padrés, *Excélsior,* Jan. 14, 1951, AGN-DGIPS, Box 807, Campaña Presidencial, Jan. 1951. A militar de carrera is someone who has dedicated his life to the armed forces, whereas a militar de carretera is one—the allusion here is to Henríquez—who has dedicated his life to using his military position to gain highway contracts.

220. "Constant intervention": Report, DGIPS, Aug. 1952, AGN-DGIPS, Box 815, 2.1/52/375, Campaña Presidencial, Feb. 1952; "never signed a single contract": Statement of the FPPM, *El Universal,* Mar. 4, 1952, AGN-DGIPS, Box 27, File 2, 2.1/061.8/15, Vol. 8, p. 13; "financial screen of his brother": *La Voz de León,* Jan. 14, 1952, quoted in *Excélsior,* Jan. 15, 1952, AGN-DGIPS, Box 815, Campaña Presidencial, Jan. 1952. The situation of a prominent Mexican politician using his influence to steer inside deals and financial opportunities to his brother is not uncommon, nor is the case of the "hidden" brother using his resources to protect the influence of his sibling in power. At least three cases are obvious: President Lázaro Cárdenas and his brother Dámaso; President Manuel Ávila Camacho and his brother Maximino; President Carlos Salinas de Gortari and his brother Raúl.

221. *La Prensa,* Jun. 20, 1952, AGN-DGIPS, Box 28, File 2, 2.1/061.8/15, Vol. 10, p. 121.

Henríquez brothers also had to deposit twenty-nine million pesos with Nacional Financiera, S.A. (NAFINSA), as surety against the debt that the government alleged they owed. On July 8, two days after the election, the assets of the three companies were "un-embargoed," but were then "re-embargoed" on July 15. On July 28, Jorge Henríquez appeared before the NAFINSA board to answer charges that he owed almost two million pesos to the federal government.[222] These legal proceedings had the dual effect of revealing the extent of Henríquez's dependence on government contracts to the public and explicitly demonstrating the fragility of that dependence to Henríquez himself.

In the autumn of 1952, Veracruz representative Manuel González Montes argued that the henriquistas "want to continue agitating in order to justify and exact some new contracts and prebends to further increase their millions."[223] While González Montes rightly viewed the continuing sporadic violence as a negotiating tactic, he was quite mistaken in one regard. The Henríquez brothers were not fighting to increase their wealth; they were battling to keep what they had. The campaign prosecuted against the Henríquez companies in the months surrounding the presidential election left no doubt about the potential cost of opposing the PRI. The Henríquez brothers faced not only the loss of political and military standing, but also the probable destruction of at least part of their formidable complex of lucrative companies that thrived on government construction contracts.

Prominent henriquistas faced similar political consequences in the aftermath of 1952, although some remarkable rehabilitations occurred. Aguilar received a presidential pardon on August 27, 1952, for his subversive activities and went to Cuba and El Salvador for a "restful vacation" on his "own volition."[224] Though reincorporated into the political system, Aguilar could not restrain himself from continuing to excoriate it. In October 1952, he declared, "It is impossible that a citizen, no matter how well-intentioned or

The companies in question were Fuentes Termales de San José Purúa, S.A., Urbanizaciones, S.A., and Compañía de Construcciones, S.A.

222. Surety against the debt: *Novedades,* Jun. 21, 1952, AGN–DGIPS, Box 28, File 2, 2.1/061.8/15, Vol. 10, p. 122; appeared before the NAFINSA board: *El Universal,* Jul. 29, 1952, AGN–DGIPS, Box 28, File 1, 2.1/061.8/15, Vol. 11, p. 138.

223. *Novedades,* Oct. 10, 1952, AGN–DGIPS, Box 29, File 17, 2.1/061.8/15, Vol. 12, p. 153.

224. *Novedades,* Aug. 28, 1952; *Excélsior,* Aug. 29, 1952 (both located in AGN–DGIPS, Box 19, File 13, 2.1/061.3/21). Also, *La Prensa,* Sep. 9, 1952, AGN–DGIPS, Box 815, 2.1/52/375, Campaña Presidencial, Feb. 1952.

how energetically he develops his ideas, can impose himself on a machinery of morally corrupted men; the huge political power possessed by those public functionaries, who will keep acquiring more in the new administration, will turn out indestructible for those few citizens who would try to govern with honor."[225] To the end, Aguilar vowed that, despite his outspoken criticism of the political system, he was "never disloyal" to the government or his military honor.[226]

Burguete, whose blunder in the CFE may have cost the FPPM its public credibility on the eve of the election, reconciled with the government after 1952 and went on to become a Supreme Court justice from 1967 until his death in 1975. He also maintained his professional status, teaching law at UNAM until 1972 and maintaining a respected law practice that served clients such as the Henríquez family and Petróleos Mexicanos.[227]

García Barragán served as the president of the FPPM from 1950 to 1952, but he was able to mend relations with the government after the election. He rejoined the army in 1958 at the behest of Adolfo López Mateos and commanded the Eleventh, Seventeenth, and Twenty-second Military Zones in turn, at the same time ascending to the rank of division general. His appointment as secretary of national defense for the period from 1964 to 1970 marked the culmination of a stunning political rehabilitation. Interestingly, García Barragán's son, Javier García Paniagua, became a trusted functionary of the PRI in his own right, serving as director of the Dirección Federal de Seguridad (DFS) from 1977 to 1978.[228] Thus, the negotiation that was crucial to the PRI's dominance of the political system allowed for the reincorporation of a once bitter opponent and then elevated his son to one of the most vital positions in defending that dominance.

Scholars have agreed that the election of 1952 solidified the new political balance between civilians and the military. Henríquez was a soldier and had the support of powerful military officers, leading Fuentes to argue that his campaign was "an attempt by the military to retake power."[229] More than that, however, the Henríquez campaign was the last ditch effort of revolutionary veterans to assert the political leverage that had once been their nearly

225. Statement of Aguilar, Oct. 17, 1952, AGN-DGIPS, Box 19, File 13, 2.1/061.3/21.

226. See Ricardo Corzo Ramírez, José G. González Sierra, and David A. Skerritt, *Nunca un desleal: Cándido Aguilar, 1889–1960* (Mexico City: Colegio de México, 1986).

227. Camp, *Mexican Political Biographies, 1935–1993,* 94.

228. Ibid., 260–61, 266.

229. Gloria Fuentes, *El ejército mexicano* (Mexico City: Grijalbo, 1983), 294.

exclusive purview. Not aiming for a military government, the military wing of the henriquistas wanted their old authority, their decision-making capacity, back from the civilians. This goal was never achieved, even as another, perhaps more lasting, one was.

The generational change that began in 1940 reached its tipping point in 1946 and accelerated during the Alemán administration: "Time was on the side of the [PRI] regime since the revolutionary generals were gradually leaving the scene."[230] As the powerful revolutionary officers aged, they became the victims of savvy legal maneuvers by the upcoming civilian elite that forced the soldiers into a secondary political role. Although the number of officers in the Ruiz Cortines and López Mateos administrations showed small increases, the gradual decay of military influence in such public posts was already well under way.[231] The election of 1952 demonstrated both the effectiveness of the civilians in excising military influence from the party and the crucial importance of maintaining a mutually beneficial relationship between the civilian and military leadership.[232]

The political aspirations of the opposition in 1952 did not wane immediately after the election. Although the registro of the FPPM was cancelled in 1954, some members of the party continued to agitate for change. By late 1956, the FPPM, PP, POCM, and the PCM were meeting to determine a strategy for the 1958 presidential election. Among the attendees were Celestino Gasca as Henríquez's representative, José Muñoz Cota, and Adan Nieto Castillo. Their goals focused partially on controlling the personalistic tendencies of the main figures of the parties. They wanted to convince Lombardo "to desist in the idea of being the *caudillo* in the next presidential campaign, since he [was] only considered such among the leftist groups." They also aimed to prevent Henríquez from "trying to be the caudillo of his party or of any others." Finally, perhaps the most ambitious aim was to dragoon Cárdenas into running for president in 1958.[233] The meetings apparently came to nothing, but Henríquez was a putative Partido Auténtico de la Revolución Mexicana (PARM) presidential candidate in 1958, a position that he actually declined.[234]

230. Sánchez Gutiérrez, "Los militares en la década de los cincuenta," 289.

231. See the table in Camp, *Generals in the Palacio,* 106, for more detailed numerical data.

232. Piñeyro, "Las fuerzas armadas," 170.

233. Among the attendees: Report, Insp. 30 to DGIPS, Nov. 26, 1956; "desist in the idea" and "caudillo of his party": Report, Insp. 30 to DGIPS, Nov. 5, 1956 (both located in AGN-DGIPS, Box 1999, 2.1/"56"/50). Nieto Castillo had been jailed in Lecumberri for a year for participating in the riots following the election of 1952.

234. Sánchez Gutiérrez, "Los militares en la década de los cincuenta," 292, n. 77.

Once a stalwart of the PRI, Henríquez reached a point in his career at which he had no viable options for political advancement but to launch an opposition campaign. One newspaper argued that "he could have come out very well and perhaps even been president if he had waited a little longer and gotten along better with the regime."[235] But Henríquez could wait no longer—not after the rebuff in 1946—and so tried to shape the political system informally through an opposition presidential campaign. His defeat at the polls on July 6, 1952, was in some ways not surprising. Violence prevailed throughout the campaign, and the sense of fear was palpable in the cities during the final weeks of the electoral season. Henríquez's coalition with other parties failed following philosophical and personal disputes, giving the PRI leadership a divided opposition it could easily quash in the election. Above all, Henríquez lacked a coherent program of political and economic change, which might have won over important labor and middle-class voters.

Nonetheless, his campaign showed the PRI leadership the danger inherent in populist movements like henriquismo, which were independent attempts to "cash in" the social legitimacy received from the Mexican Revolution. As one scholar has noted, henriquismo "brought with it a redefinition of party politics . . . and demonstrated to the group in power that such a movement could endanger [the group's] political stability."[236] Yet his effort paid few dividends, his connections provided little influence, and his campaign, in the end, bore scant fruit. His defeat marked the consolidation of a PRI discipline based on co-optation and repression. In the coming years, only the PAN would launch and maintain opposition campaigns. For the next twenty-five years, PRI presidential candidates consistently won over 80 percent of the popular vote, and opposition politics in the electoral sphere were effectively dormant.

Thus, the discipline that the PRI leadership imposed on the political system reached maturity in the election of 1952. Revolutionary military officers lost their position in high-level electoral politics, in part by the creation of the PARM, which afforded them a secondary, if still official, role in policy formation and regime support. The economic cost of opposing the PRI in elections reached such a high level that even the wealthiest and most powerful contenders could not bear the consequences. The Federal Elections Law of 1951, which strengthened requirements for the registro, further weakened

235. *El Debate,* Jan. 5, 1952.
236. Urquiza Ruiz, "El movimiento henriquista," 5.

the prospects for opposition parties. Since the PRI was dominant in the bureaucracy of Gobernación, "opposition parties exist[ed] only with the express
permission of the controlling party."[237] Finally, these steep bureaucratic obstacles effectively blocked the formation of new parties that could work in opposition to the PRI. The practice of forming a party to participate openly in
a supposedly democratic system had been evident since the election of 1940
when Almazán created the PRUN and Amaro founded the PRAC. After
1952, the PRI bureaucracy either subsumed such opposition movements or
drove them underground, later to resurface in the student and radical movements of the 1960s.

Gobernación achieved preeminence in 1952 as well. The Federal Elections Law of 1951 provided the department with enormous authority to
oversee electoral activities, count votes, and reward (or punish) political
groups. Essentially, in a system that depended on the perpetuation of a single
party in elective office, Gobernación had the power to control elections.
More than that, as chapter 4 demonstrated, through the 1940s Gobernación
developed a professional and enlarged domestic intelligence service. When
the DFS reverted to Gobernación's control in 1952, after the election, the
department gained control of almost all of the domestic surveillance and investigative bureaucracy in the country. This capacity, in combination with
the legal authority over all things electoral, made Gobernación the nexus of
political power in Mexico. From 1946 to 1970, Gobernación produced four
of the five presidents, as well as at least three politicians who were "precandidates" for the presidency or considered *presidenciable*.[238] The only other
department to have produced nearly as many presidents in the modern era
was the Secretariat of Programming and Budget.[239] As Gobernación increased
its hold on elections, so too did civilian PRI officials harden internal party
discipline. The rise of political intelligence as the basis for effective control
of the country made its keepers strikingly powerful, those dependent on it
remarkably servile, and those opposed to it undeniably futile. The election
of 1952 produced the final adjustments to the political machine in Mexico
that enabled the PRI leadership to dominate the country for decades.

237. CIA Report SR-18, "Mexico," Jan. 24, 1951, p. 7, NARA, Record Group 84, Box
130.

238. The presidents were Miguel Alemán, Adolfo Ruiz Cortines, Gustavo Díaz Ordaz, and
Luis Echeverría. Former secretaries of Gobernación who were considered presidenciable included Ernesto P. Uruchurtu, Ángel Carvajal, and Mario Moya Palencia.

239. Programming and Budget produced Miguel de la Madrid, Carlos Salinas de Gortari,
and Ernesto Zedillo. The shift from Gobernación to Programming and Budget as a formative
site for presidenciables suggests the crisis in Mexican politics in the late 1970s.

CONCLUSION

AFTER THE TURMOIL OF THE 1952 campaign and its frantic, chaotic flourish of violence, the movement that had buoyed Henríquez did not fade quickly. Supporters maintained that the *henriquista* victory had been stolen by the cynical political strategists within the PRI, dashing the popular call for a return to the *cardenista*-style reforms of the past. But it was not the henriquista elite who kept this spirit alive for the long term; it was the rank and file. The henriquista agrarian leagues continued to operate through the 1950s, provoking anxiety among PRI leaders who either coveted or feared organizations outside of their control. Yet even the determined leadership of the agrarian leagues could not long withstand the pressure toward assimilation exerted by the PRI, and they were eventually shuttered or folded into the "official" national organizations. Such relative longevity was not a fate shared by the formal electoral vehicle of Henríquez: the FPPM.

In February 1954, the FPPM lost its *registro* as a national political party.[1] Under the electoral laws of the nation, a political party could not operate without the explicit approval of Gobernación, which oversaw elections. Lacking proper paperwork from the federal government, parties could not open offices, field candidates for election, distribute literature, or secure financial support. Of course, there were many politically minded groups that

---

1. Olga Pellicer de Brody, *El afianzamiento de la estabilidad política.* Historia de la Revolución Mexicana 22 (Mexico City: Colegio de México, 1978), 59. Also, *Excélsior,* Feb. 7, 1954.

operated without a formal registro, but they did not offer candidates for election. As the PRM/PRI became more organized and adept at countering dissent, it shifted almost all of its efforts to persuading the nation of the ultimate legitimizing force of elections and then tightly controlling those elections in order to monopolize power. Throughout the 1940s and into the 1950s, the registro rule was used as a fig leaf for the bald suppression of opposition movements. The revocation of the FPPM's registro allowed the PRI to defang, once and for all, what remained of Henríquez's electoral organization. For henriquismo to have continued as an electoral opposition movement after 1954 would not only have been unworkable but also illegal. The formal suppression of the FPPM, along with the economic disincentives that Henríquez faced, drove the henriquista movement from the field in a definitive way.

Hemispheric developments soon echoed the formal suppression of the FPPM and signaled a gloomy shift in U.S.–Latin American relations. Guatemala in the 1940s had become a paragon of reformist intentions in a region beset by deep structural problems. The government of Juan José Arévalo (1945–50) represented a sincere attempt to deal with the economic and social issues that had for centuries maintained the landowning elite in power and the landless peasantry and industrial workers in a subordinate position. Arévalo encouraged the increasing organization of labor, even allowing the Guatemalan confederations to join the communist-inflected Confederación de Trabajadores de América Latina (CTAL). He trod lightly on the issue of land reform, aware of the powerful interests residing in the banana and coffee sectors. In sum, Arévalo pursued a cautious but principled policy of basic social and economic reforms. His successor, Jacobo Arbenz (1950–54), on the other hand, gambled his legacy on an accelerated and more radical menu of reforms for Guatemala.

Arbenz ascended to national prominence alongside Arévalo and Francisco Arana in the 1944 movement that removed Jorge Ubico from power. Arana's death at the hands of federal agents in 1949 cleared the path for the election of Arbenz, who became the standard-bearer for the "revolutionary" reforms promised in the Constitution of 1945. From 1950 to 1952, Arbenz tried to hew to the moderate language of the Arévalo administration, even as he edged closer to the communists and built deeper support in organized labor. The turning point for Arbenz came in 1952 with the passage of the Agrarian Reform Law. This legislation was aimed at the large landholdings of the banana industry—mainly United Fruit—in the tropical lowlands, rather than at the highland coffee estates. However, as the prospect of real land reform, including redistribution with or without compensation, loomed large, the landed elite from banana and coffee country began to agitate more vigorously against the Arbenz government. These interests were fortunate to be aligned so closely with the perceived national interests of the United States. As Guatemalan foreign policy declarations made it seem "a virtual Soviet satellite by 1954,"[2] Secretary of State John Foster Dulles began the drumbeat of war in the White House, finally convincing his colleagues (some with financial interests in United Fruit) that the overthrow of Arbenz was the appropriate response. Secretary Dulles was no doubt influenced by the recent memory of the CIA operation that successfully overthrew the Iranian government of Mohammed Mossadeq in August 1953 in defense of perceived U.S. interests. (Notably, the CIA was at that time led by his brother Allen Dulles, also a member of United Fruit's board of directors.) In June 1954, the CIA completed Operation PBSUCCESS and destroyed the democratically elected government of Jacobo Arbenz in Guatemala.[3] For Guatemala, this resulted in a decades-long political freefall that saw military dictatorships, death squads, guerrilla movements, and civil war. For the region, the U.S.-sponsored coup in Guatemala sent an unequivocal message.

The heavy-handed assertion of U.S. interests telegraphed to the region that Washington would not tolerate left-leaning governments, nor rulers who challenged the prerogatives of foreign investors, nor those who appeared to sympathize with Soviet goals or ideologies. This militant rejection of reformism in Latin America, and the insistence that the level of U.S. comfort with regimes would color hemispheric relations in decisive ways, in some sense echoed and reinforced the decision that the leaders of the PRI had already made in the Mexican presidential election of 1952. They recognized what the CIA declared explicitly in 1951: "In Mexico as in other Latin American countries, approval of an administration by the U.S. is essential to stability, and by the same token revolutionary groups would have little chance of success without either the tacit or explicit approval of the U.S."[4]

2. Ralph Lee Woodward, *Central America: A Nation Divided,* 3rd ed. (New York: Oxford University Press, 1999), 242.

3. See Stephen Schlesinger and Stephen Kinzer, *Bitter Fruit: The Story of the American Coup in Guatemala,* expanded edition (Cambridge, Mass.: David Rockefeller Center for Latin American Studies, Harvard University Press, 1999).

4. CIA Report SR-18, "Mexico," Jan. 24, 1951, p. 16, National Archives and Records Administration, Washington, D.C. (NARA), Record Group 84, Box 130.

Henríquez failed on two crucial levels. First, he was unacceptable to the dominant elite within the PRI because he broke the discipline of the party with his opposition campaign and threatened to derail the consolidation of political power through tight control of the electoral process. Second, his self-portrayal as an ideological heir of Cárdenas and his call to return to the cardenista reforms were untenable positions in the bilateral relationship with the United States. As much trouble as the United States had in dealing with Cárdenas-era reforms such as the oil expropriation of 1938, officials in Washington were in no way disposed to returning even to the nostalgia of that period, much less the reforms themselves, under a potential Henríquez administration. Had Henríquez been elected and taken office in 1952, the pressure on his government to hew a more moderate line would have been intense. Had he then chosen to defy the United States and the large segment of the elite that was disaffected with him, Henríquez may well have found himself a victim of CIA intervention, just as Arbenz did in 1954 and for very similar reasons.

The fact that the U.S. line on "communism" in the hemisphere so closely matched the strategy of the PRI in dealing with domestic opponents offered a tremendous opportunity to both sides. Indeed, it was the confluence of U.S. and PRI strategies, pursued for different reasons to be sure, that were woven together in the 1940s and early 1950s to effectively quash electoral opposition. The overthrow of the Arbenz government in 1954 was a public, visceral rejection of the reformist strain of Latin American politics. The cancellation of the FPPM's registro in the same year, in contrast, was an emotionally blank bureaucratic coda to the era of electoral opposition in Mexico. Taken together, these events sent a very clear message to the political elite in Mexico: parties and elections were no longer an open avenue of dissent.

Dissent: Cycles of Submersion

One of the core concepts that this book has addressed is political speech. Throughout the case studies and thematic chapters, the large transition under way was from physical violence as the dominant form of political speech to electoral competition. Mexico had a long tradition of rewarding the strong with access to political, economic, and social authority. The Mexican Revolution elevated countless individuals from obscurity not because of their education or pedigree but because of their prowess in leading men in battle. This process served as a sort of evolutionary bottleneck as the established lines of the political elite were taken out of the national equation—some temporarily, others permanently. The subsequent renovation of the political elite derived, then, from the new cohort that moved into the halls of power based on their innate skills rather than their family connections. The competing elites who emerged from the revolution were particularly adept at the game of subverting, intimidating, and ousting one another. The revolution had created a situation in which only the fittest political minds survived, elevating a sort of political *darwinismo* above the more familiar elite maneuvers. Therefore, the dominant elites who created the PNR, honed it into the PRM, and finally forged the PRI were among the most gifted strategic thinkers available, which in large part predicated their success in defeating challenges from smaller or lesser groups of opponents.

After the decade of revolutionary violence ended, signified ironically by the assassination of Venustiano Carranza and the subsequent election of Álvaro Obregón, the old habits of the competing elites remained strong. In 1923, Adolfo de la Huerta objected to the gradual erosion of his position within the Sonoran dynasty. Instead of attempting to enforce his claim through the presidential election process of 1924, de la Huerta assembled a large alliance of disgruntled (or opportunistic) troops to back his coup attempt against the government. The de la Huerta rebellion was comprised of competing rebel leaders along with elements of some labor unions disenchanted with the Confederación Regional Obrera Mexicana (CROM) of Luis Morones. In all, de la Huerta led a movement that included 20 percent of the officer corps and 40 percent of all army troops, along with an estimated twenty-four thousand civilians, against the imposition of Plutarco Elías Calles as Obregón's successor.[5] The failure of the de la Huerta movement served to prune the officer corps of the more politically minded leaders and those who could be tempted by the old ways of rebellion as political speech.

Yet tradition dies hard. Generals Arnulfo Gómez and Francisco Serrano had each fought well in the revolution and ascended the postrevolutionary career ladder. Gómez had tethered his higher political aspirations to his alliance with President Calles, while Serrano had the confidence of former president Obregón. Both Gómez and Serrano had been assured by their mentors

---

5. Edwin Lieuwen, *Mexican Militarism: The Political Rise and Fall of the Revolutionary Army, 1910–1940* (Albuquerque: University of New Mexico Press, 1968), 76. See also Enrique Plasencia de la Parra, *Personajes y escenarios de la rebelión delahuertista, 1923–1924* (Mexico City: Instituto de Investigaciones Históricas, Universidad Nacional Autónoma de México and Porrúa, 1998).

that in the election of 1928 they would get their opportunity to rise to the very top of the food chain: the presidency. Political calculations, however, intervened. Given the relative strength of Obregón by 1926, Calles was obliged to do without his man Gómez in the presidential race, as Gómez would surely lose. Serrano's reported degenerate behavior troubled Obregón to the point that, by 1927, he decided to drop his support. Obregón brimmed with confidence, concluding that only he could effectively lead the nation and that no one, even then-president Calles, could do anything to stop him. Once the Constitutional ban on reelection had been altered to allow for nonconsecutive presidential terms, the political plans of both Gómez and Serrano were scotched. Both men formed political parties to organize their supporters and give their efforts the appearance of solidity. However, before the creation of the PNR in 1929, no effective national forum existed for party disputes. The path of electoral opposition was not yet open since the legitimacy bestowed by elections did not yet enjoy wide acceptance. Force remained the dominant political paradigm, the decisive form of political speech. Acknowledging this fact, Gómez and Serrano joined in a strategic alliance to press their case through armed struggle in October and November 1927. Their efforts were ill conceived, as Obregón and Calles very capably anticipated the rebellion and easily contained the renegade troops. Within a matter of weeks, both Gómez and Serrano, each a presumptive surefire successor to the presidency only a year before, lay dead. The movement that they inspired was in shambles, and another swath of the military elite was removed from legitimate contention for political power. Gómez and Serrano had decided to pursue the path of armed rebellion as the most effective form of voicing their objections. However, the determination and competence of the Calles-Obregón alliance to nip any such insurgency in the bud offered no valid opportunity for success. The rebellion of 1927 thus represented the interstitial phase of the transition in political speech. Elections were not yet legitimating forces, although they offered the possibility of opposition without violence. Violence was still the dominant paradigm, but resistance was futile.

The succession crisis of 1928, following the assassination of the newly reelected Obregón, provided the context for the next incident of physical violence as the dominant form of political speech. The machinations of Calles to at once destabilize the power of the military elite and rely on them for political cover in the post-Obregón interregnum provoked the ire of several elite officers who saw themselves as the rightful claimants of the presidency.

Chief among them was General José Gonzalo Escobar, who resented Calles's strong-arm tactics, especially given their respective revolutionary credentials. When Calles froze Escobar and his group out of the PNR's founding convention in January 1929, Escobar determined that the only realistic path of opposition was physical violence. The rebellion posed a greater threat than the Gómez and Serrano uprising of 1927. Escobar managed to assemble a coalition of "nearly a third of the officers and thirty thousand troops."[6] Despite the large numbers involved, federal troops under Calles's command bested Escobar on the battlefield. The elite military officers who had led the failed movement were captured and either executed or exiled. As in 1923 and 1927, the elements within the military who considered armed conflict the preferred form of political speech and who fomented opposition to the emerging political order were eliminated. Armed rebellion evinced a powerful Manichaean message: choose well and be rewarded in the future, choose poorly and be removed for the long term. Ironically, the Escobar revolt aided the nascent dominance of the PNR and the elite who supported it by drawing the opponents of the new regime into the open where Calles could crush them.

The final—and to historical observers the most anachronistic—example of armed rebellion as political speech came in 1938 with the revolt of General Saturnino Cedillo. During and after the revolution, Cedillo had been a formidable power broker in his home state of San Luis Potosí.[7] Much of his authority sprung from traditional patron-client relations with agrarian workers. He provided them with security, a voice in their struggles, and the promise of protection from their enemies. They provided him with a steady supply of labor, popular support, and armed defense of his prerogatives. The so-called military colonies that Cedillo organized in San Luis Potosí are well known. These groups comprised an irregular private army that Cedillo could call upon when needed—a resource with which he could alternately support or threaten the national government depending on the circumstances. One of Cedillo's main desires was autonomy within his home region, including a certain amount of latitude when dealing with the issue of land redistribution. During the Cárdenas administration, this delicate balance was upset. Cárdenas did not fully trust Cedillo to be loyal to the federal government in times

6. Lieuwen, *Mexican Militarism*, 103.

7. The finest work on Cedillo is still Dudley Ankerson, *Agrarian Warlord: Saturnino Cedillo and the Mexican Revolution in San Luis Potosí* (DeKalb: Northern Illinois University Press, 1984).

of crisis. Further, he did not appreciate Cedillo's attempts to block or slow federal land reforms in San Luis Potosí. Finally, Cárdenas was intent on enforcing his claims to national power against all comers. If he had been able to destroy the base of Calles's power, how could he allow a caudillo like Cedillo to remain in place? All signs pointed to a confrontation.

Although Cedillo had been brought into the Cárdenas cabinet as secretary of agriculture, a post one might expect would suit his interests, he was never comfortable operating in the environment of Mexico City. Moreover, the structure of the federal bureaucracy prevented Cedillo from influencing policy the way that he could in San Luis Potosí. Intimidation and familial prerogative were not nearly as successful (for him) in the capital as they were back home. Finally, Cárdenas took advantage of Cedillo's presence in Mexico City to begin dismantling the patron–client relationships built up around the military colonies in San Luis Potosí. He also accelerated land reform in the state against Cedillo's wishes. As Cedillo protested the slow erosion of his influence in San Luis Potosí, Cárdenas removed him from the cabinet.[8]

The political feud between the men intensified after Cedillo's return to his home state, where he made preparations for the coming confrontation with the federal government. Cedillo still viewed politics from the vantage point of the nineteenth century, as a game in which force was prime leverage and violence the main form of political speech. The Cedillo rebellion began in May 1938, just two months after the expropriation of foreign oil companies. Cedillo aimed to use the instability of the international crisis as well as his alleged ties to foreign oil concerns in the Huasteca region to magnify his threat to the Cárdenas administration. However, Cedillo's antiquated sense of Mexican politics was no match for the increasingly media-savvy strategy of Cárdenas, who overtook the city of San Luis Potosí almost immediately and sent Cedillo running to the hills for cover. Cedillo's eight-month ordeal in the wilderness did not end well: he was cornered and killed by federal troops in January 1939. The ignominious end of the Cedillo movement represented a turning point in Mexican politics, as physical violence was replaced by more modern forms of political speech.

The new paradigm of political power in Mexico, institutionalized with the formation of the PNR in 1929 and its subsequent transformations into the PRM in 1938 and the PRI in 1946, was electoral competition. The

8. See Ankerson, *Agrarian Warlord*, 163, for the very interesting story of Cedillo's departure from the cabinet.

multiple and contradictory demands of all political classes could be represented in the new system by party organizations created to support particular
candidates or interest groups. After the failure of the de la Huerta, Gómez,
Serrano, Escobar, and especially the Cedillo rebellions, the surviving revolutionary elite consciously opted to pursue their interests via the vehicle of the
political party. Further, the electoral campaigns of Almazán, Amaro, Padilla,
and Henríquez forced the leadership of the dominant PRM/PRI to deal with
the party's structural and strategic problems. In agitating for change through
electoral, rather than armed, rebellion, these opposition candidates shifted
the terms of engagement in Mexican politics away from the violence of the
revolutionary past and toward the more nuanced battlefield of campaign
rhetoric. The election of 1940 took place only two years after the rebellion
of Saturnino Cedillo began. Almazán's renunciation of violence in defense of
his voting totals focused attention on a new mode of political action for
military officers, one based in legal forms and democratic rhetoric. Likewise,
Henríquez's refusal to countenance violent reaction to his loss at the polls in
1952 marked the final acquiescence of the revolutionary generation to the
new paradigm.

The obvious narrative line in this book has been the growth and subsequent defeat of electoral opposition movements. Indeed, the ability of the
strategists within the PRM/PRI to transform the Mexican political system
from one based on physical violence (perpetrated by military leaders) to one
centered on electoral competition (steered by civilian authorities) was crucial
to the long-term dominance of the party. Although the efforts were eventually frustrated, the opposition campaigns of 1940, 1946, and 1952 offer an
antidote to the common historical view that the PRI was wholly dominant
from the beginning. In fact, nothing could be more inaccurate than to pre-
suppose PRI hegemony. The dominant elite within the PRM/PRI faced a
very steep learning curve in the 1940s, a time when outside movements and
pressures forced them to improvise new rules, create political tactics, and
devise rhetorical strategies that in some cases would carry right on through
to the 1980s. Yet, with the defeats of Almazán, Padilla, and Henríquez at the
polls, it became evident that the paradigm of political parties and elections
was not a viable outlet for political dissent. Another avenue for the opposition
had been effectively closed by the rapidly evolving PRI strategy.

The submersion of political dissent continued into further reaches of Mexican society after the electoral process was cleansed of opposition. What fol-
lows is only a cursory sketch of a process that, for each stage, merits a book-
length treatment. Labor unions had long been a center of political agitation

in Mexico, since at least the foundation of the Casa del Obrero Mundial in 1912. The organization of the CROM in 1918 and its rapid growth under the leadership of Luis Morones in the 1920s offered politicians of all stripes a prime example of the potential benefits and dangers of such a large constituency. During the Cárdenas administration, the formation of the Confederación de Trabajadores de México (CTM) allowed for a closer alignment of labor activities with federal policy. The Junta Federal de Conciliación y Arbitraje (JFCA) provided arbitration in disputes and gave the unions a better opportunity to achieve their multifaceted goals, though generally in concert with governmental prerogatives. Over time, this situation led some within the union movement to become more radical in their approach. Vicente Lombardo Toledano, the erstwhile point man for labor relations during the early CTM years under Cárdenas who tended toward a procommunist line, eventually sought to create a truly Pan-American organization of workers in the Confederación de Trabajadores de América Latina (CTAL). In the broadest sense, as the industrial economy of Mexico grew from the turn of the century onward, the power of the labor unions grew as well. The rapid economic growth of the Mexican miracle, under way from 1946 onward, made some sort of reckoning with the various union leaderships crucial to the long-term PRI strategy. (Like Díaz, the PRI strategists recognized that labor peace was critical to assure foreign investors of the safety of Mexican industry.) By the late 1950s, the next stage of the submersion of dissent began as *charrazos* racked the major unions and independent, sometimes radical, leaders were replaced with an imposed leadership charged with bringing the unions to heel.[9] This neutralization of independent union voices effectively shut off yet another avenue for political dissent. Further, it constrained the space for political opposition to a smaller group of voices even lower on the social scale.

The space that remained for opponents of the increasingly dominant PRI was the realm of student activism. Mexican students, like students anywhere, have always had a penchant for reevaluating existing paradigms, debating new theoretical innovations, and pushing for reformist ideals in the public sphere.

9. See, for example, Victor Manuel Durand Ponte, *La ruptura de la nación: Historia del movimiento obrero mexicano desde 1938 hasta 1952* (Mexico City: Universidad Nacional Autónoma de México, Instituto de Investigaciones Sociales, 1986); Maximino Ortega Aguirre, *Estado y movimiento ferrocarrilero, 1958–1959* (Mexico City: Ediciones Quinto Sol, 1988); Antonio Alonso, *El movimiento ferrocarrilero en México, 1958–1959: De la conciliación a la lucha de clases* (Mexico City: Ediciones Era, 1972).

During the 1960s, with the ferment of social movements around the world percolating through Mexican campuses, students began to more actively oppose the hard line espoused by the government of Gustavo Díaz Ordaz. Student strikes became larger and more numerous, each participant emboldened by events that successfully challenged the status quo. In the buildup to the 1968 Olympics—the first Olympiad held in Latin America—the Díaz Ordaz administration had no interest in entertaining student demands for greater political freedom. The intense activism of Mexican students in the mid-1960s was the final public dissent allowed under PRI control. The tragic outcome of this confrontation between students and the state, the massacre of protestors at Tlatelolco on October 2, 1968, marked the most legible turn within a tumultuous half-century of the gradual submersion of political opposition.

Physical violence gave way to parties and elections. Parties and elections gave way to union activism. Union activism gave way to student movements. Finally, student movements gave way to the short-lived underground activities of the Mexican *guerra sucia*.[10] This "dirty war" was a last ditch effort of truly radical individuals and groups to oppose the policies of the PRI-dominant federal bureaucracy. The underground movement developed as all of the other formerly legitimate venues for dissent were closed off. After Tlatelolco, there was nowhere else to go but down. Kidnappings of high-profile figures became a useful tool for urban radicals to gain notoriety and provoke a sense of alarm and insecurity. Lucio Cabañas formed a rebel army in the mountains of Guerrero and proceeded to destabilize the region until his death at the hands of federal troops in 1974. In all, the refusal of the PRI-dominated government to countenance public dissent forced the voices of opposition ever further underground.

The political police described in chapter 4, especially the DFS but also the DGIPS, utilized their organizational and technical superiority to infiltrate, monitor, and besiege the radicals, finally smashing the fragile infrastructure of the opposition by the early 1970s. This process was not without considerable cost, however. As occurred in Argentina, the process of rooting out sometimes deeply hidden insurgents from among the nation's complex population created a profound paranoia in Mexican security circles. They found themselves in a paradoxical position of their own creation. The PRI and its supporting agencies had so effectively shuttered legitimate (and visible) forms of

10. See, for example, Alberto Ulloa Borneman, *Surviving Mexico's Dirty War: A Political Prisoner's Memoir,* trans. Aurora Camacho de Schmidt and Arthur Schmidt (Philadelphia: Temple University Press, 2007).

dissent that the remaining opposition was forced to become more ruthless and invisible. The DFS began to discern enemies everywhere, began to punish offenses disproportionately, and began to lose sight of any restraint in dealing with accused radicals who were, after all, Mexican citizens. The loss of control and institutional paranoia experienced by the DFS prefigured the type and depth of violence that more pervasively overtook Argentina during its Dirty War.

The cycle of submersion and reemergence was nudged along by the economic crises of the late 1970s and early 1980s, especially the austerity programs of the de la Madrid administration. The same kind of bureaucratic arrogance, based on claims to competence in managing economic and political affairs, that plagued Díaz's *científicos* was visited upon the generation of PRI loyalists ruling Mexico by the 1980s. Since the PRI had demanded obeisance based on these claims of expertise, the Mexican public expected that by trading away their political voice they could at least rely on a stable economy. The structural and policy failures of the late 1970 and early 1980s proved this bargain a losing one. The massive destruction in Mexico City caused by the 1985 earthquake, which measured 8.1 on the Richter scale, and the inaction or obstruction of the federal bureaucracy in dealing with it, served to forcefully end the old deal that the public had made with the PRI. The florescence of new civic organizations, their organic growth on city blocks and throughout neighborhoods, and the inability of the PRI or the federal government to control or co-opt them by the usual means, made this tragic event an accidental case of creative destruction. From the rubble of Mexico City came the framework for a new set of political rules, based not on the increasingly brittle strictures of the PRI but the widening horizons of the newly organized civic organizations.

Although this political renaissance began at the bottom, some within the dominant elite soon realized the potential energy contained in the local groups springing up all over the capital and the country. In 1986, senior PRI members Cuauhtémoc Cárdenas and Porfirio Muñoz Ledo, among others, began the process of renovating the PRI from within, attempting to set the party on a beneficial tangent alongside the new civic organizations. This effort was centered on the notion of appropriating enough of the popular ideology to bring the renewed opposition into the fold, without tainting the purity of their local connections. For the most conservative elements within the PRI, this strategy was anathema to the accrued conventional political wisdom of the previous fifty years: power breeds power, authority flows from the party, hierarchy determines influence. Cárdenas and Muñoz Ledo were thrown out of the PRI in 1987; the Corriente Democrática within the PRI was dead.

The democratic opening in Mexico that began in the presidential election of 1988 with the formation of Cárdenas's Frente Democrático Nacional (FDN) snowballed through the 1990s. The increasingly contested nature of elections was matched by the developing authority of the Instituto Federal Electoral (IFE). As the IFE became more independent from the federal government bureaucracy in terms of both financing and staffing, its commissioners were freer to serve judgments that worked against the interests of the PRI. This process played out to its greatest extent in the election of 2000, when the decades-long winning streak of the PRI was broken by the victory of Vicente Fox of the PAN. The submersion of dissent, so long a defining trait of the Mexican system, had ended and was replaced by a multifaceted political arena that offered at least the hope of a more democratic future.

The Root of Power

The late Fernando Gutiérrez Barrios served within the DFS bureaucracy from 1950 until the 1990s and was "the man who kept the secrets of the state."[11] No other figure in modern Mexican politics could be more closely linked to the security of the dominant PRI's power. Having been present for the consolidation of the PRI electoral machine in the presidential race of 1952, he recognized in the mid-1990s the root of the party's political problems: "It is necessary to return discipline to the Party. It seems that some groups or people come undone without compass, sometimes anarchically, with messianic and starry-eyed zeal, breaking what was traditional in the PRI and what is necessary in any political party: discipline, which should not be confused with hierarchical subjugation."[12] This perspective—that the essential factor in the success of the PRI had been its *discipline*—perfectly echoed the calculations of the PRI leadership in the 1940s and early 1950s. As they sought to streamline the party political machine, it was necessary to remove the threat of serious opposition movements.

11. *New York Times,* Nov. 1, 2000.
12. Gregorio Ortega, ed., *Fernando Gutiérrez Barrios: Diálogos con el hombre, el poder y la política* (Mexico City: Planeta, 1995), 158.

For the most part, the PRI leadership and U.S. diplomats achieved their respective goals through the 1940s. Mexico entered the 1950s with a military that was politically subjugated to civilian authority, a chastened political elite ready to operate within the bounds of party loyalty, and a professional domestic intelligence community to insure the new status quo. From the perspective of the United States, Mexico had become the economically stable, putatively democratic, and essentially nonthreatening southern neighbor that officials in Washington wanted. Beginning with the Alemán administration, both countries could get back to the business of business. After 1952, Mexican political life adhered much more closely to the line of discipline advocated by the PRI leadership.

The change that took place through the 1940s was the transition from a generation of politicians with personal revolutionary credentials to a generation with only inherited credentials. It was not coincidental that after 1952, when the last of the opposition challengers from the revolutionary era was vanquished, the tradition of personalizing the political movements of the elite ended. Following decades of porfirismo, maderismo, huertismo, villismo, zapatismo, carrancismo, obregonismo, callismo, cardenismo, avilacamachismo, almazanismo, amarismo, alemanismo, padillismo, ruizcortinismo, and henriquismo, there was no lopezmateísmo or diazordazismo. After 1952, there was only *priísmo*. The personalism that had marked most of Mexican political history was subsumed in the development of a dominant political party that itself became the subject of personalism. Individuals were still crucial, and the PRI, as such, did not make decisions; the PRI leadership did. But the image of the party as the standard-bearer of revolutionary ideology persisted for three decades after 1952, as the civilian leadership of the PRI succeeded in creating an organization that simultaneously appropriated the rhetorical inheritance of the revolution and arrogated political negotiation to the dominant civilian elite.

As this study has demonstrated, the obstacles to PRI electoral dominance fell one after another. In 1940, two of the most senior and powerful army generals were goaded into electoral rebellion and suffered the ignominy of defeat. The subjugation of the military within the party was evident in the dilution of its influence in the PRM, as it was reduced to one sector out of four. And the PRI leadership erased official military influence in the party in 1946 when it drowned the generals' voices in the massive popular sector. As the military lost influence in electoral politics at the highest level, younger officers seized the offer to take over one of the key internal bureaucracies that supported and defended the state: the intelligence services. These agencies became the true weapon against electoral opposition; federal agents investigated, harassed, infiltrated, and subverted any movement until its destruction or co-optation was certain. The genesis of the PRI's long electoral dominance lay within this dynamic: the removal of the military from politics, the professionalization of the domestic intelligence services, and the mastery of revolutionary rhetoric and democratic electoral forms by the dominant civilian elite. The opposition presidential campaigns of 1940, 1946, and 1952 challenged the leadership of the dominant PRM/PRI to develop and instill a harsh line of discipline among party members. Yet, in the end, the premonition of Gutiérrez Barrios held true: when the discipline that had sustained the structure atrophied, so too did the PRI's façade of authority and unity crumble.

Bibliography

Archives

Mexico

Archivo General de la Nación, Mexico City
    Dirección General de Gobierno
    Dirección General de Investigaciones Políticas y Sociales
    Presidential Papers
        Lázaro Cárdenas (1934–40)
        Manuel Avila Camacho (1940–46)
        Miguel Alemán (1946–52)
        Adolfo Ruiz Cortines (1952–58)
Archivo Histórico de la Secretaría de la Defensa Nacional, Mexico City
Archivo Manuel Gómez Morín, Mexico City
Biblioteca Mexicana de la Fundación Miguel Alemán, Mexico City
Centro de Estudios de Historia de Mexico, CONDUMEX, Mexico City
Fideicomiso Archivos Plutarco Elías Calles y Fernando Torreblanca, Mexico City
    Joaquín Amaro Papers
    Fondo Plutarco Elías Calles
    Adolfo de la Huerta Papers
    Fondo Fernando Torreblanca
Hemeroteca "Manuel Sobreira Galindo" de *El Universal,* Mexico City
Hemeroteca Nacional, Universidad Nacional Autónoma de México, Mexico City

United States

National Archives and Records Administration, Washington, D.C.
    Record Group 59: State Department
    Record Group 65: Federal Bureau of Investigation
    Record Group 84: Foreign Service Past Files
    Record Group 165: Military Intelligence Division
    Record Group 208: Office of War Information
    Record Group 226: Office of Strategic Services
    Record Group 306: U.S. Information Agency
    Record Group 319: Army Staff

University of Tennessee at Martin, Special Collections
Holland McCombs Papers
University of Texas at Austin, Benson Latin American Collection
John W. F. Dulles Papers Relating to Mexico, 1798–1961

Press and Periodicals

Atisbos
Boletín jurídico militar
El Debate
Excélsior
El Heraldo del Pueblo (FPPM)
Mobile Press
Mobile Register
El Nacional
New York Times
Novedades
El Paso Herald-Post
El Paso Times
El Popular
La Prensa (San Antonio)
Revista del ejército
San Antonio Evening News
San Antonio Express
San Antonio Light
El Siglo de Torreón
El Soldado
Time
Últimas Noticias
El Universal
Zócalo

Interviews

General de Brigada (D.E.M) Luis Garfias Magaña (Ret.). Mexico City, November 10, 2000.

Books and Articles

Abascal, Salvador. *Lázaro Cárdenas, presidente comunista*. Mexico City: Editorial Tradición, 1988.

———. *Mis recuerdos: Sinarquismo y colonia María Auxiliadora (1935–1944)*. Mexico City: Tradición, 1980.

Ackroyd, William S. "Descendants of the Revolution: Military Relations in Mexico." PhD diss., University of Arizona, 1988.

―――. "The Military in Mexican Politics: The Impact of Professionalism, Civilian Behavior, and the Revolution." *Proceedings of the Pacific Coast Council on Latin American Studies* 12 (1985–86): 93–107.

―――. "Military Professionalism and Nonintervention in Mexico." In *Rank and Privilege: The Military and Society in Latin America,* edited by Linda Alexander Rodríguez, 219–34. Jaguar Books on Latin America 8. Wilmington, Del.: Scholarly Resources, 1994.

―――. "Military Professionalism, Education, and Political Behavior in Mexico." *Armed Forces and Society* 18, no. 1 (Fall 1991): 81–96.

Aguayo Quezada, Sergio, ed. *El almanaque mexicano.* Mexico City: Grijalbo, 2000.

―――. *La charola: Una historia de los servicios de inteligencia en México.* Mexico City: Grijalbo, 2001.

―――. "The Uses, Abuses, and Challenges of Mexican National Security: 1946–1990." In *Mexico: In Search of Security,* edited by Sergio Aguayo and Bruce Michael Bagley, 97–142. Coral Gables: North-South Center, University of Miami; New Brunswick: Transaction, 1993.

Aguila M., Marcos Tonatiuh, and Alberto Enríquez Perea. *Perspectivas sobre el cardenismo: Ensayos sobre economía, trabajo, política y cultura en los años treinta.* [Azcapotzalco]: Universidad Autónoma Metropolitana, 1996.

Aguilar Mora, Manuel, and Carlos Monsiváis. "Sobre el henriquismo: El populismo de derecho y la historia escamoteada." La Cultura en México. *Siempre,* Oct. 11, 1972.

Aguilar V., Rubén, and Guillermo Zermeño P. *Religión, política y sociedad: El sinarquismo y la iglesia en México.* Mexico City: Universidad Iberoamericana, 1992.

Aguilar Zinser, Adolfo. "Civil-Military Relations in Mexico." In *The Military and Democracy: The Future of Civil-Military Relations in Latin America,* edited by Louis W. Goodman et al., 219–36. Lexington, Mass.: Heath, 1990.

Alamillo Flores, Luis. *Memorias: Luchadores ignorados al lado de los grandes jefes de la Revolución Mexicana.* Mexico City: Editorial Extemporáneos, 1976.

Alanís Enciso, Fernando Saúl. *El gobierno del general Lázaro Cárdenas, 1934–1940: Una visión revisionista.* San Luis Potosí: El Colegio de San Luis, 2000.

Alemán Valdés, Miguel. *Un México mejor: Pensamientos, discursos e información, 1936–1952.* Mexico City: Editorial Diana, 1988.

―――. *Miguel Alemán contesta: Ensayo.* Austin: Institute of Latin American Studies, University of Texas at Austin, 1975.

―――. *No siembro para mí: Biografía de Adolfo Ruiz Cortines.* Mexico City: Editorial Diana, 1997.

―――. *Remembranzas y testimonios.* Mexico City: Grijalbo, 1987.

Alexius, Robert Martin. "The Army and Politics in Porfirian Mexico." PhD diss., University of Texas at Austin, 1976.

Allen, Henry J. *The Mexican Confiscations Together with a Careful Survey of the Present Revolutionary Trends in Mexico.* [New York]: New York Herald-Tribune Newspaper Syndicate, 1938.

Almada, Pedro J. *99 días en jira con el Presidente Cárdenas.* Mexico City: Ediciones Botas, 1943.

Almazán, Juan Andreu. *El Gral. Almazán habla a la nación.* Monterrey: n.p., 1939.

―――. *Informe que el C. General de División, Juan Andreu Almazán, Secretario de Comunicaciones y Obras Públicas rinde al C. Presidente de la República con relación a su viaje por el noroeste del país.* Mexico City: Secretaría de Comunicaciones y Obras Públicas, 1930.

———. *Informe que el C. general de división Juan Andreu Almazán, Secretario de comunicaciones y obras públicas, rinde al C. Presidente de la República Ing. Pascual Ortíz Rubio sobre las observaciones que hizo durante su viaje al Dominio del Canadá.* Mexico City: Secretaría de Comunicaciones y Obras Públicas, 1931.

———. *Libertad y orden, 1940–46.* [Monterrey]: n.p., [1940].

———. "El manifiesto del General Almazán a la Nación." *El noticiero de la sucesión presidencial,* July 11, 1939. Broadside. Mexico City: Partido Demócrata Radical Almazanista, 1939.

———. "Memorias." *El Universal,* 1957–58.

———. *Memorias del Gral. J. Andreu Almazán: Informe y documentos sobre la campaña política de 1940.* Mexico City: Quintanar, 1941.

Alonso, Antonio. *El movimiento ferrocarrilero en México, 1958–1959: De la conciliación a la lucha de clases.* Mexico City: Ediciones Era, 1972.

Alvear Acevedo, Carlos. *Lázaro Cárdenas (el hombre y el mito).* Satélite, Estado de México: Ediciones Promesa, 1986.

Ameringer, Charles D. *U.S. Foreign Intelligence: The Secret Side of American History.* Lexington, Mass.: Lexington Books, 1990.

Anda, Gustavo de. *El cardenismo: Desviación totalitaria de la Revolución Mexicana.* Mexico City: G. de Anda, 1974.

———. *El verdadero Cárdenas.* Mexico City: n.p., 1988.

Anguiano, Arturo. *El estado y la política obrera del cardenismo.* Mexico City: Ediciones Era, 1975.

Anguiano Equihua, Victoriano. *Lázaro Cárdenas: Su feudo y la política nacional.* Mexico City: Editorial Eréndira, 1951.

Ankerson, Dudley. *Agrarian Warlord: Saturnino Cedillo and the Mexican Revolution in San Luis Potosí.* DeKalb: Northern Illinois University Press, 1984.

Anlen, Jesús. *Origen y evolución de los partidos políticos en México.* Mexico City: Textos Universitarios, 1973.

Applegate, Rex. *Kill or Get Killed.* Harrisburg, Pa.: Military Service Publishing, 1943.

Archer, Christon I. *The Army in Bourbon Mexico, 1760–1810.* Albuquerque: University of New Mexico Press, 1977.

Ard, Michael. *An Eternal Struggle: How the National Action Party Transformed Mexican Politics.* New York: Praeger, 2003.

Arreola Ayala, Álvaro. "La Ley Electoral de 1946." *Revista Mexicana de Sociología* 50, no. 3 (Jul–Sept. 1988): 169–87.

Ashby, Joe C. *Organized Labor and the Mexican Revolution under Lázaro Cárdenas.* Chapel Hill: University of North Carolina, 1967.

Avila Carrillo, Enrique. *El Cardenismo (1934–1940).* Mexico City: Ediciones Quinto Sol, 1987.

Azuela, Salvador. *La aventura vasconcelista, 1929.* Mexico City: Editorial Diana, 1980.

Bagley, Bruce Michael, and Sergio Aguayo Quezada, eds. *Mexico: In Search of Security.* Coral Gables: North-South Center, University of Miami; New Brunswick: Transaction, 1993.

Bailey, John, and Sergio Aguayo Quezada, eds. *Strategy and Security in U.S.-Mexican Relations Beyond the Cold War.* San Diego: Center for U.S.-Mexican Studies, University of California at San Diego, 1996.

Bantjes, Adrian A. *As if Jesus Walked on Earth: Cardenismo, Sonora, and the Mexican Revolution.* Wilmington, Del.: Scholarly Resources, 1998.

Basáñez, Miguel. *El pulso de los sexenios: 20 años de crisis en México.* Mexico City: Siglo XXI Editores, 1990.

Basurto, Jorge. *Cárdenas y el poder sindical.* Mexico City: Editorial Era, 1983.

———. *Del avilacamachismo al alemanismo (1940–1952).* La clase obrera en la historia de México 11. Mexico City: Siglo XXI, 1984.

Basurto, Jorge, and J. Aurelio Cuevas Díaz. *El fin del proyecto nacionalista revolucionario.* Mexico City: Instituto de Investigaciones Sociales, Universidad Nacional Autónoma de México, 1992.

Bazán Pérez, Javier. "El ejército en la Constitución y en la política." Unpublished thesis, Facultad de Derecho y Ciencias Sociales, Universidad Nacional Autónoma de México, 1952.

Benítez, Fernando. *Entrevistas con un solo tema: Lázaro Cárdenas.* Mexico: Universidad Nacional Autónoma de México, 1979.

———. *Lázaro Cárdenas y la Revolución Mexicana.* 3 vols. Mexico City: Fondo de Cultura Económica, 1977–78.

Benitez Manaut, Raúl. "Las fuerzas armadas mexicanas y su relación con el estado, el sistema político y la sociedad." In *Reconversión militar en América Latina,* edited by Gabriel Angel Peralta, 63–90. Guatemala City: FLACSO, 1994.

Benitez Manaut, Raúl, and Stephen J. Wager. *National Security and Armed Forces in Mexico: Challenges and Scenarios at the End of the Century.* Working Papers Series 236. Washington, D.C.: Latin American Program, Woodrow Wilson International Center for Scholars, 1998.

Bermúdez, Antonio J., and Octavio Véjar Vázquez. *No dejes crecer la hierba: El gobierno avilacamachista.* Mexico City: Costa-Amic, 1969.

Bernstein, Marvin D. *The Mexican Mining Industry, 1890–1950: A Study of the Interaction of Politics, Economics, and Technology.* New York: State University of New York, 1965.

Beteta, Ignacio M. *El ejército revolucionario: Visión histórica y social.* [Mexico City]: Partido Nacional Revolucionario, 1936.

———. *Mensaje al ejército nacional.* Mexico: DAPP, 1937.

Bethell, Leslie. "From the Second World War to the Cold War, 1944–1954." In *Exporting Democracy: The United States and Latin America.* Vol. 1, *Themes and Issues,* edited by Abraham Lowenthal, 41–70. Baltimore: Johns Hopkins University Press, 1991.

Bethell, Leslie, and Ian Roxborough. "Latin America Between the Second World War and the Cold War: Some Reflections on the 1945–8 Conjuncture." *Journal of Latin American Studies* 20 (1988): 167–89.

Bidwell, Bruce W. *History of the Military Intelligence Division, Department of the Army General Staff: 1775–1941.* Frederick, Md.: University Publications of America, 1986.

Blumenkron, Daniel, and Luis Campomanes. *Puebla bajo el terror almazanista: El libro rojo de un mal gobierno.* Puebla: n.p., 1933.

Boils, Guillermo. "Los militares en México (1965–1985)." *Revista Mexicana de Sociología* 47, no. 1 (Jan.–Mar. 1985): 169–85.

———. *Los militares y la política en México, 1915–1974.* Mexico City: El Caballito, 1975.

Braden, Spruille. *Diplomats and Demagogues: The Memoirs of Spruille Braden.* New Rochelle, N.Y.: Arlington House, 1971.

Brandenburg, Frank Ralph. *The Making of Modern Mexico*. Englewood Cliffs, N.J.: Prentice Hall, 1964.

Brenner, Anita. *The Wind that Swept Mexico: The History of the Mexican Revolution, 1910–1942*. Austin: University of Texas Press, 1943.

Browder, Earl. *Manifestaciones de Earl Browder, Secretario General y candidato presidencial del Partido Comunista de Estados Unidos, sobre la situación de México*. New York: State Election Campaign, Communist Party, 1940.

Brown, Jonathan C. *Oil and Revolution in Mexico*. Berkeley and Los Angeles: University of California Press, 1992.

Brown, Lyle Clarence. "General Lázaro Cárdenas and Mexican Presidential Politics, 1933–1940: A Study in the Acquisition and Manipulation of Political Power." PhD diss., University of Texas at Austin, 1964.

———. "Mexican Church-State Relations, 1933–1940" *Journal of Church and State* 6 (1964): 202–22.

Buchenau, Jürgen. *Plutarco Elías Calles and the Mexican Revolution*. Lanham, Md.: Rowman and Littlefield, 2007.

Buendía, Manuel. *La CIA en México*. Mexico City: Rayuela Editores, Fundación Manuel Buendía, 1996.

Caballero, Manuel. *Latin America and the Comintern, 1919–1943*. London: Cambridge University Press, 1987.

Calderón R., Enrique. *El Gobernador de Durango contesta el manifiesto que la actitud del general Andreu Almazán no es revolucionaria*. Mexico City: n.p., 1939.

Calles, Plutarco Elías, and Ezequiel Padilla. *El aspecto político de la sucesión presidencial*. Mexico City: Imprenta de la Secretaría de Relaciones Exteriores, 1933.

———. *Correspondencia personal, 1919–1945*. Mexico City: Fideicomiso Archivos Plutarco Elías Calles y Fernando Torreblanca, Fondo de Cultura Económica, 1991.

Camp, Roderic Ai. *Generals in the Palacio: The Military in Modern Mexico*. New York: Oxford University Press, 1992.

———. *The Making of a Government: Political Leaders in Mexico*. Tucson: University of Arizona Press, 1976.

———. *Mexican Political Biographies, 1884–1935*. Austin: University of Texas Press, 1991.

———. *Mexican Political Biographies, 1935–1993*. 3rd ed. Austin: University of Texas Press, 1995.

———. "Mexico." In *The Political Role of the Military: An International Handbook*, edited by Constantine P. Danopoulos and Cynthia Watson, 271–82. Westport, Conn.: Greenwood Press, 1996.

———. *Mexico's Mandarins: Crafting a Power Elite for the Twenty-first Century*. Berkeley and Los Angeles: University of California Press, 2002.

———. *Mexico's Military on the Democratic Stage*. Westport, Conn.: Praeger Security International, 2005.

———. *Political Recruitment Across Two Centuries: Mexico, 1884–1991*. Austin: University of Texas Press, 1995.

———. *Politics in Mexico: The Democratic Consolidation*. 5th ed. New York: Oxford University Press, 2007.

Campa, Valentín. *Mi testimonio: Memorias de un comunista mexicano*. Mexico City: Editorial de Cultura Popular, 1985.

Campbell, Hugh G. *La derecha radical en México, 1929–1949*. Mexico City: Secretaría de Educación Pública, 1976.

Campbell, Ralph Jan. "Client Mexico: Ambassador Morrow's Efforts to Stabilize Mexico's Finances, 1927–1930." Master's thesis, University of Texas at El Paso, 2001.

Canudas, Enrique. *La hacienda pública y la política económica, 1929–1958*. Mexico City: Fondo de Cultura Económica, 1994.

———. *La política económica en México, 1950–1994*. Mexico City: Fondo de Cultura Económica, 1996.

———. *Trópico rojo: Historia política y social de Tabasco, 1935–1988: Crónicas de las luchas de un pueblo contra las adversidades naturales, la difícil construcción de la democracia*. Xochimilco, Mexico City: Inquietudes Ediciones y Publicidad, 1993.

Cárdenas, Héctor. *Historia de las relaciones entre México y Rusia*. Mexico City: Fondo de Cultura Económica, 1993.

Cárdenas, Lázaro. *Apuntes*. 4 vols. Mexico City: Universidad Nacional Autónoma de México, 1972–74.

———. *Epistolario*. Mexico City: Siglo XXI, 1974.

———. *Message Delivered by the President of Mexico, General Lázaro Cárdenas, to the Nation, the 20th of February 1940, in Chilpancingo, State of Guerrero*. Mexico: n.p., 1940.

———. *The No-Reelection Postulate*. Mexico City: DAPP, 1938.

———. *Obras*. Mexico City: Universidad Nacional Autónoma de México, 1972.

Cárdenas N., Joaquín. *Morrow, Calles y el PRI: Chiapas y las elecciones del '94*. Mexico City: Editorial Pac, 1995.

Carlisle, Rodney P., and Dominic J. Monetta. *Brandy, Our Man in Acapulco: The Life and Times of Colonel Frank M. Brandstetter*. Denton: University of North Texas Press, 1999.

Carr, Barry. *Marxism and Communism in Twentieth-Century Mexico*. Lincoln: University of Nebraska Press, 1992.

———. *The Mexican Left, the Popular Movements, and the Politics of Austerity*. La Jolla, Calif.: Center for U.S.-Mexican Studies, 1986.

Castañeda, Jorge G. *La herencia: Arqueología de la sucesión presidencial en México*. Mexico City: Alfaguara, 1999.

Castillo Mena, Ignacio. *Nueve presidentes civiles en el poder: Del carisma desbordante de Alemán a la peligrosa indecisión de Zedillo*. Mexico City: EDAMEX, 1996.

Castro Martínez, Pedro. *Adolfo de la Huerta y la Revolución Mexicana*. Mexico City: Instituto Nacional de Estudios Históricos de la Revolución Mexicana, 1992.

Chalkley, John F. *Zach Lamar Cobb: El Paso Collector of Customs and Intelligence during the Mexican Revolution, 1913–1918*. El Paso: Texas Western Press, University of Texas at El Paso, 1998.

Chase, Allan. *Falange: The Axis Secret Army in the Americas*. New York: G. P. Putnam's Sons, 1943.

Child, John. "From Color to Rainbow: U.S. Strategic Planning for Latin America, 1919–1945." *Journal of Interamerican Studies and World Affairs* 21, no. 2 (May 1979): 233–59.

———. *Unequal Alliance: The Inter-American Military System, 1938–1978*. Boulder: Westview, 1980.

Cline, Howard Francis. *Mexico: Revolution to Evolution, 1940–1960*. New York: Oxford University Press, 1962.

———. *The United States and Mexico*. Cambridge: Harvard University Press, 1953.

Coe, Michael D. *Mexico: From the Olmecs to the Aztecs*. 4th ed. New York: Thames and Hudson, 1994.

Colson, Harold. *National Security Affairs and Civil-Military Relations in Contemporary Mexico: A Bibliography*. Monticello, Ill.: Vance Bibliographies, 1989.

Comité Nacional Director Ejecutivo Pro-Almazán. "Manifiesto a la Nación." *Excélsior*, Apr. 5, 1939.

Confidential U.S. State Department Central Files. Mexico: Internal Affairs, 1940–1944. Part I: Political, Governmental, and National Defense Affairs. Frederick, Md.: University Publications of America, 1987.

Confidential U.S. State Department Central Files. Mexico: Internal Affairs, 1945–1949. Part I: Political, Governmental, and National Affairs. Frederick, Md.: University Publications of America, 1987.

Contreras, Ariel José. "Estado y sociedad civil en el proceso electoral de 1940." In *La sucesión presidencial en México, 1928–1988*, edited by Carlos Martínez Assad, 105–22. Revised 2nd ed. Mexico City: Nueva Imagen, 1992.

———. *México 1940: Industrialización y crisis política: Estado y sociedad civil en las elecciones presidenciales*. Mexico City: Siglo Veintiuno Editores, 1977.

Córdova, Arnaldo. *La formación del poder político en México*. Mexico City: Ediciones Era, 1972.

———. *La ideología de la Revolución Mexicana: La formación del Nuevo régimen*. Mexico City: Ediciones Era, 1973.

———. *La política de masas del cardenismo*. Mexico City: Ediciones Era, 1974.

———. *La revolución y el estado en México*. Mexico City: Ediciones Era, 1989.

Corona del Rosal, Alfonso. *La guerra, el imperialismo, el ejército mexicano*. Mexico City: Grijalbo, 1988.

———. *Mis memorias políticas*. Mexico City: Grijalbo, 1995.

Corro R., Octaviano. *General Miguel Alemán: Su vida revolucionaria*. Jalapa, Veracruz: Ediciones TIV, 1945.

Corro Viña, J. Manuel. *Andrew Almazán, la reconstrucción de México y el crimen del Vasconcelismo*. Corpus Christi, Texas: El Puerto, 1930.

———. *Sucesión o reelección del Presidente Cardenas?* Mexico City: n.p., 1939.

Cortés Zavala, María Teresa. *Lázaro Cárdenas y su proyecto cultural en Michoacán, 1930–1950*. [Morelia, Mexico]: Universidad Michoacana de San Nicolás de Hidalgo, 1995.

Cronon, Edmund David. *Josephus Daniels in Mexico*. Madison: University of Wisconsin Press, 1960.

D'Acosta, Helia. *Alemanismo: Teoría y práctica del progreso de México*. [Mexico City]: Libros de México, 1952.

Dahl, Robert A. *Polyarchy*. New Haven: Yale University Press, 1971.

Daniels, Josephus. *Shirt-Sleeve Diplomat*. Chapel Hill: University of North Carolina Press, 1947.

Davis, Harold. "The Enigma of Mexican Sinarquism." *Free World*, May 5, 1943.

Dearing, Paul. "Synarchism in Mexico." *Current History*, Nov. 1943, 247.

De la Barra, Francisco, et al. *Los Presidentes de México: Discursos políticos, 1910–1988*. 5 vols. Mexico City: Presidencia de la República, 1988.

de la Madrid H., Miguel. *Cambio de rumbo: Testimonio de una presidencia, 1982–1988*. Mexico City: Fondo de Cultura Económica, 2004.

De la Vega-Leinert, Anna Marie. "El sinarquismo en México: Posibilidades de un régimen fascista en 1940." *Comercio Exterior*, Sept. 1976, 1076–92.

Del Cueto, Héctor Hugo. *Miguel Alemán: Historia de un gobierno, 1946–1952*. Mexico City: Impresiones Modernas, 1974.

Delhumeau Arecillas, Antonio. *México: Realidad política de sus partidos: Una investigación psicosocial acerca de los partidos políticos mexicanos.* Mexico City: Instituto Mexicano de Estudios Políticos, 1970.

DePalo, William A. *The Mexican National Army, 1822–1852.* College Station: Texas (A& M) University Press, 1997.

Departamento de la Industria Militar, 1946–1952. Mexico City: Talleres Gráficos de la Nación, 1952.

Díaz Babío, Francisco. *Un drama nacional: La crisis de la revolución, declinación y eliminación del general Calles, primera etapa 1928–1932.* Mexico City: Impresora M. León Sánchez, 1939.

Díaz del Castillo, Bernal. *The Discovery and Conquest of Mexico, 1517–1521.* Edited by Genaro Garcia. Translated by A. P. Maudslay. New York: Farrar, Straus, and Cudahy, 1956.

Díaz Escobar, Alfredo F. "The Spread of Sinarquismo." *Nation,* Apr. 3, 1943, 487.

Díaz Méndez, Alberto. *Lázaro Cárdenas: Ideas políticas y acción antimperialista.* Havana: Editorial de Ciencias Sociales, 1984.

Dirección Federal de Seguridad. *Henriquismo: 10. de octubre de 1950 a 30 de septiembre de 1951.* 2 vols. Biblioteca Mexicana de la Fundación Miguel Alemán, Fondo Miguel Alemán Valdés, Dirección Federal de Seguridad.

Donner, Frank J. *The Age of Surveillance: The Aims and Methods of America's Political Intelligence System.* New York: Alfred A. Knopf, 1980.

Dulles, Allen. *The Craft of Intelligence.* New York: Harper and Row, 1963.

Dulles, John W. F. *Cárdenas se impone a Calles.* Mexico City: Secretaría de Educación Pública, 1980.

———. *Yesterday in Mexico: A Chronicle of the Revolution, 1919–1936.* Austin: University of Texas Press, 1961.

Durán, Leonel. *Lázaro Cárdenas: Ideario político.* Mexico City: Ediciones Era, 1972.

Durand Ponte, Victor Manuel. *Las derrotas obreras, 1946–1952.* Mexico City: Universidad Nacional Autónoma de México, 1984.

———. *La ruptura de la nación: Historia del movimiento obrero mexicano desde 1938 hasta 1952.* Mexico City: Universidad Nacional Autónoma de México, Instituto de Investigaciones Sociales, 1986.

Dziedzic, Michael J. *Mexico: Converging Challenges.* Adelphi Papers 242. London: Brassey's for International Institute for Strategic Studies, 1989.

Eisenberg, Frank. "The Mexican Presidential Election of 1952." Master's thesis, University of Illinois, 1953.

Elam, Robert Varney. "Appeal to Arms: The Army and Politics in El Salvador, 1931–1964." PhD diss., University of New Mexico, 1968.

Enríquez, Ignacio C. *The de la Huerta Disloyalty: Events in the Pre-election Presidential Campaign of 1924 Which Led to the Betrayal of Mexico by Some of Its Politicians and Army Leaders.* [Mexico City: n.p., 1924].

Espejel y Alvarez, Manuel. *Miguel Alemán: Biografía de su obra, reportaje de la acción constructiva del régimen.* Mexico City: Talleres Gráficos de la Nación, 1952.

Estrada Correa, Francisco. *Henriquismo: El arranque del cambio.* Mexico City: Costa Amic, 1988.

Ezcurdia, Mario. *Análisis teórico del Partido Revolucionario Institucional.* Mexico City: Costa Amic, 1968.

Fain, Tyrus G., ed. *The Intelligence Community: History, Organization, and Issues.* New York: R. R. Bowker, 1977.

Falcón, Romana. "Saturnino Cedillo: El último gran cacique militar." In *Estadistas, caciques y caudillos,* edited by Carlos Martínez Assad, 363–84. Mexico City: Instituto de Investigaciones Sociales, Universidad Nacional Autónoma de México, 1988.

Falcón, Romana, Soledad García Morales, and Maria Eugenia Terrones. *La semilla en el surco: Adalberto Tejeda y el radicalismo en Veracruz (1883–1960).* Mexico City: Colegio de México, Centro de Estudios Históricos, 1986.

Fallaw, Ben. *Cárdenas Compromised: The Failure of Reform in Postrevolutionary Yucatán.* Durham: Duke University Press, 2001.

Farell, Arsenio. *Miguel Henríquez Guzmán: Esbozo biográfico.* Mexico City: Ediciones Botas, 1950.

Farias, Luis M. *Así lo recuerdo: Testimonio político.* Mexico City: Fondo de Cultura Económica, 1992.

Fernández Boyoli, Manuel, and Eustaquio Marrón de Angelis. *Lo que no se sabe de la rebelión cedillista.* Mexico: n.p., 1938.

Fernández Christlieb, Paulina, and Octavio Rodríguez Araujo. *Elecciones y partidos en México.* Mexico City: El Caballito, 1986.

Finer, S. E. *The Man on Horseback: The Role of the Military in Politics.* 2nd ed. Baltimore: Penguin, 1975.

Foix, Pere. *Cárdenas.* Mexico City: Editorial Trillas, 1990.

Fuentes, Gloria. *El ejército mexicano.* Mexico City: Grijalbo, 1983.

Fuentes Díaz, Vicente. *Ascenso y descenso: Revolucionarios bajo Cárdenas.* Mexico City: Editorial Altiplano, 1977.

———. *Los partidos políticos en México.* 3rd ed. Mexico City: Editorial Altiplano, 1972.

Furtak, Robert. *El partido de la revolución y la estabilidad política en México.* Mexico City: Universidad Nacional Autónoma de México, 1974.

Garcia, Richard A. *Rise of the Mexican-American Middle Class: San Antonio, 1929–1941.* College Station: Texas A&M University Press, 1991.

García Cantú, Gastón. *Política mexicana.* Mexico City: Universidad Nacional Autónoma de México, 1974.

García Maroto, Gabriel. *Hombre y pueblo.* Mexico City: Impreso por Industrial Gráfica, 1940.

García Marsh, Alma María. "Ideology and Power: A Study of the Mexican State under Porfirio Díaz, 1876–1911, and Lázaro Cárdenas, 1934–1940." PhD diss., Harvard University, 1982.

Garrido, Luis Javier. *El partido de la revolucion institucionalizada: La formación del Nuevo Estado en México, 1928–1945.* Mexico City: Siglo XXI, 1986.

Gellman, Irwin F. *Good Neighbor Diplomacy: United States Policies in Latin America, 1933–1945.* Baltimore: Johns Hopkins University Press, 1979.

Germán Parra, Manuel. *La industrialización de México.* Mexico City: Imprenta Universitaria, 1954.

Gilderhus, Mark T. "U.S.–Latin American Relations Since World War II." *Diplomatic History* 16, no. 3 (1992): 429–52.

Gill, Mario. *Sinarquismo: Su origen, su esencia, su misión.* 2nd ed. Mexico City: Ediciones del CDR, 1944.

Gilly, Adolfo. *El cardenismo, una utopía mexicana.* Mexico City: Cal y Arena, 1994.

Gojman de Backal, Alicia. *Camisas, escudos y desfiles militares: Los Dorados y el antisemitismo en México (1934–1940).* Mexico City: Fondo de Cultura Económica, 2000.

Gómez, Marte R. *Vida política contemporánea: Cartas de Marte R. Gómez*. Mexico City: Fondo de Cultura Económica, 1978.

Gómez Jara, Francisco A. *El movimiento campesino en México*. Mexico City: Editorial Campesino, 1970.

Gómez Morín, Manuel. *Diez años de México*. Mexico City: Partido Acción Nacional, 1983.

―――. *La nación y el regimen*. Mexico City: Partido Acción Nacional, 1940.

González, Natalicio, et al. *México en el mundo de hoy*. Mexico City: Editorial Guaranía, 1952.

González A. Alpuche, Juan. *Manuel Avila Camacho: Arquetipo de ciudadano: Discursos conmemorativos*. Mexico City: Instituto Mexicano de Cultura, 1975.

González Casanova, Pablo. *Democracy in Mexico*. New York: Oxford University Press, 1970.

―――, ed. *Las elecciones en México: Evolución y perspectivas*. Mexico City: Siglo XXI, 1985.

―――. *El Estado y los partidos políticos en México: Ensayos*. Mexico City: Ediciones Era, 1981.

González Compeán, Miguel, and Leonardo Lomelí, eds. *El Partido de la Revolución: Institución y conflicto (1928–1999)*. Mexico City: Fondo de Cultura Económica, 2000.

González del Rivero, Leticia. "La oposición almazanista y las elecciones de 1940." *Historia y Grafía* 3 (1994): 11–33.

González Galarza, Raúl. *Medio siglo sin sorpresas, 1945–1994*. Mexicali: Gráficos, 1993.

González Ibarra, Juan de Dios. *Interpretaciones del Cardenismo*. Mexico City: Dirección de Difusión Cultural, Departamento Editorial, Universidad Autónoma Metropolitana, 1988.

González Luna, Efraín. "El pensamiento agrario de los cuatro candidatos a la presidencia para el sexenio, 1952–58." *Problemas Agrícolas e Industriales de México* 4, no. 4 (1952): 351–420.

González Pedrero, Enrique. *Calles y Cárdenas: Dos instantes de la dialéctica revolucionaria nacional*. Mexico City: Partido Revolucionario Institucional, Comisión Nacional Editorial, 1972.

González Polo, Ignacio. *Bibliografía general de las agrupaciones y partidos políticos mexicanos, 1910–1970*. Mexico City: Universidad Nacional Autónoma de México, 1976.

González y González, Luis. *Los artífices del cardenismo*. Mexico City: Clío, 1997.

Gottfried, Corbett S. "U.S. Military Intelligence in Mexico, 1917–1927: An Analysis." Master's thesis, Portland State University, 1995.

Grayson, George W. *The Mexican Labor Machine: Power, Politics, and Patronage*. Washington, D.C.: Center for Strategic and International Studies, 1989.

―――. *The United States and Mexico: Patterns of Influence*. New York: Praeger, 1984.

Gregg, Robert W., ed. *International Organization in the Western Hemisphere*. Syracuse: Syracuse University Press, 1968.

Gruening, Ernest. *Mexico and Its Heritage*. New York: D. Appleton-Century, 1940.

Gutiérrez, Angel. *Lázaro Cárdenas, 1895–1970*. [Morelia, Mexico]: Universidad Michoacana de San Nicolás de Hidalgo, Instituto de Investigaciones Históricas, Departamento de Historia Latinoamericana, 1994.

Haglund, David G. *Latin America and the Transformation of U.S. Strategic Thought, 1936–1940*. Albuquerque: University of New Mexico Press, 1984.

Hamilton, Nora. *The Limits of State Autonomy: Post-Revolutionary Mexico*. Princeton: Princeton University Press, 1982.

282

BIBLIOGRAPHY

Hanighen, Frank C. "Foreign Political Movements in the United States." *Foreign Affairs* 16, no. 1 (Oct. 1937): 1–20.

Hansen, Roger D. *The Politics of Mexican Development*. Baltimore: Johns Hopkins University Press, 1971.

Harris, Charles H., and Louis R. Sadler. *The Archaeologist Was a Spy: Sylvanus G. Morley and the Office of Naval Intelligence*. Albuquerque: University of New Mexico Press, 2003.

Hayes, Robert Ames. "The Formation of the Brazilian Army and Its Political Behavior, 1807–1930." PhD diss., University of New Mexico, 1969.

Herman, Donald L. *The Comintern in Mexico*. Washington, D.C.: Public Affairs Press, 1974.

Hernández, Héctor. *The Sinarquista Movement: With Special Reference to the Period, 1934–1944*. London: Minerva Press, 1999.

Hernández Chávez, Alicia. *Historia de la Revolución Mexicana, 1934–1940: La mecánica cardenista*. Historia de la Revolución Mexicana 16. Mexico City: Colegio de México, 1979.

Hernández Enríquez, Gustavo. "La movilidad política en México." 2 vols. Licenciatura thesis, Facultad de Ciencias Políticas y Sociales, Universidad Nacional Autónoma de México, 1970.

Hernández Enríquez, Gustavo Abel, and Armando Rojas Trujillo. *Manuel Avila Camacho: Biografía de un revolucionario con historia*. Mexico City: Ediciones del Gobierno del Estado de Puebla, 1987.

Hernández García de León, Héctor. *Historia política del sinarquismo, 1934–1944*. Mexico City: Miguel Ángel Porrúa, 2004.

Hernández Rodríguez, Rogelio. *Amistades, compromisos y lealtades: Líderes y grupos políticos en el Estado de México, 1942–1993*. Mexico City: El Colegio de México, 1998.

Hodges, Donald Clark, and Daniel Ross Gandy. *Mexico, 1910–1982: Reform or Revolution?* Westport, Conn.: Zed Press, 1983.

Hofstadter, Dan. *Mexico, 1946–73*. New York: Facts on File, 1974.

Horowitz, Irving Louis. "Militarism and Civil-Military Relationships in Latin America: Implications for the Third World." In *Research in Political Sociology*, edited by Richard G. Braungart and Margaret M. Braungart, 79–100. Vol. 1. Greenwich, Conn.: JAI Press, 1985.

Huggins, Martha. *Political Policing: The United States and Latin America*. Durham: Duke University Press, 1998.

Hull, Cordell. *The Memoirs of Cordell Hull*. 2 vols. New York: Macmillan, 1948.

Hunt, Marta Espejo-Ponce. "The Mexican Presidential Election of 1940." Master's thesis, University of New Mexico, 1962.

Huntington, Samuel. *The Soldier and the State*. Cambridge: Harvard University Press, 1957.

Iturriaga, José E. *Plutarco Elías Calles: Obra revolucionaria*. Mexico City: Partido Revolucionario Institucional, Secretaría de Divulgación Ideológica, Secretaría de Información y Propaganda, 1988.

Jeffreys-Jones, Rhodri. *American Espionage: From Secret Service to CIA*. New York: Free Press, 1977.

Johnson, John J. *The Military and Society in Latin America*. Stanford: Stanford University Press, 1967.

Jones, Halbert, M. "'The War Has Brought Peace to Mexico': The Political Impact of Mexican Participation in World War II." PhD diss., Harvard University, 2006.

Joseph, Gilbert M., and Daniel Nugent, eds. *Everyday Forms of State Formation: Revolution and the Negotiation of Rule in Modern Mexico.* Durham: Duke University Press, 1994.

Juan Andreu Almazán, semblanza del candidato popular. Mexico City: Publicidad de la Sección Técnica de Organización, 1939.

Katz, Friedrich. *The Life and Times of Pancho Villa.* Stanford: Stanford University Press, 1998.

———. *The Secret War in Mexico: Europe, the United States, and the Mexican Revolution.* Chicago: University of Chicago Press, 1981.

Kilroy, James Richard, Jr. "Crisis and Legitimacy: The Role of the Mexican Military in Politics and Society." PhD diss., University of Virginia, 1990.

Kirshner, Alan. *Tomás Garrido Canabal y el movimiento de los Camisas Rojas.* Translated by Ana Mendizábal. SepSetentas 267. Mexico City: Secretaría de Educación Pública, Dirección General de Divulgación, 1976.

Knight, Alan. "Cardenismo: Juggernaut or Jalopy?" *Journal of Latin American Studies* 26 (1994): 73–107.

———. "Mexico's Elite Settlement: Conjuncture and Consequences." In *Elites and Democratic Consolidation in Latin America and Southern Europe,* edited by John Higley and Richard Gunther, 113–45. Cambridge: Cambridge University Press, 1992.

———. "The Political Economy of Revolutionary Mexico, 1900–1940." In *Latin America, Economic Imperialism, and the State: The Political Economy of the External Connection from Independence to the Present,* edited by Christopher Abel and Colin M. Lewis, 288–317. London: Athlone, 1985.

———. "The Politics of the Expropriation." In *The Mexican Petroleum Industry in the Twentieth Century,* edited by Jonathan Brown and Alan Knight, 90–128. Austin: University of Texas Press, 1992.

———. "Populism and Neo-populism in Latin America, Especially Mexico." *Journal of Latin American Studies* 30, no. 2 (May 1998): 223–48.

———. "The Rise and Fall of Cardenismo, c. 1930–c. 1946." In *Mexico Since Independence,* edited by Leslie Bethell, 241–320. Cambridge: Cambridge University Press, 1990.

———. *U.S.-Mexican Relations, 1910–1940: An Interpretation.* La Jolla, Calif.: Center for U.S.-Mexican Studies, University of California at San Diego, 1987.

Koster Fuentes, Pedro de. *Plutarco Elías Calles: Creador de instituciones.* Mexico City: n.p., 1976.

Krauze, Enrique. *Caudillos culturales en la Revolución Mexicana.* Mexico City: Siglo XXI, 1976.

Labastida, Horacio. *Cárdenas y la expropiación petrolera.* Mexico City: Centro de Estudios Históricos del Agrarismo en México, 1983.

———. *Lázaro Cárdenas: La Revolución Mexicana y el proyecto nacional.* Mexico City: Universidad Nacional Autónoma de México, Dirección General de Difusión Cultural, Unidad Editorial, 1983.

Laborde, Hernán. *El enemigo es Almazán: Informe del comp. Hernán Laborde, Secretario General del Partido Comunista Mexicano, al pleno del Comité Nacional, reunido en Mexico del 16 al 20 de septiembre de 1939.* Mexico City: Editorial Popular, 1939.

Lajous, Alejandra. *Los orígenes del partido único en México.* Mexico City: Universidad Nacional Autónoma de México, 1979.

————. *Los partidos políticos en México.* 2nd ed. Mexico y Latinoamérica 13. Tlahuapán, Puebla: Premia, 1986.

————. *El PRI y sus antepasados.* Colección Memoria y Olvido 17. Mexico City: Martín Casillas Editores, 1982.

Lamont Hernández, Alfredo. *Semblanza de un Revolucionario: El General de Brigada Miguel Henríquez Guzmán.* Mexico City: n.p., 1943.

Langston, Joy. *The Camarillas: A Theoretical and Comparative Examination of Why They Exist and Why They Take the Specific Form They Do.* División de Estudios Políticos 12. Mexico City: CIDE, 1993.

————. *An Empirical View of the Political Groups in Mexico: The Camarillas.* División de Estudios Políticos 15. Mexico City: CIDE, 1994.

————. "Political Factors in the Mexican Political System: A Theoretical and Comparative Examination." PhD diss., Duke University, 1995.

————. *The Role of the Political Groups in the Succession Process.* División de Estudios Políticos 19. Mexico City: CIDE, 1994.

————. *Three Exits from the Mexican Institutional Revolutionary Party: Internal Ruptures and Political Stability.* División de Estudios Políticos 11. Mexico City: CIDE, 1993.

————. *Why Rules Matter: The Formal Rules of Candidate Selection and Leadership Section in the PRI, 1978–1996.* División de Estudios Políticos 58. Mexico City: CIDE, 1997.

Lemus, George. "Partido Acción Nacional: A Mexican Opposition Party." Master's thesis, University of Texas at Austin, 1956.

León, Luis L. *Crónica del poder: En los recuerdos de un político en el México revolucionario.* Mexico City: Fondo de Cultura Económica, 1987.

Lerner de Shienbaum, Victoria, and Susana Ralsky de Cimet. *El poder de los Presidentes: Alcances y perspectivas (1910–1973).* Mexico City: Instituto Mexicano de Estudios Políticos, 1976.

Lester, Robert. *U.S. Military Intelligence Reports. Mexico, 1919–1941.* Frederick, Md.: University Publications of America, 1984.

Levy, Daniel, and Gabriel Székely. *Mexico: Paradoxes of Stability and Change.* Boulder: Westview, 1987.

Lieuwen, Edwin. *Arms and Politics in Latin America.* New York: Praeger, 1960.

————. "Curbing Militarism in Mexico." *New Mexico Historical Review* 33, no. 4 (Oct. 1958): 257–76.

————. *Generals vs. Presidents: Neomilitarism in Latin America.* New York: Praeger, 1964.

————. *Mexican Militarism: The Political Rise and Fall of the Revolutionary Army, 1910–1940.* Albuquerque: University of New Mexico Press, 1968.

Llinás Alvarez, Edgar. *Vida y obra de Ramón Beteta.* Mexico City: Impresora Galve, 1996.

Loaeza, Soledad. *El Partido Acción Nacional, la larga marcha, 1939–1994: Oposición leal y partido de protesta.* Mexico City: Fondo de Cultura Económica, 1999.

Lombardo Toledano, Vicente. *Campaña presidencial de 1952.* 2 vols. Mexico City: Centro de Estudios Filosóficos, Políticos y Sociales "Vicente Lombardo Toledano," 1997.

————. *La Revolución Mexicana, 1921–1967.* Mexico City: Instituto Nacional de Estudios Históricos de la Revolución Mexicana, 1988.

————. *The United States and Mexico: Two Nations, One Ideal.* New York: Council for Pan-American Democracy, 1942.

López de Nava Baltierra, Rodolfo, and Rodolfo López de Nava Camarena. *Mis hechos de campaña: Testimonios del general de división Rodolfo López de Nava Baltierra, 1911–*

1952. Mexico City: Instituto Nacional de Estudios Históricos de la Revolución Mexicana, Secretaría de Gobernación, 1995.

López Moreno, Javier. *Elecciones de ayer y de mañana*. Mexico City: Costa Amic, 1987.

López Portillo, Felícitas. *Estado e ideología empresarial en el gobierno alemanista*. Mexico City: Universidad Nacional Autónoma de México, 1995.

Loveman, Brian. *For la Patria: Politics and the Armed Forces in Latin America*. Wilmington, Del.: Scholarly Resources, 1999.

Loyo Camacho, Martha Beatriz. *Joaquín Amaro y el proceso de institucionalización del ejército mexicano, 1917–1931*. Mexico City: Fondo de Cultura Económica, 2003.

Loyola, Rafael. *Entre la guerra y la estabilidad política: El México de los 40*. Mexico City: Grijalbo, Consejo Nacional para la Cultura y las Artes, 1990.

Loyola Díaz, Rafael. *Una mirada a México: El nacional, 1946–1952*. Mexico City: Instituto de Investigaciones Sociales, Universidad Nacional Autónoma de México, 1996.

Lozano, Oscar. "Patria y nacionalismo en el México de afuera: The Extension of Sinarquismo into the United States." Master's thesis, University of Texas at El Paso, 1999.

Lozoya, Jorge Alberto. *El ejército mexicano, 1911–1965*. Mexico City: Colegio de México, 1970.

Ludlow Wiechers, Leonor. "La secularización e integración del sinarquismo a la vida política." *Revista Mexicana de Sociología* 50, no. 3 (Jul.–Sep. 1988): 201–16.

Lumen, Enrique. *Almazán: Vida de un caudillo y metabolismo de una revolución*. Mexico City: Editorial "Claridad," 1940.

Mabry, Donald J. *The Mexican University and the State: Student Conflicts, 1910–1971*. College Station: Texas A&M University Press, 1982.

———. *Mexico's Acción Nacional: A Catholic Alternative to Revolution*. Syracuse: Syracuse University Press, 1973.

MacDonnell, Francis. "The Search for a Second Zimmermann Telegram: FDR, BSC, and the Latin American Front." *International Journal of Intelligence and Counterintelligence* 4, no. 4 (1990): 487–505.

Mahoney, Harry Thayer, and Marjorie Locke Mahoney. *Espionage in Mexico: The Twentieth Century*. San Francisco: Austin and Winfield, 1997.

Maniruzzaman, Talukder. *Military Withdrawal from Politics: A Comparative Study*. Cambridge, Mass.: Ballinger, 1987.

Manzur Ocaña, Justo. *La revolución permanente (vida y obra del general Cándido Aguilar)*. Mexico City: Costa Amic, 1973.

Margiotta, Franklin D. "Civilian Control and the Mexican Military: Changing Patterns of Political Influence." In *Civilian Control of the Military: Theory and Cases from Developing Countries*, edited by Claude E. Welch, 213–54. Albany: State University of New York Press, 1976.

———. *Civilian Control of the Military: Patterns in Mexico*. Special Studies Series 66. Buffalo: Council on International Studies, State University of New York at Buffalo, 1975.

Marín, Carlos. *Espionaje político*. Mexico City: Proceso, 1980.

Markiewicz, Dana. *The Mexican Revolution and the Limits of Agrarian Reform, 1915–1946*. Boulder: Lynne Rienner, 1993.

Martínez Assad, Carlos R. *El henriquismo, una piedra en el camino*. Mexico City: Martín Casillas Editores, 1982.

———. *Los rebeldes vencidos: Cedillo contra el estado Cardenista*. Mexico City: Fondo de Cultura Económica, 1990.

Martínez Assad, Carlos R., and Rafael Loyola Díaz, eds. *La Sucesión presidencial en México, 1928–1988*. 2nd ed. Mexico City: Nueva Imagen, 1992.

Martínez Rodríguez, Antonia. "El sexenio alemanista: Modernización económica y proyecto político (1946–1952)." PhD diss., Universidad Complutense de Madrid, 1993.

Marván Laborde, Maria. "El Partido Acción Nacional." *Revista Mexicana de Sociología* 50, no. 3 (Jul.–Sept. 1988): 189–99.

Matute, Alvaro. *Contraespionaje político y sucesión presidencial: Correspondencia de Trinidad W. Flores sobre la primera campaña electoral de Alvaro Obregón, 1919–1920*. Mexico City: Universidad Nacional Autónoma de México, Instituto de Investigaciones Históricas, 1985.

McAlister, Lyle N. *The "Fuero Militar" in New Spain, 1764–1800*. Gainesville: University of Florida, 1957.

McAlister, Lyle N., Anthony P. Maingot, and Robert A. Potash. *The Military in Latin American Sociopolitical Evolution: Four Case Studies*. Washington, D.C.: Center for Research in Social Systems, 1970.

McDonald, James L. "Overriding Interests: Subversion as an Instrument of U.S. Foreign Policy." PhD diss., American University, 1997.

Medin, Tzvi. *Ideología y praxis política de Lázaro Cárdenas*. Mexico City: Siglo Veintiuno, 1972.

———. *El sexenio alemanista: Ideología y praxis política de Miguel Alemán*. Mexico City: Ediciones Era, 1990.

Medina, Luis. *Del cardenismo al avilacamachismo*. Historia de la Revolución Mexicana 18. Mexico City: Colegio de México, 1978.

———. *Civilismo y modernización del autoritarismo*. Historia de la Revolución Mexicana 20. Mexico City: Colegio de México, 1979.

———. *Evolución electoral en el México contemporáneo*. Mexico City: Reforma Política, 1978.

Medina Hermosilla, Miguel. *Almazán*. Mexico City: n.p., 1941.

Mejía Barquera, Fernando. *Un diario de contrastes*. Mexico City: El Nacional, 1991.

Memmott, Kip Richard. "Enduring Friendship: An Analysis of United States-Mexican Foreign Relations, 1950–1970." Master's thesis, Arizona State University, 1995.

Mena Brito, Bernardino. *Hablando claro: Mis trabajos por el Partido Nacional de Salvación Pública*. Mexico City: Ediciones Botas, 1939.

———. *El P.R.U.N.: Almazán y el desastre final*. Mexico City: Ediciones Botas, 1941.

Mendoza, Salvador. *Ezequiel Padilla: Breve apunte biográfico*. Mexico City: 1945.

Menéndez, Gabriel Antonio. *El cacique de las Huastecas*. Mexico City: Secretaría de Educación Pública, [1980].

Menéndez Herrero, Marcial. *Almazán*. Mexico City: La Impresora, 1939.

México y la República Española: Antología de documentos, 1931–1977. Mexico City: Centro Republicano Español de México, 1978.

Meyer, Jean. *El sinarquismo, el cardenismo y la iglesia: 1937–1947*. Mexico City: Tusquets Editores, 2003.

———. *El sinarquismo ¿Un fascismo mexicano? 1937–1947*. Mexico City: Editorial Joaquín Mortiz, 1979.

Meyer, Lorenzo. *Mexico y Estados Unidos en el conflicto petrolero, 1917–1942*. Mexico City: Colegio de México, 1968.

————. "La revolución mexicana y sus elecciones presidenciales, 1911–1940." In *Las elecciones en México: Evolución y perspectivas,* edited by Pablo González Casanova, 69–99. Mexico City: Siglo XXI, 1985.

Michaels, Albert L. "The Crisis of Cardenismo." *Journal of Latin American Studies* 2 (1977): 51–79.

————. "Las elecciones de 1940." *Historia Mexicana* 21, no. 1 (Jul.–Sep. 1971): 80–134.

————. "Fascism and Sinarquismo: Popular Nationalism Against the Mexican Revolution." *Journal of Church and State* 8, no. 2 (1996): 234–50.

————. *The Mexican Election of 1940.* Special Studies 5. Buffalo: Council on International Studies, State University of New York at Buffalo, 1971.

————. "Mexican Politics and Nationalism from Calles to Cárdenas." PhD diss., University of Pennsylvania, 1966.

————. "El nacionalismo conservador mexicano: Desde la Revolución hasta 1940." *Historia Mexicana* 62 (Oct.–Dec. 1966): 213–38.

Millon, Robert Paul. *Vicente Lombardo Toledano, Mexican Marxist.* Chapel Hill: University of North Carolina Press, 1966.

Molinar Horcasitas, Juan. *El tiempo de la legitimidad: Elecciones, autoritarismo y democracia en México.* Mexico City: Cal y Arena, 1991.

Mora García, Carlos. *Almazanismo y Salinismo, 1940–1988: Dos expresiones políticas del liberalismo revolucionario mexicano.* Mexico City: Cactus, 2001.

Moreno, Daniel A. *Los partidos políticos del México contemporáneo: 1916–1975.* Mexico City: Costa Amic, 1975.

Moscoso Pastrana, Prudencio. *El pinedismo en Chiapas, 1916–1920.* Mexico City: n.p., 1960.

Mosk, Sanford. *Industrial Revolution in Mexico.* Berkeley and Los Angeles: University of California Press, 1950.

Múgica Velázquez, Francisco José, and Anna Ribera Carbó, eds. *Estos mis apuntes.* Mexico City: Consejo Nacional para la Cultura y las Artes, 1997.

Múgica Velázquez, Francisco José, and Javier Moctezuma Barragán, eds. *Francisco J. Múgica: Un romántico rebelde.* Mexico City: Fondo de Cultura Económica, 2001.

Muñoz, Hilda. *Lázaro Cárdenas: Síntesis ideológica de su campaña presidencial.* Mexico City: Fondo de Cultura Económica, 1976.

Muñoz Cota, José. *Aquí está Miguel Henríquez Guzmán: Ensayo.* Mexico City: Costa Amic, 1978.

————. *Un gobierno de Frente Popular.* Mexico City: Partido Nacional Revolucionario, 1937.

Musacchio, Humberto. *Quién es quién en la política mexicana.* Mexico City: Plaza y Janés, 2002.

Nafey, Abdul. *Dominant Party Democracy: Political Process in Mexico.* New Delhi: Trans Asia Publications, 1987.

Narváez, Rubén. *La sucesión presidencial: Teoría y práctica del tapadismo.* Mexico City: Instituto Mexicano de Sociología Política, 1981.

Nathan, Paul. "Mexico Under Cárdenas." PhD diss., University of Chicago, 1952.

Nava N., Carmen. "La democracia interna del Partido de la Revolución Mexicana (PRM): El problema de la supresión de los consejos regionales." *Revista Mexicana de Sociología* 50, no. 3 (Jul.–Sep. 1988): 157–66.

Navarro, Aaron W. "La fusión fracasada: Almazán y Amaro en la campaña presidencial de 1940." *Boletín del Fideicomiso Archivos Plutarco Elías Calles y Fernando Torreblanca* 49, 2005.

————. "Opposition and Dominance in the Mexican Presidential Election of 1940: The Challenge of Almazanismo." Paper presented at the 24th International Congress of the Latin American Studies Association, Dallas, Texas, March 28, 2003.

Navarro Bolandi, Hugo. *Miguel Alemán: Trayectoria política.* Mexico City: n.p., 1970.

Needler, Martin C., ed. *Political Systems of Latin America.* Princeton: Van Nostrand, 1964.

————. *Politics and Society in Mexico.* Albuquerque: University of New Mexico Press, 1971.

Newcomer, Daniel. *Reconciling Modernity: Urban State Formation in 1940s León, Mexico.* Lincoln: University of Nebraska Press, 2004.

Newell, Roberto, and Luis Rubio. *Mexico's Dilemma: The Political Origins of Economic Crisis.* Boulder: Westview, 1984.

Niblo, Stephen R. *The Impact of War: Mexico and World War II.* Occasional Paper 10. Melbourne: La Trobe University Institute of Latin American Studies, 1988.

————. *Mexico in the 1940s: Modernity, Politics, and Corruption.* Wilmington, Del.: Scholarly Resources, 1999.

————. *War, Diplomacy, and Development: The United States and Mexico, 1938–1954.* Wilmington, Del.: Scholarly Resources, 1995.

Nordlinger, Eric A. *Soldiers in Politics: Military Coups and Governments.* Englewood Cliffs, N.J.: Prentice Hall, 1977.

North, Lisa, and David Raby. "The Dynamic of Revolution and Counterrevolution: Mexico Under Cardenas, 1934–1940." *Latin American Research Unit Studies* 2, no. 1 (1977): 25–56.

Novo, Salvador. *La vida en México en el periodo presidencial de Miguel Alemán.* Mexico City: INAH, Consejo Nacional para la Cultura y las Artes, 1994.

Noyola Barragán, Luis. *Como murieron los Generales Magdaleno y Saturnino Cedillo.* [Mexico City]: n.p., 1964.

Nuncio, Abraham. *El grupo Monterrey.* Mexico City: Nueva Imagen, 1984.

Nunn, Frederick M. *The Time of the Generals: Latin American Professional Militarism in World Perspective.* Lincoln: University of Nebraska, 1992.

Olguín Pérez, Palmira. "Los militares en México: Bibliografía introductoria." *Revista Mexicana de Sociología* 38, no. 2 (Apr.–Jun. 1976): 453–90.

Orozco, Jesús, and Francisco J. Núñez. *Ideología y programa de gobierno en los discursos de toma de posesión de los presidentes de Mexico, 1928–1982.* Guadalajara: ITESO, 1983.

Ortega, Gregorio, ed. *Fernando Gutiérrez Barrios: Diálogos con el hombre, el poder y la política.* Mexico City: Planeta, 1995.

Ortega Aguirre, Maximino. *Estado y movimiento ferrocarrilero, 1958–1959.* Mexico City: Ediciones Quinto Sol, 1988.

Ortiz Mendoza, Francisco. *Qué es y cómo se formó el Partido Popular Socialista: Esbozo histórico.* Mexico City: Dirección Nacional del Comité Central, Secretaría de Educación Política, 1978.

Ortiz Pinchetti, José Agustín. *Reflexiones privadas, testimonios públicos.* Mexico City: Océano, 1997.

Ortoll, Servando. "Catholic Organizations in Mexico's National Politics and International Diplomacy (1926–1942)." PhD diss., Columbia University, 1987.

O'Shaughnessy, Laura Nuzzi. "Opposition in an Authoritarian Regime: The Incorporation and Institutionalization of the Mexican National Action Party (PAN)." PhD diss., Indiana University, 1977.

Osorio Marban, Miguel. *Revolución y política.* [Mexico City: Investigaciones Técnico Educativas, 1981].

————. *El sector popular del PRI*. [Mexico City]: Coordinación Nacional de Estudios Históricos, Políticos y Sociales, PRI, 1994.

Padgett, Leon Vincent. *The Mexican Political System*. Boston: Houghton Mifflin, 1966.

Padilla, Juan Ignacio. *Sinarquismo: Contra revolución*. Mexico City: Editorial Polis, 1948.

Pani, Alberto J., et al. *Una encuesta sobre la cuestión democrática de México*. Mexico City: Editorial Cultura, 1948.

Paniagua, Edgar Acata. *The Rebellion of the Zapatistas*. Fort Leavenworth, Kans.: [U.S. Army Command and General Staff College], 1996.

Partido de la Revolución Mexicana. *Ávila Camacho y su ideología: La revolución en marcha: Jira electoral*. Mexico City: [Partido de la Revolucion Mexicana], 1940.

————. *Contra la reacción y su candidato Almazán*. Mexico City: Oficina de Prensa y Propaganda, Partido de la Revolución Mexicana, 1940.

————. *Convocatoria para la Asamblea Constituyente del nuevo partido*. Mexico City: PRM, 1937.

————. *En defensa de la soberanía nacional, 18 de marzo*. Mexico City: [Partido de la Revolucion Mexicana], 1940.

————. *The Second Six-Year Plan, 1941–1946*. [Mexico City]: Partido de la Revolución Mexicana, [1939].

Partido Nacional Revolucionario. *La democracia social en México: Historia de la Convención nacional revolucionaria: Constitución del P.N.R. Sucesión presidencial de 1929*. Mexico City: Partido Nacional Revolucionario, 1929.

————. *La jira del general Lázaro Cárdenas: Síntesis ideológica*. Mexico City: Partido Nacional Revolucionario, 1934.

————. *The Mexican Government's Six-Year Plan, 1934 to 1940: Complete Textual Translation of the Revised Plan and General Lázaro Cárdenas' Nomination Address, Explaining How He Will Abide by the Plan During His Administration*. Mexico City: Partido Nacional Revolucionario, [1934].

Partido Revolucionario de Orientación Almazanista. *Manifiesto a la nación*. Mexico: [Partido Revolucionario de Orientación Almazanista], 1939.

Partido Revolucionario de Unificación Nacional. *Who Is President-Elect of Mexico? A Question of Vital Importance to Every Believer in the Principles of Democracy*. Mexico City: Partido Revolucionario de Unificación Nacional, 1940.

Partido Revolucionario Institucional. *Hacia la institucionalidad revolucionaria: Fundación del P.N.R.* Mexico City: Partido Revolucionario Institucional, Coordinación Nacional de Estudios Históricos, Políticos y Sociales, 1993.

————. *Historia documental del partido de la revolución*. 14 vols. Mexico City: Partido Revolucionario Institucional, 1981.

————. *Memoria: Conferencia Nacional de Análisis Ideológico sobre la Revolución Mexicana (1910–1985)*. Mexico City: Partido Revolucionario Institucional, 1985.

————. *Lázaro Cárdenas*. Mexico City: Partido Revolucionario Institucional, 1985.

[————]. *El partido en el poder: Seis ensayos*. Mexico City: Partido Revolucionario Institucional, IEPES, 1990.

————. *Partido Nacional Revolucionario, Partido de la Revolución Mexicana, Partido Revolucionario Institucional: Actas constitutivas, documentos básicos*. Mexico City: Partido Revolucionario Institucional, 1991.

————. *Plutarco Elías Calles*. Mexico City: Partido Revolucionario Institucional, 1985.

Paz Salinas, María Emilia. *Strategy, Security, and Spies: Mexico and the U.S. as Allies in World War II*. University Park: Pennsylvania State University Press, 1997.

Pellicer de Brody, Olga. *El afianzamiento de la estabilidad política*. Historia de la Revolución Mexicana 22. Mexico City: Colegio de México, 1978.

———. "La oposición en México: El caso del henriquismo." *Foro Internacional* 68 (1977): 477–89.

Pérez Montfort, Ricardo. *"Por la patria y por la raza": La derecha secular en el sexenio de Lázaro Cárdenas*. Mexico City: Facultad de Filosofía y Letras, Universidad Nacional Autónoma de México, 1993.

Pérez Verdía, Benito Xavier. *Cárdenas apóstol vs. Cárdenas estadista*. Mexico City: n.p., 1939.

Philip, George, ed. *Politics in Mexico*. London: Croom Helm, 1985.

Pineda, Salvador. *El Presidente Ruiz Cortines: Itinerario de una conducta*. Mexico City: Editorial Guaranía, 1952.

Piñeyro, José Luis. *Ejército y sociedad en México: Pasado y presente*. Puebla: Universidad Autónoma de Puebla, 1985.

———. "Las fuerzas armadas en la transición política de Mexico." *Revista Mexicana de Sociología* 59, no. 1 (1997): 163–89.

———. "The Mexican Army and the State: Historical and Political Perspective." *Revue Internationale de Sociologie,* 2nd ser., 14, no. 1–2 (1978): 111–57.

Plasencia de la Parra, Enrique. *Personajes y escenarios de la rebelión delahuertista, 1923–1924*. Mexico City: Instituto de Investigaciones Históricas, Universidad Nacional Autónoma de México and Porrúa, 1998.

Ponce, Bernardo. *Adolfo Ruiz Cortines: Ensayo para una biografía política*. N.p.: Biografías Gandesa, 1952.

Portes Gil, Emilio. *Quince años de política mexicana*. 2nd ed. Mexico City: Ediciones Botas, 1941.

Prewett, Virginia. "The Mexican Army." *Foreign Affairs* 19, no. 3 (Apr. 1941): 609–21.

Primer simposio sobre historia contemporánea de México 1940–1984: Inventario sobre el pasado reciente. Mexico City: INAH, 1986.

Puente, Ramón. *Hombres de la revolución: Calles*. Mexico City: Fondo de Cultura Económica, 1994.

Quiles Ponce, Enrique. *Henríquez y Cárdenas ¡Presentes! Hechos y realidades en la campaña henriquista*. Mexico City: Costa Amic Editores, 1980.

Raat, W. Dirk. *Revoltosos: Mexico's Rebels in the United States*. College Station: Texas A&M University Press, 1981.

———. "U.S. Intelligence Operations and Covert Action in Mexico, 1900–1947." *Journal of Contemporary History* 22, no. 4 (October 1987): 615–38.

Ramirez, Félix C. *Carta abierta al C. General Lázaro Cárdenas*. Mexico City: Secretaría de la Defensa Nacional, 1943.

Ramírez, Ricardo Corzo, José G. González Sierra, and David A. Skerritt. *Nunca un desleal: Cándido Aguilar (1889–1960)*. Mexico City: Colegio de México, 1986.

Ramírez Cuéllar, Héctor. *Lombardo: Un hombre de México*. Mexico City: El Nacional, 1992.

Redmont, Bernard S. *Risks Worth Taking: The Odyssey of a Foreign Correspondent*. Lanham, Md.: University Press of America, 1992.

Reglamento general de deberes militares. Mexico City: Ediciones Ateneo, 1944.

Reglamento general de deberes militares. Mexico City: Ediciones Ateneo, 1947.

Reminiscencias al margen de una gran reminiscencia: Las fiestas de Monterrey y su nota culminante: Crónicas y comentarios sobre el gran desfile histórico organizado por el Gral. Dn. Juan Andreu Almazán. [Mexico City]: n.p., 1928.

Remmers, Lawrence James. "Nonintervention: Mexico and the Inter-American System, 1913–1948." Master's thesis, University of California at Davis, 1970.

El respeto a la Voluntad Popular. Mexico City: Comité Pro-Ezequiel Padilla, 1945.

Reveles Vázquez, Francisco. "La fundación del Partido Acción Nacional." *Estudios Políticos* 24 (May–Aug. 2000): 181–214.

———. ed. *Partido Revolucionario Institucional: Crisis y refundación.* Mexico City: Gernika, 2003.

Reyna, José Luis, and Richard S. Weinert. *Authoritarianism in Mexico.* Philadelphia: Institute for the Study of Human Issues, 1977.

Richelson, Jeffrey T. *Foreign Intelligence Organizations.* Cambridge, Mass.: Ballinger Publishing, 1988.

Richelson, Jeffrey T., and Desmond Ball. *The Ties That Bind: Intelligence Cooperation between the UKUSA Countries.* Boston: Allen and Unwin, 1985.

Rila, Carter. "Army Intelligence Collection and the Mexican Revolution, 1913–1917." Master's thesis, Defense Intelligence College, 1991.

Rivas Mercado, Antonieta. *La campaña de Vasconcelos.* Mexico City: Editorial Oasis, 1981.

Rivera Flores, Antonio. *La derrota de Lombardo Toledano y el movimiento obrero.* Querétaro, Mexico: Universidad Autónoma de Querétaro, Centro de Investigaciones Sociológicas, 1984.

Rock, David, ed. *Latin America in the 1940s: War and Postwar Transitions.* Berkeley and Los Angeles: University of California Press, 1994.

Rodríguez Araujo, Octavio. *México: Estabilidad y luchas por la democracia, 1900–1982.* Mexico City: El Caballito, 1988.

———, ed. *La reforma política y los partidos en México.* Mexico City: Siglo XXI, 1980.

Rodríguez Lapuente, Manuel. "El sinarquismo y Acción Nacional: Las afinidades conflictivas." *Foro Internacional* 29, no. 3 (Jan.–Mar. 1989): 440–58.

Rodríguez O., Jaime E. *The Evolution of the Mexican Political System.* Wilmington, Del.: Scholarly Resources, 1993.

———. *The Origins of Mexican National Politics, 1808–1847.* Wilmington, Del.: Scholarly Resources, 1997.

Rodríguez Prats, Juan José. *Adolfo Ruiz Cortines.* Jalapa, Veracruz: Gobierno del Estado de Veracruz, 1990.

Rojas, Beatriz. *La pequeña guerra: Los Carrera Torres y los Cedillo.* Zamora, Michoacán: Colegio de Michoacán, 1983.

Rojas Trujillo, Armando. *Manuel Avila Camacho: Al servicio de la patria.* Puebla: Imagen Pública y Corporativa, 1993.

Romero, Laura. *El Partido Nacional Revolucionario en Jalisco.* [Guadalajara]: Centro Universitario de Ciencias Sociales y Humanidades, Universidad de Guadalajara, 1995.

Romero Flores, Jesús. *Revolución Mexicana: Anales históricos, 1910–1974.* Mexico City: Costa Amic, 1974.

Romero Reséndiz, Alfonso. *Remembranzas: Narración complementaria novelada de sucesos del henriquismo.* Mexico City: n.p., 1996.

Ronfeldt, David F. *The Mexican Army and Political Order Since 1940.* Santa Monica: Rand Corporation, 1975.

———, ed. *The Modern Mexican Military: A Reassessment.* San Diego: Center for U.S.-Mexican Studies, University of California at San Diego, 1984.

Rosas, Javier. *50 años de oposición en México.* Mexico City: Departamento de Ciencia Política, Universidad Nacional Autónoma de México, 1979.

Rouquié, Alain. *The Military and the State in Latin America.* Translated by Paul E. Sigmund. Berkeley and Los Angeles: University of California Press, 1987.

Rout, Leslie B., Jr., and John F. Bratzel. *The Shadow War: German Espionage and United States Counterespionage in Latin America During World War II.* Frederick, Md.: University Publications of America, 1986.

Roxborough, Ian. *The Mexican Charrazo of 1948: Latin American Labor from World War to Cold War.* Working Paper 77. Notre Dame: Helen Kellogg Institute for International Studies, University of Notre Dame, 1986.

Ruibal Corella, Juan Antonio. *Calles, hombre de su tiempo.* [Hermosillo, Sonora]: Impresora La Voz de Sonora, 1989.

Sabbah, Maurice Leslie. "The Mexican Presidential Succession of 1940." Master's thesis, University of Florida, 1973.

Salazar, J. Cleofas. *Himno dedicado al Lic. Dn. Ezequiel Padilla: Candidato a la presidencia de la republica, 1946–1952.* [Mexico City]: Partido Nacional de la Defensa del Pueblo, 1946.

Salazar, Rosendo. *Del militarismo al civilismo en nuestra Revolución.* Mexico City: Libro Mex Editores, 1958.

Samponaro, Frank N. "The Political Role of the Army in Mexico, 1821–1848." PhD diss., State University of New York at Stony Brook, 1974.

Sánchez Azcona, Gloria. *El general Antonio I. Villareal: Civilista de la Revolución Mexicana.* Mexico City: Instituto Nacional de Estudios Históricos de la Revolución Mexicana, 1980.

Sánchez Gutiérrez, Arturo. "Los militares en la década de los cincuenta." *Revista Mexicana de Sociología* 50, no. 3 (1988): 269–93.

Santos, Gonzalo N. *Memorias.* Mexico City: Grijalbo, 1986.

Saragoza, Alex M. *The Monterrey Elite and the Mexican State, 1880–1940.* Austin: University of Texas Press, 1988.

Scheina, Robert L. *Latin America: A Naval History, 1810–1987.* Annapolis, Md.: Naval Institute Press, 1987.

Scherer García, Julio, Carlos Monsiváis, and Marcelino García Barragán. *Parte de guerra: Tlatelolco 1968: Documentos del general Marcelino García Barragán: Los hechos y la historia.* Mexico City: Aguilar, 1999.

Schlesinger, Stephen, and Stephen Kinzer. *Bitter Fruit: The Story of the American Coup in Guatemala.* Expanded edition. Cambridge, Mass.: David Rockefeller Center for Latin American Studies, Harvard University Press, 1999.

Schloming, Gordon Clark. "Civil-Military Relations in Mexico, 1910–1940: A Case Study." PhD diss., Columbia University, 1974.

Schmitt, Karl. "The Role of the Military in Contemporary Mexico." In *The Caribbean: Mexico Today,* edited by Curtis A. Wilgus, 52–62. Gainesville: University of Florida, 1964.

Schuler, Friedrich E. *Mexico Between Hitler and Roosevelt: Mexican Foreign Relations in the Age of Lázaro Cárdenas, 1934–1940.* Albuquerque: University of New Mexico Press, 1998.

Schulz, Donald E. *Between a Rock and a Hard Place: The United States, Mexico, and the Agony of National Security.* Carlisle Barracks, Pa.: Strategic Studies Institute, Army War College, 1997.

Scott, Robert E. *Mexican Government in Transition.* Urbana: University of Illinois Press, 1964.

Scully, Michael. "Almazán, Mexican Caballero." *Current History,* April 1940, 37–39.

Secretaría de Gobernación. *Seis años de actividad nacional.* Mexico City: Secretaría de Gobernación, 1946.

Secretaría de la Defensa Nacional. *Mensajes: General de División Matías Ramos Santos, Secretario de la Defensa Nacional, 1952–1958.* Mexico City: Estado Mayor, Secretaría de la Defensa Nacional, 1959.

Seis años de gobierno al servicio de México, 1934–1940. Mexico City: La Nacional Impresora, 1940.

Sentíes, Yolanda. *Adolfo López Mateos: Senador de la República (1946–1952).* Toluca: Instituto Mexiquense de Cultura, 1993.

Sepulveda, Bernardo, and Antonio Chumacero. *La inversión extranjera en México.* Mexico City: Fondo de Cultura Económica, 1973.

Serrano Álvarez, Pablo. *La política pública regional en el gobierno de Lázaro Cárdenas, 1934–1940.* Colima: Universidad de Colima, 1991.

———. "El proyecto sinarquista de la colonización de Baja California (1941–1943)." *Revista de Indias* 54, no. 201 (1994): 439–58.

Servín, Elisa. *Ruptura y oposición: El movimiento henriquista, 1945–1954.* Mexico City: Cal y Arena, 2001.

Servín González, Maria Elisa. "La 'oposición revolucionaria': El caso del henriquismo, 1945–1954." PhD diss., Universidad Iberoamericana, 1998.

Sherman, John W. *The Mexican Right: The End of Revolutionary Reform, 1929–1940.* Westport, Conn.: Praeger, 1997.

Siempre cerca, siempre lejos: Las fuerzas armadas en México. Mexico City: Global Exchange, 2000.

Silva Herzog, Jesús. *Lázaro Cárdenas: Su pensamiento económico, social y político.* Mexico City: Editorial Nuestro Tiempo, 1975.

———. *Una vida en la vida de Mexico.* Mexico: Siglo Veintiuno, 1972.

Sirvent, Carlos, ed. *Partidos politicos y procesos electorales en México.* Mexico City: Miguel Ángel Porrúa, 2002.

Smedley, Max Jewel. "Mexican-American Relations and the Cold War, 1945–1954." PhD diss., University of Southern California, 1981.

Smith, Peter H. *Continuity and Turnover with the Mexican Political Elite, 1900–1971.* N.p.: PHS, 1973.

———. *Labyrinths of Power: Political Recruitment in Twentieth-Century Mexico.* Princeton: Princeton University Press, 1979.

———. "Mexico Since 1946: Dynamics of an Authoritarian Regime." In *Mexico Since Independence,* edited by Leslie Bethell, 321–96. Cambridge: Cambridge University Press, 1991.

Solórzano de Cárdenas, Amalia, and Luis Suárez. *Cárdenas, retrato inédito: Testimonios de Amalia Solórzano de Cárdenas y nuevos documentos.* Mexico City: Grijalbo, 1988.

Spota, Luis. *Miguel Alemán en una semblanza.* Mexico City: Secretaría de Educación Pública, 1947.

Stegmaier, Harry I., Jr. "From Confrontation to Cooperation: The United States and Mexico, 1938–1945." PhD diss., University of Michigan, 1970.

Stepan, Alfred. *The Military in Politics: Changing Patterns in Brazil.* Princeton: Princeton University Press, 1971.

Stephenson, William Samuel, ed. *British Security Coordination: The Secret History of British Intelligence in the Americas, 1940–45.* New York: Fromm International, 1999.

Stevens, Evelyn P. "Mexico's PRI: The Institutionalization of Corporatism?" In *Authoritarianism and Corporatism in Latin America,* edited by James M. Malloy, 227–58. Pittsburgh: University of Pittsburgh Press, 1977.

Stiller, Jesse H. *George S. Messersmith: Diplomat of Democracy.* Chapel Hill: University of North Carolina Press, 1987.

Story, Emily F. "Aztec Imagery and the Invention of Mexican Revolutionary Identity, 1920–1940." Master's thesis, Vanderbilt University, 2000.

Suárez, Eduardo. *Comentarios y recuerdos, 1926–1946.* Mexico City: Porrúa, 1977.

———. "México en el pleno periodo de recuperación." *El Economista* 1, no. 10 (Jul. 16, 1939): 6.

Suárez, Luis. *Cárdenas, retrato inédito: testimonios de Amalia Solórzano de Cárdenas y nuevos documentos.* 2nd ed. Mexico City: Grijalbo, 1988.

Suárez Farías, Francisco. "La élite política." *Revista Mexicana de Sociología* 50, no. 3 (Jul.–Sep. 1988): 295–322.

Sugiyama, Shigeru. "Reluctant Neighbors: U.S.-Mexican Relations and the Failure of Cardenista Reforms, 1934–1948." PhD diss., University of California at Santa Barbara, 1996.

Talbert, Roy, Jr. *Negative Intelligence: The Army and the American Left, 1917–1941.* Jackson: University Press of Mississippi, 1991.

Tannenbaum, Frank. *Mexico: The Struggle for Peace and Bread.* New York: Alfred A. Knopf, 1950.

Taracena, Alfonso. *La vida en México bajo Avila Camacho.* Mexico City: Editorial Jus, 1976.

———. *La vida en México bajo Miguel Alemán.* Mexico City: Editorial Jus, 1979.

Tobler, Hans Werner. "Las paradojas del ejército mexicano." *Historia Mexicana* 21, no. 1 (1971): 38–79.

———. *La Revolución Mexicana: Transformación social y cambio político, 1876–1940.* Mexico City: Alianza, 1994.

Torres Bodet, Jaime. *Memorias.* 4 vols. Mexico City: Porrúa, 1969–72.

Torres Ramírez, Blanca. *Hacia la utopía industrial.* Historia de la Revolución Mexicana 21. Mexico City: Colegio de México, 1984.

———. *México en la Segunda Guerra mundial.* Historia de la Revolución Mexicana 19. Mexico City: Colegio de México, 1979.

Townsend, William Cameron. *Lázaro Cárdenas: Mexican Democrat.* Ann Arbor: George Wahr Publishing, 1952.

Trabajador: Almazán garantizara todos tus derechos. [Mexico City]: n.p., 1940.

Turner, Frederick C. "México: Las causas de la limitación militar." *Aportes* 6 (Oct. 1967): 57–65.

Ulloa, Berta. *La revolución más allá del Bravo: Guía de documentos relativos a México en archivos de Estados Unidos, 1900–1948.* Mexico City: Colegio de México, 1991.

Ulloa Borneman, Alberto. *Surviving Mexico's Dirty War: A Political Prisoner's Memoir.* Translated by Aurora Camacho de Schmidt and Arthur Schmidt. Philadelphia: Temple University Press, 2007.

Unión Nacional Sinarquista, Secretaría de Propaganda. *Sinarquismo: Summary of Its Program.* N.p.: UNS, Secretaría de Propaganda, [1942].

Uranga H., Javier. *La obra constructiva del General Cárdenas.* Mexico City: n.p., 1940.

Urdanivia, Fernando D. *La situación de México y la sucesión presidencial.* Mexico City: Editorial Helios, 1940.

Urquiza Ruiz, Gabriela. "El movimiento henriquista: La sucesión presidencial de 1952." Licenciatura thesis, Universidad Autónoma Metropolitana [Mexico City], 1973.

Vaughn, Michael Oscar. "Roosevelt's Good Neighbor Policy and Mexico, 1933–1938." Master's thesis, University of Southern Mississippi, 1993.

Véjar Vázquez, Octavio. *Autonomía del derecho militar.* Mexico City: Editorial Stylo, 1948.

———. *Derecho penal militar.* Mexico City: Ediciones Minerva, 1944.

———. *Derecho procesal militar.* Mexico City: Ediciones Lex, 1947.

———. *Discursos.* Mexico City: Comisión Nacional de Planeación para la Paz, 1945.

———. *El ejército y sus tribunales.* 2 vols. Mexico City: Ediciones Lex, 1944–46.

Véjar Vázquez, Octavio, and Tomás López Linares. *Código de Justicia Militar: Anotado y concordado por los abogados Tomás López Linares y Octavio Véjar Vázquez.* Mexico City: Ediciones "Ateneo," 1948.

Velasco Gil, Carlos M. *Sinarquismo, su origen, su esencia, su misión.* Mexico City: Ediciones Club del Libro Mexicano, 1944.

Vernon, Raymond. *The Dilemma of Mexico's Development: The Roles of the Private and Public Sector.* Cambridge: Harvard University Press, 1963.

Villarreal, Antonio I. *El General Antonio I. Villarreal repudia la candidatura del General Almazán.* Mexico City: Centro Nacional Defensor de la Revolución, 1940.

Villaseñor, Eduardo. *Memorias-Testimonio.* Mexico City: Fondo de Cultura Económica, 1974.

von Sauer, Franz. *The Alienated "Loyal" Opposition: Mexico's Partido Acción Nacional.* Albuquerque: University of New Mexico Press, 1974.

Wager, Stephen J. "The Mexican Army, 1940–1982: The Country Comes First." PhD diss., Stanford University, 1992.

———. *The Mexican Military Approaches the Twenty-first Century: Coping with a New World Order.* Carlisle Barracks, Pa.: Strategic Studies Institute, U.S. Army War College, 1994.

———. "The Mexican Military: The Dilemma of Functioning in a One-Party System." In *Beyond Praetorianism: The Latin American Military in Transition,* edited by Richard L. Millett and Michael Gold-Bliss, 103–32. Coral Gables: North-South Center Press, 1996.

Wagner, Eric Armin. *Popular Participation in Mexican Political Life: 1934–1964.* [Gainesville]: University of Florida, 1968.

Wasserman, Mark. *Persistent Oligarchs: Elites and Politics in Chihuahua, Mexico, 1910–1940.* Durham: Duke University Press, 1993.

Welch, Claude E., Jr., ed. *Civilian Control of the Military: Myth and Reality.* Special Studies 63. Buffalo: Council on International Studies, State University of New York at Buffalo, 1975.

———. *Civilian Control of the Military: Theory and Cases from Developing Countries.* Albany: State University of New York Press, 1976.

Weyl, Nathaniel, and Sylvia Weyl. *The Reconquest of Mexico: The Years of Lázaro Cárdenas.* London: Oxford University Press, 1939.

Whitaker, Arthur P., ed. *Inter-American Affairs, 1941–1945.* New York: Columbia University Press, 1942–46.

Wilkie, James W. "El complejo militar-industrial en México durante la década de 1930: Diálogo con el general Juan Andreu Almazán." *Revista Mexicana de Ciencia Política* 20 (Jul.–Sep. 1974): 59–65.

———. *Elitelore.* Los Angeles: Latin American Center, University of California at Los Angeles, 1973.

————. *The Mexican Revolution: Federal Expenditure and Social Change Since 1910.* Berkeley and Los Angeles: University of California Press, 1967.

Wilkie, James W., and Edna Monzón de Wilkie. *México visto en el siglo XX.* Mexico City: Instituto Mexicano de Investigaciones Económicas, 1969.

Wilkie, James Wallace, and Albert L. Michaels, eds. *Revolution in Mexico: Years of Upheaval, 1910–1940.* New York: Alfred Knopf, 1969.

Wionczek, Miguel. *El nacionalismo mexicano y la inversion extranjera.* Mexico City: Siglo XXI, 1967.

Womack, John., Jr. *Zapata and the Mexican Revolution.* New York: Alfred Knopf, 1969.

Woodward, Ralph Lee. *Central America: A Nation Divided.* 3rd ed. New York: Oxford University Press, 1999.

Zaid, Gabriel. *De los libros al poder.* Mexico City: Grijalbo, 1988.

Zolov, Eric. *Refried Elvis: The Rise of the Mexican Counterculture.* Berkeley and Los Angeles: University of California Press, 1999.

Index

García Barragán, Marcelino, 64, 207–8, 210, 234, 236, 252
García Paniagua, Javier, 155, 252
García Tellez, Ignacio, 46, 48
Garner, John Nance, 20
Garrido Canabal, Tomás, 202
Gasca, Celestino, 236, 253
Gómez, Arnulfo, 85, 260–61
Gómez, Marte, 221
Gómez Esparza, José, 211
Gómez Morín, Manuel, 27–31, 128, 225
Gonzales, Francisco, 58
González, Alejo G., 110
González, Gildardo, 135
González, Pablo, 201
González, Vicente, 201
González Gallo, Jesús, 200
González Luna, Efraín, 30–31, 225, 242, 244
Guevara, Gabriel R., 215
Gutiérrez, Juan, 220
Gutiérrez, Miguel, 158
Gutiérrez Barrios, Fernando, 155, 268
Henríquez Guzmán, Jorge, 249–51

Henríquez Guzmán, Miguel
  background, 200–204, 206
  election of 1946, 8, 100, 116, 129–31, 141, 204–5
  election of 1952; bases of support, 202–3, 218–22; counterintelligence, 173; opposition coalition, 237–40; overview, 8, 11, 78, 116, 120, 259; political strategy, 199, 205–8, 217–19, 227–29, 254; post-electoral strategy, 245–46; pre-campaign efforts, 206–8; union with Lombardo, 238–40; violence, 232–34, 248–49
  election of 1958, 253
  government contracts, 202–3, 206, 249–51
  support of Cárdenas, 53, 130–31, 199, 234–37
Hernández y Hernández, Francisco, 241 n. 184
Hinojosa, Cosme, 207
Hoover, J. Edgar, 58, 126, 180
"Huarache" group, 47
Hull, Cordell, 54

Innureta de la Fuente, Marcelino, 155, 184
Instituto Federal Electoral (IFE), 268
intelligence services, German, 124, 125, 128, 139, 176
intelligence services, Mexico. See also Departamento Confidencial (DC); Dirección Federal de Seguridad (DFS); Dirección

General de Investigaciones Políticas y Sociales (DGIPS)
  counterintelligence, 173
  dealings with Axis, 123, 124–25, 176
  history, 10–11, 122, 150–86
  influence of U.S., 175, 179–86
  methods, 164–75
  politicization, 166–67, 186
  professionalization, 10, 158–63
  U.S. distrust, 122–23, 127, 128, 170, 176–78

Jara, Heriberto, 15
Jones, Gus T., 182

Kruger, Hilda, 138–39

Labra, Wenceslao, 207
Legión de Honor Mexicana, 213–14
Lelo de Larrea, José, 125, 154
León, Gustavo, 44, 59
León Lobato, Othón, 184, 230
Leyva Velazquez, Gabriel, 114, 117
Lezama, Alfredo, 44, 59
licencia, 106–9, 113–15, 200, 218
Lieuwen, Edwin, 8–9, 81–82
Limón, Gilberto, 112
Lombardo Toledano, Vicente
  communist ties, 38, 65, 142
  electoral fraud in 1952, 242, 244
  presidential campaign in 1952, 223, 238–40
López, Anacleto, 110, 128, 201
López, Hector F., 57, 134, 174
López Buitrón, Jaime Domingo, 157
López Linares, Tomás, 112
López Mateos, Adolfo, 115, 212, 241
Lozano, Ignacio, 68

Macías Valenzuela, Anselmo, 47
Madero, Emilio, 69
Madero, Francisco, 201
Magaña, Conrado, 48
Magaña, Gildardo, 33
Martínez, Antonio, 135
Martínez, Miguel Z., 182
Martínez y Rodríguez, Luis Maria, 135
Martino, Cesar, 207, 221
Medina Mora Icaza, Eduardo, 157
Mena Alcocer, José de la Luz, 159
Meneses, Pablo, 153, 159
Mercado Alarcón, Agustín, 112
Mercado Flores, Alberto, 177
Messersmith, George S., 137, 141, 142, 181
microdot case, 177